CW00926818

CASE PREPARATION

CASE PREPARATION

Inns of Court School of Law

Institute of Law, City University, London

OXFORD
UNIVERSITY PRESS

OXFORD
UNIVERSITY PRESS

Great Clarendon Street, Oxford OX2 6DP

Oxford University Press is a department of the University of Oxford.
It furthers the University's objective of excellence in research, scholarship,
and education by publishing worldwide in

Oxford New York

Auckland Bangkok Buenos Aires Cape Town Chennai
Dar es Salaam Delhi Hong Kong Istanbul Karachi Kolkata
Kuala Lumpur Madrid Melbourne Mexico City Mumbai Nairobi
São Paulo Shanghai Singapore Taipei Tokyo Toronto

and an associated company in Berlin

Oxford is a registered trade mark of Oxford University Press
in the UK and certain other countries

Published in the United States
by Oxford University Press Inc., New York

A Blackstone Press Book

© Inns of Court School of Law, 2002

The moral rights of the author have been asserted
Database right Oxford University Press (maker)

All rights reserved. No part of this publication may be reproduced,
stored in a retrieval system, or transmitted, in any form or by any means,
without the prior permission in writing of Oxford University Press,
or as expressly permitted by law, or under terms agreed with the appropriate
reprographics rights organization. Enquiries concerning reproduction
outside the scope of the above should be sent to the Rights Department,
Oxford University Press, at the address above

You must not circulate this book in any other binding or cover
and you must impose the same condition on any acquirer

British Library Cataloguing in Publication Data

Data available

Library of Congress Cataloging in Publication Data

Data available

ISBN 0-19-925497-4

1 3 5 7 9 10 8 6 4 2

Typeset by Style Photosetting Limited, Mayfield, East Sussex
Printed in Great Britain
on acid-free paper by
Ashford Colour Press, Gosport, Hampshire

FOREWORD

These manuals are designed primarily to support training on the Bar Vocational Course, though they are also intended to provide a useful resource for legal practitioners and for anyone undertaking training in legal skills.

The Bar Vocational Course was designed by staff at the Inns of Court School of Law, where it was introduced in 1989. This course is intended to equip students with the practical skills and the procedural and evidential knowledge that they will need to start their legal professional careers. These manuals are written by staff at the Inns of Court School of Law who have helped to develop the course, and by a range of legal practitioners and others involved in legal skills training. The authors of the manuals are very well aware of the practical and professional approach that is central to the Bar Vocational Course.

The range and coverage of the manuals have grown steadily. All the manuals are updated annually, and regular reviews and revisions of the manuals are carried out to ensure that developments in legal skills training and the experience of our staff are fully reflected in them.

This updating and revision is a constant process and we very much value the comments of practitioners, staff and students. Legal vocational training is advancing rapidly, and it is important that all those concerned work together to achieve and maintain high standards. Please address any comments to the Bar Vocational Course Director at the Inns of Court School of Law.

With the validation of other providers for the Bar Vocational Course it is very much our intention that these manuals will be of equal value to all students wherever they take the course, and we would very much value comments from tutors and students at other validated institutions.

The enthusiasm of the publishers and their efficiency in arranging production and publication of the manuals is much appreciated.

The Hon. Mr Justice Elias
Chairman of the Advisory Board of the Institute of Law
City University, London
August 2002

FOREWORD

CONTENTS

CONTENTS

PREFACE

This Manual explains and demonstrates, in the context of the work of a barrister, the underlying skills of legal research and fact management which will ensure that a case has been thoroughly prepared so that every relevant consideration has been taken into account before the client is given any advice, any document is drafted or any case presented in court. Its purpose is to assist those who read it to develop effective techniques which, it is hoped, will ensure that the advice they give is sound, and the arguments they put forward are convincing.

The development of professional legal skills training with its emphasis on the ability to perform lawyers' tasks has underlined the need to develop case preparation skills to a high standard. If relevant law or fact is not identified, or if there is only a superficial assessment of the strength of evidence, the advice given is unlikely to be sound, and the argument presented in negotiation or before a tribunal is unlikely to succeed.

The experience of those studying and teaching on the Bar Vocational Course has identified the need to provide clear guidance on how to carry out legal research efficiently and to identify, analyse and present relevant facts to ensure the best outcome for the client. The methods and techniques adopted in this Manual are the outcome of our experience over the last ten years and our discussions with the many practitioners and academics who have kindly contributed to the debate about how best to develop effective case preparation skills.

The advice given in this Manual is not intended to be prescriptive. The aim is to provide practical advice and to demonstrate through the inclusion of worked examples how particular techniques can be applied to the preparation of a case. It is hoped that this will provide a framework which will assist each individual to develop his or her own intellectual skills in order to carry out the task of preparation competently and professionally.

Students will find that they will have opportunities to apply these techniques through-out the Bar Vocational Course. Some of the case papers will be used in specific classes. In particular, the sections assisting you with legal research and fact management processes will be invaluable when you are working with sets of papers for the skills exercises and should be particularly useful in your Group Study sessions.

ONE

SKILLS OF PREPARATION

The image of successful barristers suggests that their success depends on the ability to think on their feet, to use words persuasively, to mesmerise by their fluency, and to impress by their very presence and charisma those whom they address. Certainly those skills help. But the real basis for their confidence is effective preparation for the task they are undertaking so that they know the facts of the case thoroughly and, having considered the potential relevance of all the facts to their legal context, can respond effectively to any point made, and, having thought through and planned their argument beforehand, they can deliver it clearly and address in a convincing way all the relevant questions which must be decided.

The work of a barrister (more fully dealt with in **Chapters 12** and **13** below) although more varied than many realise, is focused on answering one question. If the case came before a court, how likely is it that the client would win? The only way that this question can be answered is for the barrister to address the underlying question which is: how can the case be presented so that evidence can be put before the court which will prove on the facts that the client is legally entitled to a finding in his or her favour?

In order to answer this question the barrister will need to look closely at the facts of the case to see what the client's problem is and what the client hopes to achieve from any legal claim. The barrister will then need to research the law to see whether there is a legal principle which will give the client a right to the outcome being sought. The facts of the case will then need to be analysed to determine whether they can be presented in such a way that all the component parts of the legal principle can be shown to be fulfilled. The barrister will also need to consider whether there are witnesses who can be called to give evidence which, if believed, will prove the facts on which the argument is based and which, it is hoped, will persuade the court of the client's entitlement to a finding in his or her favour.

This analytical process can be demonstrated in graphical form as in **Table 1.1** below.

Table 1.1

Legal framework	*Facts in support*	*Evidence*
Insert below each element of the crime, cause of action and/or defences	Insert below in relation to each legal element, facts which establish that element	Insert below in relation to each fact the evidence which proves that fact

By identifying every element of the legal principle which is relied on and the facts and evidence which support it, the barrister can test whether there is sufficient available evidence of the facts which establish the legal basis of the case. Even then the preparatory work will not be completed, for the barrister, before being able to advise on the likely success of a case, will have to consider all the arguments about fact and law which the other side might raise, and whether and how they can be countered. Only then will the barrister be able to answer, with any hope of that answer being justified, the question whether the client will win, or be able with confidence to present the case convincingly to the court.

The aim of this Manual is to explain and demonstrate some methods of legal research and fact management which, in the context of the work of a barrister, will assist in developing effective case preparation skills.

Chapters 2 to **11** show how legal research can be made more efficient by increasing familiarity with the basic sources of information and by outlining some of the main techniques of research.

Chapters 12 and **13** provide an overview of the stages of first a civil and then a criminal case. The Bar is predominantly a referral profession and a barrister may be consulted at various stages of a case; it is therefore always important that any preparation is focused on the particular instructions that have been received. As particular aspects of the case may require different emphasis at different stages it is always important to tailor one's preparation to the stage that the case has reached.

Chapter 14 describes the intellectual processes and the analytical skills which are required for effective fact management. The acronym CAP (Context, Analysis, Presentation) has been adopted to summarise the process by which the preparation of a case progresses from an initial understanding of the legal and factual context of a case to a detailed analysis of the issues and the evidence and finally to the construction of a persuasive and pertinent argument which can be presented to whatever audience is appropriate, be it the client or a tribunal.

The chapter also illustrates some of the possible techniques which can be used to ensure that the CAP process is carried out rigorously and may help you to develop your own analytical skills. One technique has already been displayed above at **Table 1.1**. Once that table has been completed in relation to any set of facts it should provide both an overview and a detailed analysis of the interrelation of the law, facts and evidence issue by issue. This should make it possible not only to assess the likelihood of success in establishing your client's case but also to carry out your specific instructions more precisely.

For instance if your advice is sought, whether in a conference or as a written opinion, the completion of **Table 1.1** should make obvious whether there is a prima facie case so that a preliminary assessment of potential success or advice on further steps necessary can be given. If the instructions are to draft a statement of claim the centre column will have identified the material facts which should be included. Moreover the inability to complete the table fully will of itself identify what further information may be needed.

If a similar analysis is also done of the case for the other side this should assist, once the strength of all the available evidence has been considered, in providing the basis for planning any negotiation or piece of advocacy and in answering the basic questions: How likely is it that the client will win? How can the case be presented most effectively?

Chapters 15, 16 and **17** explain and demonstrate the practical application of the CAP approach by showing how, in relation to a civil and a criminal case, the process and some of the techniques discussed in **Chapter 14**, can be applied to the preparation of realistic sets of papers. The papers for the civil case, *Lowe* v *Mainwaring*, and the accompanying preparatory notes showing the CAP approach in action are contained in **Chapter 16**. The papers for the criminal case, *R* v *Costas Georgiou*, and its accompanying notes are contained in **Chapter 17**.

Chapters 16 and **17** demonstrate with examples how fact management techniques can be applied by following through a civil and a criminal case and showing the detailed approach to preparation at each stage.

The remainder of the Manual sets out particular aspects of fact management such as dealing with figures and using information technology before providing a set of papers for self-assessment which can be used to put into practice some of the methods of preparation demonstrated in the Manual.

TWO

INTRODUCTION TO LEGAL RESEARCH

2.1 The Barrister as Legal Expert

If you think that the highest function of the barrister is in court-room advocacy, think again. Barristers are 'learned' counsel. This is no formal compliment (like, e.g. 'Right Honourable Member'). They have earned their traditional title, and not by their in-court resourcefulness but by being the specialists of the legal profession, lawyers whom other lawyers consult.

The ability to provide counsel's opinion, based on researches into the darker areas and novel aspects of the law, is the first requisite of the barrister — first also because it comes long before advocacy, or even drafting of statements of case, in the particular case. There is of course a close connection between all of these functions; the opinion given is one which the barrister knows he or she must be prepared to make stand up in court. It must therefore be well-founded on thorough research, to which the argumentative skills of the advocate can then be applied. It is in their ability to find the law and their facility to adapt and apply it in their client's cause that the most able barristers can be recognised.

If you ask any barrister how he or she learned to research in law, the chances are that they will say by trial and error, jumping in at the deep end, or various other vague expressions. Many will say that they have never actually 'learned' to do it at all. Until recently, the professional law schools have never attempted to teach the technique of systematic legal research. As for the universities, they expect their law students to absorb large amounts of legal doctrine and to apply it; but almost all of this is presented to them by textbooks and lectures, and the further reading these indicate. Not often are students set to find out for themselves. Even if they are, the academic law libraries do not have the materials a practitioner needs to use.

The result is that young barristers and solicitors have arrived at their first job without any real training in one of its most essential functions. They are then expected to 'pick it up' as best they can. Some never do, and perhaps never need to if they find a niche for themselves in areas of practice where research plays little part. If such limited practice is possible at the Bar, it consigns one to the least interesting and stimulating work. At all events, every aspiring barrister should as a matter of self-respect and professional pride want to acquire skill in research and to merit that title of 'learned'.

2.2 From Theory to Practice

There is of course a traditional answer from the profession to this criticism of lack of training. Seasoned practitioners may say that this, like most other vocational skills, can only be learned by doing it in practice. (But then they once said this about English law itself!) Whether this is true or not, you can't even begin to research in law without some preliminary acquaintance with the sources of legal knowledge and the technique of tapping them. What follows seeks to guide you in that direction, providing sufficient information to start you off in acquiring the necessary skill for yourself.

2.3 Legal Research and the Pupil Barrister

From the day you start in chambers, you will be faced with questions, points of law, procedure, tactics, etc., which are quite new to you. This does not mean that the cases and papers you will see are likely to be bristling with complex legal problems. On the contrary, to a seasoned practitioner, there may be very little 'law' involved, everything turning on the facts as the court eventually finds them. But when everything is new and unfamiliar you must have the facility to know how to find out. To start with you need to know what people are talking about. At a more advanced level, when you are given papers to prepare an opinion, you must know how and where to get at the law.

Some answers will come readily from your pupil master, from sharing experience with other pupils, or from picking the brains of other barristers. That is part of the comradeship of the Bar. But if they say, 'It'll be in *MacGillivray*', it does not extend to taking you by the hand and showing you what that is. You are assumed to know how legal knowledge is organised on the library shelf: statute and case law, reference works, the main practitioners' textbooks, the cumulations and indexes: and how they all cite, classify, fit together and cross-refer. These are things you can and must equip yourself with before you even set foot in chambers. So if you did not learn it all at university, you must do so now. (If you did, or think you did, quaere!)

Before setting off for the library and starting your legal research, make sure that you know exactly what information your pupil master wants and when he or she wants it.

2.4 Order of Treatment

2.4.1 THE LIBRARY

The first part of this guide, **Chapter 3**, is concerned with the basic materials of English and European Community law which you can expect to find in a practitioners' law library. This is part of the essential knowledge of the legal scene that you must now start to acquire. Without it you cannot even begin to research. It is important to get a general understanding of the way in which legal knowledge is organised, visually and spatially, in general and in your particular library. Most chambers' libraries have the basic sources only. For deeper research you will need to go to one of the Inns' libraries or further afield. But don't wait until a problem forces you to wander hopefully round the shelves. Get to know the library, its arrangement and contents, find the books described and browse through them to see the features indicated.

2.4.2 PROBLEM-SOLVING

The second part of this guide, **Chapters 4** to **8**, is about using the library. We have to go on and learn how to make it work for us in problem-solving. Problems in law vary greatly in type. The sequence adopted here is to start with problems in areas of law with which you must be familiar from your studies so far; going on to research in unknown territory; then the technique of 'following-through' to make sure your answer is completely up to date, which entails knowing how to access very recent law generally; and ending with the way in which computer-assistance can (and cannot) help.

2.4.3 THE DIAGRAMS

These have been provided in **Chapter 9** to show in graphic form a suggested sequence for researching. If these are to be useful, it can only be after you have read and understood the relevant sections of the text, to which they refer.

2.4.4 REPETITION

In this treatment of the resources for and methods of legal research, you will find that some things may seem to be repeated. This is where materials previously described as static apparatus on the library shelf are then deployed in problem-solving. This repetition has the advantage of reminding you of your earlier exploration of the shelves; or else sending you back to do it. In any case, familiarity and skill only come with repetition.

THREE

GETTING TO KNOW
THE LIBRARY

3.1 Introduction

The first thing you must do is familiarise yourself with the law library. Find out what it has and where it has it. Find out which library you can go to research in when yours hasn't got what you need, and then have a look at that library too. By the time pupillage begins, the would-be barrister should be familiar with the basic tools of practical legal research and how they all fit together. So please read carefully what follows, and then use it as a guide-book to the shelves, finding and exploring each of the materials described.

3.1.1 EXERCISES

Merely looking at the shelves, and perhaps flicking through a few pages, will not do much for you. Do the simple exercises at the end of each section so as to get some basic dexterity with each of the sources in turn. You should then be able to tackle the problems which are set in the research technique section.

3.2 Essential Parts of a Law Library

An English law library has at least five different sorts of materials: statutes, reports, journals, textbooks, and general reference works. Of these, statutes and law reports are sometimes called primary sources because their content, legislation and precedent, is The Law; whereas the other secondary sources, though they may sometimes be highly regarded, are only their writers' opinion of what the law is. It may have sufficed in tutorial to rely on a statement in the textbook but it will rarely do so in court.

3.2.1 NEW TECHNOLOGY

Nowadays the traditional part of the library – the books on the shelves – is only part of the picture. The practitioner of the future has got to get to grips with the ever-increasing amount of information in on-screen form. To use electronic sources you may need some training, but **Chapter 8** below gives some general guidance. These notes deal mainly with what is on the shelf because you must master the lawyer's traditional tools first.

3.3 Legislation

3.3.1 PRIMARY LEGISLATION

Legislation may be primary or secondary. In the UK, primary legislation takes the form of statutes (or 'enactments') which are Acts of Parliament or Measures of the Church Assembly or General Synod of the Church of England. Acts are either Public General

Acts, Local Acts, or Private and Personal Acts. Of all of these the only ones of importance for everyday practice are Public General Acts, which make up what is sometimes called our 'statute book'. Local and Personal Acts may be found in the Inns' libraries. Since 1992, Local Acts for each year are included in *Current Law Statutes*.

3.3.2 SECONDARY LEGISLATION

Secondary legislation, referred to as 'subordinate' or 'delegated', consists of law which has the full force of statute but which has been laid down not in Parliament but by lesser bodies authorised by Parliament. Thus local authorities and public utilities are often given power to make by-laws. (For how to find these, see Local Government Act 1972, s. 236 as amended.) But for present purposes we need consider only the regulations made by government departments and published in the form of Statutory Instruments (formerly called Statutory Rules & Orders).

3.4 Acts of Parliament

These appear in law libraries in three main forms:

(a) Queen's Printer's copies: these are the officially-issued Acts in the form in which they were passed by Parliament. For citation and use in court, these are the only versions the judges wish to refer to.

Each new Act on getting the royal assent is published in A4 format by the Stationery Office (formerly HMSO but now privatised), under the authority of the Queen's Printer of Acts of Parliament. On the library shelf, these Acts will be found in smaller format in bound volumes with either 'Public General Acts and Measures' or 'Law Reports Statutes' on their spine. Inside, both these series are identical, Queen's Printer's copies.

(b) Annotated statutes: *Current Law Statutes* are arranged in annual volumes. Very recent Acts arrive in loose-leaf parts during the year. The annotations, written by specialist editors, give much helpful information, e.g. the legal and Parliamentary background; references following each section to cases, regulations, or other statutes affecting that section; and often a general running commentary. For research purposes annotated statutes are much more useful than the bare official versions. *Current Law Statutes* is the only series which gives *Hansard* references. See **7.3**.

(c) Classified annotated statutes: *Halsbury's Statutes* (not to be confused with *Halsbury's Laws of England*) are not only annotated but arranged in alphabetical order of subject-headings. This set thus organises in its many volumes the entire statute law of this country, of whatever date, which is still to any extent in force. Individual volumes are re-issued from time to time when the quantity of new material warrants it and the whole set is kept up to date to the beginning of the present year by an annual cumulative supplement. This follows the same sequence of volumes and subject-headings as the main set. For still more recent developments there is a loose-leaf Noter-Up volume. A Current Statutes Service laid out in several loose-leaf volumes gives the text of Acts too recent to get into the appropriate bound volume. There is a separate index volume (*Table of Statutes and Consolidated Index*) which lists both alphabetically and chronologically every Act extant with its reference in the main set; or in the Current Statutes, indicated by a letter S.

Annotations take time to prepare. It may be a while before the edited *Current Law* or *Halsbury* version of an Act arrives. (Meantime they may issue a temporary unannotated version on coloured paper.) During that delay you will have only the A4 version to consult, and will have to do your own interpreting unaided; though usually there will have been running commentary on the Bill during its passage, which can be found in the practitioners' journals. See for these **3.12**.

3.4.1 CITATION OF STATUTES

Every modern Act of Parliament has a short title and year (e.g. Theft Act 1968), and a unique 'chapter' number (e.g. 1968 c. 60). Before 1963, chapter numbers were based on the regnal year or years during which the Parliament sat. So, for example, 15 & 16 Geo. 5 c. 20 is an old friend of yours. Personal Acts have their chapter number in italic e.g. *c. 11*. Local Acts have it as a Roman numeral (Port of London Act 1968 is 1968 c. xxxii).

3.4.2 LOOKING UP STATUTES

(a) *You know the short title:* In the annual bound volume or volumes of official versions (see **3.4(a)** above) you will find an alphabetical index of the year's Acts giving the chapter number of each. The Acts are bound in chapter number order. Or you can do the same with the *Current Law Statutes* annual volumes. Always look for the index to these in the last volume for the year, where that year had more than one volume.

(b) *You know the short title but aren't sure of the year:* (e.g. when was the Data Protection Act?) The index volume to *Halsbury's Statutes* will give it if it is still in force. Alternatively, *Current Law Legislation Citator* has at the beginning an alphabetical list of statutes which have been in any way active in the years covered by the *Citator* volumes. For the most complete alphabetical list, see *Current Law Statutes Annotated* Service File. Its Table of Statutes lists alphabetically all extant Acts of whatever date. The final volume for each year lists every Act, dead or alive, since 1700.

(c) *You don't know the short title, but do know the year and chapter number:* This is a bit unlikely, but may sometimes happen with older statutes. You can find it as in (a) above if it is a calendar year. If it is a regnal year and you have the official bound volumes, you should be able to find any Act this century by looking at the spines, which give the regnal year as well as the calendar year. For older Acts, check the chronological index in *Halsbury's Statutes* index volume, or in the official two-volume *Chronological Table* (see **3.4.3**).

3.4.3 IS THE ACT IN FORCE?

Once you have found your Act, the next most important thing to find out is whether it is in force. This is really two questions:

(a) *Is it yet in force?* Many Acts have a delayed beginning and await activation. Having found your Act, the first thing to do is to see if it is in force, and the first place to look for that is in the commencement section. Go to the end of the Act and find the last two or three sections (of the Act itself, ignoring any schedules — pronounced 'shedule' — which are often appended at the end of Acts). These last sections give the short title, the extent (geographical) of operation, and the date of commencement. This may be the date of enactment (which you can find on the first page of the Act in a square bracket immediately after the long title), or a stated date after that, or it may be left to the government department concerned (nominally 'the Secretary of State', or 'Her Majesty in Council'), to bring it into operation, and in such stages, areas, etc., as it sees fit. If the last, this is done by Commencement Order made in a Statutory Instrument (see **3.5**).

If it is not clear from the Act itself whether it (or the particular bit that you need) is in force, the simplest way to find out is to refer to *Is It In Force?* This annual volume, part of the *Halsbury's Statutes* set, covers every Act of the last 25 years, and is up-to-date to the beginning of the present year. Acts are listed alphabetically within their year. If this says 'not in force', don't rest content. It may have been activated since. Have a look at the loose-leaf Noter-Up volume. You will find an *Is It In Force?* section in the binder. Alternatively (or, better, look here too), *Current Law* latest monthly part has all the commencement dates fixed for Acts so far this year. For further confirmation, and for all Acts passed more than 25 years ago, there are lists of statutes not yet in force at the back of the current edition of *Is it In Force?*, and also in the *Current Law Statutes Annotated* Service File.

You are now up-to-date to sometime last month. The *New Law Journal* gives each week's commencement orders. To be right up to the minute, the Stationery Office publish a *Daily List* which many libraries take.

(b) *Is it still in force?* There is nothing more embarrassing than finding you have based yourself on an Act which has, unknown to you, been repealed or substantially amended. There is no way of telling this from the Act itself. *Halsbury's Statutes* plus its annual cumulative supplement plus the Noter-Up should give you the present status of the Act. Equally good is *Current Law Legislation Citator* which gives every Act's subsequent life-history, down to the end of last year. For happenings since, check the Statute Citator section in the *Current Law Statutes Annotated* Service File giving all the current year's happenings to any statutes. If you find the Act has been amended or repealed, you need then to check whether the repealing Act has itself yet been brought into force.

The most comprehensive source for all statutes' subsequent history is the two-volume *Chronological Table of the Statutes* published by HMSO. This is very helpful with older statutes, but is not issued sufficiently often to help with more recent happenings. The same is true of their *Statutes in Force*, a loose-leaf series which some libraries take. They aim to provide under subject groupings every extant Act and to update and amend the texts continually.

3.4.4 OLDER ACTS

Old Acts which are still in force will be found in *Halsbury's Statutes*. You will not often have to research old repealed Acts. If you do, and are unsure about the reference, check in the *Chronological Table of the Statutes*. You should then be able to locate the text in one of two official collections:

(a) *The Statutes Revised*: or if not there,

(b) *The Statutes of the Realm*: huge volumes covering 1235 to 1713, produced by the Record Commission in the nineteenth century.

Neither set is easy to find, though they are the required versions of Acts for citation in court: see Interpretation Act 1978, s. 19. You are as likely to find one of the unofficial collections called *Statutes at Large*. These are reasonably accurate, and in size and coverage more useful as well as more widely available.

3.4.5 OTHER SOURCES OF STATUTES

Other collections of statutes may be found in the library, mainly where Acts relevant to a particular subject or jurisdiction are provided in works written for that area of practice, e.g. *Stone's Justices' Manual*, *Paterson's Licensing Acts*, and the many encyclopaedic textbooks (Housing Law, Medical Law, etc.).

Exercise 1 — Statutes

1. What are the short titles of the following statutes?

(a) 21 Geo. 3 c. 49.

(b) 1997 c. 55.

(c) 59 & 60 Vict. c. 14.

2. Are the following in force?

    (a)   Employment of Children Act 1973.

    (b)   Suppression of Religious Houses Act 1539.

    (c)   Smoke Detectors Act 1991.

3.   What is the punishment prescribed by Piracy Act 1837, s. 2 as amended?

4.   What conduct is made illegal by the Chartered Associations Act?

5.   Which marriages are made void by the Royal Marriages Act?

6.   What is the heading to part VIII of the Law of Property Act 1925?

3.5   Delegated Legislation: the Statutory Instruments

3.5.1   PUBLICATION

The SIs are a vast series. At the end of 1999 there were some 13,500 in force, with a constant flow from Whitehall of new ones and revocations and amendments. The official texts are published as Queen's Printer's copies by the Stationery Office. Often these are just one sheet of paper. If your library takes these they will have to be carefully filed in sequence somewhere. In more durable form, the SIs will be found in one of three places in the library:

(a)   Annual Volumes: As with the statutes, the Stationery Office publishes annual volumes of SIs in sequence. They fill several large blue volumes each year, for which few libraries have the shelf space; and especially now that they, like the statutes, have swelled to A4 format.

(b)   *Halsbury's Statutory Instruments:* This set of volumes, arranged alphabetically by subject matter, lists all the SIs in force. But it prints the full texts of only a few, selecting the ones which the editors believe to be those most needed by lawyers and which (unlike, e.g. the various courts' rules) are not likely to be found elsewhere in the library. The key to the set by subject matter is the limp-bound Consolidated Index, revised annually, and supplemented during the current year by the monthly index at the back of Service Volume 1. The key to the set by SI reference number is at the front of the same Service Volume, where you will find a numerical list indexing every SI in force up to last year. This list is then updated in the Monthly Update, also in the same binder. Use the Monthly Index to check if your SI or subject area is affected by recent developments. The key by short titles of SIs is the alphabetical list in the Consolidated Index.

(c)   Textbooks: As with statutes, the main practitioners' works, especially the loose-leaf encyclopaedic textbooks, should set out the SIs relevant to the scope of the book.

(d)   Older SIs and SR & Os: If still in force, they should at least be mentioned in *Halsbury's SIs.* For the text of an older instrument some of the big law libraries have the HMSO annual volumes going back for years. (The SR & Os which preceded the SIs are in red volumes.) In addition, you may find the set of *Statutory Rules & Orders and Statutory Instruments Revised.* This is a reorganisation under subject headings of all the instruments in force at the end of 1948. There are indexes in the last volume; and the *Table of Government Orders* in a separate volume shows the impact of subsequent instruments.

(e)   SIs since 1987 are available on CD-ROM though the disks are currently updated only twice a year.

(f)   SIs are set out with their parent statutes in the STATIS file of LEXIS (see **6.3**).

3.5.2   CITATION OF STATUTORY INSTRUMENTS

Every SI is given a unique number in its year, shown as 1990/1234, or more fully as SI 1990 No. 1234. (The earlier series, before 1948, are still cited as, e.g. SR & O 1923 No. 752.) SIs also have short titles, e.g. Prison Rules 1964 (1964/388); Misuse of Drugs Regulations 1973 (1973/797).

Exercise 2 — Statutory Instruments

1.   The Access to Personal Files Act by s. 3 empowers the Secretary of State to make regulations enabling individuals to see files about them held by various bodies, and to make corrections and erasures, etc. Have any such regulations been made so far? If so, find the actual text of any.

2.   In a work on property law you find a reference, Rule 301 of SR & O 1925 No. 1093. What is this? Is it in the library? Have there been any recent cases on it?

3.   What is the date of the earliest piece of subordinate legislation that is still in force?

4.   How many SIs were issued in 2000?

3.6   Law Reports

Every law library will have series of reports which are general, covering all courts and subjects; and some which are specialised, covering a limited jurisdiction or area of law. There are now many specialised series, some of which are published as part of a practitioners' periodical. Some are also now published on CD-ROM (see **8.3.3**).

3.6.1   REFERENCES

The first problem you may encounter is deciphering the various initials used in citation. You will be familiar with WLR, All ER, Cr App R, and such commonly occurring references. For any initials which you aren't sure of, check in one of the following:

French, D., *How to Cite Legal Authorities*, London: Blackstone Press (OUP), 1996.

Raistrick, D., *Index to Legal Citations and Abbreviations*, 2nd edn, London: Bowker-Saur, 1993.

Current Law Case Citator.

Halsbury's Laws of England, Vol. 1.

The Digest, Annual Supplement.

Legal Journals Index.

Sweet & Maxwell's Guide to Law Reports and Statutes.

3.6.2   BRACKETS, SQUARE AND ROUND

Where the year is given in square brackets thus, [1990] 1 WLR 270, it is part of the reference. You therefore need page 270 of the particular volume of those reports with that date on the spine; if there were two or more volumes for that year, the reference will indicate the volume number. Most of our standard series of reports use this 'square-bracket' method. Where a date is supplied in round brackets, it is just given to you as useful but non-essential information; because in such series the publishers give each volume its own volume number in sequence in the set. For example, (1985) 80 Cr App R 117 tells you it was a case in 1985, but you wouldn't need to know the year to find Volume 80.

3.6.3   *THE LAW REPORTS*

Our major, semi-official series of reports, produced by the legal profession in the guise of the Incorporated Council of Law Reporting, are called simply *The Law Reports*. They started in 1865. There are now just four series:

(a) *Appeal Cases* cited as AC, has reports of the House of Lords and Judicial Committee of the Privy Council.

(b) *Chancery* cited as Ch, contains reports of cases on all matters heard in the Chancery Division and in the Court of Appeal therefrom.

(c) *Queen's Bench* (formerly *King's*) cited as QB or KB, contains reports of cases in that Division, including its ordinary, commercial, maritime, appellate and review jurisdictions, and in the CA (Civil Division) therefrom; and also decisions of the CA (Criminal Division).

(d) *Family* cited as Fam, containing reports of the Family Division in its ordinary and appellate jurisdiction, and in the CA on appeal therefrom. (Until 1971 this Division was called the Probate, Divorce and Admiralty Division and its reports were cited in a P series.)

3.6.4   *THE LAW REPORTS* ON SCREEN

The Law Reports from 1945 are accessible in full text on LEXIS. The whole series from 1865 are now available to subscribers to Law Reports Direct on Butterworths' website and to subscribers to the Justis website.

3.6.5   THE AUTHORITY OF *THE LAW REPORTS*

These are our senior series. They are checked by the judges concerned prior to publication. In addition to the usual headnotes, facts and judgments, they usually give a summary of counsel's arguments, which is helpful in ascertaining what points the court must have had in mind in coming to its decision. For all these reasons, these are the preferred series for citation in court. See *Practice Direction (Law Reports: Citation)* [1999] 1 WLR 1027; [1999] 2 All ER 490, para 10.1.2. Their corresponding disadvantage is that they are slow to arrive in the library, even in their unbound parts. To fill this gap lawyers go to one of the weekly series.

3.6.6   THE WEEKLY SERIES

(a) The Incorporated Council since 1953 have put out a junior series to fill the gap: the *Weekly Law Reports*. These arrive in paper parts within a month or so of a case being decided. They are grouped into three volumes each year: Volumes 2 and 3 contain cases intended to appear in *The Law Reports*. Volume 1 has cases which are not intended to get that full treatment. Each paper part may contain cases destined for Volume 1 as well as for Volume 2 or 3. Look carefully at the cover to see the exact content.

(b) Since 1936 Butterworths have provided us with the *All England Law Reports* (All ER), which in most respects are comparable with the WLR. There are now four volumes a year, but these are merely consecutive. A further volume, containing commercial cases, has recently been added to the series.

3.6.7   INDEXES TO THESE REPORTS

The Law Reports publishes during the course of each year a cumulative index in a pink booklet. This includes not only *The Law Reports* cases and WLR but also the All ER and many other current series: see its front cover for the list. These indexes are conflated with those for past years, becoming the (limp) red indexes; and each ten years of these are made into a bound red index volume. (The usefulness of these indexes for research on statutes and SIs is explained in **Chapter 6**.)

3.6.8   MORE RECENT REPORTS

Almost every day in *The Times* and the *Independent* there are citable law reports. The *Guardian*, the *Daily Telegraph* and the *Financial Times* have all carried law reports as well, but they have stopped for the time being. The *Scotsman* and *Lloyd's List* are now the only other newspaper law reports. In many law libraries the librarians extract and file these. Some of the more important may be reprinted after two or three weeks in one or more of the practitioners' weeklies (*New Law Journal, Solicitors' Journal, Law Society's Gazette*). These cases, if important, eventually get edited into full-strength law reports. But until they do, the newspaper or weekly is the only source. Many, moreover, never get reported further and these newspaper reports remain the sole source. There is now a comprehensive means of accessing them: *Daily Law Reports Index*.

3.6.9   REPORTS ON THE WEB

The citation of law reports as appearing on the Internet has now been officially approved. For this purpose a system of 'neutral' citation has been introduced. Each judgment when transcribed will be given a case number; note the use of paragraph numbers instead of page numbers. References will be to EWCA for the Court of Appeal and EWHC for the High Court. See *Practice Note* [2001] 1 All ER 193.

3.6.10   *DAILY LAW REPORTS INDEX*

DLRI started in 1988. Every case that has been in any of the dailies is included, and is indexed by parties' names, by subject matter, and by any statute, SI, regulation, treaty article, etc., involved. A digest of each report provides the facts and decision.

The bound volumes down to 1999 may still be shelved in some libraries. Since then it is only available on-line. The whole of the database back to 1988, kept very up-to-date, is accessible as 'Current Law Cases' on the Sweet & Maxwell Westlaw website.

3.6.11   OLDER REPORTS

(a)   Continuous series: There were various continuous series which started in the nineteenth century and ended in the middle of the twentieth: the *Law Journal Reports, Law Times Reports* and *Times Law Reports*. One such series survives: *Justice of the Peace Reports*.

(b)   Named reporters: Until *The Law Reports* were established in 1865, law reporting was left to private individuals, lawyers or judges, who made their own collections of cases and which eventually got printed and published. They are recognisable by their names, e.g. Coke's Reports, Vesey Senior, Meeson & Welsby, etc., or their corresponding initials and so are also referred to as the nominate reports. Some libraries may have some of these in the original volumes. However they have been more conveniently collected into 176 volumes as the *English Reports*, which can be accessed in the following ways:

(i)   If you have the case-name: the last two volumes of the set are an index of case-names. This gives both the original reporter's volume and page, and the volume and page in the ER set.

(ii)   If you have the reference but not the case-name (e.g. 1 C1 & F 527), there is a chart which comes with the ER set that lists all the reporters by name and initials, and tells you which courts they reported and in which volumes of the ER they appear. Look at the spine of the volume(s) cited and see which includes your reporter's volume reference.

(iii)   Citing the *English Reports*: Strictly, we don't. The ER is just a rationalised reprint. We still cling to the original reporter's name, volume and page when citing his reports as if we were using the old leather tomes. For this purpose you will find the original pagination preserved in the midst of ER pages by numbers in square brackets in the text.

(iv) A CD-ROM edition of the whole of the ER has been published by Juta-Hart of Oxford with a program which makes word-searching possible.

(c) The *All England Law Reports Reprint* (All ER Rep): this somewhat misleadingly-named series selects older cases reported in the LT and LJ reports and from the named reporters ((a) and (b) above) which still have practical importance. It is therefore a useful alternative source, especially in smaller modern libraries which may lack the older series.

(d) The oldest reports: the anonymous law reports known as the Year Books run from the late 1200s into the sixteenth century. 1535 was the last year to be printed. These are very rarely needed in modern litigation.

3.7 To Find a Specific Case Report

If you have absorbed the above information you should with a little practice be able to find any case to which you have the reference. Where you have a case by name only, or the reference seems to be wrong, you need a comprehensive case index. This is provided by the citator volumes of the *Current Law* service.

3.7.1 *CURRENT LAW* CASE CITATOR

This lists the names of every case — *of whatever date* — which has had any 'life' (decided, distinguished, followed, not followed, etc.) in the period since 1947. It is arranged alphabetically by case name in two bound volumes, 1947–76 and 1977–97. Each year since a green booklet appears and will eventually make a third bound volume. Every report of the case is given, as well as cases in which it has subsequently been cited and where it is digested in the *Current Law Year Book*. In other words, you have the subsequent case-history of every case that has had any. The cumulative table of cases in the latest monthly part of *Current Law* continues the case citator into the present year, giving new cases in capitals and citations of older cases in small type.

3.7.2 HUMAN RIGHTS CASES

This very important new area of jurisprudence, being Europe-wide, may be hard to research in our domestic sources. A new *European Human Rights Case Locator 1960–2000* published by Cavendish, lists decisions of the European Court of Human Rights alphabetically, chronologically, by country, and by Convention or Protocol article. A companion volume provides case summaries.

3.8 To Find Case Law in General

If you know that you need to find cases on a topic or line of authority, the sensible place to look may be the practitioners' textbook, where they should all be at least in the footnotes. If however you want to know of cases since a definite date, try the subject indexes in *Current Law Year Book* and the current year's latest parts, or *Halsbury's Laws* Annual Abridgment volumes; and *Daily Law Reports Index*. All of these have good subject-matter or key-words indexes. However, the widest trawl through case law of any date is achieved by searching *The Digest*.

3.8.1 *THE DIGEST*

This is a multi-volume encyclopaedia of case law, organised under subject-headings. It was formerly called the *English & Empire Digest* and that name reveals one of its virtues: as well as English cases, it digests selected cases from the common law world outside the USA (its coverage of earlier such cases is particularly full). It now also includes cases on European Community and Human Rights law. It is slightly complicated to use, because of its copious indexes, tables of contents, replacement and continuation volumes, and its system of numbering cases. It is kept up to date by quarterly cumulative supplements; but it can be misleading in that it never seems to jettison cases which have been, for example, overruled in effect by statute, or whole areas of law which are defunct, such as copyhold. Nevertheless it is a most valuable source once you have learned how to use it, and provided you are sure that it is instances of precedent that you need. It is particularly useful in extending the library both historically and geographically: if you have a reference to an old case, or one from outside England, a glance at *The Digest* via its cases index may save you a lot of unnecessary outside research.

Exercise 3 — Cases

1. What are BCLC, BWCC, WWR, Co Rep, WN, NILR, Com Cas, EG, STC? Which of them does your library have?

2. How many reports are there of *Street* v *Mountford* in the House of Lords?

3. Find the most recent cases in the library on:

    (a) trishaws;

    (b) whether the Court of Protection can seal a will if the testator is already dead;

    (c) the attitude of courts to TV crews accompanying police operations.

    (d) whether the prosecution are obliged to reveal their witnesses' previous convictions to the defence.

4. What types of goods were involved in *Hurry* v *Mangles* (1808)?

5. Find a case reported in 1989 that says that for canon law purposes there is no difference between a corpse in a grave and cremated ashes.

6. Using *The Digest*, find:

    (a) a case from Australia on whether the ringing of church bells on a Sunday morning could be a nuisance;

    (b) a case involving Switzerland which says that a corporation has no right to freedom of conscience or religion.

3.9 Sources for Words and Phrases

A very high percentage of legal problems boil down in the end to the meaning of words. It then becomes essential to discover what meaning, if any, has been given to specific words and phrases by the law in the past. A law library must have several sources from which these meanings can be ascertained.

3.9.1 DICTIONARIES OF WORDS AND PHRASES

These very useful compilations seek to expound every word or phrase to which any judicial, legislative or other recognised legal meaning has been attached. In doing so, they give detailed references, examples of usage and other helpful information. The two works are *Stroud's Judicial Dictionary* and *Words & Phrases Legally Defined*. Both are multi-volume sets with periodic supplements keeping them up to date. Although covering much the same ground, their manner of treatment can be quite different and it is always wise to consult both works. Incidentally, should you ever need to use the American equivalent to these compilations, it is called *Words and Phrases*. The set contains about 90 large volumes, plus supplements!

3.9.2   *HALSBURY'S LAWS*, VOLUME 56 AND ANNUAL ABRIDGMENT

Following the general index to this encyclopaedia there is in Vol. 56 an index of words and phrases occurring anywhere in it. This sometimes throws up a phrase missed by the dictionaries. This is carried on for each year by the Annual Abridgment volumes which have a separate section of the year's words and phrases listed near to the beginning, and updated in the loose-leaf Current Service.

3.9.3   THE PINK AND RED INDEXES

The indexes to *The Law Reports* have a section of words and phrases under the letter 'W' in the subject-matter index. The *All England Law Reports* annual and cumulated indexes have a similar list.

3.9.4   *CURRENT LAW*

Each year book has a section of words and phrases as interpreted by the courts that year. The monthly parts have a cumulative list, so by looking at the latest monthly part you will find a list of all the present year's words.

3.9.5   *DAILY LAW REPORTS INDEX:* INDEXES BY KEY-WORDS

Although not strictly the same as words and phrases, you can get useful further leads here to recent cases and those not reported elsewhere. Moreover the editors of law reports and *Current Law* don't single out as many cases on words as they might, so a further source is welcome.

3.9.6   LEXIS

The computer is at its most useful in searching for usage of words and phrases, if not necessarily for their interpretation. But unless your word or phrase is very unusual, just offering it to the Cases file will give you far too many instances to check. You should give it W/5 of constr! or defin! or mean! or interpret!

3.9.7   ORDINARY DICTIONARIES

Don't forget that it is quite proper and sometimes necessary to have one or two of the standard dictionaries' definitions available. A good law library should have at least the two-volume *Shorter Oxford*.

3.10   Foreign Legal Vocabulary

You can expect to have to translate from time to time legal terms from and to other European languages. There are professional legal translators who specialise in this work for big transactions, court documents, etc. But where it is just a term or concept in, say, a letter to or from a lawyer on the continent, it may suffice to refer to a foreign law dictionary. These may be two-way or they may be polyglot, giving legal equivalent terms across several languages. Most law libraries now have such dictionaries, covering at least the major European languages. Check to see which yours has. Also, if your library has the *Official Journal* of the European Community, check if it has the Eurovoc Thesaurus, volume 3 of which gives corresponding terms in the Community's languages. That brings us at last to EC documents in general.

Exercise 4 — Words and Phrases

1.   Find the most recent judicial explanations of:

   (a)   'car park';

   (b)   'reasonable time';

       (c)   'family life';

       (d)   'past known address'.

2.   Has it been held defamatory to describe a lawyer as 'a dunce'?

3.   An Act requires a notice to be 'displayed outside' premises. Is it sufficient to stick it to the inside of the window of the building so that it is visible outside but remains inside?

4.   A recent will left a large legacy 'to X, if he returns to England'. X has returned from Australia, where he lives, and is claiming the legacy. He says that he intends to go back as soon as he has it. The executors say this isn't what the testator meant. Are they right?

5.   What do '*purger une hypothèque*' and '*Übertragung einer Schuld*' mean in foreign legal documents?

3.11   European Community Legal Documents

The legal literature of the EC is vast and ever-increasing. A few official and university libraries have been designated European Documentation Centres and as such receive automatically all official publications of the various organs of the Community. The larger firms of solicitors and some chambers hold a selection of EC legal materials. The selection tends to be rather arbitrary and to vary greatly. See what your library has. You may find it has unofficial publications put out by commercial publishers: these can be more helpful than the EC's own sources. But find out where your nearest Documentation Centre is. It will be listed in what is a very useful source for EC law finders: *Directory of EC Information Sources*. If you can, see how the Documentation Centre is organised and what the legal documents consist of.

The EC produces various types of law. These correspond in type with UK domestic law: legislation, both primary and secondary, and case law. They are also comparable in the way they are either judicially noted or proved. (See European Communities Act 1972, s. 3.)

3.11.1   EC LEGISLATION

3.11.1.1   Primary
This consists of the treaties which established the three communities (EEC, ECSC, Euratom), plus amending treaties and the Single European Act. There is an official edition of these, *Consolidated Treaties* 1997. But in most libraries they may be found in Sweet & Maxwell's *European Community Treaties*, or the same publisher's *Encyclopedia of European Union Law: Constitutional Texts*. Some libraries may have Smit & Herzog's *Law of the European Economic Community* (New York: Matthew Bender).

3.11.1.2   Secondary: regulations, directives or decisions
(For the difference between these, see Art. 249 (formerly 189) of the EEC Treaty.) These are cited by their year, community and running number, year second for regulations, e.g. Reg (EEC) 123/88; year first for directives and decisions, e.g. Dir 85/123, Dec 89/123.

3.11.2   FINDING SECONDARY LEGISLATION

All EC secondary legislation, including draft legislation, and also recommendations and opinions, are published in the *Official Journal* (OJ) which is the main organ and official gazette of the EC. In theory, with a reference to a particular instrument, it can be found in the OJ via the index (alphabetical order, by subject) or methodological table (numerical order, for each type of instrument). In practice this may be difficult. Not many libraries have the entire OJ in hard copy: there are about 40 volumes a year! It is in microfiche down to 1999 and thereafter accessible in a combination of CD-ROM and Internet; whilst the current paper parts continue to arrive almost daily. The existing indexes are only monthly and annual, not cumulative. For recent OJ texts, the electronic sources make searching much easier. See further **3.11.2.5**.

Various commercial publishers produce collections of EC secondary legislation. In this country there is Sweet & Maxwell's loose-leaf multi-volume *Encyclopedia of European Community Law*, C volumes and the *Encyclopedia of European Union Law*; and CCH's *Common Market Reporter*, despite its name, gives legislation arranged under subject matter.

3.11.2.1 Is it in force?

EC secondary legislation is constantly amended and supplemented. As with UK legislation you must check to see the present state of any particular instrument. The EC publishes a *Directory of Community Legislation in Force* twice a year. Volume 1 contains an Analytical Register, classifying by subject-matter. Volume 2 has a chronological index, if you know the number; and a broad subject-category alphabetical index, which is useful for getting into the subject-matter headings used by Volume 1.

A more up-to-date and easier to use service for updating is provided by Butterworths' *European Communities Legislation: Current Status* in 3 volumes, supplemented by fortnightly news-sheets and a telephone service for subscribers.

3.11.2.2 Subject-headings

Searching for EC legislation by subject-matter can be difficult because the legal vocabulary of the European Community is more varied and at times more obscure than our own. Some help can be got from the Eurovoc volumes which come as an annex to the OJ. These are a thesaurus: alphabetical, subject-oriented and multi-lingual, to aid in word- and concept-searching. Once you have an acceptable subject-heading, the index to *Current Status* should lead you to the applicable legislation.

3.11.2.3 Implementation of directives

Directives tell member States to legislate but leave them to do it in their national way. It may be easy enough to find the directive but often difficult to find if it has been put into law by the UK, let alone by other member states; and if so, how. Butterworths' *EC Legislation Implementator*, a soft-cover twice-yearly volume sets out most of the EC's directives since the UK's accession (continued by fortnightly blue sheets) giving for each the instrument of implementation, if any, by the UK. The latest monthly part of *Current Law* lists the current year's SIs implementing EC directives, as well as those assisting EC regulations to achieve their intent.

3.11.2.4 Draft legislation

Generally speaking, the Commission proposes new directives and the Council eventually approves them, but the progress can be tortuous. The Commission's proposals first appear in their numbered COM series. These should be noted in the various current news sources, and are carried by the *House of Commons Weekly Information Bulletin*, which some law libraries take especially for these EC pages. The proposals may go to the European Parliament and also to the Economic and Social Committee, in which case their discussion of them will appear in due course in the OJ's C Series. When finally adopted, the directive will appear in the OJ's L Series. The EC website enables us to observe its law-making process when at these earlier stages of debate and decision-making: europa.eu.int/prelex.

3.11.2.5 EC law on the web

There are now very many websites, both official and unofficial, which give access to European law. europa.eu.int/eur-lex/en is the official website for all manner of EC law. The EC's own database, Celex, is accessible officially at europa.eu.int/celex as well as through various commercial servers.

3.11.3 EC LAW REPORTS

Decisions of the European Court at Luxembourg (abbreviated CJEC or ECJ) and the more recently formed Court of First Instance (CFI) are reported in an official series, the

European Court Reports (ECR). The Reports are now divided into three series: Court, Court of First Instance, and Staff cases. A few libraries get transcripts of judgments straight from Luxembourg. These are the quickest of all their reports — but you may have to translate them from French! A compromise, slightly less up-to-date, is the Court's *Proceedings* series, which come weekly in duplicated sheets, about three months after the decisions. These summarise case facts and extract the vitals of the judgments.

More useful for most purposes are the *Common Market Law Reports* (CMLR), and they also include relevant decisions of the courts of member states. The CCH *Common Market Reporter*, mentioned earlier, gives selected recent cases and these are then re-published in a bound companion series, *European Community Cases* cited as CEC. The *All England Law Reports* now also have a separate series of European cases, cited as, e.g., [1998] All ER (EC) 123. Another home-grown series is Sweet & Maxwell's *European Commercial Cases,* from 1978.

3.11.4 DIGESTS OF CASE LAW

The EC is in the process of producing a loose-leaf *Digest of Case Law* which seeks to summarise the effect of decisions. The *Gazetteer of European Law: Case Search* series, in two volumes continued monthly, attempts to provide up-to-date summaries, with a cumulative index. Our own *Digest* (**3.8.1**) has a European volume, Volume 21. It cannot be as comprehensive as the specialised sources but may have enough of a particular case to which you have been referred to spare you a trip to a more specialised library. Even with its supplement, however, do not take it as the last word.

3.11.4.1 Finding EC Cases
Butterworths' *EC Case Citator* is based on the ECR and CMLR, but also gives OJ references to assist in finding cases not in those series. It indexes every EC Case by every means of reference: name, nick-name, subject-matter, docket number, etc. Butterworths continue it with a fortnightly Case Citator Service, pink sheets listing all the most recent cases by number, name and subject-area.

3.11.5 PERIODICAL LITERATURE

A large number of official periodicals emanate from various organs of the EC. The most important general one is the monthly *Bulletin of the European Communities.* Various publishers produce their own journals: *Common Market Law Review, European Law Review, Journal of Common Market Studies,* etc. All significant articles on EC law relevant to the UK are indexed in *Current Law* (**6.4.1**) and *Legal Journals Index* (or, from 1993, the separate *European Legal Journals Index*) (**6.4.3**).

3.11.6 GENERAL SURVEYS OF EC LAW

There are now many textbooks by individual authors explaining EC law and legal structure to beginners, as well as monographs on particular aspects, e.g. competition. Every library differs in its holdings of these, but all will have *Halsbury's Laws*, Volumes 51 and 52 and Supplement, which attempt to give a wide-ranging survey of all aspects of EC law, as part of their encyclopaedic treatment of English law.

3.11.7 REGULAR NEWS BULLETINS

Such is the ferment of EC law-making, proposals and commentaries that several publishers offer monthly, weekly, or even daily news-sheets of current legal intelligence. The following are just a few examples.

(a) On-line: Butterworth's weekly *EC Brief* has now been replaced by an on-line service: EU Direct, in 'gold' and 'platinum' versions to subscribers. Sweet & Maxwell offer a EU newsletter at www.smlawpub.co.uk/

(b) *European Access.* Published six times a year by Chadwyck-Healey, gives very detailed references and some useful descriptions of current EC activities, literature and comment.

(c) *Current Law.* The monthly editions have a 'European Union' subject-heading and happenings are now also digested under the UK headings of law affected. A specialised *European Current Law* covers every country in Europe, cumulating monthly and with a year book. If your library does not take it, it would be well to remember that the ordinary *Current Law* will now contain rather less European matter than formerly. Conversely, *Current Law* will continue to list major articles on European law because *European Current Law* does not list any periodical articles.

3.11.8 ON-LINE RESOURCES

In addition to the official EC databases mentioned above, there is now an ever-increasing array of on-line sources and search engines for European materials: legislation, cases, bulletins of current awareness, catalogues of publications, etc. A useful guide to all of these is in *Law-Links* by Sarah Carter, published by Cavendish. The most comprehensive guide is published by Euroconfidential: the 'Beige Book'. Meanwhile, since the source most likely to be initially available to you will be LEXIS, you should note how it accesses EC materials. LEXIS can get into much of Celex, the official database mentioned earlier. LEXIS's EURCOM library leads to all the ECR and CMLR reports as well as EHRR. COMDEC has Commission decisions on competition matters. Details of these and more are in the literature supplied to subscribers.

The DTI has its own website for single market information. This very usefully gives the name and phone number of its staff members with their area of responsibility. The former DTI database Spearhead, which summarises all relevant legislation, is now maintained by a commercial publisher, ILI. See www.dti.gov.uk

Exercise 5 — European Community Law

1. Find out what the following are about and whether they are still in force: 1677/88/EEC; 87/153/EEC.

2. Find the regulation fixing the quality standard for kiwi fruit.

3. The ECJ a few years ago ruled that the Commission, having mistakenly awarded too large an amount of aid to an applicant, could not after two years withdraw the award and make a fresh one for a lesser amount. Who was the Advocate-General in the case?

4. Which is the EC Directive which gave rise to the Consumer Protection Act 1987? Who signed it?

5. Find the EC Directive which enables lawyers and other professionals to be qualified to practise in any other EC country. What are the two 'compensatory mechanisms', one or other of which the host country may require?

3.12 Legal Journals

Practitioners' libraries may have some periodicals you will recognise from your academic studies but the emphasis will be on practitioners' specialised periodicals. The weeklies (NLJ, SJ, LSG) keep up a running commentary on all current and pending legal happenings, professional news and opinion. A browse through one of these every week must now become a habit for you in order to be well-informed. In every specialised area of legal practice there are now legal or professional periodicals which you will want to scan if those areas are of concern to you. It is however virtually impossible to keep up with the vast range of periodical literature now offered to lawyers. The usefulness of *Current Law* in listing periodical articles was mentioned earlier. However, we now have some more efficient ways of accessing this literature.

3.12.1 *LEGAL JOURNALS INDEX*

This started in 1986. It lists every article in some 300 periodicals by title, subject-matter, and author's name; and where it is a case-note or statute-note, by the case or statute name. Until 1999 it came out in hard copy and also on-line. Some libraries still shelve the annual volumes. If yours does, you will see their immense size and scope. It now exists only on-screen, in the Westlaw website.

LJI is a most valuable tool for research in recent developments anywhere in the law. It can be your first port of call before venturing into the unknown; as well as your final checkpoint, when you think you have the answer from primary sources.

Exercise 6 — Journals

1. Find an article in 1988 about pupillage in chambers being more like unpaid labour than education.

2. Find the most recent article you can on: (a) *Romalpa* clauses; (b) lawyer-client confidentiality; (c) vibration white finger.

3. How many articles did H. W. Wilkinson publish in 2000?

FOUR

STARTING TO RESEARCH

Having now surveyed the apparatus of the law, we have to bring it to bear in solving specific problems. This and the following chapters aim to show how this is done. The order adopted here is to start with searching in more familiar areas of law; then going on to research in unknown territory; then to updating and to accessing very recent law; some further thoughts on construing words and phrases; and a few remarks on computer-assisted research. Exercises are set for each section. In **Chapter 9** there are some diagrams presenting a suggested sequence in graphical form.

Although reference to **Chapter 3** may be necessary, some of its content has been repeated from a problem-solving standpoint as a reminder.

There are a few preliminary observations which need to be kept in mind throughout:

(a) *The Right Way:* there is no one invariable or correct way to research in law. There are almost always two or more parallel routes to the same destination. With experience and instinct practising barristers know where and how to look up the law (or whose brains to pick). Many a pupil must have had the experience of sweating for two or three days to produce an opinion on some seemingly esoteric point. Their master scans it with a faint smile and then dictates a full (and very different) opinion off the cuff. But this need not discourage you. In legal research everyone makes mistakes, misclassifies, follows false trails to dead ends. The important thing is to learn from mistakes and to develop an approach which avoids them. For the beginner there *is* one right way: be very methodical and thorough.

(b) *Subject-Headings:* the most usual point of entry into the law books is by way of the subject-matter of the problem, which you have first to recognise and classify. An initial difficulty here is that legal labelling tends to vary from one period to another and from one law publisher to another. For example, if you have a matrimonial dispute to advise on, do you look under 'husband and wife', or 'divorce', or 'family law' or 'domestic relations'? Similarly with what used to be called 'master and servant' and is now called 'employment law' (or is it 'labour law', 'industrial law', 'trade union law', 'equal opportunities', 'discrimination', or whatever?) One discovers with experience, trial and error, which category is used by which publisher.

(c) *The End-Product:* the pupil barrister's ultimate purpose is to produce an opinion which is a well-constructed statement of thoroughly-researched law applied to the essential facts. The proper approach to opinion-writing, described elsewhere in the Manual, has to affect the way you research. Counsel's opinions are not broad and discursive overviews of an area of law such as might have won you high marks in university law school. They have to be clear, concise, realistic, reliable, client-oriented applications of the law to the facts as stated. If you bear this in mind it will help to keep your feet on the ground and to ensure that your research does not pull you in all directions. Be resourceful but not perfectionist.

(d) *Finding Nothing:*   the problems set in the exercises which follow all have more or less 'correct' and ascertainable solutions in the law. That this should be so is necessary, or at any rate desirable, for learning purposes. However, to some extent this may give a false picture of law in practice, where sometimes there is no clear-cut answer, and sometimes no discoverable law at all. Finding nothing, no case on the point, no legislation, nothing written about it, is not necessarily failure. Always provided you have done your researches thoroughly, it is success. If there is really no authority, you are free to construct what arguments or analogies you can. But of course your instinct should tell you when and where there is likely to be some relevant law on the point and should prompt you to search more widely or thoroughly before accepting a nil finding. Anyway, in the accompanying exercises there will always be something to find. In one situation, finding 'nothing' is quite normal, and usually good news: in the process of following-through. See further below.

(e) *Further Reading:* There are several books dealing with aspects of legal research. These include:

   (i)   Cope C. & Thomas P.A., *How to Use a Law Library*, 3rd ed. (London: Sweet & Maxwell 1996).

   (ii) Holborn G., *Butterworths Legal Research Guide*, 2nd ed. (London: Butterworths 2001).

   (iii) Stott D., *Legal Research*, 2nd ed. (Cavendish 1998).

   (iv) Tunkel V., *Legal Research: Law Finding and Problem Solving* (London: Blackstone Press 1992).

But no amount of book-learning will give you the skill necessary for effective research in law. So read and absorb these pages, do the exercises and learn from your successes and failures.

4.1   Finding Familiar Law

Although in pupillage you will be thrust into areas of law totally strange and new to you, there will be occasions when the ground seems slightly familiar, where you recognise the legal context (contract, tort, crime, procedure, etc.) even though you do not know the actual answer.

Exercise 7
Consider how you would go about looking up the law on these:

   (a) What is the maximum fee on counsel's brief allowable in a 'fast track' trial where the claimant recovered £10,000?

   (b) What is the maximum fine for an offence under the Tattooing of Minors Act?

   (c) While on holiday in France, John, an Englishman, found some valuable jewellery in the hotel. He kept it and brought it back to England. The jewels (in his possession) have now been identified as stolen and on these facts he has now been charged in London with handling stolen goods, How would you advise him?

Analysis
However blank you may feel about any of these, you do actually know enough at least to set off in the right direction. A moment's reflection should suggest that the answer to (a) will be somewhere in the Civil Procedure Rules. For (b) you will have first to find the Act: either by knowing or discovering its date, or by reference to a comprehensive work on criminal law. These will not necessarily give you the answer, but will point you in the right direction. You must have realised that for (c) you will have to go first to the

relevant sections of the principal statute, and that you will then have to see if there has been any case law to interpret them.

4.2   Use of Textbooks

Where you recognise the area of law involved and have some acquaintance with it, it makes sense to go straight to the known appropriate source: the Act or case itself, if you know it; or, better, the general secondary source, the textbook. Until now textbooks for you have meant students' textbooks. These may still be a useful starting-point, but do remember that you need to switch to the corresponding practitioners' works, with their detailed indexes, comprehensive coverage, multiplicity of decisions cited, updating supplements and general in-court citability. Academic books have the advantage when it comes to speculation about uncertainties in the law, answering difficult questions as yet unresolved in litigation, perhaps drawing inspiration from other jurisdictions. For this purpose some of the major academic works in, for example, criminal law and evidence, are cited from time to time in court. But it will usually suffice to get leads from these rather than to cite the writers' opinions verbatim.

You need to familiarise yourself with what is the practitioners' text in each area of law you are likely to have to research.

Exercise 8
Identify and find the main practitioners' books in the following fields:

contract, conveyancing, company law, civil procedure, landlord and tenant, evidence, custody of children, defamation, licensing, town planning, damages, jurisdiction of magistrates, insurance, motor vehicles, industrial tribunal cases, professional ethics of barristers.

Which, if any, of these do not have supplements?

If you were correct in your guess at the subject area of your problem, you should by intelligent use of the appropriate textbook index (or table of contents), plus the supplement, have obtained one or more useful references. Find these in the law reports, statutes or wherever and see if they are what you want.

Can't find them? If your difficulty is in decoding the reference itself, you may need to refer to one of the legal citation manuals. You have been reminded in **Chapter 3** how we cite and find statutes (short title, regnal/calendar year etc.) and the more common series of law reports (round and square brackets etc.). More cryptic initials are explained in any of:

Current Law Case Citator.

Halsbury's Laws of England, Vol. 1.

The Digest. Supplement Volume.

Legal Journals Index.

Raistrick D., *Index to Legal Citations and Abbreviations*, 2nd ed. (London: Bowker-Saur, 1993).

Various law dictionaries.

Exercise 9
What do the following commonly used legal abbreviations stand for?

LGR, CLY, OFT, FSR, SI, SFO, CPS, H & N, RPC, CCR.

4.3   The Right Case or Act?

In law reports a quick scan of the lines of catchwords which are provided between the case name and the headnote may help to eliminate unwanted cases. Statutes don't have catchwords but the annotated series (*Current Law Statutes Annotated* and *Halsbury's Statutes*) offer introductory notes, explanations of sections and cross-references which may be helpful for the same purpose. Annotated statutes are much more useful for the researcher than the official Queen's Printer's versions. Remember, however, that it is the official version that you will need for citation in court.

4.4   Following Through

Never be satisfied with what you have found until you have checked that it is still extant, unoverruled, unrepealed etc. A glance at a supplement taking only a few seconds may transform what the body of the book says.

Exercise 10
1.   Mary was left property by the will of her husband, Tom, who died in June. Tom's will, made in November 1982 when Tom and Mary were engaged, stated that Tom was looking forward to marrying Mary. He did marry her in March 1983. Mary wants advice on her rights under the will. She has been told by Tom's family that her marriage to Tom revoked it.

2.   Percy, a company director, wants to borrow £20,000 from the bank. He has offered his company as guarantor. The bank manager has agreed, 'if it's allowed'. Can the company guarantee the loan?

3.   Daphne employed a firm of heating contractors to replace the central heating system in her house. She warned them of the special need to take care of art treasures in the house. One of the workmen using a blowlamp set fire to a priceless tapestry. The fire was soon put out and little damage was done but Daphne suffered nervous shock. The contractors' insurers have agreed to pay for the damage but not for the nervous shock, since Daphne was admittedly not in fear for her own safety but only for her property. Can she nevertheless claim against the contractors for nervous shock?

4.5   Other Members of the Bar as a Resource

Other barristers can be a very useful research resource in many cases. It is a strong tradition of the Bar that one barrister will help another, and it is natural to talk informally to other members of chambers when you have a problem. This point is fairly obvious and will only be dealt with briefly here. Of course, consulting others should not replace doing proper research yourself, but it can be a valuable addition in many circumstances.

Amongst the circumstances in which you might wish to consult another member of the Bar are the following:

(a)   Where an aspect of a case involves an area of law you are not entirely familiar with, you might consult a person who regularly practises in the area. (If the whole brief is in an area with which you are not familiar, you should consider returning it to the solicitor.)

(b)   Where you wish to check you are up to date on a particular point.

(c)   Where you are aware that another barrister has recently acted in a similar case to the one you are presented with.

(d)   Where you have a legal or factual hypothesis about your case and you wish to try it on someone.

Ethical considerations must be kept clearly in mind if you do wish to discuss a case. The case is the client's and the client has a right to privacy. Names should not be used and personal details should not be revealed. If it is valuable to discuss points in a case with another practitioner only relevant facts without names should be given, and points may usefully be discussed in an impersonal or hypothetical way, for example, 'I'm appearing for a man who . . .' or 'If a person does not know that . . .'.

FIVE

COLD-STARTING

You can be set a legal problem that has no obvious starting point. The area of law may be just about recognisable, or not even that. This rarely happens to an experienced lawyer. If it does, he or she will apply some thoughtful analysis to the facts, consider the source or origin of the problem, probe the client for background knowledge, do some brain-picking etc. until some pointers emerge sufficient to indicate the right approach.

5.1 Unfocused Problems

Sometimes one is starting cold not so much because the area is unrecognisable as because the problem is unfocused, i.e. you are asked to advise generally in a situation where no actual problem has yet arisen, in order to forestall any problem. If a client comes with a summons in his hand you know broadly what the issue is and will seek out the facts and then the law. If, however, he says 'I am thinking of doing so-and-so. Is that all right?', you may have to pose problems to yourself in thinking of all foreseeable snags which might arise.

5.2 Keywords

Obviously any problems set for you here as an exercise have to be hypothetical, so you cannot do any of these things except the first: analysis. This involves a careful examination of the facts, attempting to identify the area of law involved and/or to establish what keywords the facts provide. Keywords are any terms which are legally significant and therefore index-worthy (or LEXIS-worthy, but see later for that). The broadest general index in the law library is in the index volumes to *Halsbury's Laws of England*. It descends to factual subjects, not just legal categories. When you have no idea where to begin, begin here. *Halsbury's Laws of England* is a legal encyclopaedia and provided you use it properly (index, volume, supplement, noter-up service) and see where it tells you to go, it is one of your best friends in the library. It is now accessible on-line as Halsbury's Laws Direct on the Butterworth website.

Example
A Bar students' magazine wants to run a competition. Readers are asked to guess the number of Bar exam candidates this year who pass in all subjects. Entry is free. Only one entry is allowed per reader, who must be a Bar Finals student. If no one gets exactly the right figure, the prize (new edition of the *Civil Court Practice*) will go to the closest guess. Some officious BVC lecturer says he thinks the magazine ought to get legal advice in case there are any restrictions or regulations applicable. You are asked to check.

Analysis
Can there be any legal objection to this? What area of law would it be? It doesn't look like wagering or betting. No money is involved. It's not a lottery with tickets. Indeed, some skill is involved. Freedom of the press? Competition law? Prize law? (Surely they are something quite different?) But maybe 'competition' or 'prize' could be worth trying as keywords.

Assuming that you have succeeded in finding the answer, it is worth noting that the above problem could have been formulated without using the actual words 'prize' or 'competition'. The point is that you must not expect that the keyword which unlocks the law will always be explicit and obvious. You may have to find synonyms or paraphrases before the particular index you are using will respond. A good index will usually give cross-references (drunkenness — see intoxication; drug — see narcotic, pharmaceutical, prescription). But not all indexers are so helpful. You will often have to use your imagination, stretch your vocabulary, and translate from plain lay terms to legal concepts to arrive at the vital keyword.

Exercise 11 — Simple Keyword Problems
1. When is the close season for snipe?
2. Must London taxis have meters?
3. In what circumstances may a coroner hold an inquest on a Sunday?
4. Why are there quarter-mile posts along the railway track?
5. Where exactly is high-water mark?
6. Are there any age limits applicable to the appointment of bishops?
7. North Sea gas is odourless but when it comes into our houses it smells. In legal terms, why is this so?
8. When did Parliament decide to have 366 days in 2000?
9. How old must one be to get a licence to operate a CB radio?
10. Are the winnings of a successful gambler or the earnings of a prostitute subject to income tax?

5.3   Concealed Keywords

The keyword approach will not work if, for example, the statutory source we need uses a precise and narrow word which we tend to widen or paraphrase in ordinary usage.

Example
Henry, a landlord, granted tenancies of rooms in a newly converted house on weekly terms. To avoid giving security of tenure under the Rent Act he installed a free coffee-machine in the basement kitchen so that his tenants can help themselves in the mornings. Henry would like you to confirm that his tenants are thus not protected.

Analysis
The landlord's thinking is that if he is providing more for his tenants than merely lodging, they are, like paying guests, outside the Act. This is an inevitable distinction which the Acts have always recognised. So a trawl through one of the standard textbooks should eventually reveal how far the law allows it to be pushed. Alternatively, we could try 'food' or 'drink' as keywords. But the books don't respond to these (and they are too general for LEXIS). The real keyword is 'board', but no one not knowing it would be likely to guess it. That, however, is the Act's word, and all the cases are based on it, including a House of Lords case in 1988 which you will need to find.

5.4   Red Herrings

There may be a plethora of keywords in a problem. Some careful analysis is called for to identify the narrow issues and focus on them to the exclusion of all else.

Exercise 12 — Less Obvious Keywords
1. Charles's house was badly damaged in a severe gale last night. The upper part is in danger of falling. Charles's surveyor says it must be pulled down and made safe without delay. Workmen are standing by to do the necessary. But the house is a listed building and no authorisation has been obtained. Can Charles go ahead?

2. Peter, Paul and Mary want to go carol singing for charity on Christmas Day. They intend to stand together, each with a collecting box, in Trafalgar Square. They have also trained their dog to carry a collecting box. Any advice?

3.   Waxmell owns a newspaper with a daily circulation of nearly half a million copies. He wants to buy another paper, a local with a circulation of about 20,000 and falling, which its owner, Burdock, wants to sell. Advise Waxmell if he can go ahead or if there are legal steps he has to comply with.

4.   The City Council is divided equally between Conservative and Labour members. The mayor, who presides, is a Labour member. Whenever the Council votes on what is a politically loaded matter, the result is a tie. So the mayor, who has already voted with the Labour side, then purports to vote for that side again, tipping the balance. The Conservatives wish to challenge his right to do this. Will they succeed?

5.   Clients are a firm of auctioneers. Their sale catalogue described a piece of furniture as Georgian. An experienced dealer purchased it at the auction. He says (and they now agree) it is Victorian and that this amounts to a false trade description. The auctioneers point out that their catalogue conditions state that being merely auctioneers, they are not responsible for vendors' statements of authenticity, origin, date, etc. of any article. They also say that anyway the purchaser is himself an expert who did not rely on their description. They therefore say that they are not liable for false trade description. Are they right?

6.   While eating in your local café you see the owner put up a notice 'Waitress Wanted. Mornings Only. Good Wages.' What advice would you give him? What may happen if he doesn't heed your advice?

SIX

FOLLOWING THROUGH

Just as you should not be discouraged if at first you do not succeed, so conversely you should not be satisfied when you find what seems to be the right case, section, regulations or whatever. Because until you have checked its current status you cannot be sure you have found the last word on the matter. You must get into the habit of searching cumulatively, right up to date.

6.1 Statutes

The first question to ask of a statute is: is it operative? That is really two questions: is it yet in force? and is it still in force?

Is it yet in force? Do not assume this. Look first at the commencement section. Nowadays this is always at the end of the Act proper, before any schedules. (Or almost always: see, however, Local Government Act 1985.) Does the commencement section indicate that the bit you want has a delayed start, waiting for the Secretary of State to activate it? If so, check *Is It In Force?* or the *Current Law Legislation Citator.* If according to these it is not yet activated, check the citator part of the *Current Law Statutes* service file, and then the latest monthly part of *Current Law* for the table of this year's commencement dates. Commencement orders even more recent than that are given in the legal weeklies, and in the *Daily List.*

Is it still in force? You will look pretty silly if you base your opinion on a statute or section since repealed. *Current Law Legislation Citator* and the latest monthly part index will tell you of any repeals or amendments and the later Act which made them. Remember that the citator gives you every statute — of whatever date — to which anything has happened since 1947. Alternatively, if you are using *Halsbury's Statutes,* you must check its supplement and current service, updating your information to the beginning of the current year and month respectively. Notice that both series give not only subsequent statutory happenings, but also SIs with regulations and orders which flesh out the sections; and, most helpfully, cases on the section.

This exercise in cumulative checking is essential. It is made easy for you by the sets (all three *Halsbury's, The Digest, Current Law*) which have cumulative supplements. We are often too lazy or rushed to follow through properly. Yet it takes only an additional minute, or not even that when, as one hopes, there are no subsequent entries to affect the information got from the main set. (Remember what was said earlier about finding 'nothing'.)

6.2 Subsequent Happenings

There are four main ways in which the law as we know or discover it can be affected by later happenings:

(a) statutes affecting earlier statutes;

(b) cases interpreting earlier statutes;

(c) cases affecting earlier case law;

(d) statutes affecting earlier case law.

Of these, the methods of checking for (a) and (b) have been considered already. Checking for (c) is easily ascertained by the use of the *Current Law Case Citator* volumes. These give every case — of whatever date — of which anything like a report exists, which has had any happenings (decided, distinguished, overruled, etc.) since 1947. Again, it is necessary to continue your follow-through to the latest monthly part of *Current Law* with its cumulative case citator for the current year.

It is (d) which is the most difficult to find out; at least where a well-known case or body of case law has been affected by recent legislation. The statute may not yet have reached the textbook's supplement. The authors may not even see it as relevant, if its impact is an incidental side-effect. One cannot expect law reports on the library shelf to be annotated to take account of later legislation. One might have thought that the *Current Law Case Citator* or *The Digest* could have indicated when a case they cite has been completely overturned by Parliament. But they do not.

Example
Any effective example depends on recentness. It will therefore quickly lose its point as the standard books and sources catch up. However, to illustrate the general point, consider the following problem:

Loveless, a youth of 17, became infatuated with Cherie, a fashion model, after seeing her photo in a magazine. Having discovered where she lived, he would hang around outside her flat all day and follow her wherever she went. He never approached or spoke to her but she was always aware of his presence. This began to tell on her and it affected her to such an extent that she feared to go out, lost modelling work and became ill and withdrawn.

In 1997, a student or pupil asked to advise with this type of problem would probably have had at least some background knowledge of the stalking cases, discussed in their criminal law course two or more years previously. So he or she would have looked up the decisions on the adaptation of assault to include psychological injury, the meaning given to 'harm' and 'inflict' in the Offences Against the Person Act 1861; as well as the availability of injunctive relief. The cases are all there in the reports, sometimes with helpful commentaries. But these sources would not have indicated that Parliament had meantime intervened to supplement these makeshift approaches by the Protection from Harassment Act 1997. This does not repeal or amend anything in the 1861 Act so one would not be alerted to it by statutory annotations in the ordinary way. How, pending the arrival of the new editions of textbooks and supplements, is one to discover the impact of legislation on existing case-law, and especially in less well-publicised instances than this? A search by key words in Legal Journals Index and in the ALLJNL file of LEXIS should reveal any contemporary discussion of current happenings anywhere in the law, including reforms advocated, officially proposed and actually in progress.

6.3   Statutory Instruments and their Subsequent Happenings

Statutory instruments are something of a law unto themselves, with their great bulk and constant flow, their manner of creation, amendment and revocation, their separate literature, their low profile (for the general public, at least), and the complications of accessing them. Section **3.5** has outlined the various ways they are found and updated in the library. They are also now contained on the STATIS file of LEXIS, on CD-ROM and on the Badger database (see **8.3.2.4**). So with a little practice you should be able to find them by their number, by their parent Act or by their subject-matter, on the shelf or the screen.

6.3.1 RESEARCHING IN THE STATUTORY INSTRUMENTS

6.3.1.1 Why might you be looking for a SI?

(a) You have an Act which is to commence on an appointed day, and want to see whether there has been a commencement order and, if so, what it says: if that is all you want, don't bother to look for the SI (if any) unless you have some very special reason for wanting its exact words. Instead:

   (i) Check *Is It In Force?* and continue as explained in **3.4.3** above.

   (ii) Alternatively there is a list of commencement and appointed day orders in the first loose-leaf volume of *Halsbury's SIs* updated to the present month by the Monthly Survey section in the same binder.

   (iii) In either case, follow through for the most recent orders by checking the weekly lists in the NLJ or SJ.

   (iv) If you feel you must see the full text of a recent commencement order, you should find it in the *Current Law Statutes* Service File, or in a previous year's Volume 4.

(b) You have a section of an Act which says 'regulations may be made under this section. . .' or words to that effect, and you want to know if there have been any. You can find out in various ways:

   (i) the annotations to that section in *Halsbury's Statutes*, with Cumulative Supplement and noter-up;

   (ii) *Current Law Legislation Citator* and latest monthly index under subject-matter;

   (iii) the Table of Statutes in *Halsbury's SIs* indexes all enabling Acts with their implementations;

   (iv) the *Index to Government Orders*, supplemented by the *List of Statutory Instruments* published monthly by the Stationery Office;

followed in all cases by a scan of the last few issues of one of the weeklies which lists all newly published SIs. To be right up-to-date, the Stationery Office publishes a daily list.

(c) You have been referred to a SI by its number:

   (i) *Halsbury's SIs* first loose-leaf service volume has a chronological (i.e. numerical) list. This will tell you under which title in the main volumes of the series the SI is located. If your SI number is higher than that of the last listed, check the Monthly Index section at the back of the same service volume.

   (ii) If the number is missing from the chronological list, this suggests that the SI is no longer in force. You will discover why in *Halsbury's Statutory Instrument Citator*, a new annual volume. This gives almost every SI back to 1801 (over 50,000 of them!) listed both alphabetically and in reverse chronological order, with its current status.

   (iii) Alternatively, if you have access to the blue, official annual volumes of SIs, you can find the SI by scanning the years and numbers on their spines. But do not assume that these Queen's Printer's copies are still in force or unamended, especially as these compilations take a long time to be published.

(d) You have the name of a SI but not its number (e.g., the Road Vehicles (Construction and Use) Regulations, of uncertain date). There is a comprehensive alphabetical list of short titles in *Halsbury's SIs* Consolidated Index. Annual lists appear in *Current Law Year Book* and *Halsbury's Laws* Annual Abridgments. *Current Law's* latest monthly part indexes all the present year's SIs. Some loose-leaf subject encyclopaedias also have tables of SIs arranged by title.

(e) You think your problem is in a typical SI area of law, but don't know any more than that (e.g. are there any restrictions on the movement of radioactive substances?) This isn't a very likely point of entry and you should do more preparatory research before plunging in. You could try the Consolidated Index of *Halsbury's SIs* or the current *Index to Government Orders*, the official two-volume index by subject-matter. However a more methodical approach would be to go to the appropriate practitioners' textbook; or to *Halsbury's Laws of England* index and follow through.

(f) You have the SI but don't know if it has been considered in any cases:

(i) At the back of the pink annual index to the *Law Reports* is a list of SIs etc. considered. Depending on the date of your SI, check also the cumulated red indexes for previous years. Note that these indexes relate not only to the *Law Reports* themselves but many other series. Nevertheless bear in mind that SIs are very often on minute areas of technical law, too specialised to be reported in any of these series. If yours is such, you should check if there is a multi-volume loose-leaf specialised textbook on the subject-area, or an appropriate specialised series of reports which have a running index.

(ii) The indexes to the *All England Law Reports* have a similar index to SIs referred to, but covering only cases reported in their series. The remarks above apply with added force.

(iii) *Daily Law Reports Index* (see **6.4.4**) has a Legislation Index which includes SIs by name which have had cases based on them reported by any of the dailies.

(iv) The CASES file of LEXIS can be searched by the SI number, name or key words.

(v) The *Legal Journals Index* or UKJNL file of LEXIS can be searched to find not only discussion of such case law, if any, but any other professional discussion of the particular SI which you think there might have been recently.

(vi) *Current Law Statutory Instrument Citator* works in the same way as its much older brethren, the *Current Law Citators* for legislation and cases: it gives every SI, of whatever date, which has had anything happen to it since the citator began, e.g. made, amended, revoked, inserted, substituted or litigated and interpreted. The new citator is limited to happenings since January 1993. However, as the years go by and it cumulates it will become increasingly useful. For 1993–95 the *SI Citator* is the rear half of the *Legislation Citator 1989–95*. From 1996 it has its own bound volume. It is continued for the present year in the Service File of *Current Law Statutes Annotated* (but not in the monthly *Current Law*).

(g) Your SI is ambiguous? Could its purpose have been explained during Parliamentary scrutiny? Very few SIs are debated. If yours was, it will usually have been debated in both Houses. For the Lords, go to the main *Hansard*. For the Commons, go first to the main *Hansard*; if it was referred to the Standing Committee on Delegated Legislation (formerly the Standing Committee on SIs) go to the Standing Committee debates (see **7.3**).

(h)   What you are looking for, although a SI in origin, is better known in another form. The best examples are the various courts' rules. These are in the Queen's Printer's SIs as issued but are more conveniently to be found in the *Civil Court Practice*, *Stone's* or *Archbold*, etc., or their supplements.

Finally, when dealing with SIs, remember that with such an active and prolific series, whatever answer you may have found in the above sources must be checked to ensure it is right up to date. All the sources mentioned have supplements, current services, etc. If your library subscribes to *Halsbury's SIs*, the publishers offer a telephone inquiry service; and will supply a copy of any SI if it is only summarised in their volumes.

Exercise 13 — Statutory Instruments

1.   What is the daily maximum fine for breach of the Insolvency Act 1986, s. 109(2)? Has the Secretary of State increased it since the Act was passed?

2.   When you have contact lenses fitted, to what after-sales service are you legally entitled?

3.   After an evening out, Reg drove his girlfriend Gloria home. They parked outside her house talking in the car. As it was a cold night, Reg kept the engine running, revving it from time to time. PC Killjoy was pushing his bike along the pavement, approaching the parked car from the rear. As he drew level with the car, Gloria opened the front passenger door to get out. The door struck the PC's bike but he managed to take evasive action and no damage was done. PC Killjoy told Gloria that she would be prosecuted for not looking before opening the door. He also told Reg that he would be reported with a view to prosecution for keeping his engine running. Reg and Gloria say they have never heard of such offences and ask you to advise them.

4.   Uplift, while travelling by hovercraft across the Channel, was injured in an accident caused by the negligent navigation of the craft; and some of his luggage was damaged. What is the maximum Uplift can claim for his injuries and loss?

6.4   Very Recent Happenings

More than any other professional, the practising lawyer has to be right up to date, aware of this morning's law reports, this afternoon's debate in Parliament. When it comes to research, the need to find very recent law arises in two main ways: one may have a vague recollection that there was something about this not long ago; or, more methodically, one should be following through to update what one has found.

In big law firms the librarians each day prepare and circulate to members all manner of current legal news. These circulars may be filed and even indexed. Barristers' chambers offer no such service to their members, other than by subscribing to the legal weeklies. How, then, do we find cases which are too recent for the WLR and All ER (which usually appear two months or more after their deciding), new legislation or newly activated legislation?

6.4.1   *CURRENT LAW*: MONTHLY PARTS

These appear about the middle of the month following. *Current Law* tries to capture every occurrence in the law; legislation, cases, articles, books, committee reports etc., under subject headings. Make yourself thoroughly familiar with its contents, layout and classification scheme. Note specially that its index is cumulative: you only need to look at the latest month's index to cover the whole year to then. There is also now a newsletter, *Current Law Week*, highlighting important developments prior to the fuller monthly parts.

Note also that at the end of year the contents of the monthly parts are reorganised into an annual volume or volumes: *Current Law Year Book 1999* has all the law fully indexed for that year. So if you know that it is a 1999 case, statutory instrument or whatever that you need, you may as well start here. Or where, for example, your textbook goes up to end 1998 or early 1999, the [1999] CLY subject heading, plus any later *Year Book* and the latest monthly index, will cover all developments since.

6.4.2 *HALSBURY'S LAWS OF ENGLAND*: CURRENT SERVICE

This keeps the main encyclopaedia up to date to the current month if read together with the supplement volumes. It is not as easy to use as *Current Law* but covers similar ground. It also has annual volumes, the Annual Abridgment, which contain much the same as CLY. The on-line Halsbury's Laws Direct was mentioned earlier (see **5.2**).

6.4.3 *LEGAL JOURNALS INDEX*

This, now on-line only, was described in **3.12.1**. Since it indexes not merely names of articles but their subject-matter, and names any case, statute or SI written about, you will realise that it is not only a comprehensive source for recent comment on all manner of law, but also an indirect source for the law itself; and even for things which have not yet happened, such as the impact of pending changes.

6.4.4 *DAILY LAW REPORTS INDEX*

We met this in **3.6.7** and noted that it is now on-line only. People often remember — or think they remember — a recent case of relevance in one of the newspaper reports. DLRI indexes by key words — finding perhaps six or more in a case — as well as by case or legislation names. Cases not yet reported and perhaps never to be further reported are included.

Exercise 14
Find the following:

(a) The largest award so far this year for personal injuries.

(b) A ruling in 1989 about barristers who accept two briefs for trials starting the same day.

(c) Any recent decision on the Insolvent Debtors Relief Act (2 Geo. II c. 22).

Find the most recent article on:

(d) Barristers' liability for negligence.

(e) The police leaking high-profile cases to the media.

SEVEN

RESEARCHING WORDS AND PHRASES

Sometimes a legal problem comes down to the precise meaning to be given to a word or words. The uncertain words may be in an Act or regulations; or they may occur in a contract, insurance policy, lease etc, between the parties. Or, conversely, you may be at the drafting stage and trying to find an expression which will have the legal effect you want without any risk of unwanted side-effects. What follows deals mainly with the first type of situation: the expression is already there, imposed on you by the document, and you need to know how strictly or flexibly the law allows it to be interpreted. Where you are drafting and have a free hand, the research process is ultimately the same: checking against future problems instead of present ones.

You already know something of the interpretation of statutes and documents, the various approaches (literal, mischief, etc.) and subrules (*eiusdem generis,* etc.). Those may be needed if at the end of all your researches and interpretative efforts, you are left with ambiguity. However, the initial question is whether the law has already defined the term used, giving it an authoritative interpretation. How is this discoverable?

7.1 Stages of Inquiry

There are four stages of inquiry here. It is really only stage (c) which concerns us for present purposes but to be methodical we need to glance at all stages.

(a) Does the Act or document provide its own definitions? Look for these. If the expression is defined, that should end doubt. But it may not be, e.g., where it is an inclusionary definition, or where it is expressly subject to exception 'where the context otherwise requires'. Even a definition section may sometimes need interpreting.

(b) Does the Interpretation Act 1978 help? It lays down some very basic clarifications (e.g. masculine includes feminine, singular interchangeable with plural, England includes Wales, etc.). It only applies to statutes, however.

(c) Has any other statute or case provided a definition? (See below.)

(d) Would dictionaries help? They are quite often produced in court to assist in establishing the accepted meaning of words, on the assumption that Parliament (or the parties) had that in mind. An example is *R* v *Fulling* [1987] QB 426 which shows this can be done even where there is a definition in the statute, provided the definition is not exhaustive.

7.2 Definitions of the Term in Other Contexts

The task for the legal researcher: to find whether the law has defined the word already. Research is necessary to find out if the word or expression has been given any authoritative construction elsewhere in the law. This could be a definition in another statute, or in a case. But before commencing the search, consider whether what you may find will be relevant to the legal context from which you are starting:

(a) Other statutory definitions. To make what should be an obvious preliminary point, one cannot mechanically import a definition of the same word from one statute to another. A definition of, say, 'child' in an Act dealing with succession is unlikely to be thought applicable to the construction of the same word in a statute on, say, employment conditions or education. On the other hand Acts on the same subject (tax, theft, road traffic etc.) have to be read together, including their definitions, so that, for example, 'income', 'deception' and 'motor vehicle' have a consistent meaning throughout. Between these two obvious extremes lie Acts which to varying extents may be arguably *in pari materia*, i.e. on legally comparable or equivalent subject-matter. If so, their definitions may be worth borrowing for the purposes of your argument. The index to *Halsbury's Statutes* may be a helpful place to start looking.

(b) Precedents of interpretation. More commonly the situation is that you are faced with an undefined word in an Act and you want to know if it has been previously defined judicially, either in the same context or more generally.

Example
A new Act of Parliament allows compensation for disturbance in certain circumstances. The disturbance must be shown to be of 'significant proportion or degree'. The Act does not define this expression. You are consulted by a (slightly) disturbed client. How would you advise him?

Analysis
The problem is the word 'significant'. The dictionaries do not help; it can mean substantial, appreciable, more than negligible, or just showing signs. Has it perhaps been defined in any other statute and been construed by a court? Where do we look?

Reference works for words and phrases: some of these were mentioned in **3.9.1**. Most libraries have *Stroud's Judicial Dictionary* and *Words and Phrases Legally Defined*. These are multi-volume works. They not only give the words and their established judicial meanings, but full references to the cases and statutes involved. They are kept up to date by supplements. But for more recent information the indexes to the *Law Reports*, the WLR and All ER all have a section of 'words and phrases'. Then, following through, we go to the latest *Current Law* monthly part where there is a list of all the words and phrases construed this year so far, with references.

So if you now return to your quest for 'significant' you should find a case about a sex shop. See what it says and use your judgment whether, notwithstanding that it is far from being *in pari materia*, it could be applied to your case.

While on the subject and in that part of the library, take the opportunity to look at the other, general, law dictionaries. You will probably find *Jowitt's Dictionary of English Law*, *Wharton's Law Lexicon*, and the *Oxford Companion to Law*. They cover a wider field, including all manner of legal terms, maxims, concepts and institutions, with references. It is no shame not to know the meaning of some technical expression or piece of lawyers' Latin on the first occasion it confronts you. You have less excuse on subsequent occasions.

7.3 Unresolved Ambiguity: Using *Hansard*

If you have to construe an enactment and no help is found in the sources above, the decision of the House of Lords in *Pepper* v *Hart* [1993] AC 593 now permits recourse to *Hansard* to see what was said during the passage of the Bill through Parliament. As a pupil you may well find yourself being delegated to carry out the task of researching *Hansard*.

7.3.1 THE DECISION IN *PEPPER* v *HART*

In *Pepper* v *Hart* [1993] AC 593 at p. 640, Lord Browne-Wilkinson sets out the three criteria which have to be met if *Hansard* is to be used as an aid to statutory construction. They are:

(a) legislation is ambiguous or obscure, or leads to an absurdity;

(b) the material relied upon consists of one or more statements by a Minister or other promoter of the Bill together if necessary with such other Parliamentary material as is necessary to understand such statements and their effect;

(c) the statements relied upon are clear.

The first of these three criteria, if strictly applied, means that the ambiguity must be patent before any recourse to Parliamentary material is made. A provision is ambiguous if it is fairly capable of more than one meaning; obscure if it is not capable of any clear meaning; and absurd if the clear meaning makes the provision nugatory, or self-contradictory or would subvert fundamental legal principle (e.g., no confiscation without compensation, no retrospective effect). Having said that, whether a provision meets this criterion is often very much in the eye of the beholder.

The second criterion means that what is said by someone other than the Minister, or other promoter of the Bill, such as a backbencher in the case of a private member's Bill, is not admissible. Thus, strictly speaking, a statement by an opposition MP in moving an amendment would be inadmissible (though what the Minister said in opposing the amendment might be admissible).

The third criterion is designed to prevent the statements being themselves subject to minute construction.

In *Pepper* v *Hart* [1993] AC 593, the House of Lords described the circumstances in which recourse to *Hansard* as an aid to statutory interpretation *may* now be made, but in practice once there is a possibility of the first of these three criteria being met, *Hansard* research *ought* to be undertaken. Indeed, it would be negligent not to do so. If a matter is urgent and counsel has not had the time to carry out full *Hansard* research in a case where a point of statutory interpretation arises, any advice given by counsel (whether given in the form of a written opinion or in conference) should make that clear.

The decision has since been subject to voluminous commentary and to frequent application by the courts. Three subsequent decisions are worth noting in particular. In *Melluish* v *BMI (No. 3) Ltd* [1996] 1 AC 454, Lord Browne-Wilkinson took the opportunity to reiterate the strictness of the criteria of admissibility, and warned that attempts by counsel to introduce material outside their scope were liable to be met with wasted costs orders. That case also added in effect a fourth criterion, namely that the statements relied upon must be directed to the particular statutory provision in issue, not to other, albeit similar or related, provisions.

Clarke J's judgment on a preliminary point of admissibility in *Three Rivers District Council* v *Bank of England (No. 2)* [1996] 2 All ER 363 is of interest in holding *Hansard* admissible, not to construe a particular provision as is usually the case, but to establish the purpose or object of the statute as a whole (in this case one implementing an EC Directive).

The third noteworthy case is *R* v *Secretary of State for the Environment, Transport and the Regions, ex parte Spath Holme Ltd* [2001] 2 AC 349, in which the House of Lords discussed the scope of *Pepper* v *Hart* at length. Once again it was unanimously reiterated that Lord Browne-Wilkinson's three conditions had to be met before resort could be had to *Hansard*. However, there were differing views on whether they had indeed been met in this case, which turned not on the meaning of a statutory expression — the usual circumstance for invoking *Pepper* v *Hart* — but on the scope of a statutory power, in this case to make a statutory instrument (see **7.3.2**). The majority thought that the first *Pepper* v *Hart* criterion was not met since none of the words or phrases used in the section of the Act that gave the power to make the statutory instrument were ambiguous — any ambiguity was as to the ambit of the power. Lord Nicholls and Lord Cooke, on the other hand, considered that 'ambiguity' in the first criterion extended to the very problem of construction which they faced. However, Lord Nicholls accepted that the third criterion was not met — the ministerial statements were not unequivocal. Lord Cooke alone considered that the ministerial statements referred to were not only properly admitted but provided 'real help' if not 'decisive help'. Nonetheless, of the majority, Lord Bingham and Lord Hope did concede that if, improbably, a minister gave a categorical assurance that a power would not be exercised in a particular way, the statement would be admissible. Another issue in the case was the proper approach to construing a consolidation Act — whether it was permissible to do so by reference to the enactments replaced (see **7.3.6.1**).

7.3.2 APPLICATION TO STATUTORY INSTRUMENTS

Pepper v *Hart* was concerned with a statute. Before that decision the House of Lords had already ruled that *Hansard,* in certain circumstances, was admissible when construing a statutory instrument (*Pickstone* v *Freemans plc* [1989] AC 66). But of course many statutory instruments, by their nature, receive no debate in Parliament. Only if the Act under which it is made provides that the statutory instrument must be approved by a resolution of both Houses of Parliament will there definitely be some debate (albeit usually very short), but that procedure is reserved for particularly important statutory instruments — perhaps one in ten. For a greater number the enabling Act provides that once the statutory instrument is made, a motion to annul it may be brought before either House within a certain period, but Parliamentary time is rarely allocated to debate such negative resolutions. The majority of statutory instruments are subject to neither the affirmative resolution nor the negative resolution procedures — they are simply 'laid' before Parliament after they are made, which is a formal procedure entailing no debate.

In *Denny* v *Yeldon* [1995] 3 All ER 624, the court, in construing a statutory instrument was prepared to look at *Hansard,* not on the statutory instrument for it was not debated, but on the enabling Act for statements on how it was envisaged the regulation-making power might be exercised. There are also examples of *Hansard* on the enabling Act being used where the question has been whether the statutory instrument was made ultra vires. In the latter eventuality, however, *Ex parte Spath Holme Ltd* (see **7.3.1**) must now be borne in mind.

7.3.3 PUTTING EXTRACTS FROM *HANSARD* BEFORE THE COURT

The procedure to be followed if you were going to cite *Hansard* in court was originally sct out in thc *Practice Dircction (Hansard: Citation)* [1995] 1 WLR 192. The requirements were:

(a) a copy of the extract together with a summary of the argument which relies on the extract must be served on the other parties and the court;

(b) the extract must be from the Official Report [i.e. *Hansard* itself];

(c) service must be five clear days in advance of the first day of the hearing.

These same requirements appeared in the early versions of the CPR, but only in the practice directions relating to the Court of Appeal. Those have gone and there is no longer any specific reference to citing *Hansard.* However, the editors of *Blackstone's Civil Practice* point out (2001 edn., para. 71.38) that in the Court of Appeal there is now the requirement to file bundles of authorities 28 days before the hearing, and they go on to suggest that the previous guidance would be a sensible approach to follow in other cases.

Though it was not mentioned in the *Practice Direction*, one small point to note is that *Hansard* is first published in daily and weekly unrevised parts, and then subsequently in official bound volumes which may contain editorial (but not, in theory, substantive) revisions. It thus obviously makes sense to use copies from the official bound volumes if they have been published. Apart from any changes in the text, the column numbering is often adjusted.

7.3.4 PARLIAMENTARY PROCEDURE

To find your way around *Hansard* and to use the material found effectively it is essential to have some grasp of Parliamentary procedure and how a Bill gets to the statute book. There is not space here to cover more than the basic procedure as it relates to a typical government Bill that ends up as a public general Act. For the numerous complications and exceptions that can arise, for procedure on private members' Bills, private Bills and statutory instruments, and for further guidance generally refer to Holborn, Guy, *Butterworths Legal Research Guide*, 2nd edn., London: Butterworths, 2001, chapter 4 '*Pepper* v *Hart* research and the background to legislation'. The two main textbooks on Parliamentary procedure are *Erskine May's Treatise on the Law, Privileges, Proceedings and Usage of Parliament*, 22nd edn, London: Butterworths, 1997, and Griffiths, J.A.G., and Ryle, Michael, *Parliament: Functions, Practice and Procedures*, London: Sweet & Maxwell, 1989 (2nd edn. due 2002). If you are stuck, the House of Commons Information Office can be very helpful (contact details on www.parliament.uk).

7.3.4.1 Pre-Bill
Before a Bill is published the government will often issue a green paper for consultation and then a white paper outlining firm proposals in light of consultation. Or, the proposals may have their origin with the Law Commission, which again usually first issues a consultation paper and then a final report, often with a draft Bill attached. These documents may of course be admissible, apart from *Pepper* v *Hart*, under the mischief rule of statutory interpretation, but they are often useful to consult in any case because they may be referred to by the Minister and may come under the category of 'other Parliamentary material' in the second *Pepper* v *Hart* criterion. The reports may also themselves be subject to separate Parliamentary proceedings, such as a debate on major reports, Parliamentary questions, or come under the scrutiny of a select committee. Such proceedings may provide amplification of the reports.

7.3.4.2 Which House first?
A Bill may be introduced in either House, but most major government Bills and all Finance Bills start in the Commons. If a Bill starts in the Lords '[HL]' appears after its title, and such Bills will include those for which the Lord Chancellor is the Minister responsible, e.g., 'law reform' Bills, and consolidation Bills; but it is now the practice, for timetabling reasons, for a few government Bills each session to start in the Lords. A Bill will go through the same stages wherever it starts. Incidentally, where a speaker in one House refers to the other, the convention is that it is not called 'the Commons' or 'the Lords' but 'another place'.

7.3.4.3 Some procedural differences between the two Houses
Unlike the Commons, there is no guillotine or other formal method of curtailing debate in the Lords. It is very frustrating to wade through Commons *Hansard* only to find that they never reached your clause because of a guillotine motion – at least there might be something in the Lords. There is also no selection of amendments for debate in the Lords, so there is greater chance of a particular point being aired.

These differences, together with the facts that the Lords are notably conscientious in their revising role and are more free of party political considerations, often make their debates more fruitful hunting grounds for *Pepper* v *Hart* material than the Commons'.

7.3.4.4 Parliamentary sessions
Unless a general election intervenes, a Parliamentary session normally starts with the Queen's Speech at the end of November and continues to the beginning of November

the following year. Most business has to be completed by the start of the summer recess, but both Houses return for a short period in the autumn before Parliament is prorogued and many Bills complete their passage in the Lords during this period. A general election may result in a Parliamentary session being unusually short or unusually long, depending when it falls. Bills and most other Parliamentary materials are published and referred to in accordance with the session (e.g. 1995–96) rather than calendar year. This can occasionally cause confusion, particularly with Finance Bills where there is more than one or where the Parliamentary session is not of standard length, because the resulting Acts are cited and numbered according to the calendar year.

A Bill usually has to complete all its stages within the Parliamentary session, otherwise it falls in its entirety, and if it is to be proceeded with has to be introduced afresh in the next session. Since 1999 a Bill may, exceptionally, with all-party agreement, be carried over from one session to the next.

7.3.4.5 Parliamentary stages of a public Bill: the basic pattern
A Bill introduced in the Commons will go through the stages below. Although some stages are more fruitful than others for *Pepper* v *Hart* material, it is usually necessary to follow a Bill through its entire passage, not only because a relevant amendment or statement may appear only at a very late stage, but also in case the Minister at a later stage varies what he said at any earlier stage.

Commons introduction and first reading
This stage is purely formal and takes place without debate. The Bill is ordered to be printed and a date is set for the second reading.

Commons second reading
This is a debate on the general principle of the Bill. There are no amendments at this stage. The Bill will normally be introduced by the Minister who will outline its provisions and explain any background, such as green papers and white papers. The debate is usually wound up by the Minister (or often a junior Minister) speaking again in response to points made. Although the Minister, whether in his or her opening or closing remarks, may provide useful elucidation of major clauses, the second reading will rarely include the detailed discussion of a particular clause that is usually needed. But it should be looked at and is useful for the background. The House will have before them the Bill as first printed.

Commons committee stage
This is when detailed clause-by-clause consideration of the Bill is given and amendments are first moved, and so is usually the most fruitful stage. The committee stage is usually taken off the floor of the House in a Standing Committee (lettered A, B, C, etc.). However, certain clauses or the whole Bill may instead be taken by a 'committee of the whole House' on the floor of the House. Finance Bills have been split between the floor and Standing Committee since 1968–69 (before that they were taken on the floor in their entirety) and matters of constitutional or similar importance will also be reserved for the floor (the Human Rights Bill, session 1997–98, was a recent example). The practical implication is that only debates on the floor of the House are reported in the main *Hansard*. Standing Committee debates form a different series. The Bill before the Committee is that first printed for the Commons.

Commons report stage
This is also sometimes referred to as the consideration stage. New amendments may be moved, especially government amendments made in response to undertakings given at committee stage. The procedure on making amendments and speaking, however, is more circumscribed than in committee. Usually the House will have before them a fresh print of the Bill as amended in Standing Committee (with corresponding changes to the clause numbers as originally published).

Commons third reading
This provides a chance for final consideration of the Bill. However, no further amendments, other than pure drafting corrections, may be moved. It is usually taken without

a gap immediately after the report stage and is generally purely formal with no debate. The Bill is not usually reprinted for this stage.

Lords introduction and first reading
As for the Commons.

Lords second reading
As for the Commons, though it will be introduced by the government spokesperson or a junior Minister in the Lords. His or her brief will the same as that of the Commons Minister and so there will be little difference between what they say, though remarks in the Lords may be modified in light of the debate that took place in the Commons. The House will have before them the first print of the Bill in the Lords series of Bills, which will be the text as amended by the Commons.

Lords committee stage
This, as for the Commons, is the detailed clause-by-clause consideration. Although there may be no debate on a particular clause, each has to be separately moved and agreed. Unlike the Commons, the committee stage is almost always taken by a committee of the whole House on the floor of the House, so the debates will be in the main Lords *Hansard*. However, the Lords in recent years have been experimenting with taking some Bills off the floor of the House as in the Commons. These are taken by a Public Bill Committee, a Special Public Bill Committee (which hears evidence from outside parties), or a Grand Committee (a committee of the whole House off the floor of the House). The last of these has now become quite common and the relevant debates appear in the main Lords *Hansard* but with separate column numbering prefixed with 'CWH'. The first two forms of committee off the floor of the House, however, have proved less popular. When they have been used their debates have been published separately. The Bill at committee stage is that first printed for the Lords.

Lords report stage
As for the Commons.

Lords third reading
Unlike the Commons, this is usually taken separately from the report stage, and furthermore substantive amendments may be and frequently are, moved; again, these are often government amendments on undertakings given in committee or at report. The consequence is that a particular section of any Act may have its origin in such a clause that was introduced only at the eleventh hour having bypassed all previous stages. The Bill is usually reprinted as amended at report stage for consideration at third reading.

Commons consideration of Lords amendments
Having gone through the Lords, the Bill returns to the Commons for agreement to the amendments made by the Lords. The whole Bill is not reprinted, but all the amendments made by the Lords are brought together with reference to the Bill as first printed for the Lords. The Commons may disagree with the Lords, in which case it returns once more to the Lords. In theory a bill can yo-yo back and forth indefinitely, but usually an accommodation is reached. In the very rare event of the Lords not conceding, the Bill will fall, but may be reintroduced in a subsequent session and can proceed without the agreement of the Lords under the Parliament Acts 1911 and 1949.

Royal assent
This is the final stage and is recorded in *Hansard,* but is purely formal without debate.

7.3.5   PARLIAMENTARY MATERIALS

7.3.5.1   Categories
The following are the main categories of Parliamentary publications.

Hansard

Its title proper is *Parliamentary Debates: Official Report,* and it is sometimes referred to as the *Official Report.* It has been the 'Official' report since 1909. The earlier series, produced by the private enterprise of the publisher Luke Hansard, go back to 1803, but they were unofficial and are not necessarily complete or verbatim – the earlier one goes back the less complete they are,

The modern debates are published in two series, one for the Commons and one for the Lords (before 1909 they are in one series).

Both series are issued in daily and weekly unrevised parts, and then in official bound volumes covering, in the Commons, a fortnight. As well as carrying a near-verbatim record of all proceedings on the floor of the House, they include written questions and their answers, which have separate column numbering.

Standing Committee debates

The procedure in the Commons of taking the committee stage in Standing Committee off the floor of the House was introduced in 1907, but their verbatim proceedings were not at first published, so there are no debates for the period 1907–1919, but fortunately the use of the Standing Committee procedure did not become a matter of routine until after the Second World War.

The debates are published separately from *Hansard,* in individual parts for each sitting (a morning or afternoon) and then in sessional bound volumes published by HMSO and its successor the Stationery Office, and arranged by Committee letter (though some libraries may bind up the loose parts for themselves). Unlike *Hansard,* the HMSO bound volumes do not contain revised text, but lists of errata are inserted at the front of the proceedings on each Bill. For large Bills there may be 20 or more sittings.

Bills

There are two series of Bills, those printed for the Commons and those printed for the Lords. The distinction between the two series is not to be confused with the House in which the Bill was introduced. A Bill introduced in the Lords (which has [HL] after its title) is printed with the Commons Bills like any other when it comes to that House.

Each series is separately numbered for each session. Fresh prints as amended at various stages get fresh numbers. Amendments to be moved are printed and issued with the Bills in the case of the Lords, but are not issued to subscribers in the case of Commons Bills (they form instead part of the 'vote bundle' issued to MPs which is not otherwise widely available). In the Lords on the day of the relevant debate all the amendments are gathered together and printed as a marshalled list of amendments. If the relevant stage lasts longer than a day, a fresh marshalled list of amendments still outstanding is issued each day. The Lords amendments bear the same number as the print of the Bill to which they refer.

Explanatory notes

From session 1998–99 Explanatory Notes, prepared by the sponsoring government department, have been issued to accompany each government Bill. These replace the Notes on Clauses, which were only made available to MPs and peers, and the rather terse Explanatory Memorandum that formed part of the first print of the Bill in each series. The Explanatory Notes are issued with the first print of the Bill in the Commons, and then again, with any necessary revisions, with the first print of the Bill for the Lords. On Royal Assent they are issued in third and final form as Explanatory Notes on the Act. When they first appeared it seemed likely that the courts would consider them permissible aids to statutory interpretation, either in order to discern the mischief the legislation was meant to remedy, as Law Commission reports are used, or as 'other Parliamentary material' in the second *Pepper* v *Hart* criterion. And indeed, they have now been used for the first time in a reported case. Since that case was in the House of Lords, it would seem safe to use them in appropriate circumstances. See *R* v *A (No. 2) (Complainant's Sexual History)* [2001] UKHL 25 at [82], [2001] 2 WLR 1546 at p. 1574, where Lord Hope gained assistance from the Explanatory Notes prepared for the Youth Justice and Criminal Evidence Act 1999. He considered them to be analogous to the Explanatory Notes that have always been printed with statutory instruments and which on occasion the courts have referred to in interpreting an ambiguous SI.

House of Commons papers
This category comprises a great variety of material both emanating from the House and printed for the House, but included are the reports and minutes of select committees (not to be confused with Standing Committees). The papers are not needed routinely for *Pepper* v *Hart*, but may occasionally be needed for background on a Bill or for certain exceptional categories of proceedings on a Bill. They are numbered each session and cited as, for example, HC (1994–95) 231.

House of Lords papers
These are a similar category to the House of Commons papers. They include the reports, minutes and verbatim proceedings of Special Public Bill Committees, where the committee stage is taken in that form.

Command papers
These are government papers presented to Parliament, and include white papers and Law Commission reports. Green papers are also sometimes command papers, but often they are simply published by the Stationery Office or by the government department concerned. Since 1986 command papers have been published with the abbreviation 'Cm' and a running number. Earlier series have different permutations of the abbreviation.

7.3.5.2 Availability
Consult your librarian as to the best place to go for Parliamentary publications. The biggest problem is with Standing Committee debates as only a handful of libraries in the country have complete sets going back to 1919. All the Inn libraries take some Parliamentary publications, but Lincoln's Inn has a complete set except for Standing Committee debates, which it holds only from 1987–88 with a small selection of volumes for the sessions 1954–55 to 1971–72. The Information Office at the House of Commons can also advise, and the House of Commons Library publishes a list: *Parliamentary Holdings in Libraries in Britain and Ireland* (1993, edited by David Lewis Jones and Chris Pond).

A substantial amount of Parliamentary material is now freely available on the Internet (at www.parliament.uk) (see **8.3.4**), but this is only of limited assistance for *Pepper* v *Hart* research, for the time being at any rate because of the limited retrospective coverage — by no means does *Pepper* v *Hart* research only arise with recent Acts. Commons *Hansard* starts with session 1988–89 and Lords *Hansard* with session 1995–96, but the Standing Committee debates, without which any research would almost always be dangerously incomplete, only start with session 1997–98. Further-more, Bills, which are often needed too (see **7.3.6.2**), are replaced with the Act once passed. The new Explanatory Notes to Acts (see **7.3.5.1**), however, are available on the Legislation part of the HMSO site (www.hmso.gov.uk).

7.3.6 FINDING DEBATES ON A SECTION OF AN ACT

Before embarking on the steps below, be aware that *Pepper* v *Hart* research can be time-consuming. As a pupil you may well be asked to do the research. If a thorough and competent job is to be done, do not allow your pupil master to set unrealistic deadlines. With all the materials at your fingertips, and if the provision in question is contained in a very short Act, the research might possibly be done in half an hour; much more commonly it will take half a day, or longer.

7.3.6.1 Step 1: Are you looking for debates on the right Act?
Is it a Consolidation Act? Some Acts consolidate a number of previous Acts without changing the law, and the long title of the Act will say that that is its purpose. Under the Consolidation of Enactments (Procedure) Act 1949, Bills for such Acts are referred

to the Joint Committee [of both Houses] on Consolidation Bills who have to certify that the Bill contains corrections and minor improvements only and not any change in the law. Consequently, when the Bill goes through each House there is no debate on the substance of the provision, and often no debate at all.

Thus if *Hansard* is to be used it is the debates on the original Act which first introduced the provision that need to be found. Before looking, bear in mind the basic *Pepper* v *Hart* rule that the provision in the consolidation Act must be ambiguous. In *Ex parte Spath Holme Ltd* (see **7.3.1**) the House of Lords recently held that it was ordinarily impermissible to construe a consolidating provision by reference to the enactments it replaced except where (a) the language of the provision was ambiguous, or (b) its purpose could only be understood by examining the context in which it had originally been used. In the case, the majority held that it had been proper for the Court of Appeal to have examined earlier enactments because of exception (b), but not proper to do have done so with the benefit of *Hansard* because the *Pepper* v *Hart* criteria were not satisfied.

Derivations may usually be found either in annotations to the particular section or in a separate table of derivations in either *Halsbury's Statutes* or *Current Law Statutes Annotated*. From 1967 the official annual volumes of public general Acts also include tables of derivations, which will be found in the last, Tables and Index, volume for the year. In the unlikely event of all those sources failing, examine any Acts repealed that are listed in the schedule of repeals at the end of the consolidating Act. Sometimes, for instance with the Companies Acts, it may be necessary to trace the section back through several successive consolidations. Here old editions of standard textbooks are sometimes helpful. The *Justis Statutes* service on the Internet or CD-ROM, which contains the full text of all Public General Acts as enacted, is another possibility, since the same wording is usually, though not invariably, recycled.

It could conceivably arise that the ambiguity in your section has arisen as a consequence of the consolidation process — the drafting of the provisions of the earlier Act may have been recast to some degree. You will need to compare the two versions. If that is the case, light may be shed by the report and minutes of the Joint Committee which will have taken evidence from the drafter of the Bill. The reports are published as House of Commons papers.

Has the section been inserted or amended by a later Act? If the source of your text of the Act is one that reprints text as amended, e.g., *Halsbury's Statutes* or a Butterworth's subject handbook, check that the relevant text is as originally passed. Lettered section numbers or text in square brackets point to an insertion. The notes to the section will usually give the source of any amending Act, and your *Hansard* research may then have to be directed to that Act rather than, or as well as, the original Act.

7.3.6.2 Step 2: Look at the Bills

Although in the case of short Bills this step may be skipped, with long Bills it usually saves time in the long run if you look at all the prints of the Bill from both Houses before you start. First, this enables you to establish whether your clause was in identical form throughout its passage and if not at what stage it reached its final form — that stage is then likely to be the most fruitful, though bear in mind the possibility that an amendment that is successful at one stage may have been debated without being agreed at an earlier stage. Secondly, you can note the clause number of your provision at each stage — this may change several times and almost certainly will not be the same as the section number in the final Act. You will find this helps when leafing through the debates to find your bit. Usually there will be two complete prints of the Bill in the Commons and three in the Lords.

7.3.6.3 Step 3: Find the *Hansard* references for each stage

See **7.3.5.1** on *Hansard* and its constituent parts and see **7.3.4.5** on the various stages of Parliamentary procedure.

Typically, there will be eight stages for which *Hansard* references will need to be found: (1) Commons second reading; (2) Commons committee; (3) Commons report and third reading; (4) Lords second reading; (5) Lords Committee; (6) Lords report; (7) Lords third reading; (8) Commons consideration of Lords amendments (see **7.3.4.5**).

There are a number of approaches to this but the safest is to use the sessional indexes to the *Hansard* for each House, bearing in mind that (as described below) the Commons Committee stage will usually have to be sought, as a separate exercise, in the Standing Committee debates. Each series has an index for each session either as a separate volume at the end of the session or in the back of the last volume for the session (usually November but note what is said in **7.3.4.4** about the duration of Parliamentary sessions). Under the title of the Bill, all stages are given with both dates and volume and column numbers. Ignore those with an asterisk which are formal only without debate.

The sessional indexes, however, are produced slowly and are usually two or three years behind. If the Bill went through in the current session, look at the latest issue of the *House of Commons Weekly Information Bulletin*, taken by many libraries. There is a complete list of public Bills with the dates (though not the volume and column numbers) of each stage. For earlier sessions use the *Sessional Digest* which is an annual cumulation of the *Weekly Information Bulletin*.

For statutes passed from 1993, an equally good alternative to the above sources is *Halsbury's Statutes*. At the start of each Act this now gives full details of each stage with *Hansard* references.

Current Law Statutes Annotated may also be used, but there are a couple of caveats. The annotations to the particular section, especially for recent Acts, may well draw attention to any particularly crucial debates on the section (as may sometimes nowadays *Halsbury's Statutes*). This is a helpful short cut, but does not preclude the need to check all of the debates for yourself if you wish to be thorough. *Current Law Statutes* have always included references to the Parliamentary debates at the start of each Act. However, until 1998 these appeared only as a string of *Hansard* references without stating which stage each referred to. Although the recent volumes, certainly since *Pepper* v *Hart*, give all references, the earlier volumes suffer from editorial laxity and do not necessarily include every stage where there was debate, and are not therefore to be relied upon.

Bear in mind that some editors of textbooks are now taking pity on the *Pepper* v *Hart* researcher. For example, *Copinger on Copyright* now includes a full section-by-section table of *Hansard* references for the Copyright Acts and *Hansard* references or extracts abound in the many books on the Human Rights Act 1998.

When it comes to finding Commons Standing Committee debates on the shelf, it will depend how they are arranged in the library. If they are in the form of the official bound volumes, you will need to know the letter of the relevant Standing Committee (Bills are not assigned to a particular Committee in any order, except that Standing Committee C usually considers private members' Bills). The letter is not given in the sessional indexes to *Hansard*, but all the other sources mentioned above do. Otherwise look at the listing of the individual parts of the debates in the annual *Catalogue of Government Publications* published by the Stationery Office or at the contents list in each volume.

7.3.6.4 **Step 4: Find the debates on your clause at each stage**
Having noted your *Hansard* references, it is usually then simply a question of leafing through them until you find the debates on your clause, remembering that every stage has to be checked. But with large and complicated Bills it can help if you are aware of the usual order of consideration at each stage, and of what to do if the clauses are not considered sequentially as can sometimes happen.

At the Commons committee stage the usual order of consideration is: each clause in the original Bill and amendments thereto, new clauses not in the original Bill at all, schedules in the original Bill, new schedules. A distinction is thus made between new matter introduced as an amendment to an existing clause and new matter in the form of a separate clause. However, this order may be varied, for example, to take a schedule with its parent section. If the debates do not seem to be going in the usual order, look at the debate for the first sitting where the proposed order will have been agreed. In the official bound volumes of Standing Committee debates there is a usually an index by clause number.

At the Commons report stage, the usual order is different: new clauses, amendments to clauses, new schedules, amendments to schedules. If this order is varied, look at the start of the first day's debate.

The Lords do not distinguish between amendments to clauses and new clauses, so the latter are usually debated where they naturally arise. If a sequential order is not followed, the order of debate can be established either by looking at the marshalled list of amendments with the print of the Bill or by looking at the 'motion for approval' in *Hansard*. These motions to approve the order of consideration appear in advance of the particular stage, not usually with it, but they are indexed in the *Hansard* sessional indexes together with the other stages of the Bill.

Finally, having eventually found your clause at each stage, do not be surprised if it is not debated at all; if it is debated do not be surprised if it is of no assistance whatsoever.

In **Chapter 9** there is a diagram setting out a suggested sequence in which to approach problems on the meanings of words, especially in construing statutes.

Exercise 15

1. The police called at the office of Snoop, a private detective, and found there a bugging device for listening in to telephone conversations. Snoop was charged under a statute which makes it an offence to use such apparatus without a licence. His counsel made a submission that, since there was no evidence of his actually using the device he could not be found guilty of the offence. The magistrates rejected this saying that he must have had the device for use. Snoop was convicted. Advise him if he should appeal.

2. Peter insured his factory against damage from 'flood, bursting or overflowing of water tanks, apparatus or pipes'. While moving some office furniture, his employees dropped a heavy metal cabinet on to a water pipe which fractured, flooding the office and causing extensive damage to the firm's records. Peter's insurers say this loss is not within the insured perils. Advise him.

3. Fred took out holiday insurance. While on holiday in Spain he got heat-stroke and died. His policy covered him against 'accidental bodily injury caused by outward visible means'. His widow is claiming against the insurers. Advise them if they should pay her claim. They think there was litigation on a similar clause a few years ago but can't find any report of it.

EIGHT

USING ELECTRONIC RESEARCH TOOLS

This chapter is not intended to give detailed instruction on every electronic source you may need to use. Although a good deal may be picked up by trial and error, mastering the mechanics of different systems is best achieved by taking the time to read the manual or on-screen help provided with most systems, or better still attending a course or asking for a demonstration from an experienced user (such as your law librarian). Such effort will pay dividends.

Awareness of two general points is essential at the outset. One is the importance of knowing the precise scope of the database you are using. The same point of course applies to printed sources, but the mystique of technology can lure the naive user into a false sense of security. Secondly, the risk of failing to retrieve material that is there is greater for the untrained user of electronic sources than it is with printed sources. The correct formulation of search strategies is all-important.

8.1 Electronic Formats

There are three main methods of delivering, and hence accessing, electronic databases: the traditional on-line database, the Internet and CD-ROM. The first, which involves dialling-up the specific host computer and on-line charges, is now rapidly dwindling, though it remains an option with some databases, for example LEXIS. Most commercial providers now prefer to mount their data on the Internet. Such commercially provided services on the Internet are usually subscription based. The Internet is now also of course the universal medium for providing free information in electronic format. How much of that free information is currently of use to the English lawyer is discussed below (**8.3.7**).

Despite the explosion in Internet use, CD-ROM remains a popular medium. There are no usage or phone charges to worry about — you can search at your leisure. Compared to the Internet, searching can be quicker and often more sophisticated. The main drawback is currency, with updated disks being issued usually quarterly, or monthly at best. Some providers try to get the best of both worlds by supplying the main database on CD-ROM, but then giving access to updated material on-line or via the Internet. Another drawback to CD-ROMs is that, unlike on-line and the Internet, they are inherently limited in storage capacity. If for example you are using law reports, you will have to look at several different CD-ROMs and even then will not nearly match the coverage of LEXIS.

8.2 Types of Database

Databases fall into two broad categories: full-text services on the one hand and abstracting or indexing services on the other. The former, in which the data is loaded wholesale on to the system, such as LEXIS, CD-ROMs of law reports and many web sites, give the possibility of greater flexibility and depth of retrieval, but require greater finesse in searching if you are not to miss relevant material or be overburdened with irrelevant material — you are your own indexer. Abstracting and indexing services, such as *Current Law* or the *Legal Journals Index*, may give greater precision and yield less unwanted material, but they depend on the intervention and judgment of another person — the indexer — in extracting from the full text the concepts and terms that might be sought.

8.3 Main Electronic Sources Currently Available

8.3.1 LEXIS

This is the major on-line full-text service in this country, though it now has a number of competitors, notably Westlaw UK from Sweet & Maxwell (see **8.3.6**). It is particularly comprehensive for case law. However, there is now one caveat with regard to *reported* case law. While it used to contain the full text of nearly all series of law reports since 1945, with the introduction of Westlaw UK it no longer carries series published by Sweet & Maxwell, LEXIS being a Butterworths product. The gaps are being filled as far as possible with original transcripts and other series, but it does mean that it is no longer quite the one-stop source it was. Its coverage of transcripts of unreported cases, however, remains the fullest simply because it goes back to 1980. This retrospective coverage is particularly important since reference copies of transcripts only exist for the Court of Appeal and certain other limited categories of case, and the shorthand writers who prepare the transcripts do not keep their tapes for more than six years. Bear in mind that both its retrospective and current coverage, as with the other transcript services, are selective for ordinary first instance High Court judgments. On citing unreported cases in court see the note at the end of this chapter (**8.5**).

LEXIS also covers all statutes and statutory instruments in force. The need to use LEXIS for legislation arises fairly seldom, but one example where it would be useful is if you wished to search for the occurrence of a particular word or phrase in a range of otherwise unrelated legislation.

Traditionally LEXIS has always carried in full text a few English law journals, such as the *New Law Journal* and *Estates Gazette*. Recently they have embarked on a major expansion, aiming to get 70 or 80 titles on. This will remain only a relatively small proportion of all legal journals published in the UK, and so will not obviate the need to use the *Legal Journals Index* (LJI) (see **8.3.2.2**) to find articles. But LJI is only an indexing and abstracting service, and there may well be occasions when it is advantageous to do full-text searches of journals, for example for mentions of particular cases that do not feature sufficiently prominently to have been indexed by LJI.

LEXIS holds a vast amount of other material — European, Commonwealth, international and especially American — if you need it.

LEXIS is a commercial service. Except in academic institutions where special arrangements may exist, access is normally only available to subscribers who have undergone training and have been assigned their own ID number. However, LEXIS will undertake one-off searches on behalf of non-subscribers, though naturally the charge is somewhat greater than would be incurred by a subscriber. While LEXIS continues to be available separately as a traditional dial-up database, the Internet version is now accessed as an option on the Butterworths web site, re-branded as Butterworths LEXIS Direct (see **8.3.5**), on which various Butterworths' services, such as *Halsbury's Laws*, are also made available. Having the LEXIS brand name on the web site, and indeed now on all Butterworths products and publications, is somewhat confusing. LEXIS as we have known it is now dubbed LEXIS Professional.

8.3.2 *CURRENT LEGAL INFORMATION (CLI) DATABASES*

This suite of databases, provided by Sweet & Maxwell, must now be regarded as indispensable for almost any legal research. They are not full-text databases but a common feature of them is that they are indexed using the same set of carefully controlled subject terms (the 'keywords' field), which means that searching can be more precise than relying only on words that may happen to appear in the title or summary of an item.

One possible source of confusion is the different formats in which the databases may be delivered. They can currently be accessed by three main methods. One is as a subscription service via Sweet & Maxwell's web site, where they are updated daily. Alternatively, many libraries will take the CD-ROM version, which is updated monthly and runs under Folio Views search software. Thirdly, the data, though not labelled as CLI, has been incorporated into Westlaw UK, Sweet & Maxwell's premium Internet subscription service (see **8.3.6**). However, historically CLI was supplied in other formats too, according to the preference of the subscriber, and a few libraries continue to receive it in those formats. One ran under Blackwell Idealist search software and was updated fortnightly — that continues to be the case at Lincoln's Inn Library. Another, also updated fortnightly, incorporated the data into the Unicorn Library Management System, as continues at Inner Temple Library.

The constituent databases, which, if the search software used allows it, may be searched simultaneously, are as follows.

8.3.2.1   *Current Law Cases*

This contains the complete text of every case entry in the printed *Current Law Year Book* and *Monthly Digest* from its start in 1947. The electronic version has the added advantage of being distributed slightly ahead of the printed version. Since *Current Law* aims to cover nearly all reported cases, and also includes otherwise unreported '*ex relatione*' cases sent in by barristers and solicitors (particularly on quantum of damages), the usefulness of this for case law goes without saying. The summaries of legislation covered by the printed version of *Current Law* are now available in the *Badger* database (see **8.3.2.3**).

Also available in electronic form are the *Current Law Case Citator* from 1947 and *Legislation Citator* from 1989. Like the main *Current Law*, the advance distribution of the electronic versions gives a slight edge in currency over the printed versions. Other than that, the electronic *Citators* currently offer no particular advantages in terms of data, though they may well be more convenient to use than hard copy.

8.3.2.2   *Legal Journals Index*

This indexes virtually all legal journals published in the UK from 1986. Since 1993 it has also indexed selected European journals in English. It now holds over 350,000 records. As well as specific subjects in the 'keywords' field and broad topics in the 'subject' field, there is also a brief abstract in amplification of the title of each article.

Although its ostensible function is to find literature on a subject, it is an excellent entry point for case law since it indexes by case name both articles commenting on cases and reports of cases that appear in journals (be they full reports, such as those in the *Estates Gazette,* or brief reports, such as those in the *Criminal Law Review*). Searches can be confined to the case field if necessary.

Similarly, there is a separate legislation field (embracing not only statutes and statutory instruments but also treaties and conventions and EU Directives and Regulations). This can help in tracing the existence of legislation as well as in finding material on legislation whose existence is already known. A small tip when looking for material on statutes is to avoid using the word 'Act' as part of your search. Often commentary appears in the journals while the statute is still going through Parliament, in which case the title in the legislation field will be 'Bill'.

It is worth knowing that Sweet & Maxwell, who prepare the index, offer a document delivery service for photocopies of articles (except, for copyright reasons, from a few titles), if you cannot get hold of them locally.

8.3.2.3 *Badger*

This covers legislation and a variety of forms of miscellaneous 'grey literature', starting for most sources from 1 May 1993. Its legislative materials comprise Bills, Acts, and statutory instruments. It is particularly useful for the latter since they are very numerous and, as well as subject information, details of amendments and revocations and the enabling Act under which the SI is made are provided.

Government press releases and articles of legal interest in the newspapers, other than law reports proper, are also covered, as are government publications and some European material. For details of the full coverage of *Badger* see the contents list that may be displayed as a front screen.

8.3.2.4 *Financial Journals Index*

This covers journals, in the same format as the *Legal Journals Index*, in the fields of banking, insurance and pensions from 1992. While it may contain some legal information of general interest, it is particularly aimed at lawyers, such as solicitors in City firms, whose practice requires them to have access to ancillary information in these areas.

8.3.2.5 *Case Transcripts Database*

A recent addition to the CLI suite of databases is an index to transcripts of selected judgments, starting in 1999. The full text of the judgments is *not* provided, but indexing terms and, usually, a short abstract are given. This is sufficient to decide whether it would be worth the expense of ordering a copy of the transcript from the shorthand writers (whose names are given). If a case is subsequently reported or included in *Current Law*, this is indicated.

The scope of the database should be appreciated. Included are House of Lords and ECJ (and CFI) cases. Otherwise, the bulk of the transcripts for indexing are supplied from Smith Bernal who currently are the shorthand writers covering the Court of Appeal and Queen's Bench Divisional Court. Other High Court (and tribunal) decisions are included, but only on a very selective basis.

On citing unreported cases in court see the note at the end of this Chapter (**8.5**).

8.3.3 LAW REPORT SERIES ON CD-ROM/INTERNET

For some while individual series of law reports have been published in electronic format as well as in hard copy, traditionally on CD-ROM. One of the leading electronic publishers in this field is Context who have made available, running under their Justis software, the following series: the *Law Reports* (from 1865), *Weekly Law Reports, Common Market Law Reports, Criminal Appeal Reports, Family Law Reports, Industrial Cases Reports, Lloyd's Law Reports, Times Law Reports*. The *European Court Reports* are also available on the EU Celex database supplied by Context and also other vendors. As well as being available on CD-ROM, most of the above series can now be accessed from Context's web site, if the Internet is preferred. Other publishers also produce their own series on CD-ROM, for example, *All England Law Reports, British Company Law Cases, Industrial Relations Law Reports*. Even the *English Reports*, the reprint of all the pre-1865 nominate reports, is now available on CD-ROM. Both Butterworths and Sweet & Maxwell also include series of law reports for which they are the publishers with other materials, such as loose-leaf encyclopedias, in topic 'bundles', available on CD-ROM or on the Internet. For example, *Butterworths Company Law Cases* and *Simon's Tax Cases* are included in Butterworths' company and tax products. The above list is not exhaustive, and new titles are being made available all the time.

The usefulness of such series as research tools needs to be carefully evaluated. They all provide the full text of the report, and so have all the advantages of full-text searching. They are particularly good at retrieving cases and legislation judicially considered and also fact-situations or unusual topics and concepts that would not be indexed in conventional printed sources. One drawback is that one generally has to search each series as a separate exercise, though in the case of the Justis software for

Context products this problem has thankfully been solved — provided all the relevant CDs have been cached to the hard disk or are available on a network, they can be searched simultaneously. The more serious limitation to bear in mind is that the search is by definition selective — only a proportion of all reported case law is available in this form. This can sometimes be an advantage. For example, if you use just the *Law Reports*, *All England Law Reports* and *Weekly Law Reports*, you know that by and large you will be retrieving only leading authorities of general importance. Likewise, in the case of the specialist series, one can hope that all the important cases in a particular area will be covered. However, they are not a substitute for LEXIS Professional if near-comprehensive full-text case research is required. Nonetheless, they are a very good preliminary if you intend to do a LEXIS search because you have the opportunity to refine your search strategy before going on-line: you will know what words best to pick and you may also retrieve some leading cases whose names would be good search targets. And if you do not have access to LEXIS (or your search does not warrant the cost), they are certainly better than nothing for many types of research.

8.3.4 LAWTEL

The greatest strengths of this subscription service provided via the Internet are its coverage of recent unreported cases and its currency. It is now comprehensive for the House of Lords, Privy Council, Court of Appeal (Civil Division) and High Court handed down decisions, and with wide coverage of other transcripts. It is updated daily, and cases of any importance generally get on very quickly. Originally it was not a full-text service, but provided very full summaries. Recently the full-text of transcripts have started to be added, and can be accessed from the summary at no extra charge. Where the transcript has not been added, hard copy of the full text can be ordered for a charge.

As well as covering unreported cases, it covers law reports in the *All England Law Reports*, *Weekly Law Reports*, *The Times* and the *Independent* back to 1980. Other parts of the service are summaries of statutes and statutory instruments, tables of commencements and repeals, progress of bills, index of command papers, personal injury quantum awards and an index to articles in selected journals. Of these the coverage of statutory instruments is probably the most useful, again for reasons of currency. There is also a daily update for current awareness, as well as separate modules for human rights and EU materials.

8.3.5 BUTTERWORTHS LEXIS DIRECT

Originally called 'Butterworths Direct', with the addition of the option of accessing LEXIS, it has been re-branded as 'Butterworths LEXIS Direct'. There are a number of separate services that can be subscribed to independently of each other. The most useful for general case law research, if LEXIS Professional is not subscribed to, is All England Direct. This has three components. First there is the 'All England Reporter' which provides summaries (quite full, with catchwords, etc.) of selected cases, updated daily. Links to the full text are added when the transcript is approved, and to the All ER version as well if it is subsequently reported there. Cases from this component are cited in the form [2001] All ER (D) 46, where the last element is the number of the whole case rather than a page number. This component, but without the links to the transcript, is now also available on Butterworths' free site, Law Direct. Secondly, there are the official transcripts in full-text of all Court of Appeal and Divisional Court cases and selected other High Court cases back to October 1997. Many but not all of these transcripts are summarised in the 'All England Reporter' just described. The third component is a complete archive of the All ER.

Halsbury's Laws Direct provides the consolidated text of the printed version and Legislation Direct provides the on-line equivalent of *Halsbury's Statutes*. There are now quite a number of other services which are mostly subject-based, providing collections of legislation, case law, other primary materials and commentary — they are rather more sophisticated and complete electronic equivalents of the traditional loose-leaf encyclopedia.

8.3.6   WESTLAW UK

This recent commercial Internet service comes from Sweet & Maxwell, and is branded with the name of Westlaw, the main competitor to LEXIS in the United States. Most of its data is drawn from, or coincides with, three sources: Sweet & Maxwell's Current Legal Information databases (see **8.3.2**), full-text material from Sweet & Maxwell's own publications, such as law reports and journals, with the addition of selected materials from other publishers, and transcripts of cases. There is a strong emphasis on currency with updates three times a day. For coverage of recent transcripts of cases, which starts from 1999, it is a competitor to Lawtel and to All England Direct. For research of the full text of law reports, it is not as comprehensive as LEXIS, since apart from series published by Sweet & Maxwell, it only includes *The Law Reports* and *Lloyd's Law Reports*. For cases from other series the data provided on the case law database, which starts in 1947, is the digest from *Current Law*. The full text of consolidated legislation is also offered.

8.3.7   FREE SOURCES ON THE INTERNET

Commercially provided subscription services that might in the past have been made available on-line or on CD-ROM, such as those mentioned above, are not usually what are in mind when the question is asked 'Can I get this off the Internet?'. Rather, the expectation raised is access to free information. Highly recommended as a starting point is the book by Nick Holmes and Delia Venables, *Researching the Legal Web: A Guide to Legal Resources on the Internet*, 2nd ed., London: Butterworths, 1999. As well as being a guide to particular sources, it offers a good deal of general practical advice on research on the Internet. Direct links to all the sources listed are provided on the authors' web sites. Their web sites are in effect organised and structured indexes to legal materials on the Internet, in the jargon 'portals'. The two portals have links to most of the same sites, but are prepared independently and are differently organised — take your choice. The addresses are *www.venables.co.uk* and *www.infolaw.co.uk*. The authors make the sound point that gateways or portals are often far more effective than using general Internet search engines, such as Google, Alta Vista, Lycos, Yahoo and so on. For one thing, somebody has already done much of the work for you. But more importantly there are large quantities of information on the web that they are unable to access — the so-called invisible web. Information in the form of databases, rather than documents or text, accounts for most of it. The web crawler can get as far the entrance to the database, but will not be able to index the content, even if the database is a free one. For example, searching on a case name with a general search engine will not retrieve the transcript, even though it is freely available via the Smith Bernal web site. The portals provided by Nick Holmes and Delia Venables are by no means the only ones to use. Also deserving particular mention is that compiled by Sarah Carter at the University of Kent: *www.ukc.ac.uk/library/lawlinks*. It is also published in printed form by Cavendish.

Nonetheless general search engines have their place. For example, if you know a database exists, but cannot remember its address, a search engine may be quicker than working your way through the links on a portal. If you are looking for a particular document that is likely to have loaded directly onto the web, a search engine may be preferable to trying to work out on whose site it might be. A very large number of government publications in particular are published as a matter of course on the web. Of the various search engines Google (www.google.com) is probably and justifiably the most popular at the moment. The number of pages that it indexes, the relevancy of the results and its sheer speed are impressive. But a particular bonus is that it indexes pdf documents (the ones you have to view with an Adobe Acrobat reader), which most other search engines do not. Government publications are very frequently only loaded in pdf format. It also caches all the pages reached by its web crawler, so at least something can be viewed, even if the direct link to the relevant site no longer works, as quite often seems to happen.

The following is a small selection of the most useful sources relevant to the English lawyer. They are all easily found from any of the three portals listed above (so web addresses, which in any case sometimes change, are not given here).

- BAILII (the British and Irish Legal Information Institute), a recently piloted independent body that aims to provide access, in a uniform format with hyper-text links, to all British and Irish case law and legislation currently available for free on the Internet. For case law it includes the material listed in the five bullet points below, though until BAILII is fully established, they may need to be separately checked for recent additions.

- House of Lords judgments from 14 November 1996 on the Parliament site.

- Privy Council judgments from 1999.

- Court of Appeal and Queen's Bench Crown Office List transcripts prepared by Smith Bernal from April 1996 to the end of 1999 on their Casebase service (but more recent cases and full free-text searching are available only on their subscription Casetrack service).

- An increasing number of cases on the Court Service site (but randomly selected).

- Some recent tribunal decisions, e.g. Employment Appeal Tribunal, Social Security Commissioners.

- Notes on forthcoming cases to be reported in the *Law Reports* and *Weekly Law Reports* on the Incorporated Council of Law Reporting site.

- Public General Acts from 1988 and statutory instruments from 1987 on the HMSO site (but only as passed or made — amendments not incorporated).

- Civil Procedure Rules 1998 and related materials on the Lord Chancellor's Department site (there are also several other 'Woolf' sites).

- Parliamentary materials, including current Bills, recent *Hansard* and Standing Committee debates (see **7.3.5.2**), and the POLIS database (see **8.3.9** under Parliament).

- Official publications — masses of material, e.g., consultation papers, Law Commission reports, government press releases, departmental circulars, etc.

- European Union materials, including ECJ judgments on the Europa site.

- European human rights materials, including HUDOC, a fully searchable database of Court and Commission cases, on the Council of Europe Human Rights site.

Also to be borne in mind is that some law publishers do offer bits of free information on their subscription sites, for example Law Direct on Butterworths LEXIS Direct, which may be useful, particularly for current awareness (again, the Delia Venables site gives links to such services and other free newsletter-type material).

8.3.8   PRACTITIONERS' BOOKS AND MATERIALS ON CD-ROM

The legal publishers continue to produce a number of their large works on CD-ROM, such as *Archbold, Blackstone's Criminal Practice* and loose-leaf encyclopedias. In contrast to the material described above, the benefits for *research* purposes of having this type of material in electronic format are not so marked. But there are other advantages for the practitioner, such as portability and the ability to transfer text to a word processor. The latter advantage means that forms and precedents for drafting are popular candidates for electronic publishing.

8.3.9   OTHER ELECTRONIC MATERIALS

The range of electronic materials is expanding all the time. The following is a selection of other materials that you might well wish to use.

- **Justis Statutes** — the full text of all Public General Acts as passed back to Magna Carta with hypertext links to amending and amended statutes; particularly useful for tracing the history of a provision and for repealed legislation. Available via the Internet or on CD-Rom.

- **Justis Statutory Instruments** — the full text of all SIs made from 1987; available via the Internet or on CD-Rom; useful where full-text searching needed but if using the CD-Rom version check the Release Note at the initial database screen to see how up to date it is.

- **Celex EU database** — the official EU database containing the full text of the treaties, legislation (with details of national implementation of directives), proposals for legislation, and ECJ cases; made available by a number of different vendors on CD-ROM and on-line, including Context, with varying amounts of added-value material.

- **Parliament** — contains the official parliamentary database, POLIS, prepared by the House of Commons Library since 1979; indexes (not generally full-text) *Hansard*, Early Day Motions, parliamentary and other official publications, and materials held by the House of Commons' Library; in the case of parliamentary questions (which appear in *Hansard*) full text of the answers as well as the questions are now provided; available as a subscription Internet service from Context. A free version of POLIS, but only going back to May 1997 and with more limited searching facilities, is available on the parliament web site.

- *Hansard* **on CD-ROM** — though recent sessions are on the Internet, some earlier sessions are also available on CD-ROM in full-text.

- *The Times* **and other newspapers** — on CD-ROM and the Internet; there are several major news on-line services, including NEXIS, the sister database to LEXIS, which contains the full text of hundreds of titles.

8.4   Search Strategies with Electronic Sources

Electronic sources, especially full-text systems, are strong on finding facts, names and concrete entities; by their nature they tend to be weaker on finding concepts. So it is often productive to try to convert a concept in which you are interested into an equivalent concrete term which might stand for it, such as the name of a case, the title of a piece of legislation or a fact situation in which the concept might be applied. This is a function of the computer being literal-minded. The computer being literal-minded also means you must be conscious of keying errors, either your own or — and it is not unheard of — the publisher's.

Electronic searching, like successful gambling, is all about hedging your bets — there is rarely any guarantee of absolute retrieval of all that might be relevant. Striking a balance between missing relevant material and retrieving too much irrelevant material — the balance between precision and recall — involves using on the one hand widening techniques and on the other narrowing techniques.

8.4.1   WIDENING TECHNIQUES

8.4.1.1   OR

The logical (or 'Boolean') connector OR is the main widening technique on most systems. Either or both of the words specified using it may appear in the record. It is used for:

(a) related terms, e.g., doctors OR nurses;

(b) broader and narrower terms, e.g., intellectual property OR copyright OR trade-marks OR patents OR designs;

(c) synonyms, e.g., 'retention of title' OR 'reservation of title' OR 'Romalpa clause';

(d) antonyms, e.g., creditor OR debtor.

8.4.1.2 Truncation

Provided on nearly all systems, it is a short cut to 'ORing' the different permutations of grammatical word ending. So, POLLUT* (on e.g., Justis, Alta Vista) or POLLUT! (on LEXIS and Westlaw) gets pollute, pollutes, polluting, pollution, pollutants etc. It is particularly important for getting both singulars and plurals (though some systems, e.g., LEXIS, do this automatically). The internet search engine Google is unusual in not offering truncation or wildcards. Lawtel uses automatic right truncation whether you want it or not.

8.4.1.3 Wild card characters

These function within a word as truncation does at the end of a word, though the wild card can usually only stand in for a single character. So wom*n (LEXIS) or wom?n (Justis) gets woman and women.

8.4.2 NARROWING TECHNIQUES

8.4.2.1 AND

The logical connector AND combines two or more terms, e.g., air AND pollution — both have to appear somewhere in the record. On full-text systems this tends to be fairly crude since one of the words could appear right at the start of the record and the other, in an entirely different context, right at the end. On a number of systems, including many internet search engines such as Google, AND is implicit if two or more terms are first entered as a string (see **8.4.3.1**).

8.4.2.2 Proximity searching

To overcome this last limitation most full-text systems provide for a search where the two words, otherwise to be 'ANDed', appear near each other. Proximity searching is often also safer than searching for a precise phrase. With most systems adjacency is expressed by number of words. So to find 'product' within 10 words of 'liability':

LEXIS: product w/10 liability

Folio Views: "product liability"@10

With Justis it is expressed by number of *characters*: product within 50 of liability

In the above examples the words can appear in any order; there are usually commands if you wish to specify that one word comes before another. Some systems also have a general 'near' command, which for example on Alta Vista means within 10 words, and on Justis means within 40 characters.

8.4.2.3 Fields

Most systems divide their records into a number of separate fields, and searches can be confined to a specified field. For instance, if using law reports your search of the whole text yielded an unmanageably large number of hits, you could confine the search to the headnote field or the catchnotes field, where the terms in question are more likely to appear only if they are in point. Most systems have boxes of forms to fill in but on some, such as LEXIS, the field has to be specified in the search Syntax, e.g.:

COUNSEL (Farmer) (for cases argued by a barrister by the name of Farmer)

8.4.3   PROBLEMATIC SEARCHES

There are a few situations in which you should be aware of the limitations of electronic searching and the foibles of the particular system you are using.

8.4.3.1   Phrases

How systems search for phrases varies. On LEXIS and Justis, for instance, the phrase can be entered unadorned, and nothing but the exact phrase will be retrieved. However, on Folio Views and Google, for example each word in the phrase will be searched for separately and retrieved whether they occur in a phrase or not, as if a Boolean AND had been inserted between the words; instead simply enter the phrase in double quotation marks, e.g. "product liability". Less commonly but for example on the Internet search engines Excite and Alta Vista (in its simple version) the two words are treated as having an implicit OR between them. Again, use quotation marks.

Double quotation marks should also be used on Justis where a phrase would otherwise contain a logical connector. For example, the search BREACH OF CONFI-DENCE, without quotation marks, would generate a syntax error message because the word 'of' is used in the proximity connector.

As noted above (**8.4.2.2**), it is often wise to avoid searching for precise phrases and use proximity searching instead.

8.4.3.2   Hyphenated words

Systems vary as to whether they treat a hyphen as a space or a character. Also there may be inconsistencies in editorial practice. So, for example, enter 'Trademarks OR Trade marks OR Trade-marks' to be on the safe side.

8.4.3.3   Stop words

On most systems there is a list of very common words, such as 'is' and 'have', that are not searchable. Rephrase your search so as to avoid them. On Google you can search for stop words, except 'the', by putting them in double quotes.

8.4.3.4   Section numbers

If searching for a particular section of an Act, it is advisable on most systems to avoid using the word 'section' or abbreviation 's.' because 'section' may or may not be abbreviated, and if abbreviated it may or may not have a stop. The bare number is sufficient. Trying to specify subsections is also almost always counter-productive.

With Idealist, for example, do the search in two steps:

Legislation = Employment Act 1980
NARROW Legislation = 7

This will get material on s. 7 of the Employment Act 1980.

On full-text systems, use proximity searching because the section number may appear either before or after the title of the Act. The same search on LEXIS might be:

employment w/4 1990 w/15 7

8.4.3.5   Capitals

Most systems are not case-sensitive. However, on Alta Vista generally enter all the letters of the search word in lower-case to retrieve all occurrences whether in lower-case or capitals. A search with capitals will retrieve occurrences with capitals *only*, though this is sometimes useful for names of people or bodies, e.g. 'Park' or 'Relate'. LEXIS, which is otherwise not case-sensitive, will do the same with the CAPS command.

8.4.3.6   Combining Boolean operators

Most systems allow the construction of complex searches where several operators are used. Use parentheses to make clear to the system the logical order of the search:

(copyright OR patent) AND software

8.5 Citing Unreported Cases in Court

If you have the transcript of an unreported case, the chances are that you would have found it by electronic means; hence the Chapter finishes with this topic. The coverage of unreported cases has long been a selling point of LEXIS but, as described above, a number of other sources now either provide the text of transcripts, or index them so that a hard copy can be ordered — Westlaw UK, Lawtel, CLI Transcripts, All England Direct, Smith Bernal, BAILII and the Court Service web site. Recently there have been two important developments on citing them in court.

First, in order to aid reference to judgments in electronic form a system of neutral citation of judgments was officially introduced with effect from 11 January 2001 (see *Practice Direction (Judgments: Form and citation)* [2001] 1 WLR 194). The system initially operated for judgments of both divisions of the Court of Appeal and the Administrative Court. The format was [2001] EWCA Civ 1, 2, 3. etc.; [2001] EWCA Crim 1, 2, 3 etc.; [2001] EWHC Admin 1, 2, 3 etc., where the number is a unique number for each case. A further *Practice Direction* [2002] 1 All ER 351 now extends that system to all High Court cases heard in London with effect from 14 January 2002. The format is [2002] EWHC 1, 2, 3 etc., with the addition *after* the number of an abbreviation for the division of the High Court or of the specialist court within it, e.g. [2002] EWHC 123 (QB) or, for a case from the Technology and Construction Court, [2002] EWHC 67 (TCC). The format for the Court of Appeal remains unchanged, but cases from the Administrative Court are to follow the rest of the High Court which is very slightly different from the original format, so now [2002] EWHC 86 (Admin) rather than [2001] EWHC Admin 86. Furthermore, both *Practice Directions* provide for all judgments to be officially prepared with paragraph numbers, and no page numbers. The paragraph numbers are cited in square brackets, thus: *Smith v Jones* [2001] EWCA Civ 10 at [59].

Secondly, the *Practice Direction (Citation of Authorities)* [2001] 1 WLR 1001 issued by the Lord Chief Justice on 9 April 2001 now places strict limits in civil cases on the citation of authorities in court whether they be reported or unreported. Hitherto, although unreported cases are no different from reported cases as far as the doctrine of precedent goes, the courts had attempted to stem the perceived problem of the over-citation of cases by issuing a series of practice directions whereby permission had to be sought to cite an unreported case as an authority. The new practice direction goes much further: counsel must justify the citation of certain categories of case, state on their list of authorities the proposition of law that each stands for, justify citing more than one authority for any particular proposition, and justify citing cases from courts other than the English courts, the European Court of Justice, and the European Commission or European Court of Human Rights. Although this affects reported and unreported cases alike, it may affect the citation of unreported cases most, because by their nature they are less likely to contain propositions of law, as opposed to being merely illustrative, than reported cases, and it will be relatively seldom that counsel will wish to use up their ration of citable authority on a case that has not been reported. The main class of unreported case that may continue to be cited is the case of importance, destined to appear in a law report, but simply too recent to have done so. It should be reiterated, however, that the practice direction only applies to *civil* courts, not to criminal courts (which include the Court of Appeal (Criminal Division)). Nor does it apply to the House of Lords, which has its own practice directions. Note also that, if an unreported case is to be cited, the full approved transcript should be put before the court, not a summary from, for example, Lawtel (see *Hamblin v Field, The Times*, 26 April 2000).

NINE

LEGAL RESEARCH TECHNIQUE

9.1   Diagrams

The diagrams which follow are meant to offer suggested sequences for tackling basic research. They are necessarily very generalised and introductory, and after a few exercises you should have found your way around sufficiently to be able to dispense with them.

The diagrams are not self-sufficient. They presuppose that you have read the relevant sections of the text of the preceding chapters, and, in particular, that you have looked at all the source-materials there described.

The stages in these diagrams should give you some guidance not only on how to carry out research, but how to make notes to present the research in written form. Notes could usefully follow a sequence like that set out in these diagrams, a separate paragraph being used to cover the results of each stage in following the diagram.

Suggested technique

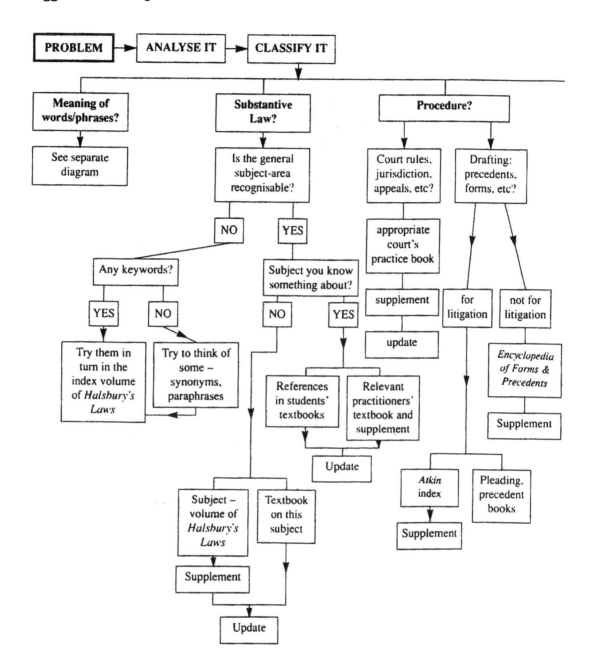

NOTES

1. This diagram is only a rudimentary outline, indicating some of the main directions that might usefully be pursued in legal problem-solving. In so far as you find that it states the obvious, you must already have some skill or instinct for basic legal research.

2. Where, having followed one particular line, the result suggests that your original classification was incorrect, go back and recommence at the appropriate heading.

3. 'Supplement' means that you must refer efficiently to all the supplement(s) and services supplied with the source indicated.

4. 'Update' means go through the appropriate updating procedures, some of which are indicated under the 'Law Known' heading.

5. LEXIS-searching may be useful at many points, either initially or once a certain amount of information has been obtained. LEXIS has been left out of the diagram, however, to avoid overloading it.

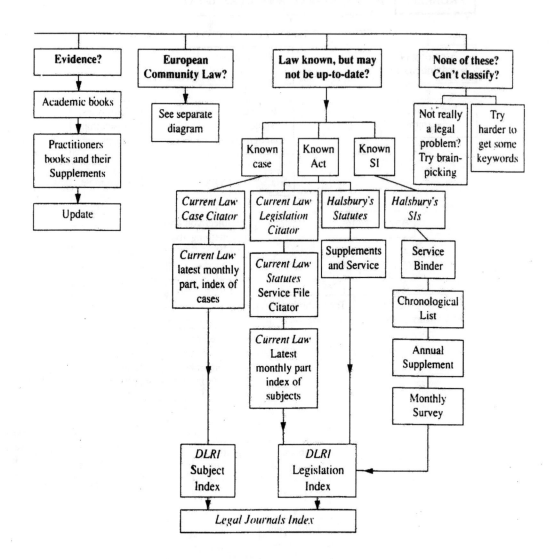

Words and phrases in statutes, etc.

There follows a suggested sequence for construing their meaning. It may also be used for construing documents, by analogy; and when drafting your own. The sequence may not need to be followed through every stage if a definition or interpretation is revealed early, e.g., in the annotations to a statute. Similarly, if a meaning before or after a specific date is sought, *CLYB* or *Halsbury's* Annual Abridgment may be a useful approach.

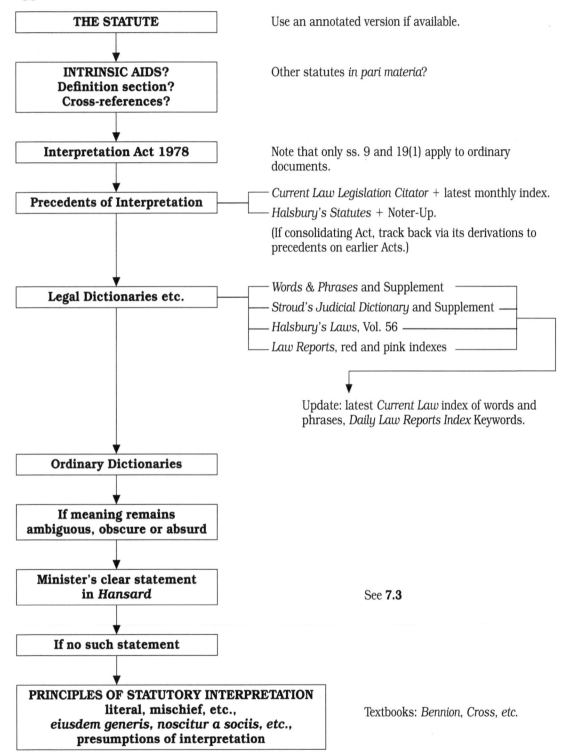

THE STATUTE

Use an annotated version if available.

INTRINSIC AIDS?
Definition section?
Cross-references?

Other statutes *in pari materia*?

Interpretation Act 1978

Note that only ss. 9 and 19(1) apply to ordinary documents.

Precedents of Interpretation

— *Current Law Legislation Citator* + latest monthly index.
— *Halsbury's Statutes* + Noter-Up.

(If consolidating Act, track back via its derivations to precedents on earlier Acts.)

Legal Dictionaries etc.

— *Words & Phrases* and Supplement
— *Stroud's Judicial Dictionary* and Supplement
— *Halsbury's Laws*, Vol. 56
— *Law Reports*, red and pink indexes

Update: latest *Current Law* index of words and phrases, *Daily Law Reports Index* Keywords.

Ordinary Dictionaries

If meaning remains
ambiguous, obscure or absurd

Minister's clear statement
in *Hansard*

See **7.3**

If no such statement

PRINCIPLES OF STATUTORY INTERPRETATION
literal, mischief, etc.,
***eiusdem generis, noscitur a sociis*, etc.,**
presumptions of interpretation

Textbooks: *Bennion, Cross*, etc.

Researching European Community law

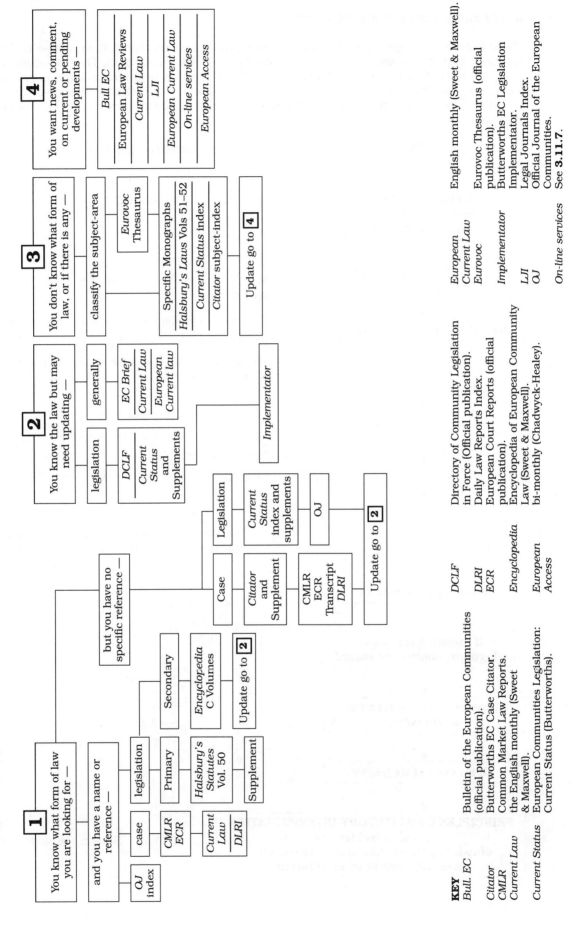

TEN

BOOKS FOR THE PRACTITIONER

10.1 Introduction

We are all familiar with such legal textbooks as Smith and Hogan on *Criminal Law* and *Cheshire, Fifoot and Furmston's Law of Contract*. It therefore comes as a shock to learn that, while such books are excellent for students and may still assist a practitioner on occasions, they are not often used in practice. The likely effect of this is a bookshelf of out-of-date legal textbooks and a large bill to replace them with practitioners' works!

That being said, most chambers have an extensive chambers library, with all having at least a basic selection of law reports, statutes, precedents and practitioners' books. It is therefore unlikely that you will need to purchase more than one or two books in your first year of pupillage or practice.

The following is a guide to some of the most common books used in practice. They have a more detailed coverage than a general encyclopaedia like *Halsbury's Laws*. You will see them time and again in the court room or under the arm of counsel on his or her way to court; you will hear many of them being cited as authority in court. The list, however, is not exhaustive: there are many excellent, practical books on the market which are not included here. Indeed, it is difficult to find a legal subject which has not been covered extensively by at least one author. The purpose of this list is to provide a basic guide to the main practitioners' books so that you become familiar with using them for your practical work on the course and during pupillage. Some specialist law reports are included where appropriate. Other books can be located via the subject index in a law library.

It is vital that you use the latest editions of these or any books. Those which are not re-edited annually are normally updated by supplements. The law changes so rapidly that it is foolhardy to rely on out-of-date material. If the textbook is in loose-leaf format it will be regularly updated. The front page of each section should tell you how up-to-date it is. Recent developments may be set out in a service volume rather than in the main text. Bound texts may have soft-cover supplements which deal with recent developments. The following list is up-to-date as at March 2002.

10.2 A Guide to Practitioners' Books

10.2.1 ADMINISTRATIVE LAW

Aldous & Alder: *Applications for Judicial Review*, 2nd ed. (Butterworths, 1993).

Clayton & Tomlinson: *Judicial Review Procedure* (Hart Publishing, 1997).

De Smith/Woolf/Jowell: *Judicial Review of Administrative Action*, 6th ed. (Sweet & Maxwell, 2001).

Fordham: *Judicial Review Handbook* (Hart Publishing, 2001).

Gordon: *Judicial Review: Practice and Procedure*, 3rd ed. (Sweet & Maxwell, 1998).

Lewis: *Judicial Remedies in Public Law*, 2nd ed. (Sweet & Maxwell, 1999).

Payne & Bibby: *Effective Use of Judicial Review* (Tolley, 1995).

Supperstone & Goudie: *Judicial Review* (Butterworths, 1997).

Wade & Forsyth: *Administrative Law*, 7th ed. (Oxford University Press, 1994).

10.2.2   AGENCY

Bowstead/Reynolds: *Law of Agency*, 16th ed. (Sweet & Maxwell, 1995), updated.

10.2.3   ARBITRATION

Merkin: *Arbitration Law* (Informa, 1999).

Mustill/Boyd: *Commercial Arbitration*, 2nd ed. (Butterworths, 1989).

See also: *Lloyd's Arbitration Reports*.

10.2.4   BANKING

Byles: *Bills of Exchange*, 27th ed. (Sweet & Maxwell, 1995).

Encyclopaedia of Banking Law (Butterworths), updating service.

Paget: *Law of Banking*, 12th ed. (Butterworths, 2001).

10.2.5   BANKRUPTCY AND INSOLVENCY

Muir Hunter: *Personal Insolvency* (Sweet & Maxwell), updated.

10.2.6   BUILDING

Emden *et al: Construction Law* (Butterworths), updated.

Keating: *Building Contracts*, 7th ed. (Sweet & Maxwell, 2000).

See also: *Construction Law Reports*.

10.2.7   CHARITIES

Tudor/Maurice/Parker: *Tudor on Charities*, 8th ed. (Sweet & Maxwell, 1997), updated.

10.2.8   CIVIL LITIGATION

See **Practice and Procedure**.

10.2.9   COMPANY LAW

British Company Law and Practice (CCH), updated.

Butterworths' Company Law Service, updated.

Gore-Browne: *Companies*, 44th ed. (Jordans, 1994), updated.

Palmer/Schmitthoff: *Palmer's Company Law* (Sweet & Maxwell), updated.

See also: *British Company Cases*; *Butterworths Company Law Cases*.

10.2.10 COMPETITION LAW

Bellamy/Child: *Common Market Law of Competition*, 5th ed. (Sweet & Maxwell, 1999).

Butterworths' Competition Law, updated.

Korah: *Introductory Guide to EC Competition Law and Practice*, 6th ed. (Hart Publishing, 1997).

Sweet & Maxwell's *Encyclopedia of Competition Law*, updated.

Whish: *Competition Law*, 4th ed. (Butterworths, 2001).

10.2.11 COMPUTERS

Encyclopedia of Data Protection (Sweet & Maxwell), updated.

Encyclopedia of Information Technology Law (Sweet & Maxwell), updated.

10.2.12 CONFLICT OF LAWS

Cheshire/North: *Private International Law*, 12th ed. (Butterworths, 1992).

Dicey/Morris: *Conflict of Laws*, 13th ed. (Sweet & Maxwell, 1999).

10.2.13 CONTRACT LAW

Chitty/Guest: *On Contracts*, 28th ed. (Sweet & Maxwell, 2000), updated.

Goff/Jones: *Law of Restitution*, 5th ed. (Sweet & Maxwell, 1998).

10.2.14 CONVEYANCING LAW

See also **Real Property**.

Emmet/Farrand: *Emmet on Title* (Sweet & Maxwell), updated.

Encylopaedia of Compulsory Purchase (Sweet & Maxwell), updating service.

Fisher/Lightwood: *Law of Mortgage*, 10th ed. (Butterworths, 1988), updated.

Preston/Newsom: *Restrictive Covenants Affecting Freehold Land*, 9th ed. (Sweet & Maxwell, 1997).

Ruoff/Roper: *Law and Practice of Registered Conveyancing* (Sweet & Maxwell), updated.

Sweet & Maxwell's Conveyancing Practice, updated.

10.2.15 CORONERS

Jervis: *Coroners*, 11th ed. (Sweet & Maxwell, 1994), updated.

10.2.16 CRIMINAL LAW

Archbold: *Criminal Pleading, Evidence and Practice* (Sweet & Maxwell, 2001), plus supplement.

Blackstone's Criminal Practice (Blackstone Press (OUP), annual).

Stone's Justices' Manual (Butterworths, annual).

Wilkinson: *Road Traffic Offences*, 20th ed. (Sweet & Maxwell, 2001), updated.

See also: *Criminal Appeal Reports, Criminal Appeal Reports (Sentencing), Criminal Law Review.*

10.2.17 CRIMINAL LITIGATION

See **Practice and Procedure**.

10.2.18 DAMAGES

Butterworths' Personal Injury Litigation Service (Butterworths), updating service.

Kemp/Kemp: *Quantum of Damages* (Sweet & Maxwell), updating service.

McGregor: *Damages*, 16th ed. (Sweet & Maxwell, 1999) updated.

10.19 DATA PROTECTION

Carey: *Blackstone's Guide to the Data Protection Act 1998* (Blackstone Press, 1998).

Lloyd: *A Guide to the Data Protection Act 1998* (Butterworths, 1998).

Singleton: *Data Protection: The New Law* (Jordans, 1998).

10.2.20 ECCLESIASTICAL LAW

Hill: *Ecclesiastical Law* (Butterworths, 1995).

10.2.21 EMPLOYMENT LAW

Encyclopedia of Employment Law (Sweet & Maxwell), updating service.

Encyclopedia of Health and Safety at Work Law (Sweet & Maxwell), updating service.

Harvey: *Industrial Relations and Employment Law* (Butterworths), updating service.

Redgrave: *Health and Safety* (Butterworths, 1998).

See also: *Industrial Relations Law Reports, Industrial Cases Reports.*

10.2.22 ENVIRONMENTAL LAW

Encyclopedia of Environmental Law (Sweet & Maxwell), updated.

Encyclopedia of Environmental Health Law and Practice (Sweet & Maxwell), updated.

Garner: *Environmental Law* (Butterworths), updated.

10.2.23 EQUITY AND TRUSTS

Snell: *Equity*, 30th ed. (Sweet & Maxwell, 1999).

Underhill/Hayton: *Law Relating to Trustees*, (Butterworths, 2002), updating service.

10.2.24 EUROPEAN COMMUNITY LAW

Bellamy/Child: *Common Market Law of Competition*, 5th ed. (Sweet & Maxwell, 1999).

Butterworths' Competition Law Service (updated).

Encyclopaedia of European Community Law (Sweet & Maxwell), updating service.

Green/Robertson: *Commercial Agreements and Competition Law*, 2nd ed. (Kluwer, 1997).

O'Malley/Layton: *European Civil Practice* (Sweet & Maxwell), updated.

Vaughan: *Law of the European Communities* (Butterworths), updating service.

See also: *European Law Review* (Sweet & Maxwell).

10.2.25   EVIDENCE

Andrews/Hirst: *Criminal Evidence*, 3rd ed. (Sweet & Maxwell, 1997).

Cross and Tapper: *Evidence*, 9th ed. (Butterworths, 1999).

Keane: *The Modern Law of Evidence*, 5th ed. (Butterworths, 2000).

May: *Criminal Evidence*, 4th ed. (Sweet & Maxwell, 1999).

Phipson et al: *On Evidence*, 15th ed. (Sweet & Maxwell, 1999), updated.

10.2.26   FAMILY LAW

Bevan: *Child Law*, 2nd ed. (Butterworths, 1998).

Bird/Turner: *Forms and Precedents in Matrimonial Causes*, 3rd ed. (Sweet & Maxwell, 1992), updated.

Butterworths' Family Law Service, updating service.

Clarke/Hall/Morrison: *On Children* (Butterworths, 1990), updated.

Hershman/McFarlane: *Children: Law and Practice* (Jordans, 1991), updated.

Jackson: *Matrimonial Finance and Taxation* (Butterworths, 1996).

Practical Matrimonial Precedents (Sweet & Maxwell), CD-ROM.

Rayden/Jackson: *Divorce and Family Matters*, 17th ed. (Butterworths, 1997), updated.

See also: *Family Law Reports*; *Family Court Reporter*.

10.2.27   HEALTH AND SAFETY

Encyclopedia of Health and Safety at Work (Sweet & Maxwell, 1996), updated.

Redgrave's Health and Safety, 3rd ed. (Butterworths, 1998).

10.2.28   HOUSING LAW

Arden/Partington: *Housing Law*, 2nd ed. (Sweet & Maxwell, 1994), updated.

Encyclopedia of Housing Law and Practice (Sweet & Maxwell), updating service.

See also: *Housing Law Reports*.

10.2.29   HUMAN RIGHTS

European Human Rights Reports (Sweet & Maxwell).

Emmerson: *Criminal Law and the ECHR* (Sweet & Maxwell, 2001).

Simor: *Human Rights Practice* (Sweet & Maxwell, 2000).

10.2.30 IMMIGRATION

Butterworths' Immigration Law Service, updating service.

MacDonald: *Immigration Law and Practice*, 5th ed. (Butterworths, 2001).

10.2.31 INSURANCE LAW

Encyclopedia of Insurance Law (Sweet & Maxwell), updated.

Hardy Ivamy: *General Principles of Insurance Law*, 6th ed. (Butterworths, 1993).

10.2.32 INTELLECTUAL PROPERTY

Copinger/Skone James: *Copyright*, 14th ed. (Sweet & Maxwell, 1998), updated.

Cornish: *Intellectual Property: Patents Etc.*, 4th ed. (Sweet & Maxwell, 1999).

Encyclopedia of UK & European Patent Law (Sweet & Maxwell), updated.

Kerly: *Law of Trade Marks and Trade Names*, 13th ed. (Sweet & Maxwell, 1999).

Merkin/Black: *Copyright and Designs Law* (Sweet & Maxwell), updated.

Terrell: *Law of Patents*, 15th ed. (Sweet & Maxwell, 2000).

10.2.33 LANDLORD AND TENANT

Hill/Redman/Barnes: *Landlord and Tenant* (Butterworths), updated.

Woodfall/Wellings: *Landlord and Tenant Law* (Sweet & Maxwell), updating service.

10.2.34 LEGAL AID

Legal Aid Board: *Legal Aid Handbook* (Sweet & Maxwell), annual.

10.2.35 LIBEL

Carter-Ruck: *Libel and Slander*, 5th ed. (Butterworths, 1997).

Gatley: *Libel and Slander*, 9th ed. (Sweet & Maxwell, 1997), updated.

10.2.36 LICENSING

Hyde/Rossen: *Licensing Procedures and Precedent* (Sweet & Maxwell, 1990), updated.

Paterson: *Paterson's Licensing Acts* (Butterworths), annual.

10.2.37 LOCAL GOVERNMENT

Cross/Bailey: *Cross on Local Government Law*, 8th ed. (Sweet & Maxwell, 1991).

Encyclopedia of Local Government Law (Sweet & Maxwell), updating service.

Ryde: *Rating and Council Tax* (Butterworths), updated.

10.2.38 MEDICAL LAW

Powers/Harris: *Medical Negligence*, 2nd ed. (Butterworths, 1994).

10.2.39 MENTAL HEALTH

Gostin: *Mental Health Services: Law & Practice* (Shaw & Sons), updated.

Whitehorn: *Court of Protection Practice*, 12th ed. (Sweet & Maxwell, 1991).

10.2.40 PARTNERSHIP LAW

Encyclopedia of Professional Partnerships (Sweet & Maxwell), updated.

Lindley/Banks: *Law of Partnership*, 17th ed. (Sweet & Maxwell, 1995).

10.2.41 PERSONAL INJURY

See **Damages**.

10.2.42 PLANNING LAW

Butterworths' Planning Law Service, updating service.

Encyclopedia of Planning Law and Practice (Sweet & Maxwell), updating service.

See also: *Planning Law Reports; Estates Gazette Law Reports*.

10.2.43 PRACTICE AND PROCEDURE

Anthony/Berryman: *Magistrates' Court Guide* (Butterworths), annual.

Archbold: *Criminal Pleading, Evidence and Practice* (Sweet & Maxwell) 2001, with supplements.

Blackstone's Civil Practice (Blackstone Press (OUP)), annual.

Blackstone's Criminal Practice (Blackstone Press (OUP)), annual.

Bullen/Leake/Jacob: *Precedents of Pleadings*, 14th ed. (Sweet & Maxwell, 2000) updated.

Butterworths' Civil Court Precedents, updating service.

Butterworths' Costs Service (updated).

Chitty/Jacob: *Queen's Bench Forms* (Sweet & Maxwell, 1991), updated.

Civil Court Practice ('Green Book'), annual.

Practical Civil Court Precedents (Sweet & Maxwell), updated.

Stone's Justices' Manual (Butterworths) annual.

White Book (Sweet & Maxwell, annual), updated.

For judicial review see **10.2.1**.

10.2.44 RATING

Brown/Haslam: *Rating Digest* (Sweet & Maxwell), updated.

Encyclopedia of Rating and Local Taxation (Sweet & Maxwell), updated.

Ryde: *Rating & Council Tax* (Butterworths), updated.

10.2.45 REAL PROPERTY

See also Conveyancing at **10.2.13**.

Butterworths' Property Law Service (updated).

Encyclopedia of Compulsory Purchase (Sweet & Maxwell), updated.

Megarry/Wade: *Law of Real Property*, 6th ed. (Sweet & Maxwell, 1999).

Sara: *Boundaries and Easements*, 2nd ed. (Sweet & Maxwell, 1996).

See also: *Estates Gazette Law Reports; Property, Planning and Compensation Reports.*

10.2.46 ROAD TRAFFIC LAW

Bingham & Berrymans: *Motor Claims Cases*, 10th ed. (Butterworths, 1994).

Butterworths' Road Traffic Service (updated).

Encyclopedia of Highway Law and Practice (Sweet & Maxwell), updated.

Encyclopedia of Road Traffic Law (Sweet & Maxwell), updated.

Wilkinson: *Road Traffic Offences*, 20th ed. (Sweet & Maxwell, 2001), updated.

10.2.47 SALE OF GOODS AND CONSUMER LAW

Benjamin: *Sale of Goods*, 5th ed. (Sweet & Maxwell, 1997), updated.

Butterworths' Law of Food and Drugs, updating service.

Butterworth's Trading and Consumer Law, updating service.

Encyclopaedia of Consumer Credit Law (Sweet & Maxwell), updating service.

Encyclopedia of Consumer Law (Sweet & Maxwell), updating service.

Goode: *Consumer Credit Law* (Butterworths, 1999).

Miller: *Product Liability & Safety Encyclopedia* (Butterworths), updated.

O'Keefe: *Law of Weights & Measures* (Butterworths), updated.

O'Keefe/Smith: *Law Relating to Trade Descriptions* (Butterworths), updated.

10.2.48 SENTENCING

Thomas: *Current Sentencing Practice* (Sweet & Maxwell), updating service.

10.2.49 SHIPPING

Carver/Treitel: *Carriage by Sea*, 14th ed. (Sweet & Maxwell, 1999).

Hardy Ivamy: *Marine Insurance*, 4th ed. (Butterworths, 1985).

Sassoon/Merren: *CIF and FOB Contracts*, 4th ed. (Sweet & Maxwell, 1995).

Scrutton: *On Charterparties*, 20th ed. (Sweet & Maxwell, 1996).

See also generally: *British Shipping Law* series.

10.2.50 SOCIAL SECURITY AND WELFARE LAW

Encyclopaedia of Social Services Law (Sweet & Maxwell), updating service.

Wikeley: *Law of Social Security*, 5th ed. (Butterworths, 2001), updated.

Social Security and State Benefits (Tolley), annual.

10.2.51 TAXATION

Bramwell/et al.: *Taxation of Companies*, 6th ed. (Sweet & Maxwell, 1996), updated.

British Tax Encyclopedia (Sweet & Maxwell), updating service.

Butterworths' Orange Tax Handbook, annual.

Butterworths' Yellow Tax Handbook, annual.

De Voil: *Value Added Tax* (Butterworths), updating service.

Foster's Inheritance Tax (Butterworths), updated.

Simon's Taxes (Butterworths), updating service.

Sumption: *Capital Gains Tax* (Butterworths), updating service.

Whiteman/et al.: *On Capital Gains Tax*, 4th ed. (Sweet & Maxwell, 1989), updated.

Whiteman/et al.: *On Income Tax*, 3rd ed. (Sweet & Maxwell, 1989), updated.

See also *British Tax Cases: Simon's Tax Cases*.

10.2.52 TORTS

Charlesworth/Percy: *On Negligence*, 10th ed. (Sweet & Maxwell, 2001), updated.

Clerk/Lindsell: *On Torts*, 18th ed. (Sweet & Maxwell, 2000), updated.

Jackson/Powell: *Professional Negligence*, 5th ed. (Sweet & Maxwell, 2001), updated.

10.2.53 WILLS AND PROBATE, SUCCESSION

Butterworths' Wills, Probate & Administration (Butterworths), updated.

Clark: *Theobald on Wills*, 16th ed. (Sweet & Maxwell, 2001), updated.

Sherrin/Bonehill: *Law and Practice of Intestate Succession*, 2nd ed. (Sweet & Maxwell, 1994).

Tristram/Coote: *Probate Practice*, 28th ed. (Butterworths, 1995), updated.

Williams/Mortimer: *Executors, Administrators & Probate*, 18th ed. (Sweet & Maxwell, 2000).

Williams: *Wills*, 8th ed. (Butterworths, 2001), updated.

ELEVEN

PRACTICAL LEGAL RESEARCH

11.1 The Purpose of this Chapter

The preceding chapters of this Manual have set out in detail the legal research process. This chapter is intended to serve two purposes: to summarise the key points contained in the earlier chapters, and to emphasise the distinction between academic research and practical research.

11.1.1 WHAT IS 'PRACTICAL' LEGAL RESEARCH?

The important hallmarks of a practitioner's research are these:

- A practitioner may start the research with a textbook, but will base the advice to the client on primary sources (that is, cases, statutes or statutory instruments) unless there is no primary source which adequately answers the question.

- Research carried out by a practitioner has a very narrow focus: the practitioner will only search for the law which is needed to answer the specific questions which have to be answered in order to deal with the specific matters on which the client needs advice. As **Chapter 8** of the *Opinion Writing Manual* makes clear, the law is a means to an end, not the end itself.

- A practitioner's research must be quick ('time is money') but it must also be accurate (since getting it wrong may well amount to negligence).

11.1.2 IDENTIFYING THE ISSUES

The first step is, of course, to digest the facts of the problem. Once you have done this, the next step is to identify the issues which need to be researched. In some cases, your instructing solicitor will already have done this, and your instructions will contain a series of questions for you to answer. Even if this is so, you should consider whether there are any other questions which the solicitor should have asked you. In other cases, the solicitor will seek general advice and so you will have to identify the specific questions yourself.

Remember that some problems with which you may be faced might involve basic principles of law and so need little or no legal research, or the problems may raise purely factual questions which actually involve no law.

11.1.3 WHAT SOURCES SHOULD I USE?

If the problem is one where you need to do some legal research, you must first decide what source(s) you are going to use.

In most cases, there will be more than one starting point to solving the problem. It will often be the case that another user of the library has got the source you wish to consult, and so you will have to think of an alternative. All libraries have lists (usually on computer), arranged according to subject-matter, of the titles they hold. There is also the list of practitioner books in **Chapter 10**.

11.1.4   TEXTBOOKS

If you are unfamiliar with the area of law in question, you will probably want to use a textbook. You should use textbooks written for practitioners, not those written for students. For example, *Chitty on Contracts, Clerk and Lindsell on Torts, Charlesworth on Negligence* or 'looseleaf' works (such as *Harvey's Industrial Relations and Employment Law* and *Butterworth's Family Law Service*). These may look rather off-putting at first, but they function in exactly the same way as ordinary textbooks. If you cannot identify an appropriate practitioners' text, or the one you want is not available, *Halsbury's Laws of England* is often a good starting point.

Unless you are looking for commentary on a particular case or a particular statutory provision (in which case you will use the table of statutes or table of cases in whichever book you are using), the best starting point in any textbook is the index. This is the essential tool which enables you to find the part of the book you are looking for. To use an index you need to be able to formulate the question which you are trying to answer by using words which are likely to be found in the index. This involves identifying 'keywords'. If you cannot find the word(s) you are looking for, try to reword the question. To take a rather trite example, you might have to look for 'taxi' instead of 'cab'.

11.1.5   PRIMARY SOURCES

In some instances, you might want to bypass textbooks and go straight to the 'primary' sources (in other words statutes, statutory instruments, or cases). You might know, for example, that the basic law governing a particular subject is statutory, and so the statute is likely to provide the starting point you need. For example, the statutory provisions relating to unfair dismissal are in the Employment Rights Act 1996, so you might decide to start your research there.

If you want to find a statute, you should choose an annotated version, since this will give you assistance in interpreting the Act. *Current Law Statutes Annotated* contain commentary written when the statute was first enacted (including references to Parliamentary debates for *Pepper* v *Hart* research). However, *Halsbury's Statutes* has two advantages over *Current Law*. First, the volumes are periodically reissued; this means that where the statute has been amended, the amended version is shown and the footnotes take account of cases decided after the enactment of the statute. Secondly, there is a very useful Cumulative Supplement which gives up-to-date information about the statutes printed in the main volumes and in the loose-leaf binders which contain more recent statutes. Many textbooks also reprint statutes, although the commentary will often be in the main body of the text and not in the form of annotations to the statute itself. When you are trying to find your way around a statute, remember that the list of sections (headed 'Arrangements of Sections') at the start of each Act will help you to find the section(s) you need.

If you are looking for case law, the likely starting point will be to use a textbook. When reading cases themselves, it is best to use the official law reports published by the Incorporated Council for Law Reporting (the *Weekly Law Reports, the Appeal Cases* etc.) or the *All England Law Reports*. However, do not forget that there are several very useful 'specialist' series of law reports. For example, the *Industrial Relations Law Reports*, the *Family Law Reports*, the *Criminal Appeal Reports* and the *Justice of the Peace* reports.

11.1.6   ELECTRONIC RESOURCES

You should also be aware of the range of electronic databases available for legal research. Quite a lot of information is available free of charge on the Internet, including statutes from 1996 and statutory instruments from 1997 (via the HMSO web site), House of Lords decisions from 1996 (via the Parliament web site), and Court of Appeal and Crown Office decisions from 1996 (via the SmithBernal web site). A useful link to freely available legal information is http://www.bailii.org. There is also an ever-increasing range of CD-Roms: many series of law reports (including the 'official' law reports and the *All England Law Reports*) are available in this format. Finally, there are various on-line subscription services, such as *Butterworths' Direct* (which includes an electronic version of the *All England Law Reports*, *Halsbury's Laws of England* and *Halsbury's Statutes*), LEXIS, *Current Legal Information* (from Sweet & Maxwell) and *Lawtel*.

If you are using an electronic resource, you have to decide what words you are going to ask the computer to search for. Each database has its own rules regarding how the search should be phrased, but all search engines perform the same basic function of looking for words or phrases. You can specify where in the database the search should take place (often called a 'field'). Remember too that if you ask the computer to look for negligen* (the * is called a 'wildcard') it will look for 'negligent', 'negligently', 'negligence'.

Bear in mind that if you are searching through an electronic law reports database, each case begins with a series of 'catchwords' (which list the keywords to which the case relates), and a headnote. If the case is going to be really helpful, the word or phrase you are looking for is likely to be in either or both of these. It is therefore sensible to confine your search to the catchwords and/or head notes.

Searching for combinations of words will also make your research more focused. For example, if you are trying to find cases on sentencing in theft cases, you will get far too many hits if you just look up 'theft' or if you just look up 'sentencing'. If you confine your search to the catchwords or to the headnotes and search for < theft AND sentenc* > you should get a far more manageable number of hits.

Another way of defining your electronic search to get a more manageable number of hits is to ask the computer to look for words within a specified distance from each other. For example, if you are looking for cases involving theft in breach of trust, you could ask the computer to look for 'theft' within 10 (say) words of 'trust'.

11.1.7 FINDING RELEVANT MATERIAL

Once you have found the law you are looking for, you must be able to sort through it. You will generally find more law than you need to answer the particular question you are dealing with. You therefore need to be able to distinguish between what is relevant and what is irrelevant. The acid test of relevance is whether the source you have found actually helps you to answer the question or whether it is merely background material.

If when you are giving your advice you cite a case, be clear what proposition you derive from it. It is a mistake to cite cases without making it clear what proposition of law is to be derived from each case you are citing.

11.1.8 INTERPRETING THE LAW

In some cases, the law will be so clear that only one interpretation is possible. However, this will not always be so.

If the language of a particular statutory provision is obscure, look to see if there is a definition section and/or relevant case law on that section.

In an area governed by case law, you may well have to distil the relevant legal principles from dicta in a series of cases.

It may be necessary to consider whether the facts of the case upon which you are advising can be distinguished from the facts of the authorities you have found. If there are conflicting authorities, it may be necessary to predict which is more likely to be followed.

If you cannot find a clear answer to the problem you are researching, it may well be that you can find a case (or series of cases) setting out a narrow principle which you can then use to establish a wider principle.

Textbooks (or the commentary in *Halsbury's Laws of England*) will often show how various authorities relate to each other, pointing out any inconsistencies and suggesting ways in which apparently conflicting case law can be reconciled.

11.1.9 FOLLOWING THROUGH BETWEEN SOURCES

You must also be able to 'follow through' from one source to another. For example, if a textbook sets out a proposition of law which seems to answer the question you are researching, and the book cites a particular case as authority for that proposition, you should ensure that the case really does say what the textbook asserts. It is rarely sufficient (although very tempting!) to rely on what textbooks say about primary sources.

11.1.10 UPDATING

You must remember to make sure that the answer you have found is current. Has the case on which you base your advice been overruled (or distinguished)? Has the section of the statute on which you base your advice been brought into force? Has that section been repealed? Has it been amended?

If you are using a textbook, check how up-to-date the book is (the publishing information at the front will tell you the year in which it was published and the author's 'foreword' will usually say something like 'I/we have endeavoured to state the law as at [date]'. Many textbooks have supplements, so remember to see if there is one for the book you are using (and to check how up-to-date it is). If you are using a loose-leaf book, you should check the front of the relevant section to see how up-to-date it is. Armed with this information, you will know what period your check for more recent material should cover.

If you are using *Halsbury's Laws* or *Halsbury's Statutes* remember to check both the hardback cumulative supplement and the supplement in the appropriate loose-leaf 'current service binder' to make sure that you are as up-to-date as possible.

Similarly, if you think the answer is in a case, look the case up in the Index to the official law reports or whichever series you found it in, or look it up on an appropriate electronic database, to see if anything has happened to it.

11.1.11 USING THE LAW THAT YOU HAVE FOUND

Once you have done all this, you need to be able to summarise the relevant law and apply it to the facts of the case you are dealing with, so that you can give accurate and succinct advice to your client.

A barrister does not carry out abstract legal research. The purpose of the research is to give the best advice you can to your client, or to ensure that the strongest possible case is put before the court on behalf of your client. You must therefore apply the law to the facts of the case in a realistic and practical way. Your advice must not be an essay on the law: it must be specific to the case in which your advice is sought.

You must attempt to answer all the questions or issues raised in your instructions. It may or may not be possible to give a definite answer. If you are unable to give a categorical answer, you must try to assess the likely result and the degree of probability that the court will come to the conclusion you suggest.

Each answer you reach must be 'satisfactory' in the sense that it has a reasonable prospect of being upheld by the court.

11.2   Notes to Pupil Master

In most cases, your pupil master will not require you to produce a full opinion, but rather the notes which could form the basis for an opinion. The notes must be clear, concise and accurate. The following guidelines may help you:

(a) You may write in note form (rather than writing complete sentences which conform with the rules of grammar) if you wish to do so, but do remember that the result must be intelligible to another reader (i.e. your pupil master).

(b) Your answers must be satisfactory, in the sense of being sustainable given the present state of the law which applies to the questions you are answering.

(c) Your answers must be supported by relevant authority (usually, statutory or case law):

(i) Only cite relevant authority, as the citation of irrelevant sources adds to the length of your notes and tends to create confusion. Something is relevant if it actually makes a difference to your answer.

(ii) Show how the authority you cite is relevant. This will involve relating that authority to the facts of the case upon which you are advising. When you are citing precedent, you will normally find it easier to show its relevance by referring to a particular dictum rather than simply referring to the case as a whole. If you do not set out your legal reasoning, your pupil master cannot check the soundness of your reasoning.

(iii) Correct citations must be given for all the authorities you cite. For example, 'the Ecclesiastical Judges and Legal Officers (Fees) Order 1991 (SI 1991 No. 1756)'; or *R* v *Roberts* [1993] 1 All ER 583, at p. 590 *per* Lord Taylor CJ'. If you do not give the correct citation for the authority which supports your conclusion, your pupil master will not be able to find that authority quickly.

(iv) Verbatim quotation of statutes and judgments should be kept to a minimum. If the passage upon which you wish to rely is very short, or the precise words are crucial, then you will have to write it out in full. Otherwise, you should simply distil the essentials, which will involve paraphrasing the material rather than copying it out.

(v) You should always cite 'primary' sources (i.e. statutes, case law, etc.) in preference to 'secondary' sources (textbooks, articles etc.). However, if there is no authority, or there are conflicting authorities, then it may be appropriate to cite academic opinion. In that case, you should wherever possible refer to a source which could be cited in court (that is a textbook written for practitioners rather than students, or an article in a publication which is aimed, at least in part, at practitioners).

(d) Finally, some guidance on the incorporation of background detail in your notes. If you are unfamiliar with an area of law, it may well be that you will have to do a certain amount of background reading before you can put the questions which you have to answer into context. However, your notes should contain only reasoned answers to the questions which are posed (expressly or by implication) in your instructions. Otherwise you will find that you are writing a legal essay, not the notes which form the starting point for an opinion.

11.3 Summary

To summarise, these are the basic steps of legal research:

(a) Analyse the issues raised by your instructions so that you can identify what questions of law (if any) have to be answered.

(b) Classify the questions (e.g. magistrates' court procedure, criminal law, tort, highways). This will help you to decide what source(s) to look for. Remember that if the source you want is unavailable, there is almost certain to be another one that you could use.

(c)   Decide what word(s) you are going to look up in the index or on the database ('keywords' or 'catchwords'). To do this, you must be able to formulate the question(s) you are trying to answer and then see what keywords appear in that formulation. If the word you are looking for is not in the index or database, try to think of another one.

(d)   If you have found what you are looking for, distil what you have found. Set out the statement of law and the authority for that statement.

(e)   Ensure that the law you have found is up to date. Is the statute in force? Has the statute been amended? Has the statute been repealed? Has the case you have found gone on appeal to a higher court? Has the case been considered, followed, distinguished or overruled by a later case?

(f)   Check that you have answered the question(s) completely. If not, look for other relevant sources, distil the contents and check that what you have found is up to date.

(g)   Summarise the relevant law, apply it to the facts of the case you are dealing with, and advise the client.

11.4   Criteria by which you may Assess your Legal Research

To assess the standard of your performance in carrying out a legal research exercise, you may use or adapt the following basic criteria. In carrying out legal research, you should be able to:

(a)   identify the legal issues raised by your instructions (expressly or by implication) correctly and completely;

(b)   identify relevant sources and materials, disregarding those which are irrelevant;

(c)   extract the key points from, and correctly cite, those sources and materials;

(d)   apply the law to the facts of the case so as to produce satisfactory answers to the questions posed (expressly or by implication) in your instructions;

(e)   give brief reasons for the answers you have arrived at, showing how those answers have been reached;

(f)   produce clear and concise notes which encapsulate the results of your research.

There now follows a worked-through example demonstrating the legal research process from beginning to end.

11.5   *Re Colonel Jack Hayward* — A Sample Exercise in Legal Research

There is no single 'right' way of conducting legal research. However, we now consider one way of approaching a particular exercise. It is not the only approach that is possible.

So that the rest of this chapter has the greatest general value, we are going to assume that specialist books are not available and that the researcher has access only to *Halsbury's Laws of England* and *Halsbury's Statutes*. It should be borne in mind that the method of research would be very similar using other books.

Re COLONEL JACK HAYWARD

INSTRUCTIONS TO COUNSEL TO ADVISE

Chalice & Co.
11 High Street
Lower Gumtree
Norchester

Instructions to Advise

Counsel is instructed to advise on various matters raised by Colonel Jack Hayward, a churchwarden at St. Mary's, Upper Gumtree. Instructing solicitors have acted on behalf of St. Mary's Parochial Church Council on previous occasions. However, the partner who normally deals with such matters is unwell and it would appear that the advice is needed as a matter of some urgency. Enclosed with these instructions is the letter received from Colonel Hayward setting out the matters upon which he requires advice.

Tode Hall
Upper Gumtree
Norchester
26 September

Chalice & Co.
11 High Street
Lower Gumtree
Norchester

Dear Sirs

You may remember that you have kindly advised the PCC of St. Mary's, Upper Gumtree, on several previous occasions. I would be most grateful if you could now help me on the following questions.

(1)   A young couple have asked to be married at St. Mary's even though neither of them lives in the parish. They have been attending Evensong here and seem to appreciate the fact we are one of the few Church of England churches in the area to use the Book of Common Prayer. However, that is by the way. Their banns have been published in the parishes where they each live. However, banns for this couple have not been published in this parish. The wedding is fixed for next Saturday. I need to know if their banns should have been published here, and if they should have been, does this mean that the wedding will have to be postponed?

(2)   My second question is also about banns. You may have heard that we now have a new Rector. One of the changes he has made is that he asks me, or the other churchwarden, to read out the banns at the start of the Parish Communion, rather than doing it himself. I have never heard of this being done elsewhere, and I wondered if it is legal.

(3)   On a completely separate matter, and in fact nothing to do with the PCC, I have taken over as Secretary to our local Music Society. We are a bit short of funds, and I have had this brilliant idea for fund raising. We propose to set up what I have called 'The Hundred Club'. The Society has got some 200 members and I hope to persuade about 100 of them to pay an annual subscription of £5 (in addition to their membership fee for the Society) to the Hundred Club. At the last concert each year the names of the Hundred Club members would be put into a hat and there would be a draw. The first prize would be £75, the second £50, the third £25. This would leave £350 to go into the Society's funds. I know this sort of thing can have all sorts of legal implications and I wondered if there was anything I ought to be aware of.

I would be grateful if I could receive your advice as soon as possible, especially given the urgency of the first question. Finally, please send your account to me personally rather than to the PCC.

Yours faithfully

Jack Hayward (Col.)

11.6   *Re Colonel Jack Hayward* — The Research Process

11.6.1   INTRODUCTION

In the text which follows:

(1)   The questions are reformulated in a way which should facilitate the research process.

(2)   The relevant law is found and set out.

(3)   The law is applied to the facts so as to produce answers to the questions contained in the instructions.

11.6.2   GETTING STARTED: FORMULATING THE QUESTIONS

In order to carry out the necessary legal research effectively, the questions to be answered have to be formulated with some care. This is for two reasons:

(a)   First, because the keywords with which the research process starts should be contained in the question you are researching.

(b)   Secondly, because (so far as possible) the question should include all that is relevant and exclude all that is irrelevant.

The first of these two objectives may require that the question be reformulated if the words which comprise the question do not provide suitable keywords. The second objective also requires the question to be kept under review, in that something which appeared irrelevant turns out to be relevant or something which seemed relevant at the start of the research process turns out to be irrelevant.

The questions contain the following facts.

Question 1:

(a)   Neither the bride nor the groom reside in the parish in which they want the marriage to take place (St. Mary's).

(b)   Both have been attending Evensong at St. Mary's (though the instructions do not say for how long they have been doing so).

(c)   The banns of marriage have been published in the parishes in which they live.

(d)   The banns of marriage have not been published at St. Mary's.

(e)   The wedding is due to take place in a few days' time.

Question 2:

A churchwarden is asked by the Rector to read out the banns of marriage at a communion service.

Question 3:

A Music Society with 200 members wants 100 of them to pay £5 to take part in a draw with the chance of winning £75, £50, or £25.

Sifting through these facts and discarding those which are clearly irrelevant, you will then find that the three questions to be researched may be set out as follows:

Question 1:

Whether a marriage can take place in a church in which the banns have not been published, though the banns have been published in the parishes in which the prospective bride and groom reside.

Question 2:

Whether a lay person is permitted to read out the banns at a communion service.

Question 3:

Whether there are any restrictions on groups of people running prize draws amongst themselves.

11.6.3   FINDING THE LAW

Now that the questions have been formulated, it is possible to find the relevant law. This involves deciding, first, what book or books to use and, secondly, what words to look up in the index of the book (or books) chosen. The first decision may well be helped by the list of practitioner books contained in **Chapter 10** of this Manual, or by the subject-matter index of the library being used. The research route for the three questions under consideration might go as follows.

Question 1

The answer to a question about marriage is likely to be found in a book dealing with family law and so a source such as Butterworths' *Family Law Service* (see **10.2.23**) would be a sensible starting point. Alternatively, since the marriage is to take place in a church, the question could be seen as one of ecclesiastical law and so a source such as Hill's *Ecclesiastical Law* (see **10.2.17**) could also be appropriate. Another option would be to look up the word 'banns' in the Consolidated Index to *Halsbury's Laws of England* (this does not involve classifying the question under a particular area of law).

The Consolidated Index to *Halsbury's Laws of England* gives 'BANNS OF MARRIAGE — place of, marriage elsewhere than' and refers the reader to volume 14, paragraph 1006. Note that looking up 'MARRIAGE — banns' simply gives 'see BANNS OF MARRIAGE': it is usually better to try a more specific keyword and only use a more general one if the specific one yields nothing of use.

Volume 14, paragraph 1006 is headed 'Place of solemnisation of marriage'. It says that marriage after banns must normally be solemnised in one of the churches in which banns have been published (s. 12(1), Marriage Act 1949 is cited). The paragraph then goes on to deal with specific situations brought about by the structure of the Church of England and with marriage by 'common licence'.

Reading on (it is often the case that an index will take you only to more or less the right part of the book and so a certain amount of reading around may be called for), paragraph 1007 says that banns of marriage between two persons must normally be published in the parish church of the parish in which they reside or, if they reside in different parishes, in the parish church of each parish (s. 6(1), Marriage Act 1949 is cited).

Paragraph 1008 says that banns may also be published in any parish church which is the usual place of worship of the parties to the intended marriage, or one of them, even though neither of them is resident in the parish to which the church belongs, but this publication is in addition to and not in substitution for the publication required under the provisions set out in the previous paragraph (s. 6(4), Marriage Act 1949 is cited). The paragraph goes on to say that no person can claim as his usual place of worship any parish church unless he is enrolled on the electoral roll of that church (s. 72(1), Marriage Act 1949 is cited).

The subsequent paragraphs on banns are clearly irrelevant.

Paragraph 1017 states that banns have to be published on three Sundays preceding the solemnisation of the marriage (s. 7(1), Marriage Act 1949 is cited). This information can be found either by skim-reading the paragraphs which deal with banns or by looking up 'banns of marriage — publication of — mode of' in the index at the back of volume 14 of *Halsbury's Laws*.

After the paragraphs of *Halsbury's Laws* which deal with banns the next section of *Halsbury's Laws* (from para. 1023) is headed 'Marriage Licences'. Marriage by common licence was mentioned in paragraph 1006 where it was said that marriage by common licence must be solemnised in the parish church of the parish in which one of the persons to be married has had his or her usual place of residence for 15 days immediately before the grant of the licence or in a parish church which is the usual place of worship of the parties or one of them (s. 15(1), Marriage Act 1949 is cited).

Paragraph 1023 says that an archbishop and bishop may grant a common licence for the solemnisation of marriage without the publication of banns (s. 5, Marriage Act 1949 is cited).

Paragraph 1024 states that before a common licence is granted, sworn declaration must be made by one of the parties before a surrogate (the footnote refers the reader on to paragraph 1275) to the effect (1) that the party believes that there is no impediment of kindred or alliance or any other lawful cause to bar or hinder the solemnisation of the marriage; (2) that for 15 days immediately before the grant of the licence one of the parties has had his or her usual place of residence in the parish in which the marriage is to be solemnised or that the parish church in which the marriage is to be solemnised is the usual place of worship of the parties or one of them (s. 16, Marriage Act 1949). The paragraph goes on to deal with the situation where one of the parties is a minor. Paragraph 1026 (citing s. 16(3), Marriage Act 1949) says that a licence is valid for three months.

Paragraph 1023 also refers to the power of the Archbishop of Canterbury to grant a 'special licence' for the solemnisation of marriage without the publication of banns at any convenient time or place throughout all England (citing ss. 5(b) and 79(6), Marriage Act 1949). *Halsbury's Laws* says no more about this topic, and so it may be assumed that such licences are rare creatures.

Reading on further, paragraph 1028 says that a marriage according to the rights of the Church of England may be solemnised on the authority of a certificate of a superintendent registrar (ss. 17 and 26, Marriage Act 1949 are cited). Footnote 2 says that the superintendent registrar may issue a certificate for the solemnisation of marriage in any parish church which is the usual place of worship of the persons to be married or of one of them, notwithstanding that the church is not within a registration district in which either of those persons resides. Footnote 3 says that a marriage on the authority of a superintendent registrar's certificate may be either by licence issued by the superintendent registrar or without a licence but adds a proviso (for which s. 26(2), Marriage Act 1949 is cited) that he may not issue a licence for a marriage according to the rites of the Church of England. The effect of this proviso is spelt out in paragraph 1029. This says that a marriage according to the Church of England may not be solemnised on the authority of a superintendent registrar's certificate within 21 days after the day on which notice was entered in the marriage notice book (s. 31(4), Marriage Act 1949 is cited); the certificate remains valid for three months (s. 33(2)).

The latest Cumulative Supplement and the Noter-up in the Current Service contain no relevant entries in respect of these paragraphs.

Question 2

The Consolidated Index to *Halsbury's Laws of England* gives 'BANNS OF MARRIAGE — publication of — layman, by' and refers the reader to volume 14, paragraph 1018. That paragraph is headed 'Who may publish banns'. This paragraph says that where a clergyman does not officiate at the service at which it is usual in that church to publish banns, the publication may be made either (1) by a clergyman at some other service at which banns may be published; or (2) by a layman during a public reading authorised by the bishop of a portion or portions of Morning or Evening Prayer, such public reading being at the hour when the service at which it is usual to publish banns is commonly held or at such other hour as the bishop may authorise, and the incumbent or minister in charge of the church, or some other clergyman nominated in that behalf by the bishop, must have made or authorised to be made the requisite entry in the register book of banns of the church. Apart from this, no person other than a clergyman may publish banns of marriage. The footnotes to this paragraph refer to s. 9(1) and (2), Marriage Act 1949. The text in *Halsbury's Laws* follows the statutory wording very closely and so it is not usually necessary to refer to the statute itself. Alternatively, having found that paragraph 1018 contains the answer and is based on s. 9 of the Marriage Act 1949, the researcher might go straight to the statute. In the present case, the wording of paragraph 1018 and of the statute on which it is based are virtually identical.

The latest Cumulative Supplement and the Noter-up in the Current Service contain no entries in respect of this paragraph.

Question 3

The keyword with which to start researching this problem is not so easy to work out since it is not given in the instructions. Indeed it is difficult to classify the question under a particular area of law. Where the particular area of law is difficult to identify, *Halsbury's Laws* provides a useful starting point.

The Consolidated Index contains the word 'PRIZE' but none of the subjects listed under this word appear to be relevant. The Index does not contain the word 'draw'. The question therefore has to be reformulated. It is here that an ordinary English dictionary is useful. The *Collins* dictionary defines a 'draw' as (amongst other things), 'something taken at random, as a ticket in a lottery' and it defines a 'prize' as 'something given to the winner of any game of chance, lottery, etc.'.

The Consolidated Index to *Halsbury's Laws of England* contains the keyword 'LOTTERY'. One of the items under this heading is 'club, in', but following up the reference (to volume 6, paragraph 325) shows that this is not relevant. Another item under the heading 'LOTTERY' is 'legislation' and the reader is referred to volume 4(1), paragraph 9. This paragraph refers to the Lotteries and Amusements Act 1976. The researcher now has two options: either to persist with *Halsbury's Laws of England* or to find the statute itself. If the first option is taken, it should be noted that once it is clear that the relevant law is in a particular volume of Halsbury's Laws, the index to that particular volume may be used instead of the Consolidated Index.

Assuming that the second option is chosen, the research route carries on as follows. Assuming also that an annotated version of the statute is wanted (and an annotated version is generally a better medium of legal research), the statute is located either by turning to *Current Law Statutes Annotated* for the relevant year or by turning to the Tables of Statutes and General Index to *Halsbury's Statutes*. The latter shows that the Lotteries and Amusements Act 1976 is to be found in volume 5 of *Halsbury's Statutes* at page 221. This volume was re-issued in 1998.

There is no statutory definition but the case law cited in the footnotes to s. 1 of the Act in *Halsbury's Statutes* defines a lottery as a scheme for distributing prizes by lot or chance. The distribution must depend wholly on chance: if merit or skill plays a part in determining the distribution it is not a lottery. A large number of cases are cited. The more recent cases include *Readers Digest Association Ltd v Williams* [1976] 3 All ER 737 and *Imperial Tobacco Ltd v Attorney-General* [1980] 1 All ER 866.

The structure of the 1976 Act is clear from the 'Arrangement of Sections' which appears at the front of the statute and sets out its contents. Section 1 makes lotteries unlawful except as provided by the Act. Section 2 sets out a number of criminal offences. Sections 3 to 6 set out the lotteries which are lawful, i.e., the exceptions to the general rule in section 1.

Section 3 deals with lotteries which are incidental to entertainments such as a bazaar, a fête, a dinner or a sporting event. Clearly, this section is not relevant.

Section 4 is headed 'Private lotteries'. A 'private lottery' is defined in section 4(1) as (inter alia) one 'which is promoted for, and in which the sale of tickets or chances by the promoters is confined to . . . (a) members of one society established and conducted for purposes not connected with gaming, betting or lotteries'.

Section 4(1A) says that 'the lottery must be promoted by persons each of whom — (a) is one of the persons for whom the lottery is promoted; and (b) in the case of a lottery promoted for the members of a society, is authorised in writing by the governing body of the society to promote the lottery'.

Section 4(1B) says that 'the sale of tickets or chances in the lottery must be confined — (a) to the persons for whom the lottery is promoted; and (b) in the case of a lottery promoted for the members of a society, to any other persons on the society's premises'.

Section 4(3) provides that:

> A private lottery is not unlawful, but the following conditions shall be observed in connection with its promotion and conduct, that is to say —
> (a)   the whole proceeds, after deducting only expenses incurred for printing and stationery, shall be devoted to the provision of prizes for purchasers of tickets or chances, or, in the case of a lottery promoted for members of a society, shall be devoted either —
>> (i)   to the provision of prizes as aforesaid; or
>> (ii)   to purposes which are purposes of the society; or
>> (iii)   as to part to the provision of prizes as aforesaid and as to the remainder to such purposes as aforesaid;
> (b)   there shall not be exhibited, published or distributed any written notice or advertisement of the lottery other than —
>> (i)   a notice of it exhibited on the premises of the society for whose members it is promoted or, as the case may be, on the premises on which the persons for whom it is promoted work or reside; and
>> (ii)   such announcement or advertisement of it as is contained in the tickets, if any;
> (c)   the price of every ticket or chance shall be the same, and the price of any ticket shall be stated on the ticket;
> (d)   every ticket shall bear upon the face of it the name and address of each of the promoters and a statement of the persons to whom the sale of tickets or chances by the promoters is restricted, and a statement that no prize won in the lottery shall be paid or delivered by the promoters to any person other than the person to whom the winning ticket or chance was sold by them, and no prize shall be paid or delivered except in accordance with that statement;
> (e)   no ticket or chance shall be issued or allotted by the promoters except by way of sale and upon receipt of its full price, and no money or valuable thing so received by a promoter shall in any circumstances be returned; and
> (f)   no tickets in the lottery shall be sent through the post.

Section 5 is headed 'Societies' lotteries'. Section 5(1) defines a 'society's lottery' as:

> a lottery promoted on behalf of a society which is established and conducted wholly or mainly for one or more of the following purposes, that is to say —
> (a)   charitable purposes;
> (b)   participation in or support of athletic sports or games or cultural activities;
> (c)   purposes which are not described in paragraph (a) or (b) above but are neither purposes of private gain nor purposes of any commercial undertaking.

Under s. 5(3) a society's lottery is not unlawful if:

(a)   the lottery is promoted in Great Britain; and

(b)   the society is registered under the Act; and

(c)   the lottery is promoted in accordance with a scheme approved by the society.

Registration is under Schedule 1A to the 1976 Act (registration by the Gaming Board) if the total value of tickets or chances is more than £20,000, or if the total value of tickets or chances in the present lottery together with all earlier lotteries held by the same society in the same year (i.e., the period of 12 months beginning 1 January) is more than £250,000, or if either of these conditions have applied to any earlier lottery held by the same society in the same year or any of the three preceding years. Otherwise, registration is under Schedule 1 to the 1976 Act (registration with the registration authority, defined in Schedule 1, para. 1(2), as the district council).

Section 5(4) requires that the whole proceeds of a society's lottery, after deducting expenses and prizes, must be applied to the purposes of the society.

Section 10 (in its amended form) empowers the Secretary of State to limit the number of lotteries which a society may promote in any period of 12 months and to prescribe a minimum number of days which must elapse between the dates of any two lotteries promoted by the same society.

Section 11 (again in its amended version) sets out further rules applicable to a society's lottery:

(1)   (a)   The promoter of the lottery must be a member of the society authorised in writing by the governing body of the society to act as the promoter.

(1)   (b)   Every lottery ticket distributed or sold must specify the name of the society, the name and address of the promoter and the date of the lottery.

(2)   No ticket or chance shall be sold at a price exceeding £1.

(3)   The price of every ticket or chance must be the same.

(4)   No person shall be admitted to participate in a society's lottery in respect of a ticket or chance except after payment to the society of the whole price of the ticket or chance, and no money received for or on account of a ticket or chance shall in any circumstances be returned.

(4A)   No payment other than the price of a ticket or chance may be required of a person as a condition of his admission to participate in the lottery.

(5)   No prize in a society's lottery shall exceed in amount or value £25,000 or 10% of the total value of the tickets or chances sold in the lottery (whichever is the greater).

(6)   The total value of tickets or chances sold in any one lottery must not exceed £1,000,000.

(7)   The total value of tickets or chances sold in lotteries promoted in any one year by the same society must not exceed £5,000,000.

(11)   The amount of the proceeds of a society's lottery appropriated for the provision of prizes must not exceed 50% of the whole proceeds of the lottery.

(12)   Limits are placed on the amount which may be appropriated on account of expenses.

Section 12 of the Act provides for the making of regulations concerning participation in a society's lottery. The annual supplement shows that the present regulations are to be found in the Lotteries Regulations 1993 (SI 1993/3223). Looking up this statutory instrument in the List of Instruments in the Service Binder of *Halsbury's Statutory Instruments* leads the reader to the title on 'Betting' (volume 3 of *Halsbury's Statutory Instruments*). The section on betting in volume 3 begins with a chronological list of instruments and SI 1993/3223 can thus be found. These regulations apply (*inter alia*) to a society's lottery. No ticket or chance may be sold to a person who has not attained the age of 16 (regulation 3), no ticket or chance may be sold to a person in any street (regulation 4) or by means of a machine (regulation 5), no ticket or chance may be sold in a person's home by someone visiting in an official, professional or commercial function not connected with lotteries (regulation 6).

Breach of any of the rules, whether an offence under s. 2 of the 1976 Act or under the 1993 Regulations, renders the promoters guilty of an offence which is punishable on summary conviction with a fine up to £5,000 (see footnote for definition of 'prescribed sum' and check in supplement that the footnote is still correct) and on conviction on indictment with up to two years' imprisonment and/or a fine: ss. 2 and 20 for the 1976 Act.

Section 6 of the Act, which applies to 'local lotteries' deals with lotteries promoted by a local authority so is clearly irrelevant.

11.7 Producing the Answers to the Questions

The preceding paragraphs are somewhat indigestible. If counsel were simply to send such bare statements of the law to instructing solicitors, the latter would not be very impressed. So, the law has to be related to the facts in a way that produces answers which are correct, clear and concise.

In many cases, the contents of a statute or the dictum found in a case will have to be paraphrased (rather than quoted) so as to shorten and simplify what is said.

Much of the law found is not really relevant to the answers to the questions under consideration, and so much of it will be discarded when it comes to setting out the answers.

Those answers may look something like what follows.

Question 1

Marriage by banns is governed by the Marriage Act 1949. Section 6 says that banns must be published in the parish where the parties reside or, if they reside in different parishes, then in both those parishes (s. 6(1)). That requirement has been satisfied in the present case.

Section 6(4) says that the banns may be published in the church which is the usual place of worship of either or both of the parties. Section 72(1) of the 1949 Act requires enrolment on the church electoral roll as a precondition to that church being a person's 'usual place of worship'. It is unclear whether either of the parties in the present case is so enrolled.

Section 12(1) of the 1949 Act stipulates that parties can only be married in a church in which their banns have been published.

It follows from this that the couple may marry in either of the parish churches of the parishes where they live (since the banns have been published in them), but they can only marry at St. Mary's if two conditions are satisfied: at least one of the couple must be enrolled on the church electoral roll and their banns must have been published at St. Mary's. Since s. 7(1) of the Marriage Act requires banns to be published on three Sundays preceding the solemnisation of the marriage, there is insufficient time for that to be done in the present case.

A marriage can proceed by licence instead of publication of banns. A 'common licence' may be obtained from a person (called a 'surrogate') who acts on behalf of the diocesan bishop. One of the parties must swear before the surrogate that there is no legal impediment to the marriage, that one of the parties has been resident in the parish where the marriage is to take place for 15 days before the granting of the licence or that the church in which the marriage is to take place is the usual place of worship of either or both of them. So (since neither of the parties lives in the parish of St. Mary's) a common licence may only be granted if either or both of them is on the electoral roll of St. Mary's.

A licence granted by a superintendent registrar (the only way that a superintendent registrar can authorise a marriage according to the rites of the Church of England) is not valid until 21 days have elapsed (and so the couple would be no better off than if they had their banns called).

That leaves the possibility of a special licence. That would enable the couple to marry anywhere (so it would not matter that they do not live in the parish of St. Mary's nor that their banns have not been published there) but it is unlikely that such a licence would be granted save in exceptional circumstances.

Question 2

In general, banns must be published by a clergyman (Marriage Act 1949, s. 9(1)). However, a layman may publish banns at a service of morning or evening prayer at which a clergyman is not officiating (s. 9(2)). Since the service referred to in Colonel Hayward's letter is a Parish Communion, not morning or evening prayer, the practice adopted by the Rector of St. Mary's is unlawful: a clergyman taking part in the service should publish the banns.

Question 3

What is being proposed seems to fall within the definition of a lottery. There is no statutory definition but case law defines a lottery as a distribution of prizes by chance (rather than skill): *Readers Digest Association Ltd* v *Williams* [1976] 3 All ER 737 and *Imperial Tobacco Ltd* v *Attorney-General* [1980] 1 All ER 866.

Lotteries are illegal unless permitted by the Lotteries and Amusements Act 1976 (see s. 1 of that Act).

The scheme proposed might fall under one of two categories: a society's lottery or a private lottery.

Section 5 of the 1976 Act governs society lotteries. Colonel Hayward's Music Society is engaged in 'cultural activities' and so satisfies s. 5(1)(b) of the Act. However, the society would have to be registered with the district council (s. 5(3)) and ticket prices could not exceed £1 (Colonel Hayward's scheme involves a payment of £5).

Section 4 of the 1976 Act governs private lotteries. A private lottery is one which is confined to members of one society, that society being established for a purpose other than gaming (s. 4(1)(a)). Various requirements are imposed on private lotteries. These include:

(a) that the lottery should be confined to members of the Society (s. 4(1B));

(b) all the proceeds, after deducting only expenses incurred for printing and stationery, must be devoted to the provision of prizes and/or to the purposes of the Society (s. 4(3)(a));

(c) the lottery must not be advertised except at the premises of the Society and/or on the tickets themselves, if any (s. 4(3)(b));

(d) the price of every ticket or chance of winning must be the same, and the price of any ticket must be stated on the ticket (s. 4(3)(c));

(e) every ticket must bear the name and address of each of the promoters, a statement of the persons to whom the sale of tickets or chances by the promoters is restricted, and a statement that no prize won in the lottery shall be paid to anyone other than the person to whom the winning ticket or chance was sold, and no prize may be paid except in accordance with that statement (s. 4(3)(d));

(f) all tickets or chances must be paid for at their face value (s. 4(3)(e));

(g) no tickets in the lottery may be sent through the post;

(h) participants in the lottery must have attained the age of 16.

These rules are not particularly onerous, though it should be noted that breaching them renders the promoters guilty of an offence (punishable on summary conviction with a fine up to £5,000 and on conviction on indictment with up to two years' imprisonment and/or a fine): ss. 2 and 20 of the 1976 Act.

11.8 And Finally, Some Useful Tips

You might find this non-exhaustive list of tips helpful in carrying out your legal research. You may like to add to the list as you do your own research and discover for yourself useful shortcuts.

11.8.1 PAPER SOURCES

- If you are unfamiliar with an area of law, it is often best to start with a paper source rather than an electronic source: it is easier to browse through a paper source to get an overview of a subject.

- Once you have formulated the legal question(s) you are trying to answer and you have found an appropriate textbook, it is usually best to start with the index at the back of the book rather than the contents pages at the front.

- Do not forget to go through the up-dating process: e.g., check to see if the textbook you are using has a supplement. Remember that even if there is a supplement it is likely to be at least a little out-of-date, so check the supplement to see when it was issued and update from then; similarly, even loose-leaf publications can be out-of-date, so check to see when the publication was last updated.

- If your answer is based on a statute or statutory instrument, check that it was in force at the relevant time.

11.8.2 ELECTRONIC SOURCES

- Remember that in most databases you can make your search more efficient by the use of 'Boolean searches', i.e. using connectors such as AND, OR, NOT.

- Sometimes the use of brackets is needed in a search, e.g., '(transfer OR transaction) AND illegal' if you are not sure whether the appropriate noun is 'transfer' or 'transaction'.

- You can narrow your search by using 'proximity searching', e.g., looking for one word within (say) 10 words of another word, e.g. solicitor w/10 negligence.

- Truncation (use of 'wildcards') enables you to look for words with a common stem; with most databases the symbol to use is an asterisk (*), with others it is an exclamation mark (!). For example, neglig* would find negligent, negligently, negligence.

- When searching a case law database, it is often wise to confine your search to a specific field, e.g., 'catchwords' or 'headnote': that is likely to ensure that only relevant case law is produced.

- The best way of searching for a particular section of a statute, e.g., s. 246 of the Insolvency Act 1986, is usually to search for: 246 AND insolvency AND act AND 1986.

- If you want to find out whether a particular word appears in the file you have currently opened, click on 'edit' — 'find' and type in the word you are looking for.

- If you do not know the web address for the site you want to use for your legal research, try using a link site such as *http://www.venables.co.uk/legal* or *http://library.ukc.ac.uk/library/netinfo/intnsubg/lawlinks.htm*.

- Most databases have an 'about' function which will give you further information about what that particular source covers.

- If you want to copy information from the Internet or a CD-ROM into a word processing document, highlight the text you want to copy by dragging the cursor over the relevant text with the left-hand mouse button held down; then you have three options: click on 'edit', then 'copy', and then go to your word processed document and click on 'edit', then 'paste' (or click on the paste icon); or press 'ctrl' and the letter 'c' simultaneously, then go to your word processed document and press 'ctrl' and the letter 'v' simultaneously; or press the right-hand mouse button, highlight 'copy' and click with the left-hand mouse button, and when you are in your word-processed document, press the right-hand mouse button, highlight 'paste' and click with the left-hand mouse button.

- If you cannot remember how you got to where you are on the Internet (or in most CD-ROMS), you can use the 'history' function to retrace your steps.

- Remember that a case reported in one set of reports may be referred to in a later case that is not reported in the same set of reports: *Current Law*, or the electronic version *Current Legal Information*, or Lawtel are good sources for tracking down the later case.

TWELVE

OVERVIEW OF A CIVIL CASE

12.1 Introduction

This section outlines the different contexts in which you will be working and what may be required of you at the different stages of a case by setting out the main stages in a civil case, explaining the different roles of the solicitor and barrister, the work done by the solicitor at each stage, the stages at which the barrister will generally be consulted and the work done by the barrister at each of these stages.

12.2 Stages in a Civil Case

12.2.1 INTRODUCTION

Civil disputes cover a broad range of cases including those involving general common law, family matters, insolvency, Chancery claims and claims to statutory tribunals such as employment tribunals. The steps set out here relate to those in the most common types of common law cases taken in the High Court and county courts, e.g., suing for debts and damages in tort and contract. This is not a civil litigation manual and does not cover the detailed rules but rather the main stages in a civil case and the work to be done by the lawyers at each stage. The Woolf reforms implemented as the Civil Procedure Rules 1998 (CPR) on 26 April 1999 have made major changes to the terminology used and procedure followed in both courts, simplifying them and attempting to cut the cost and delay of litigation in many cases. This has been done by introducing the concept of 'proportionality' by which the court will attempt to balance the need for disputes to be resolved as quickly and cheaply as possible with the need for cases to be properly prepared and fairly heard. Although the changes have altered what is required or possible at any particular stage of a case, the main stages in the preparation of a case remain the same.

12.2.2 MAIN STAGES

The conduct of a civil case through the courts can be divided into seven main areas of work from the time the client first sees a lawyer to the closure of the client's file:

(a) *Before action:* involves ascertaining how the costs will be paid, analysis of the case and decisions by the client and the lawyer, in particular whether court action is appropriate. In some cases the client may also need to obtain a court order before proper proceedings are initiated, e.g., a tenant claiming to have been unlawfully evicted may seek an injunction to be reinstated pending determination of his or her right to remain by a full trial.

A big change introduced by the Woolf reforms in certain standard cases, is the introduction of the concept of 'pre-action protocols', which requires parties to exchange a fair amount of information before initiating proceedings. The first two such 'protocols' were for personal injury and clinical negligence cases and it is envisaged that such 'protocols' will be written for as many standard types of cases as possible. The idea is to break down the present adversarial and secretive approach and promote settlement as early as possible.

(b) *Initiating proceedings*: involves deciding which court to use, the drafting and issue of proceedings, and exchange of statements of case by the parties.

(c) *Interim*: involves all the intermediate steps between the exchange of statements of case and the trial, some taken automatically and some requiring applications to the court.

(d) *Trial*: involves the preparation immediately before the trial and the actual day(s) of the trial.

(e) *Enforcement*: involves the winning party taking formal steps to force the losing party to obey the order of the court where there is any failure to do so.

(f) *Appeal*: involves any party dissatisfied with the court's judgment or order considering whether an appeal is possible and appropriate and taking the formal steps necessary to appeal.

(g) *Payment of costs*: involves ensuring all costs of the litigation have been assessed, where appropriate, and been paid to the relevant person or authority.

Clearly, the first four of these areas of work occur in succession. However, the parties may decide not to proceed further or to discontinue the case at any time during the process, for example, if the parties agree to settle the case. A case may not involve enforcement or appeal. Payment of the various costs of litigation occur throughout the process.

12.2.3   WOOLF REFORMS

The main areas in which the Civil Procedure Rules 1998 affect the work of barristers and solicitors are:

(a) The 'overriding objective' which the court and parties must bear in mind throughout. One of the principal concepts is that of 'proportionality' by which the court, parties and lawyers must, throughout the case, deal with the case expeditiously and efficiently and keep the preparation involved proportionate to the value and importance of the case.

(b) The use of pre-action protocols (see **12.2.2(a)**). These result in the costs of a case being moved earlier as much of the information will have been exchanged before proceedings are even issued. It also sometimes means that barristers are more involved in cases before proceedings are issued (see **12.3.5**).

(c) Case management by the courts. The idea behind this is that the control of the timescale and costs of the litigation should be vested in the courts. This is done partially through tracking of cases (see (d)) where the steps allowed in preparation are kept commensurate with the value and importance of the case. It is also done by 'procedural' judges keeping an eye on cases and, where necessary, having case management hearings with the lawyers to ensure that the case is proceeding in a way which is efficient and cost effective.

(d) Tracking of cases. There are three tracks, each with its own set of rules to ensure that the cost and speed with which the case comes to trial is proportionate to the value and importance of the case. The three tracks are:

(i) Small claims (basically where the value of the claim is under £5,000 with some exceptions) — very simple procedure with minimal steps before the hearing which will be informal with strict rules of evidence not applying. Similar to the old 'small claims' cases pre-Woolf, these are often conducted by litigants in person because of the restrictions on lawyers' costs.

(ii)   Fast track (basically where the value of the claim is over £5,000 but under £15,000) — slightly more detailed procedure with limited steps to ensure sufficient disclosure of documents, witnesses and expert evidence (where relevant) and a trial date set for 30 weeks after the case has been allocated to this track. In addition, the time for the trial will be limited to one day. These rules attempt to ensure that the case does come to trial as quickly as possible and the costs of preparation are controlled.

(iii) Multi-track (basically where the value of the claim is more than £15,000) — more detailed procedure which allows for more detailed disclosure and preparation of evidence to reflect the greater complexity of the case. In addition, judges are more likely to become actively involved in managing the case through procedural hearings such as 'case management conferences' (held early on to determine the main issues, steps to be taken in preparing the case etc.), 'listing hearings' (to assist the parties and court in the decisions necessary for fixing the date for trial) and 'pre-trial reviews' (to set out how the actual hearing will be conducted — e.g. the length of time for speeches, witnesses etc.).

Thus the amount of work involved in the interim and trial stages (see (c) and (d) in **12.2.2** above) will vary depending on the 'track' to which the case is allocated and the specific requirements of the individual case.

12.3   Roles of Solicitor and Barrister

12.3.1   BAR IS REFERRAL PROFESSION

Although there are now some cases where clients have direct access to barristers, the Bar is a referral profession which, generally, gets its work from solicitors. A solicitor will use counsel for specialist advice or advocacy either because the solicitor lacks the relevant expertise or rights of audience or because it is more cost-effective for the solicitor to use a barrister than to do the research or advocacy personally. It is the solicitor who decides when to use a barrister and if he or she fails to instruct counsel when it is necessary, the solicitor may be liable to the client in negligence.

12.3.2   SOLICITORS' WORK

The level of expertise and specialisation of solicitors' firms varies enormously, from a firm which offers a broad range of legal services, from drafting wills to acting for defendants in criminal cases, to one which specialises, e.g., doing largely personal injury work. In any firm, work will be done by the partners, who must be solicitors, employed solicitors and paralegals who are often qualified legal executives. Most firms will assign the contentious and non-contentious work to different people. The litigation department may also be divided into criminal, family and civil, with solicitors specialising in one or two areas, e.g., personal injury and housing. Paralegals usually do the more routine aspects of civil litigation such as service of documents or sitting behind counsel and taking notes in a hearing.

Technically a client instructs a firm of solicitors to act. All correspondence and instructions or briefs to counsel will be in the firm's name. Once the other side has been notified that they are acting, it is improper for any other lawyer to communicate with the client directly (although there is nothing wrong with the parties dealing with each other directly). When court proceedings are issued, the firm (but not the individual solicitor) is on the record at court as acting for the client in the particular proceedings and will remain so until this is altered or the case is concluded or withdrawn. Although the firm as a whole technically acts for the client, an individual solicitor will usually conduct the case. Most firms will try to ensure that the solicitor who first sees the client takes the case on and sees it to completion.

The individual solicitor with conduct of the case will decide when to consult a barrister. Within the seven areas of work set out above, barristers will frequently be involved in pre-action, initiating proceedings, interim work, the trial and appeals. However, they are rarely involved in enforcement, and their involvement in costs is minimal (aside from ensuring they receive their own fees).

12.3.3 DEALING WITH COSTS

Prior to taking any steps, including instructing counsel, the solicitor must explain the costs of litigation to the client and ascertain how they will be paid. The bulk of the costs will be the fees to cover the work done by the solicitor and any barrister involved. The bulk of the solicitor's fees will usually be calculated on the basis of an hourly charge, with even small firms charging £100 an hour. Barristers' fees are usually calculated on a piecework basis, for a particular opinion or statement of case or court appearance. The level of the fee depends on the seniority of the barrister doing the work and its complexity, and is agreed between the solicitor and the barrister's clerk, but the minimum charge even for a junior barrister on a short application would be £100. Other expenses include court charges and the costs of obtaining expert reports. The client must be made aware of the fact that every consultation with the solicitor, and every step taken in the case, adds to the costs. The solicitor must also make clear that if the case is lost the client may be liable for the other side's costs and that, even if successful, the client may still be liable for all of his or her own costs, and in any event, will almost certainly have to pay some of his or her own costs.

The method of paying costs in civil litigation is changing rapidly. The client may simply pay privately, i.e. pay the costs from his or her own pocket. Alternatively, the client and solicitor may enter a conditional fee agreement whereby, if the client loses no legal fee will be charged by the client's own lawyers, but if the client wins the lawyers are entitled to payment of the usual rate plus a success fee. A client conducting litigation on a conditional fee basis remains potentially liable for the other side's costs if the claim is unsuccessful, but this liability can often be covered by insurance. Some people have legal expenses insurance whereby the costs are met by the insurance company. This is sometimes called 'before the event' insurance, and is increasingly common as part of motor insurance and household insurance policies. Finally, some people qualify for public assistance by way of legal aid or its replacement, help under the Community Legal Service. The manner in which public funds are made available for litigation is changing dramatically. The new method requires firms to apply to the Legal Services Commission to obtain a franchise. This franchise enables the firm to conduct publicly-funded work on the basis of being given a budget from public funds for each period for which the firm has a franchise. The old method required firms to apply to the Legal Aid Board in each case and often for each step in the case, and if the Board approved the application, a 'legal aid certificate' was issued by the Board. As old cases are completed, this method will gradually disappear.

12.3.4 INSTRUCTING AND BRIEFING COUNSEL

The solicitor with conduct of the case will also decide which barrister to consult and when 'booking' the barrister will officially deal through the clerk to the barrister's chambers. Most solicitors build up a 'stable' of several barristers in any one field of work whom they use regularly because they are good, fast, efficient, get on well with clients or with whom they have a particularly good rapport. Solicitors new to litigation or a particular area of work without such a 'stable' will select on the basis of recommendations of those working in the firm, solicitors working in the same field or, possibly, the clerk of a set of chambers which the solicitor has used. Lacking such recommendations, a solicitor may select on the basis of the specialisation of the chambers which can be obtained from the various directories.

A solicitor will use a range of barristers from very junior barristers for fairly simple matters, generally because it is cost-effective, to very senior Queen's Counsel for their highly specialist knowledge and advocacy skills on particularly complex cases. The cab-rank rule (see para. 601 of the Code of Conduct for the Bar) requires barristers not to refuse to do work except for specified reasons which include lack of expertise and inadequate time and opportunity to prepare. Within the rule, when taking on work for the barristers in their set, clerks do try to take into account the work preference of the barristers. However, in early years of practice most barristers have no particular area of expertise and will usually take a broad range of cases.

12.3.5 THE BARRISTER'S INVOLVEMENT

A barrister's involvement in any civil case is limited to doing specific tasks as requested by the solicitor. The three types of tasks which solicitors will usually ask a barrister to undertake are:

(a) Advising on:

    (i) merit and/or quantum,

    (ii) difficult or obscure points of law,

    (iii) evidence.

(b) Drafting documents, e.g., statements of case, affidavits.

(c) Advocacy at:

    (i) interim hearings,

    (ii) trial.

The solicitor consults the barrister separately on each specific step. Most solicitors will want continuity of barrister throughout a case so, for example, will ask the same barrister who advised on the merits at the beginning to draft the statement of case and do the advocacy at the trial. In the civil brief in **Chapter 16** the same barrister has been instructed at three stages: to draft a Defence; advise on merits; and appear at an interim hearing. However, if the solicitor is not satisfied with the work done at any stage he or she may ask someone else or decide to do the work personally. A solicitor may also use barristers of different call for different aspects of the same case, e.g., one of very junior call for simple interim hearings but a more senior barrister for advising on evidence and the trial. Finally, briefs for interim hearings or for trial may pass from one barrister to another because the original barrister briefed is not available, e.g., when he or she is 'double booked' because a case is taking longer than expected.

12.3.6 FORM AND CONTENT OF INSTRUCTIONS OR BRIEF

Although solicitors may consult counsel by phone on occasion, it is more usual for them to consult in writing. Technically a solicitor 'instructs' counsel to advise or draft documents and 'briefs' counsel to attend hearings. The solicitor will send a fresh set of 'instructions' or 'brief' each time the barrister is consulted. Instructions or briefs from solicitors should include copies of all relevant documents, follow a fairly standard format (see **16.1** for an example) and include:

(a) the heading which sets out the names of the prospective parties if proceedings have not yet been issued or the title of the case as drafted if proceedings have been issued;

(b) the party for whom counsel is instructed or briefed;

(c) a list of the documents enclosed;

(d) the name of the instructing firm and the name, reference and extension of the particular solicitor conducting the case within the firm;

(e) a brief summary of the case which should identify the relevant issues, information and documents and explain the solicitor's opinion, advice to the client and steps taken to date;

(f) specific directions as to what work the barrister is instructed or briefed to do, for example, to advise on merit and quantum or represent a client at a hearing;

(g) a 'back sheet' which contains the heading, the barrister's name and chambers address, the solicitor's firm name, address, telephone number, fax number and e-mail address, the reference or name of the individual solicitor dealing with the case and the words 'public funding' if the client is publicly funded or counsel's fee where briefed to appear on a hearing for a private client.

12.3.7 RETURNING THE WORK AND ENDORSING THE BRIEF

The barrister does the work as instructed or briefed and returns the instructions or brief to the solicitor with all the enclosed documents and an endorsement on the back sheet of the work done, the date and the fee. The endorsement is important as it is the statement of the work done. Where an opinion or draft is enclosed with the returned brief (as in the case of *Lowe* v *Mainwaring* at **16.2**), the endorsement merely signifies the work done, the date and the counsel who did it. Where court hearings are attended, it is important to ensure that the endorsement fully and accurately sets out the order made or the settlement reached. It should contain all the relevant details including the date, the judge, the order made and be signed by counsel. An example of such an endorsement after a hearing in a criminal case is shown at **17.2**.

The barrister retains none of the papers once the work under any particular set of instructions or brief has been completed. When solicitors instruct or brief counsel they should include any previous instructions or briefs together with their enclosed documents and any written advice or opinion. However, it is useful for a barrister to keep a copy of any written work done for the solicitor and a note of any relevant detail about the case, e.g., factual analysis of the case or legal research done, for future reference.

12.3.8 SOLICITORS AND BARRISTERS AS CLIENT'S AGENT

Solicitors and barristers act as the client's representatives and as such the rules of agency apply. The actual authority of the solicitor conducting the case will depend on the instructions of the client and the solicitor should obtain specific instructions from the client before taking any step. The actual authority of the barrister at any stage will be limited to the work required by the current set of instructions or brief. Both solicitor and barrister may be liable to the client if they act outside their actual authority. The apparent authority of solicitor and barrister to bind the client may be wider or narrower than their actual authority. The solicitor's apparent authority will extend to accepting service on behalf of the client and progressing the case to trial. It will also extend to making admissions and, in certain circumstances, compromising or settling the case. The barrister's apparent authority extends to speaking for the client in court and may also extend to making admissions and settlements on behalf of the client.

12.4 Pre-claim Stage

12.4.1 THE BARRISTER'S INVOLVEMENT

A barrister's involvement at this stage is usually confined to being:

(a) instructed to advise on merit and/or quantum,

(b) briefed to appear in court to obtain pre-action orders.

In both situations, the solicitor will have dealt with the legal costs and how these will be paid. The solicitor will almost invariably have interviewed the client, should have obtained full details of all relevant matters and sent instructions or a brief to counsel including all the relevant information and documents. How much barristers will become involved with satisfying pre-action protocols (see **12.2.2(a)**) remains to be seen.

12.4.2   OPINION ON MERITS AND/OR QUANTUM

The solicitor will seek counsel's opinion if he or she wants a second opinion of the case, feels further legal research or a more expert view is required to assess the case or it is required, e.g., by the insurance company where the client has legal expenses insurance.

Prior to seeking counsel's opinion, the solicitor should have obtained full information from the client on personal details, the problem, details of any loss suffered and the solution the client is seeking. The solicitor should have discussed with the client what the best course of action is, given the remedy the client is seeking, taking into account all relevant factors including a provisional view on the merits of the client's case, the position of the potential defendant(s) (e.g., easily located, in the country, financially good for the sum to be claimed, likely to pay up if proceedings are issued), the time it will take to bring proceedings to trial if necessary and whether some other alternative, such as mediation or complaint to an ombudsman, might be more appropriate.

Having reached a provisional view that litigation is at least worth investigating, the solicitor may then seek counsel's opinion by sending instructions setting out clearly all the relevant information, the solicitor's own view and advice to the client to date and any steps already taken, for example, an attempt may have been made to mediate or settle the case which has failed. The instructions should set out clearly exactly what advice is sought from counsel.

When advice is being sought at this preliminary stage, the solicitor will have been conscious of not taking any steps which might cost the client and be wasted because the advice is not to proceed. Thus the instructions may not contain, for example, expert reports, all the necessary documentation, or much in the way of evidence, e.g., proofs from witnesses. The solicitor may also have felt that, in the circumstances, despite the additional cost to the client, a conference with counsel might be advisable prior to any written advice being given. However, if the instructions do not suggest a conference, counsel should advise on the basis of the information in the brief. Clearly if essential information has not been provided, counsel could contact the solicitor to obtain this before advising.

The date of receipt of instructions in chambers will be noted on the instructions. Once the barrister has written the opinion, which should be signed and dated by counsel, it will be returned to the solicitor together with the original instructions to counsel with the back sheet properly endorsed with the fee and date the work was completed. One of the criticisms of barristers is the time taken to return written advice. It is important therefore to ensure you develop efficient methods which enable you to achieve a reasonable turnaround time. With ever more efficient methods of communication being used (e.g. fax, e-mail) what is a 'reasonable' turnaround time gets shorter and shorter.

Although the instructions to counsel will rarely be shown to the lay client, solicitors frequently do either give or show a copy of counsel's opinion to the lay client. The client will then make a decision on whether or not to issue proceedings. Depending on the type of case and client, the solicitor may call the client in for an interview and give or show the client a copy of the opinion. Alternatively, a copy of the opinion may just be sent to the lay client with a covering letter setting out the solicitor's view and seeking the client's decision.

12.4.3   MAKING APPLICATIONS BEFORE ISSUE

There are a variety of orders which can be obtained prior to issue. Most of these are done by application to the court for a hearing at which the matter can be determined on the basis of written evidence. Although solicitors may have the right to appear on such an application, counsel is frequently instructed. The more common of these orders are set out below.

12.4.3.1 Injunctions
A client may require an immediate court order to be protected from an alleged wrong. Thus, for example, the client's neighbour may be doing building work which is

undermining the client's house and an application is made to court to order the neighbour to cease the building work until the case can be determined at trial. A client may fear that property relevant to his claim held by the wrongdoer may be destroyed and a search order will be sought to permit the client to search and seize the property pending trial. A client who fears that the wrongdoer will dissipate assets or transfer them out of the country so as to render judgment hollow may seek a freezing injunction to freeze those assets.

12.4.3.2 Orders to assist collection of evidence

In order to ascertain whether or not a client has a sufficiently good case to issue proceedings, it may be necessary to obtain documents or inspect property which is in someone else's possession. If access is refused, an application can be made in certain circumstances for a court order that inspection be given.

12.4.3.3 Making the application

In these situations, particularly where injunctions are sought, counsel may receive extremely short notice of the hearing, e.g., an hour, and very little written information from the solicitor (sometimes only the back sheet). The written evidence which forms the basis of the application is that of the client but will be drafted by the barrister or the solicitor. Counsel may only be involved in making the application on the basis of the written evidence drafted by the solicitor. Alternatively counsel may also be instructed to advise in conference (where time is short the whole thing may be done in one telephone call) and/or draft the written evidence (faxed to the solicitor's office). If time is very short, the written evidence may be drafted outside the court door.

Where a detailed order is also sought, e.g., an injunction, counsel should have a draft order ready to present to the court. Again this may have been prepared by the solicitor or by counsel. Clearly care must be taken in the drafting of the order to ensure that it does give the client the protection sought and is within the court's powers.

Those attending court should, in theory, include the barrister, the solicitor and the lay client. However, often the solicitor will not attend. If the case is sufficiently straightforward there may be no representation from the solicitor's firm. Alternatively, the solicitor may send an 'outdoor clerk', i.e., a file carrier from the solicitor's office who may be extremely bright and au fait with the client and the case or a part-timer who has no idea about the case and very little, if any, legal knowledge. In addition, there is strictly no need for the client to attend as he or she will have no role to play in the hearing (the evidence being that contained in the written statement). However, if possible it is desirable for the client to attend in case something unexpected arises. Thus the barrister at the hearing may have access to fairly comprehensive information where both the solicitor and the lay client attend. However, he or she may equally have to rely solely on information from the brief including the written evidence.

At court, there may be attempts to settle the matter, either just the immediate application or the whole matter. Although the solicitors may have been negotiating prior to this, once at the court door, negotiations will usually be between counsel. Thus the barrister needs to be aware of the wider context of the the case and be ready to receive and process information very quickly indeed. If a settlement is reached, the barrister should ensure that he or she knows exactly what has been agreed and that it is within the client's instructions. Clearly this will be extremely difficult, if not impossible, where the client is not present and the solicitor is represented by an uninformed 'outdoor clerk'.

In making the application, the barrister will be responsible for obtaining the best possible outcome from the court for the lay client. The barrister should be fully aware of the facts, law and evidence before the court, and must present the case and respond to his or her opponent to further the client's claim. The barrister should note the precise wording of the order, and check that it is within the power of the court to make and is enforceable. The barrister should also make sure that the costs of the application have been dealt with and (where necessary) that a certificate for counsel has been granted. Counsel should also be clear who must draft and serve the order.

Once outside court, counsel should ensure that the solicitor (or whoever attended from the office) and the lay client (if attending) understand exactly what has been ordered, both in terms of the substantive order and as to costs. The brief should be properly endorsed (see **12.3.7**).

12.5 Instituting Proceedings

12.5.1 INTRODUCTION

If the client decides to take proceedings on the basis of the solicitor's advice or counsel's opinion, a 'letter before action' should be sent to the proposed defendant or his or her solicitors warning that proceedings will be issued if the client's claim is not satisfied. The client will have to pay court costs if no such letter is sent and the defendant satisfies the claim on receipt of the court documents and argues that this would have been done if warned of the impending proceedings. In those cases where there are pre-action protocols the requirements set out in them will also have to be satisfied. The proper court documents must also be drafted, served and, where necessary, filed with the court. A barrister will rarely be involved in writing the 'letter before action' but will frequently draft court documents. In addition, there are a variety of orders which may be sought early in the litigation process and the barrister may be briefed to obtain these.

12.5.2 COURT DOCUMENTS

12.5.2.1 The claimant's case

The documents required to take court proceedings consist of the statement setting out the facts (but not generally the law or evidence) of the claimant's case sufficient to inform the defendant of the nature of the case which has to be met and the formal document(s) containing basic information such as the name and address of solicitors acting for the claimant.

It is vitally important that the statement of the claimant's case is properly drafted as it sets out the issues which the claimant wishes the court to consider and the remedies being sought. It is usual to instruct counsel to draft the statement and the instructions should contain all the relevant information and documents. If counsel has already advised on the merits and/or quantum, the instructions seeking this advice and the advice given should be included in the instructions to draft the statement of the claimant's case. Claims are commenced by issuing a claim form and 'particulars of claim'.

Usually, counsel will draft only the particulars of claim. His or her clerk will then arrange for the instructions together with the draft document to be returned to the solicitor. The solicitor (or a clerk in the firm) will then complete the formal documentation, which includes the client or solicitor signing a 'statement of truth' verifying the content of the particulars of claim, and arrange for sufficient copies to be sent or taken to the court where they are stamped (the date of issue). Service on the other parties will be arranged by the court or by the solicitor by posting or personal delivery (by clerk or process servers).

Once served, the defendant will have a set period of time to respond by serving a defence. If the defendant fails to respond within the period, the claimant, in many cases, can get 'judgment in default' (i.e., of the defendant responding). This is a routine step in which the barrister will not be involved. A defendant who does respond may also consult a solicitor, who in turn may instruct counsel to draft the statement of his or her case.

12.5.2.2 The defendant's case

Counsel instructed to draft a response to particulars of claim should receive a proper set of instructions with all the relevant documents and sufficient information for the drafting of a defence and, where appropriate, a counterclaim (where the defendant, in addition to a defence, has a claim against the claimant) and/or a Part 20 claim (third-party notice) (where the defendant alleges someone else is wholly or partly responsible for any damages which the claimant may obtain against the defendant). The barrister will return the instructions with the relevant documents which have been drafted to the solicitor who will serve them on the relevant parties. Strict time limits apply and counsel must ensure that the necessary work is done in sufficient time for the solicitor to keep to those limits.

12.5.2.3 Reply by claimant

Where the defendant makes a counterclaim, which is relatively common, the claimant must serve a defence to that claim. If the defendant merely serves a defence, the claimant only needs to serve a 'reply' if the defence raises a good answer to the claimant's claim. The need for a 'reply' is rare. The barrister who drafted the initial statement will almost invariably be instructed to draft the subsequent responses. Again there are time limits for these to be served.

12.5.2.4 The statement of case

The particulars of claim, defence, counterclaim, defence to counterclaim and any reply constitute the 'statement of case'.

If any of the parties consider that the statement of case served on them does not give sufficient information to enable them to prepare their case properly, he or she may request further information. The further information provided will be available at trial.

The statements of case set out the issues to be determined by the court and the parties are confined to arguing the issues in dispute as set out in the statements of case. Although all statements of case can be amended throughout the litigation process, there are limits on the amendments which can be made and there are cost implications for a party seeking amendments. Thus it is very important that counsel draft the statements of case carefully. In drafting particulars of claim, counsel must ensure that all relevant matters are set out. In drafting defences, counsel must ensure that an answer has been given to each allegation made in the particulars and made clear whether it is admitted, denied or, while not denied, puts the claimant to proof (not admitted), and must include any additional facts on which the defendant intends to rely. Any statements of case must be signed and dated by the barrister who drafts them and then verified by a statement of truth signed by the lay client or solicitor. Examples of statements of case can be found in the civil brief in **Chapter 16**.

12.5.3 APPLICATIONS TO THE COURT

12.5.3.1 Introduction

In any civil proceedings there are a variety of applications which the parties can make to shorten the process or obtain payment or some form of court order without having to wait for the full hearing. Although some of these can be used at any stage in the proceedings, they will more commonly be employed relatively early in the process and before much of the evidence has been collected.

Applications are usually heard by judicial officers known as masters (in the High Court) and district judges (in a county court). Although solicitors have rights of audience in these matters, they often instruct counsel. The hearing will generally be in public but often in a smaller room than a courtroom with counsel being invited to sit rather than stand. The master or district judge will hear argument from counsel for both parties on the basis of the statements of case served to date and written evidence. Counsel may have drafted the statements of case and also have been instructed to draft the written evidence for the hearing. However, applications often have to be made on the basis of statements of case and written evidence drafted by someone else, whether it be the solicitor or another barrister. The most common of the applications in which counsel may be involved are set out below.

12.5.3.2 Summary judgment

The claimant may apply to the court for 'summary judgment' where there is no real prospect the defence will succeed and therefore no real need for trial. The defendant may also apply for summary judgment where the claimant's case has no real prospect of success. The purpose of this process is to dispose of the case without the expense and delay of a full trial. In drafting the written statements and doing the advocacy at the hearing, counsel will need to balance the need to present the best case for the client with the fact that, as the purpose is to dispose of the case without extra expense, the application will be made at a stage before much of the evidence has been collected.

12.5.3.3 Interim payments

Although there are now procedures to attempt to bring cases to trial much faster than in the past, interim payment procedure recognises that even this delay may cause hardship to a claimant and allows an application for early payment of at least some of the money being claimed. An interim payment will be ordered only where it is clear that the claimant will be at least partially successful and it would be unjust to delay immediate payment of that entitlement.

12.5.3.4 Security for costs

A defendant who considers he or she has a strong case may be worried that, though he or she will win at trial, the claimant will be unable to pay his or her costs. In certain circumstances, a defendant can apply to the court for an order that the claimant give 'security for costs', usually by paying a specified amount into court.

12.5.3.5 Other orders

The orders which can be sought prior to issue can equally be sought after issue and before the full hearing (see **12.4.3** above).

12.6   Interim Stage — Preparing the Evidence

12.6.1   INTRODUCTION

Once statements of case have been exchanged, the issues between the parties have been defined and they now move to collecting and preparing their evidence for trial, including any relevant documents, real evidence (e.g., goods which are claimed to be faulty), expert reports and witness statements.

The evidence at trial is that of all the parties, and the solicitor for each party must ensure that he or she collects all the evidence relevant to his or her client's case and exchanges evidence and information with the other parties where mutual disclosure is required or appropriate.

12.6.2   OBTAINING INFORMATION FROM OTHER PARTIES

There are formal steps by which all parties are obliged to exchange information about their evidence. This will be done by the solicitor, sometimes with counsel's assistance. The steps involved include the following.

12.6.2.1   Disclosure

This is the process by which the parties exchange information about the potential documentary evidence which they hold. All parties are obliged within a set time period to make a list of all relevant documents (even those they themselves do not intend to use at the trial) which are or have been in their possession, custody or power and serve the list on the other parties who then have the right to inspect all those still in possession and for which privilege is not claimed. Inspection may be by exchange of photocopies of documents or actual inspection at the solicitors' offices. From this exchange of lists and inspection, both sides collect the documents and information contained in them which may form evidence for or against them. The process, which it is essential to carry out carefully, can be extremely tedious and, fortunately, counsel is rarely involved in it, unless problems occur as in the case of *Lowe* v *Mainwaring* at **16.3**.

12.6.2.2   Requests for further information

A party can request 'further information' from other parties on matters which are reasonably necessary and proportionate to enable the party to understand the case he or she has to meet or to assist in the preparation of his or her case. The request could be for clarification/further information of the statements of case (see **12.5.2.4**) or other matters, such as witness statements. Prior to the Woolf reforms, counsel was frequently instructed to draft both the request and answers to equivalent procedural steps (called request for further and better particulars and interrogatories). Although the procedure for seeking such information has been simplified by the Woolf reforms, as the requests and answers will be available at trial, counsel may still be involved in drafting both.

12.6.2.3 Notice to admit facts

The length and cost of trial will depend to a degree on the number of disputed issues which need to be determined. The statements of case limit the issues to those which the defendant denies or does not admit (i.e., puts the claimant to proof). A party may attempt to limit the issues further by seeking admissions from the other side through the formal process of serving a notice to admit. A party who fails to admit facts in response to such a notice may have to bear the cost of proving them at trial. Counsel may be asked to draft notices and replies.

12.6.2.4 Exchange of witness evidence

Within a set period parties must simultaneously exchange both witness statements and expert reports of all those they intend to call and are basically confined at trial to the evidence in the statements and reports exchanged. The actual wording of them is therefore very important and counsel will frequently be involved in the drafting of them. The solicitor then arranges the exchange with the other parties.

12.6.3 ADVISING ON EVIDENCE

The solicitor may seek counsel's advice on evidence at any stage in the litigation process, either through formal instructions seeking written advice or a conference with counsel, with or without the lay client. Even where this is done in conference, counsel is frequently asked to confirm the advice in writing. Counsel's involvement in collecting and preparing the evidence for trial is usually confined to advising on the strengths and weaknesses of the evidence and what further evidence should be collected.

When advising on evidence, counsel should be acutely aware of the overriding principle of 'proportionality' (see **12.2.2(a)**). This involves two aspects. First, the amount of time involved and difficulty in obtaining the evidence. The actual work of collecting the evidence falls to the solicitor who will interview witnesses to obtain statements, ensure all the relevant documents and items of real evidence are assembled and, where necessary, instruct and obtain a report from an expert. Counsel must weigh up the need to have all relevant evidence available for the hearing with the feasibility of the solicitor actually being able to produce it in the time available. Secondly, collecting and preparing the evidence increases the client's costs. The solicitor charges for any work done on the case. In addition there will be 'disbursement costs' incurred which will be passed on to the client where a charge is made to the solicitor to obtain information, copy documents, advice etc. from others. Experts will charge for their work as will counsel. Counsel must therefore also weigh up the need for the evidence against the cost of obtaining it.

12.6.4 DRAFTING WITNESS STATEMENTS AND EXPERT REPORTS

12.6.4.1 Witness statements

Until recently, all witnesses except expert witnesses gave evidence orally at trial. The solicitor drafted statements (or 'proofs' as they were sometimes called) for use by the advocate in court as the basis for questioning in examination in chief. These statements or proofs were not revealed to the other side and the evidence of the witness in chief was what was said orally at the trial. Any errors or omissions in the statements or proofs could therefore be rectified by counsel's careful questioning in court.

In virtually all cases now, witness statements must be in a particular format and exchanged prior to the hearing. The statements themselves stand as the bulk of the witness's evidence in chief. The actual wording of the witness statements is therefore incredibly important.

Although the witness statement is technically that of the witness, it is usually drafted by the solicitor or barrister. The Bar's Code of Conduct (para. 705) prohibits 'witness coaching' and sets out some guidance for discussing the evidence with witnesses. Generally, a barrister drafting statements will do so on the basis of the solicitor's instructions and enclosed documents including records of interviews with the client, letters, client's files and attendance notes by the solicitor. Alternatively, a barrister may be instructed to 'polish' a statement drafted by the solicitor. The statement represents the witness's evidence in chief and should cover all the issues in the statements of case on which this witness can give evidence. It is written in narrative form in the first person with appropriate reference to the relevant documents and items of real evidence which the witness is to produce. It must also fulfil the formal requirements as to form and content. The witness signs it as an acknowledgement that he or she accepts the truth of its contents and the solicitor should, therefore, ensure that the witness has the opportunity to check and amend the contents prior to signing and exchange.

12.6.4.2   Experts and their reports

The success of many cases will depend on the expert evidence. Thus, for example, in personal injury cases, the court will usually determine the extent of the claimant's injuries on the basis of medical evidence. In building disputes, the parties may rely on the opinion of surveyors, e.g., as to the extent of disrepair and what is required to rectify it. Expert evidence is basically opinion evidence of a suitably qualified or experienced person. Experts can differ in their opinions. In order to prevent the trial disintegrating into the swapping of numerous expert opinions, parties are usually each confined to a certain number, frequently one or two, experts. In addition, the procedure has for a number of years encouraged the parties to limit as far as possible the need for experts to be called at trial by directing exchange of expert reports and meetings of experts to attempt to limit the issues and have the reports agreed if possible. The Woolf reforms have increased the limitations on numbers of experts, including requiring the appointment of a single joint expert in some cases.

Obtaining expert evidence can be a complicated task which requires great skill to choose the right experts, instruct them properly and ensure that their evidence is well presented.

The involvement of counsel in obtaining expert evidence will depend on the level of expertise of the instructing solicitor. Most solicitors who specialise will have a 'stable' of experts on which they can rely and will be sufficiently au fait with the area to instruct them. The solicitor will obtain the report and counsel will have no involvement with the expert prior to the evidence being given in court aside from, possibly, where the expert evidence is complicated or in an area not known to counsel, a conference with the expert for counsel to ensure he or she has sufficient understanding of the evidence to deal with it properly at court. Alternatively, the solicitor may be new to the area and look to counsel for advice throughout including seeking advice on which expert to instruct.

The basis of expert evidence is the reports which the experts will write themselves. The report will be considered by the solicitor, who may also seek counsel's view of it, to ensure that it covers all relevant matters and does not include irrelevant ones. If an expert report is not favourable, the lawyer (solicitor or barrister) can discuss the contents of the report with the expert. Clearly there are professional conduct issues in the lawyers becoming too involved in the drafting of the report and attempting to 'rework' the opinion of the expert. If the expert's view is genuinely not favourable to the client, the lawyers need to decide whether or not to seek the opinion of another expert. The report of the first expert remains privileged and will not be shown to the other parties. However, if the other parties have discovered that the expert has been consulted there is nothing to stop them from calling that expert to give evidence.

Counsel must be able to deal with expert evidence at whatever level is required by the solicitor, and so should maintain information to assist in dealing with expert evidence, including a list of names of experts and copies of relevant books and diagrams to assist in deciphering reports, e.g., medical dictionaries, surveying terminology etc. A barrister dealing with experts must understand fully and in detail what the expert evidence is about, including any diagrams or plans. Counsel must be prepared to press an expert to clarify and explain technical terms, underlying principles or rules etc. in order to be able to put the relevant evidence before the court.

12.7 The Trial — Final Preparation and Hearing

12.7.1 INTRODUCTION

Having gone through the stages of exchanging statements of case to define the issues to be tried, and collecting and exchanging the evidence as required by the rules, the final preparations for trial involve ensuring that all the parties, witnesses and lawyers attend court properly prepared and that the evidence is put into a format which is convenient for all, including the judge.

12.7.2 TRIAL DATES AND TIMETABLES

Cases assigned to the small claims and fast tracks will almost invariably be given trial dates when allocated to that track. In cases where no trial date has been given (in multi-track cases and some fast track cases) a trial date will have to be obtained from the court. In addition, in both fast track and multi-track cases, a few weeks before the trial date, the court will make directions as to the evidence to be called, the documents to be used (see **12.7.4**), how the trial should be conducted (trial timetable which will include limitations on the amount of time for each step in the trial) and any other matters it considers are required to prepare the case for trial. Where it is intended that counsel act as advocate, he or she should be involved in providing the information to the court on which decisions as to trial date and directions for trial are made (whether done in writing or by way of a procedural hearing at court).

12.7.3 WITNESSES

It is the solicitor's duty to ensure that the witnesses attend court on the hearing day. The solicitor should therefore make sure that all the witnesses (and the client, if not also a witness) are given as much information as possible about likely hearing dates and, when it is actually fixed, the precise date. If there is any likelihood that a witness will not attend, the solicitor should consider compelling attendance by issuing and serving a witness summons.

12.7.4 TRIAL BUNDLES

The claimant's solicitor must, within a set number of days before the date fixed for the trial, prepare and lodge with the court copies of all the documents which will be used or referred to at the trial by the claimant or defendant (the defendant's solicitor having given notice to the claimant's solicitor). The division of labour becomes more complicated where there is a claim and counterclaim (i.e., the defendant taking on the role of claimant in respect of the counterclaim).

The purpose of preparing and lodging the bundles of documents is to ensure that they have been put into a usable format for the court. The rules set out the number and format (e.g., paginating) of bundles to be lodged; the principal documents lodged include:

(a) the claim form and all statements of case;

(b) a case summary and/or chronology where appropriate;

(c) all requests for information and the answers;

(d) all witness statements with an indication of whether the contents are agreed;

(e) all expert reports with an indication of whether the contents are agreed;

(f) all documents which any of the parties wish to have before the court.

The claimant's solicitor will arrange for sufficient copies of the bundles to be provided for all parties (the other parties paying a reasonable fee for their copies). Each party will usually have three or four copies, one for the solicitor, one for counsel, one for the witness and, possibly, one spare.

Ensuring that the bundles contain all the relevant documents and are compiled in accordance with the rules is an extremely important but tedious task. Fortunately, counsel's only involvement in this will be to advise on which statements, reports, documents etc. are to be included.

12.7.5   BRIEFING THE ADVOCATE

Where the solicitor has decided not to do the advocacy personally, his or her choice of counsel will depend on a variety of factors including the type of case, its complexity and whether counsel has been involved in the preparation stages. Whoever the solicitor decides to use should be properly briefed (see **12.3.6** for general format) and should include copies of the following:

(a) any bundles lodged at court;

(b) all previous advice and opinions of counsel;

(c) any additional proofs of evidence from witnesses (i.e., updating their statements).

The detail in the brief will depend on counsel's previous involvement. Thus, where counsel has been actively involved, and the documents enclosed include previous opinions and advice, the brief itself may be relatively short as counsel is au fait with all the detail.

The barrister's fee for the case will depend on his or her standing and the complexity of the case. It is agreed on the basis of a 'fee' of £x for the first day (a sum which includes preparation time) and a 'refresher' of £y (a lower sum than the fee, a daily charge) for subsequent days. Although technically the full fee is payable once the brief is delivered even if the case settles or folds before then, in practice many barristers agree to accept no fee if, e.g., the case settles before a deadline date which is calculated to give them time to prepare.

Ideally, where the trial is of any substance, briefs should be delivered to counsel at least two weeks before the hearing date.

Counsel should consider whether a skeleton argument is required. This may have been included in the case management directions, or it may be required by a specialist court guide. Skeleton arguments are generally required for High Court trials (and in the Court of Appeal). Otherwise, it is a matter of professional judgment based on the complexity of the issues. Skeletons should be served on the other side and filed at court 24 or 48 hours before the hearing (except for the Court of Appeal, when they must be lodged early on in the process).

While some solicitors are very professional and do ensure counsel has the brief in adequate time, some more often than not deliver it very late. On the reverse side of the coin, barristers who have been booked to do the hearing may become unavailable, e.g., because of being 'part heard' (i.e., in the middle of a case which has overrun its estimated time). Counsel's clerk should notify the solicitor as soon as the problem arises so the solicitor can choose another barrister to take the brief. Some chambers are very good at notifying solicitors and some delay the notification, hoping the barrister will in the end be free. The clerk may suggest someone else in chambers to take over. The advantage of this is that counsel taking over has more opportunity to discuss the case with counsel who was initially briefed.

12.7.6 THE TRIAL

When counsel is instructed as the advocate at trial, there may or may not be a representative of the instructing solicitor's firm present. The representative may be the solicitor, where the case or the client is worth a reasonable amount, or a 'file carrier' who may or may not know anything about the case or the law.

At trial, the advocate has control of and responsibility for the conduct of the case. There are numerous matters which require some attention immediately before going into court, e.g., there may be last-minute checking of information, updating of statements, reassuring witnesses who are nervous, ensuring the court has the advocate's name etc. It is the advocate's duty to ensure the smooth running of the case, e.g., that all the witnesses are present, all the documents are before the court and available for those who need them, e.g., witnesses when giving evidence etc.

Once the hearing has started, the advocate will be fully occupied either addressing the court or dealing with witnesses. Any attendant solicitor (or representative) should take a full note of what is said. However, the barrister should be making notes as well, partially because it is not possible to turn constantly to the solicitor (or representative) for their notes and partially because of the varying quality of their notes.

Once all the evidence has been called and the closing speeches given, the court will deliver judgment. This may be done immediately or, where the case has been long or complex, may be reserved, by an adjournment to the next day or to a much later date where the judge requires more time to consider it. Counsel should take a full note of the judgment and endorse the brief properly (see **12.3.7**). Counsel should also check that any orders are within the court's power, the details are accurate and that he or she understands the judgment or order in detail.

The advocate for the successful party will ask for costs. It is important that the court makes orders on all the costs before it including any which are outstanding from interim hearings. In addition, the court should deal with the summary assessment of costs if it is a fast track trial, or make an order for detailed assessment, including the detailed assessment of any public funding costs.

The judgment and/or order of the court cannot be enforced until it is formally drawn up. This will usually be the task of the court. Counsel must ensure that his or her notes and endorsement are sufficient for the solicitor to check that the court has done the task properly before serving the order on the party against whom it has been made.

12.8 Settlement during the Process

A very high percentage of cases never get to trial but settle at some stage along the way. Although there is nothing preventing the parties themselves from negotiating a settlement, once proceedings are issued, negotiations are usually conducted through the lawyer, usually the solicitor. Counsel may be involved in negotiations, most frequently at the court door prior to the full trial or possibly at interim hearings. All such negotiations are conducted on a 'without prejudice' basis which means that they cannot be revealed to the court if settlement is not reached.

A defendant who wishes to put some pressure on the claimant to settle can use one of two devices. If the claimant's claim is for money (damages or a debt), a 'payment in' to court may be made. Under this procedure the defendant pays a sum into court which the claimant can then accept, which ends the matter, or refuse, in which case the case will still go to court. However, if the claimant does not win more than the sum paid in, he or she will have to pay the defendant's costs from the date of the 'payment in'. Where 'payment in' is not possible, e.g., the claim is not for money or raising the money would require the sale of an asset which would be unreasonable to do prior to acceptance of the offer, the defendant can make an offer in a 'Part 36 offer'. This procedure may also be used by claimants. The contents of the letter cannot be revealed at trial prior to judgment but will be used in much the same way as a 'payment in' for costs. Counsel may be asked to advise on the level or format of the offer or its acceptance.

12.9 Enforcement

Many parties against whom judgments are given or orders are made comply with them without any further steps being required. However, if a party fails to comply, further formal steps are required to force compliance, e.g., the issue by the court of a warrant for possession to instruct the bailiffs to evict a person whom the court has ordered to deliver up possession or a warrant of execution to instruct the bailiffs to seize goods and sell them to obtain money a person has been ordered to pay. All of this falls to the solicitor and the barrister is rarely, if ever, involved.

12.10 Appeal

A party may wish to appeal a decision of the court, e.g. because judgment has been given against them or because, although an order has been made in their favour, they disagree with the terms set by the court. Counsel will frequently be involved both in advising on whether or not to appeal and in drafting the grounds of appeal.

12.11 Costs

The costs incurred which form the subject of a costs order include court fees, lawyers' fees and other costs such as photocopying costs and expert witness fees. Although the general rule is that 'costs follow the event' which means that the losing party is ordered to pay the winning party's costs, this is not always the case and the court may refuse to make the order, e.g., where there has been a 'payment in' which has not been exceeded at trial.

Even where a costs order is made, the winning party will rarely have all of his or her costs paid by the loser. There are three different methods for determining the actual amount which the loser must pay:

(a) 'agreed' costs – the parties agree how much of the winner's costs the loser will pay;

(b) 'summarily assessed' costs – used in 'fast track' cases where, immediately after giving judgment, the court assesses and states the costs payable;

(c) 'detailed assessed' costs – the solicitor whose client's costs are being paid submits a bill of costs to the court and a court officer decides the costs which should be allowed, reduced or disallowed on either a 'standard' or 'indemnity' basis. The 'standard' basis is the usual basis used and allows a reasonable sum in respect of all costs reasonably incurred, any doubts being resolved in favour of the paying party. The 'indemnity' basis, under which all costs are allowed except in so far as they are unreasonable, is far more generous and is ordered against the loser only in exceptional cases.

The solicitor has overall responsibility for keeping a record of all the costs incurred, including the barrister's fees, paying the various expenses, including the barrister's fees, having the bill assessed where a costs order is made and getting payment from the paying party and/or the client and/or the Community Legal Service.

Where a costs order is made, the winning party still has to pay his or her solicitor the full amount of the bill and is reimbursed by the losing party paying what was agreed or assessed. However, the winning party may feel that the bill is too high and have it assessed (which will be done on the indemnity basis). Only the amount allowed on assessment need be paid.

Counsel's brief fee will generally be what was agreed between the clerk and the solicitor. However, where the client has had the costs assessed, counsel will only be entitled to the amount deemed to be reasonable. On interim hearings, costs will generally be assessed summarily, and the amount of counsel's brief fee will be considered by the procedural judge at that time.

THIRTEEN

ANATOMY OF A CRIMINAL CASE

13.1 Introduction

The purpose of this chapter is not to act as a textbook on criminal procedure, nor as a guide to criminal advocacy. Rather, its function is to set out the stages of a case in which counsel may be involved so that this involvement can be put in its proper context. Further details regarding the procedure adopted by the criminal courts may be found in the *Criminal Litigation and Sentencing Manual* and in the *Advocacy Manual*.

The popular picture is of the barrister acting as an advocate in the courtroom. However, counsel's role is invariably much wider than that. This chapter sets out some of the tasks which a barrister instructed in a criminal case may have to perform. You should compare and contrast this chapter with **Chapter 12** (especially **12.3**), which deals with civil cases.

Although counsel may be briefed only for a particular stage in a case, real life does not exist in tidy compartments. For example, counsel may be instructed to apply for bail, but in the course of talking to the client about the bail application may be asked questions about what plea the defendant should enter or (in cases where there is a choice) which court should try the case. It is therefore vital for the barrister to be able to take an overview of the case as a whole.

Although reference is made to the role of the Crown Prosecution Service, most of this chapter is written from the perspective of a barrister representing the defendant. This is because barristers in private practice are generally required to have gained several years' experience in the criminal courts as defence advocates before being allowed to prosecute cases.

13.2 Role of the Defence Barrister

A barrister only represents a defendant if 'briefed' to do so by a solicitor. Solicitors themselves have complete rights of audience in the magistrates' court, and so there is nothing a barrister can do there that a solicitor cannot.

In the Crown Court, any solicitor may appear at the hearing of an appeal (against conviction and/or sentence) from a magistrates' court and at the sentencing hearing which follows a committal for sentence by a magistrates' court, provided that the solicitor is from the firm of solicitors which represented the defendant in the magistrates' court.

Solicitors who have been granted rights of audience in the higher courts under the Courts and Legal Services Act 1990 may also conduct a Crown Court trial or appear at hearings in the Crown Court prior to the trial.

If a barrister is instructed the brief (generally entitled 'Instructions to Counsel') usually consists of a short introduction to the case, written by the instructing solicitor, together with a proof of evidence (i.e., a written statement) from the defendant. In the criminal brief in **Chapter 17**, the same barrister has been instructed at three stages of the same case.

At the early stages of a case, the brief sent to the barrister may consist of very little. Indeed, there will be cases where the barrister is the first lawyer the defendant sees in connection with this particular offence. In that case, the brief may consist of only a 'back sheet' (i.e., a piece of paper containing the name of the defendant, the court in which that defendant is appearing and the name and address of the solicitors).

When the barrister meets the client it is necessary to go through the proof of evidence (assuming there is one) with the client. It may be that there are things the client wishes to correct or to add. Where the barrister is taking instructions from the client at court (shortly before the hearing), there may only be a short time available and counsel should give priority to eliciting information which is relevant to the hearing which is about to take place. For example, if the reason for the appearance is to make a bail application, then the information which counsel needs to draw out first from the client should relate to matters which are relevant to bail. Other matters can be dealt with after the important information has been discovered.

By the time the case is ready for trial, counsel should have a much fuller brief which contains not only a proof of evidence from the client, but also statements from any witnesses whom counsel is to call in support of the defence case. In the case of Crown Court trials, defence counsel will also be in possession of the written statements made by the witnesses whom the prosecution intend to call. In the case of magistrates' court trials, counsel for the defence *may* have copies of the witness statements made by the prosecution witnesses; if the offence is one which is triable either way (i.e., triable either in the magistrates' court or in the Crown Court), counsel will at least have a summary of the prosecution case.

If the solicitor has not already done so, defence counsel should make sure that the defendant looks through the statements made by the prosecution witnesses and so has a chance to comment on those statements; this may give counsel very useful ammunition with which to cross-examine those witnesses when the time comes.

In the magistrates' court, where counsel has been instructed on behalf of the defendant, no representative from the solicitor's office will be present. If the defendant brings witnesses who have not made statements to the instructing solicitor, counsel will have to take statements from those witnesses.

In the Crown Court, a representative from the instructing solicitor should be present (although this will usually be an 'outdoor clerk', that is, a representative who is not legally qualified).

13.3 Criminal Defence Service

From April 2001 the existing system of criminal legal aid has been abolished and is replaced by representation through the Criminal Defence Service (established by the Access to Justice Act 1999).

Schedule 3, para. 5(1) to the 1999 Act provides that any question as to whether a right to representation should be granted shall be determined according to the interests of justice. Paragraph 5(2) provides that, in applying the interests of justice test to an individual defendant, the following factors must be taken into account:

(a) whether the defendant would, if convicted, be likely to lose their liberty or livelihood or suffer serious damage to their reputation;

(b) whether the determination of any matter arising in the proceedings may involve consideration of a substantial question of law;

(c) whether the defendant may be unable to understand the proceedings or to state their own case;

(d)   whether the proceedings may involve the tracing, interviewing or expert cross-examination of witnesses on behalf of the defendant; and

(e)   whether it is in the interests of another person that the defendant be represented.

These criteria mirror the criteria which applied to the grant of criminal legal aid under the Legal Aid Act 1988.

Under the 1988 Act there was also a means test (some defendants being ineligible for legal aid because of their means, others having to pay a contribution to the costs incurred on their behalf). Representation through the Criminal Defence Service is dealt with differently. Section 17 of the Access to Justice Act 1999 provides that an individual for whom representation is provided by the Criminal Defence Service shall not be required to make any payment in respect of the services except in specified circumstances, set out in s. 17(2). This provides that where representation is provided by the Criminal Defence Service in any court other than a magistrates' court, the court may make an order requiring him to pay some or all of the cost of any representation so funded for him (in proceedings in that or any other court). In other words, representation in the magistrates' court will be provided by the Criminal Defence Service irrespective of the defendant's means. Where the defendant appears in the Crown Court, that court will have the power to require the defendant to pay for some of the costs incurred (including any costs incurred in the magistrates' court) by the Criminal Defence Service acting on his behalf. Obviously, the defendant's means (disposable income and disposable capital) would be an important consideration.

13.4   Crown Prosecution Service ('CPS')

At a very early stage in the case, papers are sent by the police to CPS. A Crown Prosecutor will decide whether to proceed with the case.

In the magistrates' court, CPS is represented by a Crown Prosecutor or by an 'agent' (that is, by a solicitor or barrister instructed by CPS); in the Crown Court CPS will usually be represented by a barrister.

In the magistrates' court, the CPS file takes the place of the brief for the prosecutor. In the Crown Court, prosecuting counsel receives a brief which is very similar in form to the brief sent to counsel for the defence. The file or brief, as the case may be, will contain an introduction written by a Crown Prosecutor, copies of written statements made by the witnesses to be called on behalf of the prosecution, and details of the defendant's previous convictions (if any).

In the Crown Court, a representative from the CPS should be available to assist counsel, and the police officer in charge of the case will also be present. In the magistrates' court the prosecutor will be alone, although the police officer in charge of the case will be present for the trial (but not for any hearings which precede the trial).

13.5   Stages of a Criminal Case: a Thumbnail Sketch

To help you make sense of the rest of this chapter, this section aims to provide a thumbnail sketch of criminal procedure in so far as counsel may be involved.

Where proceedings were commenced by the laying of an information (followed by the issue of a summons), counsel is likely to attend only for the trial itself. This is because the question of bail does not arise (and so remand hearings, where the question of bail is dealt with, do not take place); furthermore, most offences where proceedings are commenced in this way are triable only in the magistrates' court, and so there is no mode of trial hearing (i.e., a hearing to determine which court should try the case).

The other method of commencing proceedings is to arrest and charge the suspect. The suspect will be arrested and will usually then be interviewed at the police station. At the police station, the suspect is entitled to legal advice; that advice will invariably be provided by a solicitor, not by a barrister. If the suspect is charged with an offence, he or she may either be granted bail by the police or else held in custody until the next sitting of the magistrates' court (when the magistrates can be asked to grant bail to the defendant). If police bail is granted, counsel may attend remand hearings but, assuming the prosecution do not subsequently oppose bail, the grant of bail is a formality and so there is little for counsel to do.

Whether proceedings are begun by the laying of an information or by the arrest and charging of the suspect, the police will send the papers to the CPS. A Crown Prosecutor will decide whether the proceedings should be continued. In coming to this decision, the Crown Prosecutor will have regard to the strength of the evidence against the suspect and to whether it is in the public interest to continue the prosecution. In complex cases, CPS may seek the advice of counsel.

If proceedings were commenced by the arrest and charge of the suspect, and police bail was withheld, counsel may be instructed to attend the magistrates' court to make an application for bail on behalf of the defendant. In many cases, however, the first bail application will be made by a solicitor. Where the prosecution oppose the grant of bail, the bail application will be opposed by the CPS representative. If that application for bail is unsuccessful, counsel may be briefed to return to the magistrates' court a week later to make a further bail application, as in the criminal brief of *R* v *Costas Georgiou* at **17.1**.

If bail is withheld by the magistrates after the second application for bail, counsel may be asked to return to the magistrates' court to reapply for bail if there is a material change in circumstances (enabling a further bail application to be made) or there may be an appeal against the refusal of bail by the magistrates; this appeal is normally to the Crown Court (although the High Court also has power to grant bail). In the Crown Court, bail will be opposed by a barrister instructed by the Crown Prosecution Service.

In addition to the remand hearings in the magistrates' court, counsel may, if the offence is triable either way, be instructed to attend the magistrates' court to represent the defendant at the mode of trial hearing: at this hearing, the defendant is asked to indicate whether he intends to plead guilty or not guilty to the 'either way' offence(s) with which he is charged. If the defendant gives no indication or indicates an intention to plead not guilty, the next step is for the decision to be taken whether the case should be heard in the magistrates' court or in the Crown Court. Again, the prosecution will be represented by a Crown Prosecutor or by a solicitor or barrister instructed by CPS.

Where the offence is triable either way and the case is to be tried in the Crown Court, counsel may also be instructed to attend 'committal proceedings'. This is the hearing at which the case is sent to the Crown Court for trial. The prosecution hand to the magistrates the statements made by the witnesses whom the prosecution intend to call at the Crown Court. The defence confirm that they do not wish to make a submission that the prosecution have failed to establish a *prima facie* case against the accused. The magistrates then commit the defendant to the Crown Court to stand trial. In those rare cases where the defence do not accept that the witness statements show a *prima facie* case against the accused (i.e., a reasonable court could not convict the accused on the basis of that evidence), the justices consider the prosecution evidence at the committal proceedings: the prosecutor reads out the statements, the defence submits that there is no case to answer, the prosecutor makes a speech in reply and the magistrates then consider whether there is sufficient evidence against the accused for him to be put on trial at the Crown Court.

Where the offence is triable only in the Crown Court, the first appearance will take place in the magistrates' court but in most cases all subsequent appearances will be in the Crown Court.

In some cases, prosecuting counsel may be asked to advise on evidence and/or on the question of disclosure to the defence of material which the prosecution have but which they do not intend to use at the trial. Defence counsel may be instructed to advise on the contents of (or even draft) the statement of the defence case which (in the case of Crown Court trials) must be served on the prosecution.

Next, counsel may be instructed to appear at the trial itself. This trial will be in the magistrates' court if the offence is a summary one or if the offence is triable either way but both the defendant and the magistrates agreed (at the mode of trial hearing) to summary trial; if the offence is triable only on indictment, or the mode of trial hearing resulted in a decision in favour of trial on indictment, the trial will take place in the Crown Court. In the magistrates' court, the prosecution will be conducted by a Crown Prosecutor or by a solicitor or barrister instructed by CPS; in the Crown Court, the prosecution will be represented by counsel.

Wherever the defendant is tried, if he either pleads guilty or is found guilty, counsel will have to make a plea in mitigation on behalf of the defendant before sentence is passed.

At the conclusion of the case it may be necessary for defence counsel to advise the defendant on the possibility of appeal against conviction and/or sentence. Where the trial took place in the magistrates' court that appeal will normally be heard in the Crown Court (although an appeal on a point of law may be made to the High Court, by way of case stated or by means of an application for judicial review). Where the trial took place in the Crown Court, appeal lies to the Court of Appeal (Criminal Division).

13.6 The Stages in Greater Detail

Having set out an overview of criminal procedure, it is necessary to examine some of the stages in more detail.

13.6.1 BAIL APPLICATION

In most cases, on the first occasion that a defendant appears before the magistrates' court charged with a particular offence, representation will be provided either by a duty solicitor (under the legal advice and assistance scheme) or by a solicitor from the firm which later instructs counsel. An application for public funding may be made at that hearing.

There will be occasions, however, where the barrister is the first lawyer the defendant meets in connection with this offence. It may be, for example, that the defendant agreed to be interviewed by the police without a lawyer being present and, after being charged with an offence and finding that police bail was withheld, contacted a firm of solicitors he or she has used before. If there is insufficient time for a solicitor from that firm to see the defendant prior to the first court appearance, counsel may receive instructions by telephone or fax (or even e-mail) to go to the magistrates' court. In that case, it will be for counsel to take initial instructions from the defendant, to give preliminary advice, to apply for public funding, and to make a bail application.

Even where counsel is in possession of a brief which includes a proof of evidence from the defendant, the role of defence counsel when attending court to make a bail application involves a number of elements: preparation, advice and advocacy.

In particular, counsel will have to:

(a) *Take instructions from the client:* If a proof of evidence from the defendant is included in the brief, it is necessary to check with the client that it is complete, accurate and up-to-date; if there is no proof of evidence, it is up to counsel to elicit all the necessary information from the defendant. In deciding what questions to ask the defendant, counsel should consider the factors set out in the Bail Act 1976, sch. 1 (e.g. risk of absconding, committing offences while on bail or interfering with witnesses, all of which are assessed in the light of such matters as the nature and seriousness of the present offence, the defendant's previous convictions (if any), the defendant's community ties and record of answering bail in the past).

(b) *Advise the client:* If this is the client's first court appearance, he or she may need reassurance; it may therefore be necessary to explain to the client what will happen in court. Furthermore, the client may seek advice about other aspects of the case. Where advice is given, a short note of that advice should be endorsed on the brief, signed and dated by counsel (so that the solicitor knows what advice has been given).

(c) *Address the court in favour of bail:* The prosecutor addresses the court first and explains to the court why the prosecution oppose bail. Counsel for the defence then replies to those submissions and will try to show that the prosecution objections to the grant of bail have no foundation or that those objections can be overcome by the imposition of conditions on the grant of bail. No witnesses are called (unless a surety comes forward, in which case that person will usually have to give evidence to show that he or she is a suitable surety).

(d) *Advising the client on challenging refusal of bail:* If bail is withheld, counsel should advise the defendant (and, later, communicate this advice to the instructing solicitor) on any steps which can be taken to increase the chance of bail being granted (e.g., the provision of a surety) and/or whether an application for bail should be made to the Crown Court.

The role of the prosecutor is rather more limited. He or she simply makes a speech opposing the grant of bail. In doing this, the prosecutor will usually have to rely on notes contained in the CPS file; those notes are based on information supplied by the police. The police officer in charge of the case is unlikely to be present at the bail application.

There may occasionally be some scope for negotiation between defence counsel and the prosecutor. It may be that the prosecutor will agree not to oppose the grant of bail if the defendant agrees that the grant of bail should be subject to certain conditions.

If the first bail application is unsuccessful, the defence may make a second application to the magistrates a week later. This is so even if the second application says nothing different from the first application (although the person making the application will normally try to find something different to say). Once the magistrates have heard two fully argued bail applications, they can only hear a further application if there is a material change in circumstances (i.e., the defence can put forward an argument which has not been put forward already).

Where bail has been refused by the magistrates following the second fully argued bail application, it may be appropriate to make a further bail application in the Crown Court. The procedure in the Crown Court is very similar to that in the magistrates' court (that is, the prosecutor sets out the reasons for opposing the grant of bail and defence counsel then replies to those submissions). However, the defendant will not be present and CPS will be represented by counsel.

If the offence is triable only in the Crown Court, the case may be transferred to the Crown Court after the first appearance in the magistrates' court. If the magistrate refuses bail, any further application for bail will be made in the Crown Court.

13.6.2 MODE OF TRIAL

Where the defendant is accused of an offence which is triable either way (that is, triable in either the magistrates' court or the Crown Court), counsel may be asked to advise the client on which court should try the case. This advice will almost always be given orally, and will generally be given just before the mode of trial hearing itself (unless it was given at an earlier remand hearing).

At this stage (if not before) the client may well need advice on plea. The mode of trial hearing in court begins with a 'plea before venue' hearing. The defendant is asked to indicate whether he intends to plead guilty or not guilty to the 'either way' offence(s) with which he is charged. If the defendant indicates an intention to plead guilty, then he is regarded as having pleaded guilty. At that point the magistrates will either proceed to sentence (if necessary, after an adjournment for a pre-sentence report to be prepared) or else commit the defendant to the Crown Court for sentence (the Crown Court having greater sentencing powers than the magistrates' court). If, on the other hand, the defendant either indicates an intention to plead not guilty, or gives no indication as to the intended plea, the magistrates then proceed to determine the question of mode of trial,

At the mode of trial hearing the magistrates have to decide whether the case is suitable for summary trial. The key question is whether, in the event of the defendant being convicted, their sentencing powers would be adequate to deal with the case. If the magistrates decide that the case is not suitable for summary trial, only trial in the Crown Court is possible. If the magistrates decide that the case is suitable for summary trial (i.e., they 'accept jurisdiction') the defendant is asked where he or she wishes to be tried. This is because, in the case of an offence which is triable either way, the defendant has an inalienable right to be tried on indictment (that is, at the Crown Court).

During the mode of trial hearing, the prosecution and the defence both have the right to make representations regarding the appropriate mode of trial. If the defendant wishes to elect trial on indictment, there is little point in the defence making any representations, because of the defendant's right to choose Crown Court trial. If, on the other hand, the defendant wants to be tried in the magistrates' court but the prosecution are seeking trial in the Crown Court, counsel for the defendant will have to try to persuade the magistrates that the case is suitable for summary trial.

13.6.3 ADVISING THE PROSECUTION

Counsel who has been briefed to prosecute in a forthcoming Crown Court trial may be asked by the CPS to advise on the evidence (and sometimes to redraft the indictment) before the trial takes place. This involves examining the witness statements made by the prosecution witnesses in order to see how strong the prosecution case is; counsel has to consider if the case can be improved (e.g., advising that the police take further statements from existing witnesses, to fill gaps or clarify ambiguities, or advising that further investigations be made).

The advice given must be realistic and practicable. It must be remembered that the police do not have limitless resources (and are not endowed with psychic powers!).

Where the trial is to take place in a magistrates' court, these matters will almost invariably be considered by a Crown Prosecutor, not by a barrister in private practice.

13.6.4 ADVISING THE DEFENDANT

Counsel for the defence may be asked to advise on evidence prior to a Crown Court trial. This advice will often be given orally, during a conference with the client, rather than in writing; such conferences usually take place in counsel's chambers or in a prison where the defendant is in custody. Sometimes, however, the only opportunity for a conference is at court, shortly before the start of the trial. Whenever it is given, the advice must be realistic and practicable: where the defendant is represented through the Criminal Defence Service, further enquiries involving considerable expense are unlikely to be covered by public funds. (See **17.3** for an example of a written advice in the case of R v Costas Georgiou.)

Prior to a magistrates' court trial, it is very rare for defence counsel to have a conference in chambers or to give written advice. The conference usually takes place in the court building, shortly before the trial is due to begin.

The function of the conference (whether held in counsel's chambers or, just before the trial is due to start, in the court building) may include some or all of the following elements:

(a) *Taking instructions from the client (that is, gathering information):* by the time of the trial, counsel will be in possession of a proof of evidence from the defendant which sets out the client's version of events. However, it is still useful to get the client to go through his or her side of the story: the solicitor may have missed something, or the defendant may remember something new. Whilst it is unethical, and therefore forbidden, for counsel to 'coach' the defendant (that is, to suggest evidence which the defendant might give), there is no objection to counsel questioning the client closely on the evidence he or she will be giving. It is helpful for the defendant to rehearse the evidence he or she will be giving in court and to prepare for cross-examination by the prosecutor.

Where counsel is in possession of the witness statements made by the prosecution witnesses, the defendant should also be asked to comment on what those witnesses say (so that counsel can decide what questions to ask them by way of cross-examination). It may be that the solicitor has already performed this task, so that the defendant's proof of evidence contains comments on the prosecution evidence; even then, it can be helpful to ask the defendant if there is anything he or she wishes to add to those comments.

(b) *Advising the defendant on plea and tactics:* Where the client has not received full advice on plea (from the solicitor, or from counsel on a previous occasion) it may be necessary for counsel to advise the defendant (based on what the client has said about his or her side of the story) on plea. It may be, for example, that the defendant has indicated an intention to plead guilty but then says something which amounts to a defence (e.g., a person accused of theft says that he or she did not realise that the property belonged to someone else).

It may also be necessary to advise on tactics, for example, what lines of cross-examination to pursue and what evidence to call.

(c) *Taking instructions on matters relevant to sentence:* Counsel should be careful to have all the information needed to make a plea in mitigation. Instructions should therefore be taken on matters which would be relevant to a plea in mitigation. This is so even where the client is going to plead not guilty, since (in the event of the defendant being convicted) there may not be time for a further conference between the defendant being convicted and the moment counsel has to start the plea in mitigation.

(d) *Advising on sentence;* Whether the defendant is going to plead guilty or not guilty, it will almost always be necessary to give advice on the sentence which is likely to be imposed in the event of conviction.

Counsel representing a defendant at an early stage of the proceedings should always be prepared to give advice about later stages of the case. On occasions, for example, counsel may be instructed to attend the magistrates' court to make a bail application, or for the mode of trial hearing, and may be asked for advice then by the defendant. Provided counsel is sufficiently well acquainted with the background to the case, there is no objection to such advice being given (although a short note setting out the advice given should be endorsed on the brief, so that the instructing solicitor, and any barrister involved in the case at a later stage, knows what was said).

13.6.5 PRE-TRIAL DISCLOSURE

A particularly important aspect of advising on evidence concerns the rules which govern pre-trial disclosure. The rules which apply to the prosecution are different from the rules which apply to the defence. The disclosure rules are contained in the Criminal Procedure and Investigations Act 1996. Further details can be found in the *Criminal*

Litigation and Sentencing Manual. As regards disclosure by the prosecution, a further distinction has to be drawn between material that the prosecution will be using as part of their case and material which they will not be using.

13.6.5.1 Pre-trial disclosure by the prosecution

If an offence is triable either way, the prosecution must (if the defence so request) supply the defence with a summary of the prosecution case or with copies of the statements made by those persons to be called as prosecution witnesses. This must be done (assuming the defence request advance information) before the mode of trial hearing (see **13.6.2**) takes place. If the case is to be tried in the Crown Court, copies of the statements made by the witnesses whom the prosecution intend to call at the trial must be supplied to the defence (if this was not done prior to the mode of trial hearing). The effect of these rules is as follows: if an offence is triable either way but is to be tried in a magistrates' court, the defence may have the prosecution witness statements prior to the trial, or they might just have a summary of the prosecution case; however, if an offence is to be tried in the Crown Court, the defence must have copies of the prosecution's witness statements before the case can be sent to the Crown Court for trial. Where the offence is triable only on indictment, the prosecution serve their witness statements on the defence after the case has been transferred to the Crown Court.

Where a case is to be tried in the Crown Court and the prosecution wish to use a witness whose statement has not already been served on the defence, a 'notice of additional evidence' (including a copy of the witness statement) must be served on the defence prior to the trial.

The prosecution are also under a statutory duty to disclose material other than the statements of the persons they will be calling as witnesses. Under s. 3(1) of the Criminal Procedure and Investigations Act 1996, the prosecutor must disclose any prosecution material which, in the prosecutor's opinion, might undermine the case for the prosecution against the accused. This applies to all trials (whether in the Crown Court, the magistrates' court or the youth court).

Section 7 imposes a further duty of disclosure on the prosecution. This additional duty applies to all Crown Court trials, and to summary (i.e., magistrates' court or youth court) trials where the accused has made disclosure under s. 5 or s. 6 (see **13.6.5.2**). Section 7(2) requires the prosecution to disclose to the defence any prosecution material which might reasonably be expected to assist the defence.

Section 9 imposes a continuing duty on the prosecution to keep the question of disclosure under review so that any material which comes to light and which might undermine the prosecution case is disclosed to the accused.

The prosecution may only withhold material under ss. 3, 7 and 9 if the court authorises non-disclosure on the ground of public interest.

13.6.5.2 Pre-trial disclosure by the defence

Section 5 of the Criminal Procedure and Investigations Act 1996 imposes a compulsory duty of disclosure on the defence, but this compulsory duty applies only to trials in the Crown Court. Section 5(6) requires the defence to inform the prosecution, in general terms, of the accused's defence and to indicate the matters on which the accused takes issue with the prosecution (and why he or she takes issue with the prosecution on those matters). Where the defence case includes an alibi, the accused must give full particulars of the alibi to the prosecution (s. 5(7)).

In the case of summary (i.e., magistrates' court or youth court) trials, s. 6 of the Act enables the defence to make voluntary disclosure of their case. The advantage of doing so is that the prosecution then have the duty (under s. 7) to disclose any material in their possession which might assist the defence (see **13.6.5.1**).

If the defence fail to comply with the compulsory duty of disclosure prior to Crown Court trial, or if the defence case at trial differs from that disclosed to the prosecution (whether the disclosure was compulsory or voluntary), then adverse inferences can be drawn by the jury or magistrates as the case may be (s. 11).

The General Council of the Bar has given guidance on the involvement of counsel in the drafting of defence statements under s. 5 or s. 6 of the 1996 Act. The guidance makes the point that it will normally be more appropriate for instructing solicitors to draft the defence statement, since counsel will generally have had little involvement in the case at this stage. Nonetheless, there is no reason why a barrister should not draft a defence statement. However, counsel must ensure that the defendant:

(a) understands the importance of the accuracy and adequacy of the defence statement, and

(b) has had the opportunity of carefully considering the statement drafted by counsel and has approved it.

13.6.6 PREPARATORY HEARINGS AND PRE-TRIAL HEARINGS

The Criminal Procedure and Investigations Act 1996 requires preliminary hearings to take place before all Crown Court trials. The nature of the hearing differs according to whether or not the trial is likely to be lengthy or complex. However, in both cases, the object of the rules is that the issues in the case should have been defined before the trial and to reduce the number of cases where the defendant was due to be tried on a 'not guilty' plea but then pleads guilty at the start of the trial (giving rise to what is sometimes called a 'cracked trial').

13.6.6.1 Complex or lengthy trials

Under s. 29 of the Criminal Procedure and Investigations Act 1996, which applies to Crown Court cases which are likely to be complex or lengthy, the judge may order a preparatory hearing to take place. The purpose is to identify the issues in the case, to see how the jury can be assisted to understand those issues, to expedite the trial, and to assist the judge's management of the trial (s. 29(2)).

To this end, the judge can make rulings on the admissibility of evidence or other questions of law likely to arise in the trial (s. 31(3)). The judge can also order the prosecution to prepare a document setting out the principal facts of the Crown's case, the witnesses who will speak to those facts, and any propositions of law the Crown will rely on (s. 31(4)(a)). The prosecution can also be ordered to prepare the evidence in a form that is likely to aid comprehension by the jury (s. 31(4)(b)). Finally, the prosecution can be ordered to provide a written notice detailing any documents the truth of which the prosecutor believes the defence should admit (s. 31(4)(c)).

The judge can then order the defence to give written notice of any points of law they will be raising (s. 31(6)) and to state which of the documents referred to in the notice given under s. 31(4)(c) the defence are prepared to admit; where the defence are not willing to admit the truth of any such documents, they must explain why this is so (s. 31(7)).

13.6.6.2 Other cases

In the case of Crown Court trials other than those which are likely to be complex or lengthy (in other words, the majority of cases) s. 39 of the 1996 Act enables a pre-trial hearing to take place. This gives statutory effect to the system of Plea and Directions Hearings which preceded the enactment of the 1996 Act.

At this hearing, the defendant is asked to enter a plea. If he pleads 'guilty', the judge proceeds to the sentencing stage (if necessary with an adjournment for a pre-sentence report). If the defendant pleads 'not guilty', a date is fixed for the trial.

Where the defendant pleads 'not guilty', prosecuting and defence counsel are expected to inform the court of matters such as: the issues in the case, the number of witnesses to be called, any points of law likely to arise (including questions on the admissibility of evidence), and whether any technical equipment (such as video equipment) is likely to be needed. It follows that it is very important that, by the time of this hearing, the factual and legal issues in the case should have been identified. (See **17.3.1** for the issues in *R* v *Costas Georgiou*.)

At this hearing, the judge is empowered to make rulings on the admissibility of evidence and on any other questions of law which are relevant to the case. These rulings are binding for the whole of the trial unless there is an application for the ruling to be altered, but such an application can only be made if there has been a material change in circumstances since the ruling was made. This is so whether or not the preliminary hearing and the trial are presided over by the same judge.

13.6.7   TRIAL

Defence counsel and the prosecutor may attend court expecting a trial to take place. However, a trial will not take place if either the defendant pleads guilty to the charge(s) or the prosecution accept a plea to a lesser offence. In the Crown Court any negotiations with the prosecution regarding the acceptance of a plea of guilty to a less serious offence than that charged will usually take place at the plea and directions hearing. Such negotiations will usually take place just before the trial where the case is to be heard in the magistrates' court.

We have already seen that counsel for the defence may have to give advice to the defendant at the conference which takes place immediately before the trial.

During the trial itself, counsel is involved in three main tasks:

(a)   *Making speeches:* In the magistrates' court the prosecutor makes an opening speech but no closing speech whereas counsel for the defence will usually make a closing speech but not an opening speech; in the Crown Court both the prosecution and the defence are usually entitled to make both an opening speech and a closing speech (although the defence often forgo the right to make an opening speech). As well as these speeches, it may be necessary for counsel to address the court on the admissibility of certain evidence or to make (or, if prosecuting, to respond to) a submission that there is no case to answer.

The purpose of the prosecution opening speech is to prepare the jury or magistrates for the evidence they are about to hear. The prosecution case is summarised so that the jury or magistrates can put the evidence they are about to hear in context.

The purpose of the closing speech is to highlight the strengths of one's case and, where possible, to minimise the impact of any weaknesses. The defence, for example, will stress any doubt in the prosecution evidence and any explanation which the defendant has given for apparently incriminating evidence.

A submission of no case to answer may be made by the defence at the end of the prosecution case. The essence of the submission is that the evidence adduced by the prosecution is so weak that no reasonable tribunal (jury or bench of magistrates) could convict the defendant on the basis of that evidence.

(b)   *Examination-in-chief:* This means getting the witness to tell the story (answering questions such as 'Who?', 'When?', 'Where?'). Care must be taken not to 'lead' the witness (that is, to suggest answers to the questions being put or to ask a question which can be answered with a simple 'yes' or 'no'). Before going into court, counsel must have decided what he or she hopes to achieve with the particular witness, since the examination-in-chief should only bring out evidence which is relevant to the case. Counsel will always be in possession of a written statement from the witness (which obviously forms the basis of the questions which will be put to the witness). Counsel should also be alert to any inadmissible evidence which is contained in the witness's written statement (e.g., references to previous dealings between the defendant and the police) so that those areas can be avoided in the questioning.

Examination-in-chief can also be used to anticipate questions which may be put to that witness in cross-examination. For instance, in a case involving identification evidence, prosecuting counsel would, in examination-in-chief, ask a witness who claims to have identified the defendant as the perpetrator about the circumstances of that identification (e.g., distance, lighting, obstructions to view etc.). The answers to these questions may well make it more difficult for counsel for the defence to cross-examine effectively on the matters.

The defendant has been present in court throughout the trial and so has heard the evidence of the prosecution witnesses. The defendant may be asked, in examination-in-chief, to comment on what he has heard (for example, 'You heard Miss Jones say . . . What do you say about that?').

(c) *Cross-examination:* This means probing the story told by the witness. In the Crown Court counsel for the defence will be in possession of the written statements made by the prosecution witnesses; in the magistrates' court counsel for the defence may have sight of the prosecution witness statements if the offence is one which is triable either way. In any event, the prosecution never have sight of the written statements made by witnesses for the defence. Obviously, it is easier to prepare a cross-examination if one has advance notice of what the witness is going to say.

Cross-examination essentially focuses on inconsistencies and on the probing of weaknesses:

(i)   inconsistencies between what the witness is saying now and what he or she has said in the written statement;

(ii)   inconsistencies in the evidence which the witness has given to the court (e.g., in the course of the witness's testimony, the colour of the car changes from dark blue to black);

(iii)   inconsistencies between what this witness has said and what another witness says;

(iv)   inconsistencies between what this witness is saying and the theory which counsel has formed about the case he or she is presenting;

(v)   inconsistencies between what the witness is saying and what common sense suggests actually happened (e.g., a witness who says that a car was travelling at 70 m.p.h. and that it braked sharply and stopped within a distance of 15 metres cannot be correct);

(vi)   probing the strength of the evidence (e.g., to find how far away the witness was from the scene of the crime and what obstructions there were to the observation). Does the witness have a motive for misleading the court?

It is important that in cross-examination you 'put your case'. In other words, if a witness called by your opponent may be able to comment on part of your case, the witness should be given the chance to do so. In the case of counsel for the defence, this will include putting to the witness those parts of the witness's evidence which differ from, or are inconsistent with, the defendant's account of what happened.

13.6.8   PLEA IN MITIGATION

A plea in mitigation is required if the defendant pleads guilty or is found guilty. Sentence is usually passed, either immediately or after an adjournment for preparation of a pre-sentence report, by the court which convicted the defendant. However, if the defendant was convicted by a magistrates' court of an offence which is triable either way, the magistrates may (if they decide that their sentencing powers are insufficient to deal with the case) commit the defendant to the Crown Court to be sentenced (the Crown Court having greater sentencing powers); in that case, the plea in mitigation is delivered in the Crown Court. It should be borne in mind that in the magistrates' court, the Bench which sentences the defendant will probably not be the same Bench that convicted him.

If sentence is passed immediately after the defendant has been convicted following trial (i.e. the defendant pleaded not guilty but was convicted), the prosecutor will simply tell the court about any previous convictions recorded against the defendant. If the defendant pleaded guilty, or the defendant is being sentenced at a hearing after the trial at which he was convicted, the prosecutor will also have to explain to the court precisely what the defendant did.

The next step is for defence counsel to make a plea in mitigation on behalf of the defendant. The essence of a plea in mitigation is to emphasise personal mitigating circumstances relating to the offender and to draw the court's attention to any mitigating factors relating to the offence itself.

The plea in mitigation will be based on information gathered from the client (in the proof of evidence and in things said by the client prior to the hearing) and, in many cases, on information contained in a pre-sentence report prepared by a probation officer. A list of the client's previous convictions (if any) should be in the brief; if not, the list can be obtained from the prosecutor. Counsel should check that the defendant agrees that the list of previous convictions is correct and that the defendant is happy with the comments made by the probation officer in the pre-sentence report. Counsel should be prepared to probe the client for details of mitigating factors relating to the offence itself or to the client's personal circumstances.

Before presenting a plea in mitigation, counsel should ensure that he or she is familiar with the approach taken by the courts to sentencing for the particular offence(s) of which the defendant has been convicted. If the 'entry point' (i.e., the type of sentence taken as a starting point) is a custodial sentence, counsel should indicate that he or she is aware of this before trying to persuade the court to impose a lesser sentence. The Sentencing Guidelines issued to magistrates by the Magistrates' Association are particularly helpful in this regard, as are the guideline judgments handed down by the Court of Appeal in respect of particular offences.

13.6.9   COSTS

A defendant who is acquitted is usually entitled to be reimbursed from State funds in respect of the legal costs incurred in defending the case. The main exception to this is where the defendant was represented through the Criminal Defence Service (and so the State has already borne the costs of the defendant's legal representation).

A defendant who is convicted may be ordered by the court to contribute towards the legal costs incurred by the prosecution. In deciding whether to make such an order (and, if so, the amount the defendant has to pay) the court must take account of the defendant's means.

13.6.10   APPEALS

13.6.10.1 Appeals from the magistrates' court

Most appeals from the magistrates' court are heard by the Crown Court. An appeal against conviction takes the form of a rehearing of the case. The prosecution will usually be represented by counsel instructed by CPS. Counsel for the defence may or may not have represented the defendant in the magistrates' court.

Leave to appeal is not required and grounds for the appeal do not have to be stated. Because the appeal takes the form of a rehearing, the Crown Court is not concerned with what happened in the magistrates' court; one corollary of this is that a witness who was not called in the magistrates' court can be called in the Crown Court and a witness who was called in the magistrates' court need not be called in the Crown Court. This means that counsel for the appellant may reconsider any tactical decisions (regarding which witnesses to call) which were taken prior to the trial in the magistrates' court.

Similarly, the hearing by the Crown Court of an appeal against sentence imposed by the magistrates' court takes the same form as the original sentencing hearing in the magistrates' court, with a prosecution summary of the facts followed by a plea in mitigation by the defence advocate.

When advising the defendant whether or not to appeal to the Crown Court, counsel should warn the defendant that the Crown Court has the power to increase the sentence imposed by the magistrates' court, up to the maximum which the magistrates could have imposed; this is so even if it is only the conviction (and not the sentence) which is the subject of the defendant's appeal. Thus, if the defendant was convicted of an offence which is triable either way and the magistrates imposed a sentence of three months' imprisonment, the Crown Court could increase the sentence to six months (the maximum the magistrates could have imposed for one either-way offence).

Alternatively, in a case which involves a point of law or jurisdiction, the defendant may appeal instead to the High Court. This can be done in two ways. The first is to ask the magistrates to state a case for the opinion of the High Court ('appeal by way of case stated'); the magistrates duly summarise their findings of fact and their rulings on the law and the High Court considers whether the magistrates reached the correct conclusion. The second way is to apply for judicial review of the decision of the magistrates' court; this method is particularly appropriate where the magistrates exceed their powers in some way or behaved unfairly. The prosecution can also appeal to the High Court by way of case stated, or seek judicial review, on a point of law or jurisdiction.

13.6.10.2 Appeals from the Crown Court

Appeals from the Crown Court against conviction and/or sentence lie to the Court of Appeal (Criminal Division).

Sometimes the appellant is represented by the same barrister who represented him in the Crown Court, sometimes a different barrister is chosen. In any event, counsel for the appellant has to examine the notes which were taken during the trial by counsel for the defence to see if any errors occurred during the course of the trial. Particular attention has to be paid to any rulings made by the judge during the course of the trial (e.g., rulings on the admissibility of a piece of evidence) and to the judge's summing up of the case to the jury. As far as the latter is concerned, counsel should consider whether the judge stated the law correctly and whether the judge summarised the case for the prosecution, and the case for the defendant, accurately and fairly. Similarly, the comments made by the judge when passing sentence should be scrutinised with care, to ensure that the correct sentencing principles were applied.

If errors were made in the course of the trial and/or in the summing up, or when sentence was passed, grounds of appeal have to be drafted; these grounds are attached to an advice by counsel in which the errors are identified and any relevant case law set out. This is an important document, since it forms the basis of the decision by a Court of Appeal judge whether to give leave to appeal or not.

Once an application for leave to appeal against conviction has been lodged, a transcript of the summing up and any other rulings made by the trial judge will be sent to the barrister who drafted the grounds of appeal; counsel then has the chance to 'perfect' the grounds of appeal (that is, to relate those grounds to the transcript).

If leave to appeal is granted, counsel has to submit a 'skeleton argument' to the court prior to the hearing of the appeal.

The hearing of the appeal itself takes the form of argument by counsel for the appellant and counsel for the respondent; no evidence is heard except in exceptional cases.

FOURTEEN

THE FACT MANAGEMENT PROCESS

14.1 Introduction to the Fact Management Process

At the heart of the practitioner's work are facts: an incident has occurred or must be prevented from occurring, a person injured, property damaged or likely to be damaged, and loss threatened or sustained. From the first moment of receiving a brief until the last stage of trial it is the facts of a case that will be the basis of the practitioner's work. 'Facts' are the basis of any evidence given, any speeches made and any questions asked. It is the barrister's ability to manage the facts, to understand their implications and to use them as the basis of argument, which will be crucial to the success of a case.

The majority of cases involve disputes of facts, not, despite the emphasis in academic training, disputes about questions of law. The ability of barristers to carry out the task of managing facts has in the past been developed by experience, and until the development of the vocational course for the Bar, very little attempt had been made to consciously define and develop this skill. Very few texts have sought to unravel the fact management process in order to teach others how to carry it out on a step-by-step basis. However, it is generally recognised that the ability to prepare a set of papers effectively depends on:

(a)   the need to have a clear picture of what you are preparing for;

(b)   being able to identify what is relevant to your task;

(c)   identifying what the issues are;

(d)   recognising what can and cannot be proved;

(e)   evaluating the strength of the case accurately; and

(f)   putting together, from the information available, the most compelling argument on your client's behalf.

The working approach advocated in this Chapter, the CAP approach (Context, Analysis, Preparation), applies these intellectual skills in a practical and structured process to case preparation. The CAP method of preparing a case demonstrates, on a step-by-step basis, every stage in the process — from initial understanding of the legal and factual context, to detailed analysis of issues and evidence, and finally the construction of persuasive and pertinent arguments to present to a tribunal or a client. The Chapter also illustrates some of the techniques which can be used to aid analysis and the presentation of a case. Thorough case preparation can be achieved by many different working methods and it is usual for these to develop and change with time and experience.

While some may think of this as an objective science, the process involves more than applying a logical method of analysis and presentation. Resourceful barristers also use lateral thinking to identify alternative interpretations of the facts. One's own perception of how witnesses see and describe events and their effectiveness as witnesses will influence a decision about whether they should be called at trial or how to question them. Finally, the ability to use different methods to communicate information in a clear and persuasive way calls for creativity and thought about how to present the facts in the best light. These qualities are part of the practical aspects of fact management which cannot be separated from the more objective tasks of collecting facts.

14.2   Starting from Scratch — Defining Basic Terms

14.2.1   'AGREED' FACTS

Every problem will contain 'facts': who the parties are, the history of the situation, what transpired on certain dates etc. **Agreed facts** are those facts which are conceded by your opponent and are not therefore issues in the case. In criminal cases they may sometimes be set out in a 'formal admission' (see **Chapter 1** of the *Evidence Manual*). More often, practitioners simply tell the court, 'It is not in dispute that . . .'. In civil cases the statements of case will disclose what is agreed between parties. Put simply, if a fact is 'admitted', that fact is not in issue and no evidence has to be adduced to prove it.

It is important to note down what facts are agreed between the parties. It helps to narrow down the issues of a case and will be likely to shorten the length of a trial. It may also assist in a negotiation situation to be able to start from some common ground between the parties.

14.2.2   FACTS AND EVIDENCE

When a 'fact' has been agreed, or can be proved by a witness or document, that fact is then considered to be 'evidence' in the case, and can be taken into account in determining the strengths and weaknesses of the case. The distinction is important: some facts are incapable of proof and (if not agreed) should not be relied upon as part of the case.

14.2.3   DISPUTED FACTS AND FACTS IN ISSUE

If a fact is in dispute between the parties, that is, the opponent does not 'agree' it, it is deemed to be a **disputed fact** in the case. In civil cases you can determine what the 'disputed facts' are by looking primarily at the court papers, although documents and correspondence may bring up other facts that are not agreed. The statements of case (particulars of claim and defence) will show which facts are 'denied' or simply 'not admitted'. If a fact is 'not admitted', the party seeking to prove the fact will have to adduce evidence. By stating 'no admissions are made as to . . .', the other party is saying 'I will not adduce evidence to contradict this fact but I reserve the right to cross-examine your witnesses to test their evidence on this point'. If a fact is 'denied', the party relying on that fact will have to adduce evidence to prove it and the opponent will probably bring evidence to contradict it.

Students often confuse '**disputed facts**' and '**facts in issue**'. First, bear in mind that it is common for a case to contain many disputed facts. Of these, there will be some that are crucial in the sense that they support points that must be proved in law in order for the case to be successful. It is these facts, i.e., the facts which are not agreed by the opponent, and which must be proved in law, that become the 'facts in issue'. For example, D is accused of assaulting the owner of a public house after D and his friend asked to play a game of snooker. D's story is that he arrived at the bar 15 minutes after his friend on the evening in question; the prosecution say that he arrived sometime before his friend. The time and sequence of arrival are 'disputed facts' between the parties in the sense that there is no agreement as to who arrived first and at what times they arrived. But bringing evidence of the truth of one version or the other is not relevant to proving the elements of the criminal offence of assault, and will not affect a successful outcome. Therefore it is not a 'fact in issue'.

The facts in issue will be determined by what legal elements (in a criminal case) or prima facie requirements (in a civil case) apply. For example, in a contract case where C is suing D for breach of contract and resulting loss, the parties may agree that a contract was made, and the terms of that agreement. However, D disputes that a breach occurred, and naturally disputes causing losses. As breach and causation are two of the prima facie requirements for a successful action in contract (and the facts on these two matters are disputed), these become the 'facts in issue' in the case. C will only win the case by producing evidence on these issues to prove that his or her version of the facts was correct, and is therefore entitled to judgment in his or her favour.

It is important to bear in mind that 'facts in issue' (sometimes called 'factual issues') can be a general heading containing several separate issues. For example, in a criminal case, the identity of the defendant might be in issue. One element of the identification evidence concerns the colour of his hair. One witness says that he had fair hair, another that he had brown hair. The colour of the hair is therefore a fact in issue. Its proof will affect whether the prosecution have proved their case in that identification of the defendant as the offender is an element of the offence. It will assist in identifying all the factual issues to divide the case into fairly broad factual issues first, and then look at the facts which are in dispute within each of those main issues. This is covered in more detail later on in the Chapter.

14.2.4   LEGAL ISSUES

These are the questions of law which will have to be answered in the case:

(a)   What are the potential causes of actions or offences?

(b)   What are the potential defences?

(c)   What are the potential legal outcomes?

(d)   What procedural and evidential questions arise?

In tort and contract cases, there are established frameworks to work from, e.g., elements that the claimant must prove in order to establish a prima facie case. In criminal cases, the prosecution must prove the elements of an offence, and in some cases, the absence of a defence. Of the host of legal issues that apply to a case, only some will need to be formally proved since often there will be no dispute between the parties on some of the relevant issues. Later on in this Chapter we look at establishing legal frameworks, and defining the issues to be resolved.

14.2.5   THE 'THEORY' OF THE CASE

After the barrister has identified a framework of the legal and factual issues in a case, and done the necessary legal research, a picture should start to emerge. For each case, it is necessary for you to consider a 'theory' of the case, that is, your explanation of how the events of the case are likely to have happened. The 'theory' of the case will influence the nature of the evidence that will be required for a successful resolution, and will also be the base for the advocacy in the case. For example, in the civil brief of *Lowe v Mainwaring* in **Chapter 16**, the claimant (tenant) alleges damages were caused by the failure of the defendants (also tenants) to keep an external pipe in good order. In representing the defendants, one theory might be as follows.

The duty was owed by the landlord (not the defendants) under the lease. If any duty was in fact owed by the defendants, there was no breach of the duty as the pipe was properly insulated and, in any event, the damage which the claimant suffered, if proved, was not caused by the flood of water from the pipe but from the pre-existing financial difficulties.

In a straightforward case, the theory may be fairly clear, and based solidly on legal and factual certainties. But often the law may not be clear, all the facts may not be available, or there may be gaps in the evidence. In those cases, you will need to develop arguments which link the facts and evidence which are available into a persuasive explanation of your client's version of events.

Developing a 'theory' is covered in more detail later in this Chapter.

14.3 The CAP Approach

Having identified the intellectual elements of fact management skills in **14.1**, there are a number of practical techniques which barristers use to produce a well-prepared case. Regardless of the task which a barrister might be asked to undertake — to advise on the merits, appear in court, or advise in conference — it is crucial to absorb and analyse the facts of the case. Without a uniform approach and structure to this process, thoughts and theories can become confused. Adopting a logical yet flexible framework will not only minimise the chances of missing important pieces of information, but will maximise productivity in terms of your time and effort.

The CAP approach is a step-by-step method of preparing and analysing a case. All barristers develop their own practical styles of working, with or without attaching formal names or titles to their working methods. In order to study the necessary stages, the CAP approach sets out the three main stages involved in efficient preparation:

(a) Context;

(b) Analysis;

(c) Presentation.

Each stage contains tasks and questions which must be answered before moving on to the next stage. The time necessary for each step depends on the complexity of the case, and the specific task you are instructed to do. The advantage of taking an overview of the preparation process is that it enables the student to see how the process develops from the first reading of the facts, through to the analysis of evidence needed in order to present a successful case. As you gain experience, it is hoped that the CAP framework will allow you to selectively determine what is required by means of thorough preparation for any given case.

In **Chapter 16**, the CAP approach is applied to the civil case of *Lowe* v *Mainwaring* to illustrate the process at different stages in the life of a case when a barrister might become involved, i.e., giving advice on merits, drafting, and appearing in an interim application.

The CAP approach is applied to a criminal action in **Chapter 17**, based on the brief for the defence in the case of *R* v *Costas Georgiou*.

It should be remembered that the CAP approach is only one method of achieving a well-prepared case as discussed in **14.1**. Even while following the CAP approach, the tasks within each stage can be done by using any number of techniques, e.g., lists, charts, mind-maps, graphs. As examples a set of proforma charts which can be used as part of the CAP approach are included at **14.8**. While their use is by no means prescriptive, they may be helpful in clarifying the various steps involved in thorough case preparation.

14.3.1   THE THREE STAGES OF CAP

STAGE 1: THE CONTEXT OF THE CASE

(a) *Understand the stage of the proceedings:* your role and instructions, and the objectives.

(b) *Understand the problem:* e.g., the history of the situation, nature and cause of the problem.

(c) *Collect the 'facts'.*

(d) *Identify the agreed facts and facts in dispute:* i.e., those facts which are disputed between the parties, for example, by use of a chart to set out the facts, queries, and each party's version.

(e) *Identify the legal framework:* in a criminal case this would be the elements of the offence, possible defences, sentence, jurisdiction and procedure. In a civil case, this would be the elements required to obtain or refuse the remedy sought.

STAGE 2: ANALYSIS OF ISSUES AND EVIDENCE

(a) *Analyse the issues:*

    (i) *Identify the factual issues:* i.e., those disputed facts which are not agreed by the opponent and which must be proved in law for a successful outcome.

    (ii) *Identify the legal issues by applying the facts to the legal framework.*

    (iii) *Identify a potential 'theory' of the case.*

    (iv) *Identify the gaps and ambiguities in the facts.*

(b) *Analyse the evidence:*

    (i) *Analyse the strengths and weaknesses of your case and that of your opponent.*

    (ii) *Establish 'proof' – turning facts into 'evidence'.*

STAGE 3: THE PRESENTATION OF THE CASE OR ARGUMENT

(a) *Revisit the chosen theory and select a theme.*

(b) *Consider how to support the legal framework.*

(c) *Consider how to carry out your instructions.*

(d) *Consider the intended audience:* e.g., who will be reading your work or listening to you, and the best method of conveying information.

(e) *The client's choice – acting on instructions.*

14.4   Stage 1: Context

14.4.1   INTRODUCTION

When you receive a set of papers, they will contain varied information. The first task is a simple one of comprehension. Specialist terminology may be used in a report, for example, to describe a part of a machine used in factory production and you may need to consult a glossary or trade manual for a full understanding of the term. This occurs frequently with medical terms used in expert reports, e.g., diagnosis of a condition, and practitioners must understand the meaning of the term and its application in the particular context. There is a glossary covering medical terms in **Appendix 1** to this Manual.

Increasingly, information is presented in numerical form and you will need to be able to analyse bank statements, sets of accounts, and possibly graphs or statistics. It is likely that you will be expected to verify any figures you have been given. Indeed, in planning for a negotiation or considering a proposed settlement package you would be expected to make accurate calculations without the need to call for an accountant except in fairly complex cases. (See **Chapter 18** on dealing with figures.) Understanding a variety of information is only part of the task. It is also important that you develop an ability to present that information to others using various modes, and for a variety of purposes (see **Chapter 19**).

14.4.2   UNDERSTANDING THE STAGE OF THE PROCEEDINGS, YOUR INSTRUCTIONS, ROLE, AND THE OBJECTIVES

Just as the facts in a case must be viewed in the context of all the surrounding information, they can be and are interpreted differently according to the standpoint of the interpreter. Before beginning a factual analysis, it is important to understand the stage that the case has reached, what you have been instructed to do and why, and what your client is hoping to achieve.

Your view of the past and present situation will be influenced by whether you are representing the claimant or defendant, prosecution or defence, employer or employee, a consumer or a manufacturer. As you read the papers, it is important to approach them with an objective frame of mind. In some cases proceedings may have already begun before you become involved in the case. In other cases, the 'present' situation is one where there is a threat of future harmful events and the 'future' solution will be some type of preventative action.

14.4.2.1   The stage of the proceedings

Fact management skills cannot be divorced from civil and criminal procedure and require a thorough knowledge of the legal process. **Chapter 16** provides an overview of the stages of a civil case and **Chapter 17** gives an outline of a criminal case. Ascertaining what stage of the process a case has reached is a crucial starting point and it is wise to make a written note of when proceedings were issued, served, previous court orders made etc. prior to embarking on further analysis of the case.

Your approach will differ according to your instructions and the development of the case to date. For example, it is common for barristers to be instructed to write an advice on evidence. This is the particular 'task' which is requested, but it can occur at different stages in the life of a case. In a civil case, advice is often requested when a solicitor is preparing for trial and wishes to know if there are any gaps in the evidence or whether to call for further evidence. It is also common for such an advice before disclosure of documents occurs or after an initial wave of disclosure has been completed, or both (see *Civil Litigation Manual* on disclosure). Advice may be requested prior to any proceedings being issued, to ascertain whether there are sufficient grounds to support a claim, and if so, the appropriate parties to be sued. In this case, you will be advising only on the evidence available at that particular time. Advice on evidence may be requested at any time before the trial.

Understanding the procedural and factual history will assist you to appreciate the task requested, define successfully your objectives for the task and to resolve the problem.

14.4.2.2 Your instructions, role and objectives

It is perhaps stating the obvious to point out the necessity of understanding the parameters of your instructions to ensure that the advice sought is in fact given, and the requested performance completed to the letter. However, the fact is that in the process of digesting a multitude of facts, documents, events and statements, particularly in a complex case, it is easy to lose sight of the specific task that has been requested.

Is your role to be the sole counsel who will see the case from beginning to end? Or are you one of several counsel who will represent the client on a variety of ancillary matters? As a junior barrister, it is common to find that you are briefed to appear on a bail application in a criminal case, or an interim hearing in a lengthy and complex civil case. The task involves one small part in the process, and it may be difficult or even impossible in the time available to understand fully the 'past' of the case. While spending hours reading through files in preparation for a hearing is laudable, two points should be remembered.

First, unless you recognise where in the litigation process you (and the court hearing) are, you will be reading the papers with the wrong purpose. A legally qualified sponge, soaking up facts without a reference point achieves nothing. Time would be better spent analysing the arguments that may be made, both for and against, at the hearing.

Secondly, you will often find that these arguments (particularly in protracted cases) will have already been considered as part of the general strategy for the case. The senior barrister with overall responsibility may have specific thoughts about the hearing for which you have been instructed. In these cases, it would be unwise to decide that the brief is yours to handle independently; the hearing may not achieve its real purpose (either long-term or short-term). The danger lies in highlighting the wrong areas, or giving away points unnecessarily because your involvement prevented you from seeing their long-term significance. In short, determine your role properly in the context of the size of case and the stage it has reached. Consultation with the instructing solicitors and the senior barrister (if there is one) is advised.

In answering 'Why are you instructed to do this task?' you will need to identify your objectives, which you should realise by now may differ from those of the client. Superficially your objective may be to win the case, or succeed at a particular hearing. Of the several aims that you might have, the most obvious is not necessarily the only one or even of primary importance. In carrying out your task, be it written work, or attending hearings, there may be latent as well as manifest reasons for your working methods. For example, when a barrister in court asks his or her own witness, 'What is your name and address?', the manifest purpose is to put on record who the witness is and his or her residence. The latent purpose is usually to settle the witness in the witness box by asking easy and comfortable questions. There may be other latent purposes, for example, to show the judge or jury that the witness comes from a deprived part of the city (if this is part of your theory or theme of the case).

One further point about objectives borrows a page from advocacy skills. Be sure that in clarifying your objectives and expectations, you have considered your audience. It is common for barristers to speak in front of magistrates, judges, juries, administrative or employment tribunals. Thought should be given to their expectations, agenda, and what methods of persuasion will produce the most successful results.

14.4.3 UNDERSTANDING THE PROBLEM

To understand the context of a case, it is essential to understand fully the history of the parties (civil), or background information about the client (criminal), and how the situation arose. For every client and fact situation, there is a past, present and future. Once you see how and why the problem arose, it will assist you in identifying how to deal with the present problem, and possible solutions for the future. In the civil context, parties may have enjoyed a good business relationship in the past which one or both parties wish to continue in the future. In a criminal case, the defendant's financial situation leading up to the alleged offence may provide an insight into the circumstances.

14.4.3.1 Looking at the cause of a problem

A crucial part of understanding a problem is appreciating the cause. Why has it occurred? What circumstances led to the problem? If an effective solution is to be found, what circumstances must be avoided to prevent recurrence? For example, your client has asked that a court order be obtained allowing him to have contact with his children on a Sunday, rather than the present arrangement on a Saturday. You will need first to investigate why this issue has arisen between the parties. More specifically you would wish to know:

(a) whether Saturday contact had been agreed or was the subject of a court order;

(b) whether the agreement or order had worked well, and the history of any difficulties;

(c) what the nature of any problems had been;

(d) whether changing the day is considered by the client and/or child carer to make arrangements easier or more difficult;

(e) how the children have responded;

(f) whether the children wish to maintain contact;

(g) why your client wants to see the children on Sundays, e.g., to go to church, because of a work schedule etc.;

(h) whether the children want to change to Sunday — any conflict with their activities or school projects;

(i) if the proposal has been refused, the possible reasons;

(j) whether there are any other difficulties between the parties which may be masked by this dispute.

Once this information has been digested, you will then be in a position to understand fully the problem and consider appropriate ways of solving it which will meet the client's objectives.

The process of 'understanding' a problem is achieved by a combination of using your individual sense of perception and intellect. Just as the results of computer output are only as accurate as the data which has been put in, the range and accuracy of facts fed into the human mind will affect the conclusions made from them. You will find that developing an approach or structure for posing generic questions (Who did what to whom, when, where and with what result?) will focus your mind on collecting the crucial facts and appreciating how and why a problem has arisen, thus paving the way to reaching a solution that is appropriate on the facts and desired by the client.

14.4.3.2 The client's objectives

One may wonder why, in a study of fact analysis, the client's objectives, or even those of the barrister, are a part of the process. Simply put, understanding the client's objectives impacts the way the problem-solving process is managed and influences the way facts can be interpreted. As you read the papers, a mental picture emerges of the appropriate ways to resolve the problem. The client's objectives may or may not be reflected in the papers. Alternatively, you may find after a conference that the client holds different or additional objectives that will require a rethink on the best method of resolving or presenting the case.

The barrister's day-to-day contact with the legal system and the constant approach to problems solely from a legal standpoint can easily allow his or her own objectives to influence the understanding of the problem and the client's objectives. For example, you may decide that the best course of action would be to negotiate a settlement or seek arbitration to avoid a court hearing. However, your client may want a public investigation (or a day in court) and/or be opposed to settlement where no commercial benefit can be seen in settling the case, for example, where the client is a supplier of faulty goods but has already received full payment. Your task is to identify your client's values and interests, to know the extent to which your own objectives may affect a proposed resolution, and base your factual analysis on the strengths and weaknesses of the case.

It should be remembered that clients may have non-legal as well as legal objectives; these may or may not be articulated. Some stated objectives may eclipse the true interests that the client has but, for whatever reason, has not verbalised. Rather than taking statements at face value, strive for more thorough questioning which may reveal additional reasons for their objectives, and which may improve the strength of their position.

It is not too soon, even at this stage of reading the papers, to bear in mind possible resolutions to the problem. In civil cases, while some disputes will ultimately go to trial for final resolution, this may not be in the client's best interest. Various forms of alternative dispute resolution (ADR), such as arbitration and mediation are becoming more popular as costs escalate and the delays of bringing an action to trial increase. Arbitration is common in construction cases and is increasingly used in commercial and civil cases. Mediation, the process where a mediator attempts to bring the parties together into an agreed resolution is often preferable to a contested trial in family and child cases and neighbour disputes. Further, there are other remedies that might be suggested by the facts including use of internal employee complaint procedures, filing formal complaints with an agency such as the Commission for Racial Equality, or with the local authority. In criminal cases, the client's circumstances may indicate that the best solution would be long-term medical treatment and you may wish to raise with the solicitor the possibility of investigating this option on behalf of the client.

14.4.4   COLLECTING THE FACTS

The next stage is to collect all the relevant facts in the case. In practice, this work is divided between the barrister and the solicitor. The degree of factual information included in the instructions to counsel will vary according to the type of case (civil or criminal), the size of the case, the stage in the proceedings and the task which you are asked to do. In the early stages, you may have only a proof of evidence from the client, and possibly a few witness statements. In civil cases, this may be sufficient to provide an advice on the merits, although it would be insufficient for providing, e.g., an advice on evidence and quantum. Where you are briefed to appear at an interim hearing and have been sent copies of the drafts and relevant witness statements, there may be no need to acquire further information, unless the facts require clarification. In defending a criminal case, the defendant is likely to be best placed to provide more information about witnesses, particularly about potential alibi evidence. Prosecuting counsel often request additional information from e.g., police who were at the scene or otherwise involved in the matter.

In some cases your written instructions to counsel may be minimal. You may need to ask what has taken place in previous conferences between the client and solicitors. If so, you will want to ensure that you understand exactly what was said or done, as different interpretations can easily arise when discussions are relayed second-hand. If the need for information or clarification can best be met by requesting a conference with the client, this is appropriate, but you will want to bear in mind that conferences increase the costs in a case and should only be requested when the information cannot be obtained by other, less expensive means.

Once you have understood the contents of your brief, and held a conference (if necessary), you can begin to clarify in your own mind precisely what is said to have occurred. It is crucial to develop a critical and questioning approach to all information which you receive. Remember that the information that is missing is as important in the context of the situation as what has been said or written. It is not sufficient merely to identify the gaps in the information or inconsistencies in the facts. You must attempt to fill the gaps by acquiring more information and ask, 'Why might these inconsistencies exist?'

It is also important to remember that fact-finding is an ongoing process. New facts will become available at different stages in a case, for instance, on disclosure of documents. As new facts emerge you must keep an open mind; your view of the case may need to be reconsidered and your original conclusions reassessed and possibly modified. You may never possess all the facts in a case.

14.4.4.1 Methods of collecting facts

Rather than start with a group of assorted facts, which at this stage may not bear a great degree of logical order, it is more helpful to approach collection with a structure or framework of main questions to be answered. The facts that are presently available can then be filled in, and the areas where more information is needed, or ambiguities exist are highlighted. Regardless of what task is requested, e.g., to advise, draft, or appear as an advocate, you will find that most practitioners undertake several routine steps in preparing a case. These preparatory steps are important because they assist in understanding the events and problem generally, and the schedules and charts produced as a result (if the information they contain is agreed) are often given to the court in hearings and at trial to assist the court's understanding of the case. As there is always that possibility, strive for accuracy, clarity and neatness as you prepare them. There are several methods which can be used, though the purpose of all of them is the same: to ensure that every aspect of the problem is explored thoroughly and from every angle. As you gain experience you will no doubt devise your personal methods of asking these important questions of who, what, where, why and how?

14.4.4.2 Construct a chronology and dramatis personae

Listing the people involved and the events in the order in which they occurred clarifies what happened, assists understanding and can be invaluable as the basis of an opening speech. Increasingly, an agreed chronology is handed up to the judge at the start of both civil and criminal trials which provides a structure for the presentation of the case.

14.4.4.3 Draw a plan of the *locus in quo*

The *'locus in quo'* simply means the place where the events occurred. It can be represented by maps, floor plans, or other types of drawings. The first plan which you prepare should be entirely uncontroversial: either delete any points which are in dispute or, if they are included, ensure that they are clearly identified as in dispute. The rationale for this is that, where a plan is produced that makes assumptions about facts which are yet to be proved, the plan tends to become fixed in the mind as the true factual scenario and may prevent you from keeping an open mind to consider other possible explanations. An 'undisputed' plan can also be useful in a client conference where asking the client to explain his or her version of events will test the credibility of the client's evidence.

You also need to devise ways to represent in the plan the areas about which you do not yet have enough information to present the data accurately. For example, in the plan of a bank robbery, you are told that a witness was on the opposite side of the road, but at this stage of the case you do not know precisely where. Guessing the position and marking it on the plan is inaccurate and could lead to subconsciously assuming its truth without obtaining further factual information. Mark it in a way that shows there is doubt, or delete it until further facts are known. Until the location is certain, it is impossible to assess the witness's line of view, obstructions etc.

It may also be helpful to draw a series of plans. Following the first which is uncontroversial, additional plans may then show various alternative explanations of what might have occurred.

14.4.4.4 Organise by sorting

This method, based on the five basic questions of who, what, why, where and how, will assist you to categorise main areas. In **Table 14.1**, column 1 contains main categories of questions; column 2 lists possible answers (or possibilities which may lead to answers).

Table 14.1 Sorting method

Column 1	Column 2
1. Who did what to whom?	Names, addresses of parties, witnesses.
2. With whom does problem occur?	Friend, employer, supplier.
3. When does the problem occur?	Date, time, season.
4. Where does it occur?	Work, home, public place.
5. In what situation does it occur?	Drunkenness, anger, lack of funds, lack of supplies etc.
6. Is there a pattern?	When contact is refused, when maintenance is unpaid, when supplies are scarce.
7. What triggers it?	Smell, noise, rain?
8. What result from the problem?	. . .

14.4.4.5 Flowcharts

Some practitioners prefer to use general-style blank flowcharts which provide an overview of the case as well as prompt heads of information which will be needed. The chart shown in **Figure 14.1** is an overview of a civil case. It could be used in its present form in fairly straightforward cases. More complex cases will require a more extensive system of collection and organisation of the facts.

Figure 14.1 Flowchart

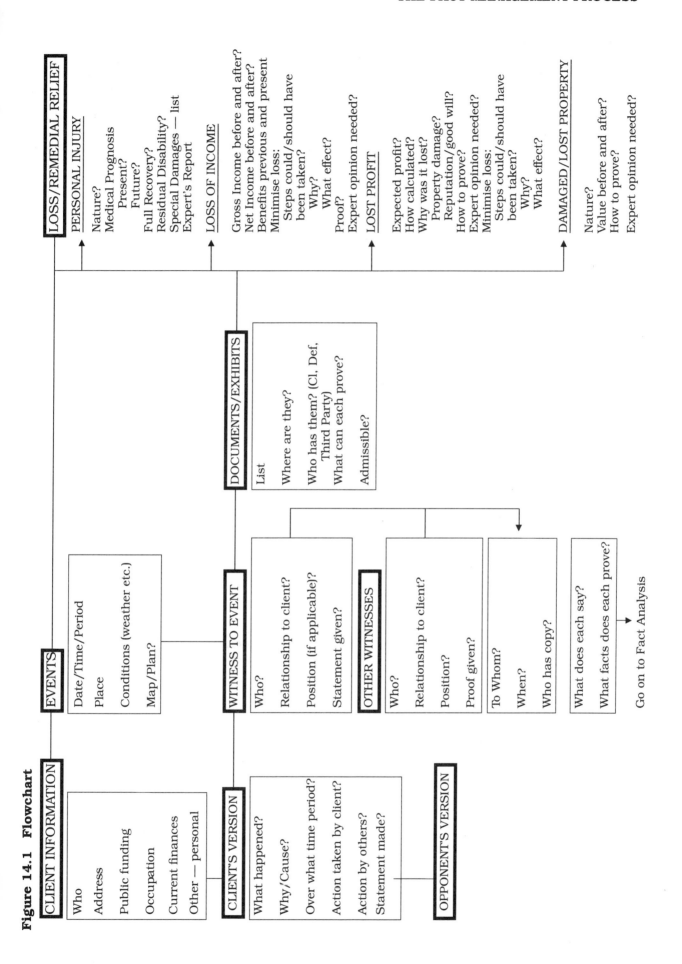

14.4.4.6 Checklists

Finally, you may prefer to develop checklists of the information which you will need when you prepare your cases. With experience, you will be able to amend and update your lists to home in on the crucial information, cover new legal developments and avoid spending time and effort on sorting through information which is not relevant to the issues as hand. Of course there may be times when papers are received at the last minute and there is not sufficient time to prepare copious checklists. However, if you have developed this structure as part of your working approach, your mind should automatically take you through the generally relevant areas, using the little time which you have to best advantage.

An example of the questions that would be included in a checklist in a civil action based on the flowchart illustrated in **Figure 14.1** is as follows:

Personal:
1. Who is your client?
2. Where does he or she live?
3. Occupation.
4. Other personal details?

Event:
5. When did event happen?
6. How does your client say it happened?
7. What did your client do or say at the time?
8. Who heard or saw what your client said or did?
9. Who witnessed it? What do the witnesses say happened?
10. Can they give evidence?
11. What points could each prove? Are they consistent with the client's story?

Exhibits:
12. What exhibits are there?
13. Where are they? Who has them?
14. What can each prove?
15. Who will produce them in court?

Loss or Damage:
16. Type of loss suffered.
17. If PI, nature of injury.
18. Medical prognosis?
19. Will there be full recovery?
20. If no, to what extent is disability permanent?
21. What experts have given or should give evidence?
22. What other losses are there, e.g., lost income, lost profit, lost or damaged property, pain and suffering etc.

If income lost:
23. What is/was client's gross and net income?
24. What payments were/are being received from State?
25. What steps could/should have been done to minimise loss?
26. Why should they have been taken?

If profit lost:
27. What profit should have been made?
28. How calculated?
29. Why was it lost?
30. What steps could/should have been taken to minimise loss?
31. Why should they have been taken?

If property lost or damaged
32. What was its value before and after the event?
33. What is its value now?

34. Can it be repaired? If so, what is the cost?
35. What could/should have been done to minimise loss?
36. If so, why should they have been taken?

Insurance:
37. Does client have insurance? With whom?
38. Does the policy cover this loss?
39. Has a claim been made? If so, when?
40. Does the other party have insurance?
41. Does that insurance cover this loss if liability can be proved?
42. Has a claim been made?

14.4.5 IDENTIFY AGREED FACTS AND DISPUTED FACTS

Once the basic facts have been digested, you will begin to identify the facts which are agreed between the parties and those which are disputed. It is necessary to crystallise these issues and ascertain, for each disputed fact, both your client's version and that of your opponent. This is an important preliminary analysis which should be recorded in a practical form which can be used later in the fact management process. The way in which this information is presented is a matter of style although its usefulness may be increased if it is neat and can be used, for example, in discussing the case with the solicitor. A suggested format can be found in **Table 14.7** at the end of this Chapter.

Example

In the civil case of *Lowe* v *Mainwaring* (see **Chapter 16**), the defendants are the tenants of the first and second floors of a property. The claimant is the tenant of the ground floor and uses the space to run the Topspin Snooker Hall. A flood occurred from a water pipe outside the building at about the first-floor level causing damage to the claimant's property. The claimant alleges that the defendants were responsible for the water pipe and their negligence caused the damage. The facts might be recorded as in Table **14.2**.

Table 14.2

A/D	Claimant	Page/ref	Defendant	Page/ref
A	At the time, C was tenant of ground floor, and Defendants were tenants of the 1st and 2nd floors of 83–87 Leeds Road.	XX		
A	The pipe located in the 1st floor outside the building burst.	XX		
D	Time: it burst between 23 and 30 December 1998	XX	Pipe was repaired within a few hours of bursting on finding it on the 30th	XX
D	D responsible for repairing and maintaining the pipe	XX	Under lease with M. Pike, D *not responsible* for repair or maintenance	XX
D	Pipe was not properly insulated	XX	Properly insulated	XX

This table is further developed at **16.1.1**.

There may be many disputed facts in a case and though it may be a tedious job, it is important that all of them are recorded. From this information you will be able to determine which of these disputed facts will actually be 'facts in issue' in the case, i.e., facts which are not agreed and which must be proved in law in order to win the case. This will be covered in more detail in Stage 2 of the CAP approach in **14.5**.

14.4.6 IDENTIFY THE LEGAL FRAMEWORK

Having started with facts, you will need to identify a possible legal framework to which the facts will ultimately be applied. This applies equally whether you are determining the best legal basis for bringing a case, or the best defence. At this stage, the aim is to identify all the legal possibilities which may lead to a resolution of the problem. Later in the analysis process, the framework will be developed and any necessary legal research done.

The process of identifying the legal possibilities may be difficult, particularly where the area of law is an unfamiliar one or several potential legal frameworks are suggested. To start, you will need to list all the possible legally relevant factors which are present. You cannot afford at this point to make snap judgments about the best legal framework or settle for a quickly identified clever answer which may have weaknesses or be less appropriate than another legal basis for bringing or defending the case.

14.4.6.1 List the potential legally relevant factors

Having taken a preliminary view of the facts, it may be tempting to place them into familiar pigeon-holes, e.g., contract, misrepresentation, mistake, theft etc. While this may assist in providing initial focus, it can be restrictive; the best legal solution may not always come from a textbook framework.

First, list all the factors of the case which may possibly have a legal ramification. The index of *Halsbury's Laws of England* or *Halsbury's Statutes* can be a source for ideas. The general categories in **Table 14.3** have legal relevance in most cases.

Table 14.3   Relevant factors

Categories	*Legally relevant factors*
People and parties	E.g., minor, spouse, joint owner, limited company, professional.
Places	E.g., occupier's liability, Factories Act, waterways, party resident in France, leased premises.
Objects/Items	E.g., animals, children's toy, car window, machine part, stereo (consumer).
Documents	E.g., contract, will, bill of lading, deed.
Acts	E.g., negligence, intentional, reckless act.
Omissions	E.g., failure to act or deliver or mitigate.
Words	E.g., inducement, fraud, misrepresentation.
Dates	E.g., limitation.

In making this list, you should include everything that underlies or surrounds the facts, as well as actual words that appear in the papers. For example, in a case that concerns a jam jar, even though there is no Jam Jars Act, you will still need to enter 'jam jar' on the list. There are laws relating to the manufacture of jam jars, filling jars either in a factory or at home (if the contents are for sale to the public), labelling them (including EC regulations), not dealing with jars negligently to cause injury to another etc. The more comprehensive your list of potential factors, the more pieces are available for choosing a framework.

The completed list of factors can then be organised and grouped together into 'legal frameworks'. The following headings might be used as general categories for grouping factors in a civil case:

(a) *Parties.*

(b) *Cause(s) of action.*

(c) *Defence(s).*

(d) *Remedy sought.*

Some factors on the list in **Table 14.3** may apply to more than one heading. For example, under 'Acts' you may have: 'Piano owned by client wrongfully taken away from his home'. This factor suggests a possible cause of action (tort of conversion) and also the relief sought (return of piano).

Some potentially relevant factors may not fit easily within one of the headings above but should not be ignored. Retain them in a general category at the end. They may prove useful, for example, by revealing a gap in the case you are preparing.

An example of how factors might be grouped in chart form is shown in **Table 14.4**. In this case example, the claimants have suffered loss and damage as a result of their neighbour (D1) who is burning industrial waste from a machine-shop business operated on the property. The neighbour rents the property from the landowner (D2) who is aware of D1's activities. Column 1 lists the facts which carry a legal implication. Column 2 contains general issue headings. The space in column 3 is for legal frameworks suggested by the facts; in this case nuisance and a possible breach of statutory obligation. This procedure is the same in criminal cases to explore bases for the offences which might be charged, and potential defences. While many methods can achieve this analysis, the benefit of the tabular form is the visual analysis on a single page.

Table 14.4 Grouping legal factors

Example of grouping legal factors towards developing a full legal framework. In this example, the clients (Mr and Mrs C) are suffering from the burning of industrial waste by a neighbour (D1) who lives on adjoining property and runs a small business. D1 leases the property from a freehold landlord (D2).

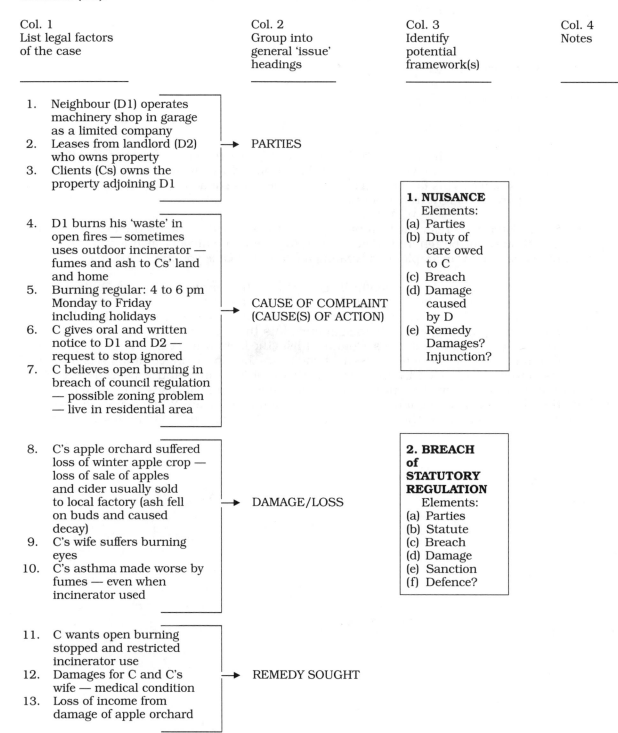

Col. 1
List legal factors
of the case

Col. 2
Group into
general 'issue'
headings

Col. 3
Identify
potential
framework(s)

Col. 4
Notes

1. Neighbour (D1) operates machinery shop in garage as a limited company
2. Leases from landlord (D2) who owns property
3. Clients (Cs) owns the property adjoining D1

→ PARTIES

4. D1 burns his 'waste' in open fires — sometimes uses outdoor incinerator — fumes and ash to Cs' land and home
5. Burning regular: 4 to 6 pm Monday to Friday including holidays
6. C gives oral and written notice to D1 and D2 — request to stop ignored
7. C believes open burning in breach of council regulation — possible zoning problem — live in residential area

→ CAUSE OF COMPLAINT (CAUSE(S) OF ACTION)

1. NUISANCE
Elements:
(a) Parties
(b) Duty of care owed to C
(c) Breach
(d) Damage caused by D
(e) Remedy Damages? Injunction?

8. C's apple orchard suffered loss of winter apple crop — loss of sale of apples and cider usually sold to local factory (ash fell on buds and caused decay)
9. C's wife suffers burning eyes
10. C's asthma made worse by fumes — even when incinerator used

→ DAMAGE/LOSS

2. BREACH of STATUTORY REGULATION
Elements:
(a) Parties
(b) Statute
(c) Breach
(d) Damage
(e) Sanction
(f) Defence?

11. C wants open burning stopped and restricted incinerator use
12. Damages for C and C's wife — medical condition
13. Loss of income from damage of apple orchard

→ REMEDY SOUGHT

14.4.6.2 Basic legal frameworks

While it would be unwise to conclude at this stage that a particular framework is the only applicable one, it is often a helpful starting point to consider established frameworks which are suggested from the facts, e.g., contract, tort, a specific criminal offence. For a specific criminal offence, you would focus on the following headings:

(a) *Offence:* What are the elements of the offence?

(b) *Defence:* applicable common law and statutory defences.

(c) *Penalty:* sanctions on summary trial, on indictment.

(d) *Jurisdiction:* type of offence, e.g., can be tried by magistrates or in the Crown Court; financial threshold e.g., if amount less than £5,000 to magistrates' court.

(e) *Procedure:* relevant procedural steps.

Table 14.5 shows how this information could be set out in relation to s. 18 of the Offences against the Person Act 1861

Table 14.5 Identifying the legal framework: example in a criminal case: Offences against the Person Act 1861, s. 18

Offence	Unlawfully and maliciously wound with intent to do grievous bodily harm.
Defences	Factual denial of elements including claiming lawfulness of wounding by reason of self-defence, prevention of crime, protection of property or other persons.
Penalty	Imprisonment up to life. Usual bracket 3 to 8 years. Provocation factor which can be taken into account. Deportation. See EC Treaty, Art. 48 and Directive 64/221, Arts 3 and 9.
Jurisdiction	Indictable offence. Crown Court only. Class 4 offence.
Procedure	Magistrates commit/transfer to Crown Court. Plea taken at plea and directions hearing. If not guilty, date fixed for jury trial.

For civil cases, the facts may suggest a tort and/or a contract claim. The following preliminary frameworks set out the elements which would be considered in determining whether a prima facie case is established.

TORT	*CONTRACT*
(a) Parties.	(a) Parties.
(b) Accident or cause of complaint.	(b) The contract.
(c) Cause(s) of action (causation).	(c) The terms.
(d) Damage or loss.	(d) Performance.
(e) Remedy sought.	(e) Breach.
	(f) Damage and causation.
	(g) Remedy sought.

Even where an established framework fits the facts well, you should in any event investigate other legal bases to ensure that your chosen framework not only applies to the facts but offers the best opportunity to achieve the client's objectives. In civil cases, it may be wise to plead alternative causes of action, join causes of action or bring in additional parties for the most effective legal solution.

14.4.6.3 Identify areas for legal research

Additional research may be necessary to determine whether the framework is the most appropriate, for example, to determine whether the specific act complained of is covered by statute or constitutes criminal activity. By stepping back and taking a critical view of the framework, it should be possible to see all the strengths and weaknesses within it, and to take decisions where there are options.

If additional research is undertaken, notes of it should be recorded for later use, possibly at trial. At a minimum, the following should be recorded:

(a) *Sources:* including the relevant page or paragraph numbers of textbooks, and full citations of case law.

(b) *Short summary of the relevant legal point.*

(c) *Your view of the answer to the question:* indicating how the point found in research will support a specific fact or issue in the case.

See **Chapters 8** and **9** above.

14.4.6.4 How to choose the best legal framework

Surrounded by a myriad of legal possibilities, it is sometimes difficult to know what particular legal framework should be chosen and why. Having an understanding of alternative ways of assessing the case, as well as using your professional judgment in filling gaps will help you to make the best decision.

14.4.6.5 Which framework makes the best use of the legal and factual strengths? The 'best-fit' approach

If the framework does not provide a single obvious answer, it should nevertheless take you some distance down the road. At a minimum it should define where there are legal and factual certainties and, if options exist, what the options appear to be. One way to proceed is simply to make an objective valuation of all the legal requirements and relevant facts. The solution that 'best fits' the framework – the one which makes the best use of the legal and factual strengths of the case while placing least reliance on its weaknesses – would be the preferred one. This approach is not suggesting that superficial analysis will do so long as it gives a roughly right answer, but that, on critical analysis of the law and facts, a particular framework would make the best use of the elements in the case.

Even in the 'best-fit' method, the elements which do not sit well with the rest of the framework should not be ignored. They may have some use in reviewing the case at a later stage, or in looking for options for a settlement.

14.5 Stage 2: Analysis of Issues and Evidence

14.5.1 INTRODUCTION

Thus far, the potential legally relevant factors have been identified and loosely grouped to suggest a possible legal framework or 'legal basis' to the problem. More than one framework may be suggested. The best legal argument has no point in a court if it is not soundly based on the facts. Equally, the facts of the case need the best legal argument to achieve the best result. Although an analysis of a case should start with consideration of the facts, as the case progresses, the role of law and fact is equally important, and the two are closely interrelated. More than that, they are interactive; one moves with the other as more legal or factual input is provided for a case.

14.5.2   ANALYSE THE ISSUES: IDENTIFY THE 'FACTUAL ISSUES' AND ANALYSE THE LEGAL ISSUES BY APPLYING THE FACTS TO THE LEGAL FRAMEWORK

By this stage you will have identified a possible legal framework and noted what facts are agreed and disputed. From the elements or legal requirements of this framework, you must then determine the 'factual issues' (also called 'facts in issue') of the case. The factual issues will be those disputed facts which, according to the legal framework chosen, must be proved in law for the case to be successful. Where statements of case have already been served, these will specify what issues have to be proved. For example, in a contract case where the claimant (landlord) is suing the defendant (tenant) for failure to maintain a gas boiler under the lease, which exploded causing damage to the claimant's property, the analysis might look like **Table 14.6**.

Table 14.6

Framework	Facts of client	Disputed/agreed
Parties	Landlord: Mr X, Tenant: Ms Y.	Agreed
Contract	By lease dated	Agreed
Terms	Tenant had obligation to maintain.	Agreed.
Performance	Tenant in occupation, rent paid.	Agreed.
Breach	On XYZ date, boiler not in order.	Denied.
Causation	Caused explosion.	Agree: explosion. Deny: causation.
Loss	Damaged property.	Loss not mitigated.

From this analysis you will see that the legal and factual issues will be breach, causation and loss. (The loss is a factual issue as the defendant's case is that the claimant's loss is due to his failure to mitigate.) Each of these factual issues must be formally proved by evidence. Thus each issue must be fully analysed to determine which facts can be proved and by what means. This information should be recorded for clarity and use later in the case.

The aim is to identify, for each factual issue, the name of the witness who can prove the fact, whether oral or documentary evidence is available, on which party the burden of proof lies, and in a civil case whether it is specifically raised in the court documents. There are various methods of recording this information and provided the relevant analysis is done, the choice is left to the practitioner. One chart which can be used for this purpose appears in **Table 14.8** at the end of this Chapter.

In finding the factual support for a framework, remember that every disputed fact will need to be proved. As the evidence is gathered, you will need to update the chart or list of all facts for which evidence is still required. Some of the possible frameworks identified early on may prove unworkable. While you can normally expect to have enough factual information for a preliminary determination, it is rare to have all the relevant facts before starting work on a case. As more information comes to light, your view on the most appropriate framework may change.

One final word on the interrelation of law and fact. It is vital to select relevant law with a sound knowledge of the facts, and then also to consider the facts in the light of the law to ensure coherence. Although law and fact become interrelated, never be deceived into thinking the law has become more important — the evidence, or the proven facts will always be just as important as the law. **Table 1.1** in **Chapter 1** showed how the correlation of law, fact and evidence could be achieved.

14.5.3 IDENTIFY A POTENTIAL 'THEORY' OF THE CASE

The theory of the case is a convincing and logical account of why and how the events in the case are likely to have happened. It is based on:

(a) the principles of law that are likely to be used at trial, i.e., the legal solution or framework;

(b) what has to be proved and/or disproved at trial for the case to succeed;

(c) consideration of which facts are capable of being proved and the inferences which can be made from them.

Formulating a theory, though based on the available facts and evidence, sometimes requires a degree of guesswork to fill in the gaps. In a sense it puts cement between the bricks of the framework to fill in any factual or legal gaps in order to make a cohesive and persuasive story. It is your theory of the case that you hope to convince the fact finder is the true version of events.

The dangers of developing an imaginative theory that is not well founded on the facts cannot be underestimated. The more gaps that are filled by guesswork, rather than proven facts, the weaker the case. It follows that the more that the theory is grounded on persuasive evidence rather than supposition the higher likelihood that it will be accepted.

In the context of fact management, developing a theory is an important stage in considering the legal and factual basis for the client's version of events and the chance of successfully obtaining a good resolution. Putting forward a theory is also a basis for persuasive advocacy, used in arguing interim applications, and submissions at trial. This is covered more fully in the **Advocacy Manual**.

The 'theory' should be an objective analysis of the events, rather than merely the best theory for the client. The opponent will also put forward a theory, and seek to disprove your account, thus it is wise to consider how the other parties may view your theory. Critically analyse the legal and factual weaknesses of the potential theory. Ensure that it is coherent and as capable of proof as possible.

In considering the theory, bear in mind:

(a) The need for the *best* explanation for the client's position from all the possible alternatives. Although alternative theories are possible it should be remembered that a single explanation is inherently more compelling.

(b) Early in a case it is desirable to develop provisional theories. The 'theory' may need to be altered as more evidence comes to light with regard to the opponent's defence, disclosure, information received in a criminal case etc.

(c) Although the theory must be logical, the ultimate form that it takes will be influenced by the 'theme' of the case, which goes beyond logic and may show that your client should be successful on, e.g., moral grounds. Choosing the theme of the case is discussed in Stage 4 (see **14.7**) after factual analysis of the case is completed.

14.5.3.1 Ways to develop the 'theory'

If you are fortunate enough to have a substantial amount of factual information, and sources of proof, it may be possible to identify the best legal framework and develop a theory fairly easily. However, where the factual information is scarce, you will have to construct, either partially or wholly, a theory of the case alongside the consideration of the best legal framework. Thus the phrase 'developing a theory' is sometimes referred to as using theory to identify the most appropriate legal framework, or, as is used here, to fit together how and why the events or problem occurred.

Identifying alternative theories can be difficult, particularly where the area of law is unfamiliar to you. The more experienced you are with an area of law, the easier it becomes to appreciate the range of different theories which may apply. If you are in uncharted waters, there are guidelines to assist you in developing a perspective of the situation.

First, the problem at hand may be analogous to another situation with which you are familiar. In civil cases, consider the basic rights and obligations of the parties; the same legal principles may apply. In criminal cases, consider how analogous conduct is treated by the law and whether defences in those situations may be applicable to the case at hand. Secondly, consider whether the conduct or acts are of a nature that may be covered by statute. Research in *Halsbury's Statutes* may suggest other legal solutions and alternative theories for the case. Finally, bear in mind that there is no need to reinvent the wheel. You may find that merely asking whether someone in your chambers or firm has experience in the area enables them to point you in the right direction. It will very likely save time, may prevent you from going down the wrong path, and also give you a different perspective on the case.

14.5.3.2 Logical and lateral thinking

Many of you have played the game where one word is given and the object is to think of all the different words that can be formed from this one word. There are many variations but the challenge remains the same: to brainstorm, or to use another phrase, to use logical thinking to come up with all plausible answers. In this context, you are presented with a proposition that X happened or did not happen. The challenge is to think logically about all the evidence that exists to support that conclusion, even if purely circumstantial. Your analysis must be based on proved — or provable — facts as far as possible. Beware of emotion, intention and knowledge elements which are particularly difficult to prove. Remember too the weakness of logical thinking: the danger of assuming because a theory is logical, it is actually true.

Lateral thinking asks, not how events are most likely to have happened, but what are all the possible ways in which they *could* have happened, logical or otherwise. It looks for explanation from different, and often unexpected, angles to a problem. An example of reaching a solution by lateral thinking follows:

Problem: John states that when he came home, he went into the living room of his house and saw immediately that Victoria was lying naked on the floor, and that she was dead. There was broken glass on the floor, and a small pool of water. The window was open, but John could not remember if he had forgotten to close it before he went out.

Logical assumptions and focus for questioning:
It is natural to assume and concentrate on:

(a) Victoria has been murdered or has died from natural causes such as a heart attack.

(b) Why was Victoria naked?

(c) Broken glass — if the window had been closed, an intruder could have broken a window or door for entry.

Logical thinkers would pursue more about Victoria, e.g., how she died and why, and about John, e.g., how long he had been gone, whether Victoria was very familiar to him etc. Stimulate lateral thinking by putting the problem in the centre of a diagram as in **Figure 14.2**. Follow the 'dos and don'ts' around the path and think of new lines of questioning.

Figure 14.2

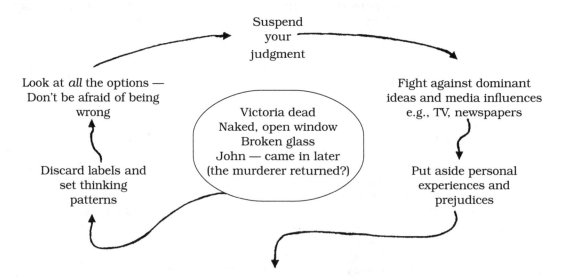

New lines should include where Victoria lived, whether she was usually clothed and in what type of clothes, who lived with John including any animals, what objects in the room were made of glass, e.g., vases, ornaments, drinking glasses.

The answer:
Victoria is in fact a fish and has died naturally after John's cat knocked the bowl over and ran out through the window!

This, of course, is an extreme example but does illustrate the trap of simple faith based on assumptions that something is true because it outwardly appears so.

Information rarely arrives in a sequential manner. A piece of information coming in early does not signify that it is particularly important, nor should it prejudice the importance of the other facts arriving later or from unexpected sources.

14.5.3.3 Mind-mapping
Another technique for developing a theory of a case is mind-mapping. When you receive information, your mind processes it in key concepts, interlinking thoughts with other ideas. Each word is received in the context of the words surrounding it, integrating the ideas and concepts to communicate certain meanings. Mind-mapping is a physical picture of the process that is occurring in the mind. Although it can take some time to become proficient at drawing them, the rewards are many as they visually present the structure of the case, and indicate where the weaknesses lie.

To start a mind-map, place the main theme or event in the centre. The branches coming out from the centre outline the main characters and events, with descriptive detail forming smaller branches. The more important elements are placed near the centre; the less important ones nearer the edge. There is an example in **Figure 14.3**.

Figure 14.3   Mind-map or concept map of facts for bail application in the case of
R v *Costas Georgiou* (see Chapter 17)

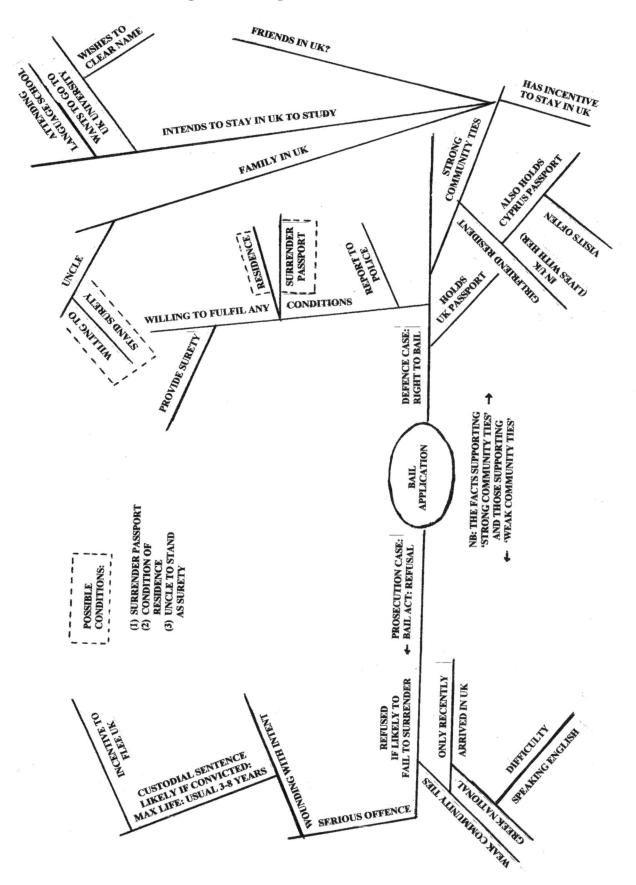

14.5.4   IDENTIFY THE GAPS OR AMBIGUITIES IN THE FACTS

The advantage of adopting a methodical approach to analysis and recording is that it tends to highlight any gaps or ambiguities in the fact scenario. Sometimes these are fairly obvious, as where some invoices in a regular pattern of trading are missing which are relevant to the disputed fact. More commonly these are spotted by putting yourself at the scene — try to picture the story and ask yourself what pieces are missing or unclear. For example, in the fact scenario about the bank robbery, there is a witness to the robbery. Before the picture can be completed you will need to know where the witness was standing, the direction he or she was facing, any obstructions to a clear view such as cars, signs, weather conditions, personal visual disabilities etc.

In some cases, the client is able to supply missing information and the most cost-effective way of obtaining this may be by requesting a conference. In civil cases, it may be necessary to serve a request for further and better particulars or interrogatories on your opponent (see the *Civil Litigation Manual*). Information may be needed from a third party and you will need to ask your instructing solicitor to take a proof of evidence if the identity of the witness is known or seek further witnesses who can provide evidence on a particular issue.

14.5.5   ANALYSE THE EVIDENCE: IMPORTANCE OF ANALYSING THE STRENGTHS AND WEAKNESSES

The question which most clients ask their barristers is 'Will I win my case?'. The answer will depend on the strength of the evidence, i.e., on what facts can be proved. Before you are in a position to answer the client's questions, you will need to assess:

(a)   What facts must and can be proved by whom.

(b)   From the facts which can be proved (the evidence), what admissible evidence is there in support of each proposition which must be proved?

(c)   The degree of conflicting or contradictory evidence.

(d)   Whether the evidence is sufficient to satisfy the standard of proof required.

In a civil case, it will be clear from the claim and defence which facts are in issue and therefore must be proved. By identifying which side carries the burden of proof on each issue, and assessing the witness statements and documentary evidence which support your case, as well as the contradictory evidence, you will then be in a position to comment on the likelihood of successfully establishing your client's case. While this information can be collated in a number of ways, you may wish to try using the chart in **Table 14.9**. This gives an overview to ascertain easily the strengths and weaknesses of a case. The importance of this assessment process, often called 'assessing the strengths and weaknesses' of the case cannot be overestimated. It is not only the key result of the fact analysis process, but is also essential before you can competently:

● give sound advice on the likelihood of success at trial;

● negotiate effectively on your client's behalf;

● advise on whether to accept a Part 36 payment (payment into court);

● advise on whether further evidence is necessary, and if so, the nature of that evidence; and

● plan the presentation of the case at the trial.

In a criminal case, the prosecution must prove the commission of the offence beyond reasonable doubt. Whether you are briefed for the prosecution or the defence, an analysis will still be required to assess whether the facts, or inferences drawn therefrom, can be established to the required standard of proof for each and every element of the offence. As in civil cases, this evidence must be balanced against the opposing evidence which may weaken the prosecution case.

14.5.6 FROM FACTS TO EVIDENCE — ESTABLISHING 'PROOF'

By this stage, you should have identified from the information which you have, the facts which are agreed and disputed, their source, i.e., who or what will (may) be able to prove the proposition, and, where available from the claim or defence and disclosure, the facts which your opponent will be putting forward. Facts become evidence when they are proved. There are various methods of 'proving' a fact: by direct evidence, inferences and generalisations. Regardless of which form the evidence takes, each required element of the case must be proved.

It is at this point that careful thought will have to be given as to whether, by reason of the rules of evidence, any facts will be (or are likely to be) excluded at trial.

14.5.7 DIRECT FACTS VERSUS INFERENCES

Direct evidence is evidence which proves the truth or falsity of a fact, and does not need an inference for proof. Evidence by inference, sometimes called circumstantial evidence, allows proof by virtue of the inference of another fact. The inferred fact may be a required element in the case or, as is more common, may prove a secondary fact which can in turn infer proof of the required element. The chain of facts which can be inferred before finally proving the required element is not limited, that is to say, a court is unlikely to reject evidence simply because several inferred facts were needed to prove an element. However, where the inferred facts are so remote from proving the element that an extensive chain is needed, there is more risk that little probative weight will be given to the evidence.

The importance of the distinction between direct evidence and evidence proved by inference is important, but not because one is necessarily more persuasive than the other. A group of inferences — or for television viewers of courtroom drama, the circumstantial evidence — may carry more probative weight than a single fact of direct evidence. The distinction is necessary to recognise where proof can only be through one or more inferences.

It is not uncommon to find in some cases the legal elements of the action or offence have been proved primarily, if not wholly, by inference (or circumstantial) evidence. In these cases, the strength of the inferences and credibility of witnesses become crucial as each offers a piece of the overall picture. Witnesses on both sides will have conflicting evidence of what was seen, or what happened. Therefore how credible, accurate and persuasive a witness is perceived to be will directly influence the weight which the inferred evidence will have.

14.5.8 USING GENERALISATIONS TO LINK INFERRED FACTS TO REQUIRED ELEMENTS

Inferences are based on premises assumed to be true. The truth is assumed possibly because it is based on widely accepted knowledge or science. But where this support is lacking it is also possible to rely on a generalisation. Generalisations are based on general life experience which permit a conclusion that something is more likely to be true. As explained by Binder, D. A., and Bergman, P., *Fact Investigation: from Hypothesis to Proof*, West Publishing Co, 1984, at p. 85, the generalisation becomes the premise which enables one to link the specific evidence (inference) to the final elements which are required to be proved:

> A generalisation is, then, a premise which rests on the general behaviour of people or objects. How does one formulate generalisations? Usually, one adopts conventional wisdom about how people and objects function in everyday life. All of us, through our own personal experiences . . . through knowledge gained from books,

movies, newspapers and television, have accumulated vast storehouses of common-ly-held notions about how people and objects generally behave in our society.

To illustrate a case example of how inferences and generalisations operate, take the criminal case of Cassie Charnel who has been charged under the Theft Act 1968, s. 1, with stealing a bottle of whisky from Super Stores plc. To establish the case, the prosecution must prove several elements which make up this specific offence. These are:

(a)   Cassie took a bottle of whisky.

(b)   The whisky belonged to Super Stores plc.

(c)   She did so dishonestly.

(d)   At the time, she intended to deprive Super Stores permanently of the whisky.

Suppose the Super Stores detective has made a statement to the police and that part of it reads as follows:

I saw the defendant take a bottle of whisky from the spirits display. She did not put it in the store's wire basket which she was carrying but instead she put it in an inside pocket in the coat which she was wearing. She went to a checkout and paid for the goods in the basket but made no attempt to pay for the bottle of whisky. She then left the store. I followed her and stopped her in the street outside.

Concentrating on proving the elements of the offence, the crucial facts contained in the detective's statement are that she took the whisky from the display at Super Stores plc, put it in her coat instead of her basket, failed to pay for the whisky at the checkout, and left the store with the whisky. However, there is no direct evidence of this. Rather they are inferences from the detective's statement to this effect.

The move from the detective's statement to the inference that what he stated was in fact true involves several generalisations:

(a)   In the absence of a motive to lie or opportunity for erroneous observation, a person's account of what he or she has seen is likely to be true.

(b)   The detective had no known motive to lie.

(c)   He had no known opportunity for erroneous observation.

In analysing the evidential support for your case, you will need to consider each fact, whether its proof is by direct evidence or inferences, and what evidence or inference exists to challenge or weaken the proposition. This should highlight where the proof is weak and requires further evidence to strengthen the proposition. It is important in carrying out the analysis that facts do not take on a theoretical superiority, if in reality they cannot be proved to exist, or for evidential purposes they would clearly be inadmissible. Tabulation can be helpful to do this and is illustrated in **Table 14.10**.

14.5.9   WIGMORE ANALYSIS CHARTS

Another method of analysing evidence is by drawing a chart based on a scheme originally proposed by Wigmore (see Wigmore, J.H. 'The Problem of Proof', *University of Illinois Law Review*, 1913, vol. 8, p. 77). The aim of this method is to identify the chain of proof, including inferences which strengthen or weaken the main proposition to be proved. This method is explained in more detail in **Appendix 2** along with examples. While it can be a time-intensive exercise, many people find it beneficial to produce a visual analysis in this way.

14.6   Stage 3: The Presentation of the Case or Argument

14.6.1   INTRODUCTION

The last stage in the CAP approach is to prepare the presentation of the case in light of the task which you have been instructed to do. Presentation is a generic term which in practice means:

(a)   Making a final decision on the theory and theme of the case.

(b)   Determining how you will support the legal framework.

(c)   Considering your task, and its intended audience.

(d)   Preparing the results of your analysis.

14.6.2   REVISITING THEORIES — SELECTING A THEME

After the fact analysis process is completed, you will need to consider the theory chosen earlier, and be prepared to amend it as required up until the end of the trial. Having chosen the theory, you will need to select a theme (or themes) to fit the theory of the case. The theme may be defined as the part of the 'story' presented in court which is used because of its persuasive effect.

In an essay entitled 'Lawyers' Stories' (originally presented at the Seminar on Narrative in Culture, University of Warwick, in 1987) in *Rethinking Evidence, Exploratory Essays* (Blackwell, 1990), Professor William Twining defines theme in the following way:

> Sometimes it is used to refer to the overall characterization of the situation or story or some element of it that appeals to a popular stereotype. For example: 'This is an example of a grasping landlord exploiting a helpless tenant'; or 'this is a case of property developers needlessly desecrating the countryside'. Another, more precise usage . . . refers to any element that is sufficiently important to deserve emphasis by repetition. An English barrister (Patrick Bennett QC) gives a vivid account of what he calls 'the mantra', as follows: 'In almost all cases there will be a key factor which has played a dominant role in the case from your point of view. It may be stupidity, fear, greed, jealousy, selfishness. Pick your word, inject it into your opening. Put it on a separate piece of paper. Repetition will have a lasting effect. If you have hit the right note and have repeated it often enough, it will echo in the jury's mind when they retire. It will be the voice of the 13th juror. Try to hit the note as soon as possible in opening.'

The theme will be used in opening and closing speeches, and will underpin the questions put to the witnesses. The 'story' should include the items of evidence which support it and exclude any matters that undermine its persuasiveness. Good themes are often very simple. They extend logic and have been defined as the soul or moral justifications of the case, put forward in such a way as to maximise the appeal to the judge or jury.

The theory and the theme must be consistent with each other. The experienced advocate can make the two so consistent that they are virtually indistinguishable. This is done because the better the theme fits with the theory, the greater the moral force of the theory and likelihood of persuading the tribunal of fact to find in your favour. Take, for example, a contested careless driving case in the magistrates' court: a pedestrian steps out on to a zebra crossing, causing the motorist to brake hard and skid. The only substantial dispute on the facts is whether the pedestrian looked to the right before stepping on to the crossing. The defence theme may well be that there is a limit to the care and foresight to be expected of the ordinary competent motorist, especially when faced with a jay-walker. If, at the trial it emerged that the pedestrian was late for an appointment, another defence theme might be 'more haste, less speed', and so on.

14.6.3   SUPPORTING YOUR LEGAL FRAMEWORK AND REASONING

Whether the law on which your case is based derives from established legal principles or is unsettled, e.g., because previous precedents conflict, a firm basis of legal sources will be required, including any legal research that is necessary to support the chosen legal solution. You may have referred to key statutes or cases in your advice or opinion. In an increasing number of trials and hearings a written 'skeleton argument' is required to be submitted prior to the hearing. These outlines of the case and the arguments will require legal support for your key propositions. You will be expected to provide your opponents and the court with a list of authorities (e.g., statutes, cases, reports) on which you will rely. Legal research is covered elsewhere in this Manual but a few considerations are included here for thought.

Statute Law

If a statutory section is relevant to the legal argument, consider its real role in the case:

- Does the entire section apply to the case, or merely a part?

- Is its effect clear or is its interpretation open to challenge? If so, how could it be challenged?

- What are the relevant principles of statutory interpretation?

- Are there cases interpreting the words of the statute?

Case Law

If a case supports your argument, you will want to defend its precedent value; if it does not, you will want to find points on which to challenge or distinguish it, e.g., on the facts, or the application of the principle involved. A case is rarely directly on point and you should consider its real value in constructing the legal arguments supporting the framework. For example:

- On what facts was the decision made?

- What precisely was the *ratio* as opposed to *obiter dicta*?

- Did all the judges agree? (Which judge gave the principal judgment; what is his or her standing?)

- What was the level of the court making the decision?

- When was the case decided?

- And finally of most importance — has the case been subsequently reviewed or overturned?

There is rarely a single case on a particular point. It is more common to find a variety or line of cases. The whole line of cases should be reviewed, not simply to make coherence of the decisions, but also to consider what pattern of thinking can be seen through them and how this will fulfil your purpose.

If appropriate, note the procedural basis on which the decision was made. In some cases it is not open to the judges to review the facts and their decision is limited to whether the lower decision was properly reached.

Textbooks
While some of the leading textbooks can be quoted in court, and indeed judges have been known to adopt passages within their judgments, the support for the legal framework in a case should be based on original sources, rather than textbook comment.

14.6.4 CONSIDER YOUR TASK AND THE INTENDED AUDIENCE

Whether there are any preliminary matters which must be dealt with before you are able to carry out your instructions will depend on the nature of the task requested; the present stage in the proceedings; and the result of your analysis of the case.

In a sense this is a chicken and egg situation for it is only after you have completed an analysis of the case that it can be determined whether, on the basis of the papers, witness statements etc. that have been sent by the solicitor, the instructions can be carried out. In some cases, no further information will be needed, save for clarification of confusing points arising in the papers. For example, where you are asked for advice on the merits based on existing facts (which can be proved).

Sometimes it may be difficult to know what further information to ask for from the solicitor. You should consider the stage of proceedings as this will influence the degree of detail and range of relevant documents which may be required. Where you are briefed to appear at an interim hearing, you will, of course, require support for the arguments to be used at the hearing, and the relevant court documents. However, it would be unreasonable to ask the solicitor to produce documents which are not relevant to the present hearing. An exception might be where the document or evidence to prove a proposition would eventually be needed in any event, and preparation for trial is inevitable. Then, it may be prudent to discuss the matter with the solicitor. The point is that requests for further information should only be made where necessary to enable you to carry out your instructions.

Where you have been asked to provide an advice on evidence, it may also be difficult in some cases to know precisely what to advise, particularly if the area of law is an unfamiliar one. By this time, however, the legal framework and factual issues will have been identified, and usually a 'theory' of the case developed. These will provide you with a focus to concentrate on what evidence will be needed to bring out the strengths of the case or highlight the weaknesses in the opponent's case. You will also want to consider the nature of the evidence, whether it is consistent in itself and with your client's story, and where more detailed facts may be needed to fill gaps. For example, the history of parties and disputes are often found in more than one medium, e.g., letters, memos, reports and faxed communications. Many disputes develop over months or years and the client's position will be strengthened if there is supporting evidence over the entire relevant period rather than patchy samples. Even at the stage of preparing for trial, it may be necessary to embark on further disclosure, where, for example, it comes to light that important evidence is in the custody of a third party and previously unseen.

Finally, it may be necessary for counsel to have a site view or product sample in order to appreciate fully the circumstances or how an injury was alleged to have occurred. This is often the case in complex or technical matters, such as engineering, manufacturing or property damage cases. Additional briefing may also be needed in cases involving complicated experts' reports and counsel must prepare the examination of expert witnesses for the hearing.

The manner of 'presenting' your analysis and the case also depends on the intended audience. When you are asked to write an advice or opinion, the audience will likely be limited to your client, the solicitors, and possibly other counsel who may become involved in the case. The knowledge that your written work will not be seen by your opponent (in most cases) allows more flexibility in how you present it. On appearances in court, however, your 'audience' will be the judge whom you are trying to persuade, and, unless it is an application without notice, the opponents and their counsel.

Careful thought must be given not only to the content of presentation, but the best methods of relaying facts and evidence in light of the audience. In studies of how people receive information it has been shown that the majority of human beings are 'visual', meaning that material shown to them using a visual medium, as opposed to, e.g., an aural medium, has the highest degree of impact and influence. A smaller number of people react more favourably to 'hearing' the information. Therefore, consider whether it might be appropriate to use charts, graphs or other visual aids in presenting the case.

14.6.5 PREPARING THE RESULTS OF YOUR ANALYSIS

Your final task will to be make sure that you have everything you need to help you carry out your instructions in a form which will support your presentation. It may be useful to present some of the work you have done in preparation to your opponent or to the court itself. Agreed chronologies, summaries of facts, schedules or plans of the *locus in quo* are frequently handed up before a case begins and can be very compelling and certainly make you appear well prepared and efficient. It is increasingly common for courts to require that lists of issues, skeleton arguments and lists of the authorities which will be relied on should be submitted before a case begins. The new Civil Procedure Rules governing civil cases provide for skeleton arguments to be used in most cases.

If you are instructed to hold a conference or to negotiate it will help you to have some notes with you so that nothing relevant is forgotten. If you are appearing at court, notes about the points you wish to make on each issue will be helpful. **Chapter 4** of the ***Advocacy Manual*** contains suggestions of the kind of notes you might find useful to prepare for your own use.

Everyone adopts a method of organising information to suit his or her own needs. Many barristers use blue notebooks for all their work done on preparing a case, from notes of conferences with clients, to preparations for trial. One particular form of organising information for trial, described as a 'trial book' is explained in detail in Anderson and Twining's *Analysis of Evidence*, chapter 5.

14.7 The Client's Choice — Acting on Instructions

At the beginning of the CAP approach, you became familiar with the client's objectives and what they hoped to achieve. These should not be forgotten as you proceed with your fact analysis and assess the strength of the case. You may be asked for an advice on the merits, or other task which will result in the client needing to take an immediate decision. Your task may alternatively be part of the overall case management. Apart from your client's overall objectives, other criteria such as costs, time efficiency, the desire to avoid stress or risk, the impact on family or business, and the desire to be exonerated may be factors which determine what decision is made. You will need to bear this in mind and ensure that you present the possible solutions to your client in such a way that all the consequences of a particular course of action are highlighted, thus aiding your client to make an informed decision about the next steps.

14.8 Suggested Charts

We have seen that the CAP approach identifies the stages necessary for efficient case preparation and that there are varying techniques which can be used to achieve those tasks. The following four charts can also be used to aid understanding and analysis. The titles refer to the stages in the CAP process.

Table 14.7 Stage 1: Context of the case: identifying agreed and disputed facts

(Note: This form may be used for either civil or criminal cases. 'Ref/page' refers to the source of the statement, e.g., witness statement of J. Bloggs, page 6, para. 2.)

A = AGREED
D = DISPUTED

	CLAIMANT'S VERSION OR PROSECUTION VERSION	REF/ PAGE	DEFENDANT'S VERSION	REF/ PAGE	QUERIES/ NOTES
[A]					
[D]					

Table 14.8 Stage 2: Analysis of issues and evidence: identifying issues and relating evidence to issues

(Note: This form can be used in criminal cases by changing the reference to the claim and defence.)

Ref.	Issue	Para. of particulars of claim	Para. of defence	Para. of reply	Burden of proof	Name of witness	Available oral evidence	Available documentary evidence	Notes/comments e.g., procedure, evidence, gaps

Table 14.9 Stage 2: Analysis of issues and evidence: analysing the strengths and weaknesses

(Note: This form can also be used as the basis for examining and cross-examining witnesses.)

Issue	(a) Evidence in support of C's version	Witness	Page	(b) Evidence which contradicts/undermines C's version	Witness	Page	(c) Evidence which contradicts/undermines (b)	Witness	Page

Table 14.10 Stage 2: Analysis of issues and evidence: analysing the evidence proving the case

ISSUE/ELEMENT:

FACTS IN SUPPORT	WITNESS	INFERENCE IN SUPPORT	CHALLENGE/ WEAKNESS	NOTES

FIFTEEN

THE CAP APPROACH IN ACTION

15.1 Introduction to Chapters 16 and 17

Once the various stages of the CAP approach have been identified and understood, they should be applied routinely to the preparation of every case until you have developed your own effective methods of preparation. Obviously the context of every set of instructions will highlight particular aspects and not every stage may be required to be considered for every piece of work.

The following Chapters demonstrate through worked examples how using the CAP approach can ensure that you are able to carry out your instructions effectively. **Chapter 16** deals with a civil case, *Lowe* v *Mainwaring,* **Chapter 17** with a criminal case, *R* v *Costas Georgiou.* The contents of each chapter are set out on the title page. Each chapter contains a series of instructions in the case at various stages of the legal process at which a barrister is commonly instructed. Each set of instructions is followed by notes entitled '**CAP in action**' which have been prepared as an example of how a barrister might apply each stage of the CAP approach in preparing to carry out his or her own instructions in the context of a civil and a criminal case (see, for instance, **16.1.1** and **17.1.1**).

15.2 Instructions to Counsel

Each set of instructions would include a back sheet similar to that shown at **16.1**. After the instructions have been carried out, the back sheet should be returned endorsed to instructing solicitors together with the completed work (if any). Each subsequent set of papers in the same case in addition to any new documents would also contain all the papers previously before counsel together with a copy of any opinion or case statement previously settled by counsel. For reasons of space, papers have only been duplicated where there is good reason for doing so, for instance in each case one back sheet is shown before and after endorsement. Not all back sheets have been printed. The contents of any set of instructions are set out in the 'Instructions for Counsel' prepared by instructing solicitors. These should always be checked to ensure that nothing has been inadvertently omitted.

15.3 The Civil Brief: *Lowe* v *Mainwaring*

In this case counsel is instructed for the defendants on three occasions. The first set of instructions at **16.1** are to draft the defence and a request for further information. The second set of instructions at **16.2** are to advise on the merits of the case and the last set at **16.3** are to make an application for specific disclosure.

15.4 The Criminal Brief: *R* v *Costas Georgiou*

In this case counsel is instructed for the defence on three occasions. The first set of instructions at **17.1** are to represent the defendant at an application for bail. The next set of instructions at **17.2** are to advise on evidence some months later. Lastly counsel receives the brief to appear at the pleas and directions hearing and to represent the defendant at trial at **17.3**.

15.5 CAP in Action Notes

The notes, prepared after each set of instructions in **Chapters 16** and **17**, show how every stage of the CAP approach to preparation can be put into practice. The particular technique used in the examples is in no way prescriptive. A variety of methods could be used and everyone will want to develop the method which best suits them. What is important is that preparation should be methodical and accurate so that it is complete and exact and nothing is overlooked which might assist the client, or the presentation of his or her case. There is no 'right' way to prepare a case: the test is whether the preparation is effective.

The notes show examples of small chronologies, lists and tables which can be used to help master the facts and law and identify the issues and evidence in a case using the techniques suggested in **Chapter 14**. You should also refer to the other skills Manuals for further assistance in preparing to carry out particular skills.

The majority of barristers keep the notes they prepare in blue books so that a complete record of a case from beginning to end is maintained. If counsel is subsequently instructed the previous notes can be referred to and built upon thus saving valuable preparation time.

15.6 Practising the Skill

All skills require practice. When you have worked through the examples of the use of the CAP approach in **Chapters 16** and **17** you should try to apply it for yourself. **Chapter 20** contains a number of self-assessment exercises, including a civil and a criminal brief, which you can use to practise your own skills in applying the CAP approach until they become second nature and you find that you automatically consider each stage as you get to grips with each new set of papers. Once this level of expertise has been reached you will no longer need to articulate the stage by stage process but can concentrate on whether you have acquired the ability to carry out your preparation effectively.

15.7 Criteria by which You may Assess Your Own Performance

When you have completed your preparation of any set of papers you may find it useful to review the list of criteria below to consider which fact management skills you have demonstrated by your preparation and which still require improvement. As these skills are required in all the work you undertake, your performance of other skills will be affected by the level of your fact management skills.

Effective preparation entails the ability to:

(a) understand data presented in a variety of ways;

(b) identify gaps, ambiguities and contradictions in information;

(c) identify and prioritise the objectives of the client both in terms of practical outcomes and legal remedies;

(d) place the information in context;

(e) identify and prioritise the factual issues;

(f) identify and prioritise the legal issues raised by the facts;

(g) select possible solutions to the client's problem;

(h) recognise the interaction between law and fact;

(i) assess the strengths and weaknesses of a case;

(j) organise information in a variety of ways:

   (i) to aid understanding;

   (ii) to prove propositions of law;

   (iii) to assist at trial;

(k) distinguish between relevant and irrelevant facts;

(l) distinguish between fact and inference;

(m) construct an argument from the facts to support the client's case:

   (i) by developing a theory of the case;

   (ii) by selecting a theme to fit that theory;

(n) evaluate the issues in response to new information and in the light of tactical considerations.

SIXTEEN

THE CIVIL BRIEF

Stage 1   The Context of the Case

    (1)   The stage of the proceedings
    (2)   Understanding the problem
    (3)   Collecting the facts
    (4)   Agreed/disputed facts: gaps and ambiguities
    (5)   The legal framework

Stage 2   Analysis of Issues and Evidence

    (a)   The Issues

       (1)   The factual issues
       (2)   The legal issues
       (3)   The potential theory
       (4)   Gaps and ambiguities

    (b)   The Evidence

Stage 3   Presentation

    (1)   The chosen theory
    (2)   Carrying out instructions

       A.   Preparing to draft the Defence
       B.   Planning the Request for Further Information

16.1   Drafting the Defence and Request for Further Information

Claim No. WF01 048972

IN THE WAKEFIELD COUNTY COURT

BETWEEN:–

ANTHONY MALCOLM LOWE

Claimant

-and-

(1) HENRY GEORGE MAINWARING

(2) ELSA ANN MAINWARING

Defendants

_____

INSTRUCTIONS TO COUNSEL

_____

Counsel: Mr. BRIAN BARRISTER

Godfrey & Co.
27 Cressey St.
Wakefield
West Yorks
WF5 3SL

Ref: BB

Date: 29.10.01

<u>IN THE WAKEFIELD COUNTY COURT</u>   Claim No. WF01 048972

BETWEEN:–

ANTHONY MALCOLM LOWE   <u>Claimant</u>

-and-

(1) HENRY GEORGE MAINWARING

(2) ELSA ANN MAINWARING   <u>Defendants</u>

INSTRUCTIONS TO COUNSEL

Counsel has herewith:

1.   Particulars of Claim;
2.   Defendants' Lease (only relevant parts reproduced);
3.   Relevant correspondence.

Counsel is instructed on behalf of the Defendants, the Tenants of the First and Second Floors of 83-87 Leeds Road, Wakefield. As Counsel will see from the Particulars of Claim, the Claimant is the Tenant of the Ground Floor of this property, which he uses to run a snooker hall business called the Topspin Snooker Hall. It appears that a flood occurred at the premises during the period between the 23rd and 30th December 2000, while the building was empty for the Christmas holiday.

The flood came from a water pipe on the outside of the building at about First Floor level. It was discovered by Mr Mainwaring when he went to his premises early in the morning to open up. He immediately switched off the water and called a plumber. Obviously, the flood caused damage to our clients' property as well as to that of the Claimant. The damage to our clients' property was relatively minimal. However, the Claimant is claiming very extensive damages, including not only costs of repairs said to be in excess of £8,000, but also loss of profits and loss of what he claims to be the value of the business. Our clients inform us that the snooker hall has been in operation since the flood, and this would seem to be consistent with our clients' evidence that the flood caused them only a small amount of damage. Nevertheless, the Claimant is claiming £45,000, said to be the value of the business which he appears to be alleging has been totally lost as a result of this flood. Regardless of whether or not the business has closed down, Counsel will also see from the papers that in any event the snooker hall appears to have been in financial difficulties before the damage from the flood happened. Indeed, bailiffs called on our clients some time last year mistakenly calling on them instead of Mr Lowe.

Those Instructing are still making inquiries into the facts of this matter, but the Solicitors for Mr Lowe have refused an extension of time for filing the Defence. Clearly most of the information relating to this claim will be in the hands of the Claimant. Counsel is requested to draft a Defence based on the information to hand, and also to draft a Request for Further Information if so advised to obtain such further information as can be obtained by this means.

Should Counsel have any questions on anything raised in these Instructions, please do not hesitate to contact Miss Pemberton of Instructing Solicitors.

> Counsel is instructed to settle the Defence and Request for Further Information.

IN THE WAKEFIELD COUNTY COURT   Claim No. WF01 048972

BETWEEN:-

ANTHONY MALCOLM LOWE   Claimant

-and-

(1) HENRY GEORGE MAINWARING

(2) ELSA ANN MAINWARING   Defendants

PARTICULARS OF CLAIM

---

1.   At all material times the Claimant has been the Tenant of the Ground Floor of a building known as and situate at 83–87 Leeds Road, Wakefield, West Yorkshire, WF4 1AP (the 'Ground Floor'), where he has traded as the proprietor of a snooker hall.

2.   At all material times the Defendants have been the Tenants of the First (the 'First Floor') and Second Floors of the building known as and situate at 83-87 Leeds Road, Wakefield, West Yorkshire, WF4 1AP, where they are and have been trading as upholstery manufacturers.

3.   Between 23rd December 2000 and 30th December 2000 the Ground Floor sustained severe flood damage when a pipe located at the First Floor level at the rear of and outside the building (the 'pipe') burst.

4.   At all material times the Defendants were responsible for maintaining and repairing the pipe.

5.   At all material times the Defendants knew or ought to have known that the pipe carried mains water at mains pressure, was not insulated and was not protected against the elements. In the circumstances the pipe was at all material times in a dangerous state of repair.

6.   The flood was caused by the negligence of the Defendants, their servants or agents.

PARTICULARS OF NEGLIGENCE

The Defendants, their servants or agents were negligent in that they:

(a)   Failed to insulate or otherwise protect the pipe against the elements whether by lagging or otherwise adequately or at all.

(b)   Failed to inspect, maintain or repair the pipe whether adequately or at all.

(c)   Failed to identify that the pipe was a source of danger to the building and in particular to the Ground Floor of the building.

(d)   Failed to eliminate the danger to the building presented by the pipe by relaying it inside the building.

(e)   The Claimant will further rely upon the doctrine of res ipsa loquitur.

7.   By reason of the matters set out above the Claimant has been deprived of his use and enjoyment of the Ground Floor and has suffered loss and damage.

<u>PARTICULARS OF LOSS AND DAMAGE</u>

(a)   Flooding damage to the Ground Floor   £9,503.40

(b)   Before the flood the Claimant's snooker hall business
       that he ran from the Ground Floor was worth £45,000
       That business has ceased trading as a result of damage
       caused by the flood and now is of no value. Loss of the
       value of the business   £45,000

(c)   Before the flood the Claimant's snooker hall business
       generated profits of £6,500 per annum. As a result of
       the flood the Claimant's business has ceased trading and
       the Claimant claims loss of profits from the 30th December
       2000 to the date of issue of this claim at the rate of £6,500
       per annum equivalent to £17.76 per day. Loss of profits
       for 295 days   £5,239.20

(d)   Continuing loss of profits at £6,500 per annum.

8.   Further, the Claimant claims interest pursuant to the County Courts Act 1984, section 69 at the rate of 8% per annum on such sums and for such periods as the Court thinks fit.

9.   The value of this claim exceeds £15,000.00.

AND the Claimant claims:

(1)   Damages

(2)   Interest thereon pursuant to the County Courts Act 1984, section 69 to be assessed.

ALISON COUNSEL

Statement of Truth

I believe that the facts stated in these particulars of claim are true.

Signed   *A. M. Lowe*

Claimant

DATED this 19th day of October 2001

Messrs Fraser & Co., of Bank Chambers, Ripon Road, Wakefield, WF1 9GR, Solicitors for the Claimant who will accept service of all proceedings on his behalf at the above address.

To: The Defendants

and to the Court Manager.

THIS LEASE is made the 18th day of October
One thousand nine hundred and ninety five BETWEEN
MARGARET PIKE of Grange House, Cleaver Street, Keighley, West Yorkshire, BD21 6EM (hereinafter called 'the landlord') of the one part and HENRY GEORGE MAINWAR-ING and ELSA ANN MAINWARING both of 18 Conniston Road, Wakefield, West Yorkshire, WF6 2UN (hereinafter called 'the Tenant') of the other part
WHEREAS:
In this Lease where the context so admits:
(1) 'the Landlord' shall include the person for the time being entitled in reversion immediately expectant on the term hereby created and 'the Tenant' shall include the successors in title of the Tenant
(2) in the event of the Tenant being at any time more than one individual 'the Tenant' shall be deemed to include also a reference to any of them and any covenant on the part of the Tenant shall take effect as a joint and several covenant
(3) 'the demised premises' means the premises (including the Landlord's fixtures and fittings) more particularly described in the Schedule hereto and all alterations and additions to such premises
(4) 'the conduits' means all ducts cisterns tanks radiators water gas electricity and telephone supply pipes wires and cables sewers drains soil pipes waste water pipes and any other conducting media under or upon the demised premises
(5) 'the Building' means the building of which the demised premises form part
NOW THIS LEASE WITNESSETH as follows:-
1. IN consideration of the rents covenants and conditions hereinafter reserved and contained and on the part of the Tenant to be paid observed and performed the Landlord hereby demises unto the Tenant ALL THOSE premises more particularly described in Part I of the Schedule hereto (hereinafter called 'the demised premises') TOGETHER WITH the rights set out in Part II of the Schedule hereto EXCEPT AND RESERVING unto the Landlord as stated in Part III of the Schedule hereto TO HOLD the same unto the Tenant for the term of twenty one years commencing from the 18th day of October One thousand nine hundred and ninety four
YIELDING AND PAYING therefor during the said term
(1) the yearly rent of Four thousand pounds (£4,000.00) (subject to the provisions for revision contained in Clause 5 hereof) such rent to be paid by equal quarterly payments in advance on the usual quarter days the first of such payments or a proportionate part thereof to be made on the signing hereof . . .
2. The Tenant HEREBY COVENANTS with the Landlord as follows:
(1) To pay the yearly rent and any increased rents as hereinbefore reserved on the days and in manner aforesaid without any deduction . . .
(6) At all times during the said term to keep the whole of the demised premises and the conduits and all Landlord's fixtures and fittings, plant, machinery and equipment therein and all additions and improvements thereto in good and substantial repair and condition (notwithstanding that any want of repair may be due to normal wear and tear) damage by any of the insured risks excepted unless payment of the insurance monies shall be withheld in whole or part by reason solely or in part of any act or default of the Tenant or the Tenant's servants or agents.
3. The Landlord HEREBY COVENANTS with the Tenant as follows:
(1) That the Tenant paying the rents hereby reserved on the days and in the manner aforesaid and performing and observing the several covenants and conditions on the Tenant's part herein contained shall quietly hold and enjoy the demised premises during the said term without any interruption by the Landlord or any person rightfully claiming under or in trust for the Landlord.
(2) To insure and keep insured the demised premises (including all the Landlord's fixtures and fittings plant machinery and equipment now or hereafter in or about the same) subject to such reasonable and usual exclusions and limitations as may be imposed by the Insurers in some insurance office of repute or with Underwriters or through such agency as the Landlord shall from time to time decide in the name of the Landlord with a note of Tenant's interest and that of any mortgagee of the Tenant from time to time notified to the Landlord to be endorsed on the Policy if required by the Tenant in such sum as shall represent the full reinstatement value thereof including Architects' and Surveyors' and other professional fees and incidental expenses against loss or damage by fire and such other reasonable risks which the Landlord shall

reasonably consider necessary and against the public liability of the Landlord arising out of or in connection with any accident explosion collapse or breakdown being referred to in this Lease as 'insured risks' . . .

IN WITNESS whereof the parties hereto have set their respective hands and seals the day and year first above written

THE SCHEDULE above referred to
Part I
The Demised Premises

ALL THAT first and second floors of the Building situate at and known as 83-87 Leeds Road, Wakefield, West Yorkshire, WF4 1AP including the floorboards on the first floor but not the joists on which the flooring is laid.

PART III
Exceptions and Reservations out of the Demise

There are excepted and reserved out of this demise all rights and privileges now enjoyed over and against the premises and the particular rights following namely:

(1) The right of the Landlord her successors in title and assigns and all persons authorised by her during the term hereby granted on prior reasonable notice to enter with or without workmen into or upon the premises for the purpose of executing repairs upon the exterior structure of the Building and such installations thereon the proper repair of which is necessary for the protection of the Building.

FRASER & COMPANY
SOLICITORS

Bank Chambers
Ripon Road
Wakefield
WF1 9GR
Tel: 01924 782364
Fax: 01924 807243
Ref: TBC/DH/00.0247

Date: 17th April 2001

Dear Sir,

Re: TOPSPIN SNOOKER HALL, 83–87 LEEDS ROAD, WAKEFIELD
Our Client: Mr A. LOWE

We have been instructed by Mr Lowe, the proprietor of the Topspin Snooker Hall at the above address. The property has been unusable since it suffered severe flooding damage in late December 2000. The cost of repairing the damage to the property and three tables damaged by the flood has been put at £9,503.40. In addition there is an element of continuing loss of profits.

Everyone is denying responsibility for this occurrence, and, if anything is clear, the blame does not rest with our client. We are instructed that the flood emanated from a mains pipe located in your property, and it is our view that the flood would not have occurred in the absence of negligence on your part. We have been instructed to commence proceedings against you without further warning if we do not hear from you in the next 14 days with sensible proposals for settling our client's claim.

A Legal Services Commission certificate was granted on the 9th April 2001 to our client to commence proceedings and the relevant notice is enclosed herewith.

Perhaps we should suggest that you pass this letter to your insurers without delay.

Yours faithfully,

Fraser & Co.

Mr and Mrs H. Mainwaring,
18 Conniston Road,
Wakefield,
West Yorkshire,
WF6 2UN

18 Conniston Road,
Wakefield,
West Yorkshire,
WF6 2UN

27th October 2001

Dear Miss Pemberton,

Thank you for agreeing to take on our case, and it was good to speak to you this morning. We don't have many papers relating to this case, but what we have we are sending you with this letter.

My husband runs an upholstery business from the upper floors of 83-87 Leeds Road. Downstairs on the ground floor there is a snooker hall run by Mr Lowe. During Christmas week there was a flood when a water pipe burst at the back of the property. My husband found it when he went in on the 30th. He noticed as soon as he went in through the front door that the place was very damp, and when he investigated he found a pipe on the rear of the building had burst. He immediately telephoned the plumber, who arrived about two hours after he telephoned. In the meantime he stopped any further damage being done by turning off the mains. I arrived at the workshop at about 10 a.m. The plumber was still working at the back on the pipe. It had happened on the back wall of the first floor, so our property took the brunt of the damage. A lot of water had got in and a fair amount of stock was soaking wet where it had been stored near the rear wall. The floor was awash, and, together with Paula I set to with buckets and mops in drying the place out.

I don't know how Mr Lowe comes to say he suffered such a lot of damage that the repairs will come to over £9,000. Our soiled stock came to about £800, of which we salvaged about £300. Although the back wall and floors were soaked, and you have to remember that the pipe was immediately outside our part of the building, after a few days they were back to the same condition they were beforehand, and you would never know that anything had happened. Henry asked the plumber when he arrived how long the water had been escaping, and he was told that it could have been only a few hours.

About six months ago the bailiffs came to our property trying to get arrears of rent. They had called on us by mistake, because when we read the warrant we saw that it was for the ground floor where Mr Lowe's snooker hall is. My understanding is that his business has not been doing at all well for some time, and that, in addition to problems with his rent, he has also had problems with other creditors. I think that most of his claims as set out in the court documents are an excuse for a failing business, and not too much store can be placed on them.

My husband tells me that all the pipes on the outside of the building are insulated, so we don't understand why Mr Lowe is saying that this one was not. Fraser & Co. seem to be unsure whether we are in fact responsible for the pipes at the back of the building. Surely they come under the landlord's responsibility as common parts of the building?

As we discussed, we have no insurance against this sort of claim, and we enclose the £500 you asked for on account of your costs.

Yours faithfully,

H. & E. Mainwaring.

16.1.1   CAP IN ACTION

Notes for drafting the Defence and Request for Further Information.

STAGE 1   THE CONTEXT OF THE CASE

(1)   THE STAGE OF THE PROCEEDINGS

(a)   What steps have been taken?
Particulars of Claim filed at Wakefield County Court 19.10.01

(b)   Your Instructions
Draft Defence and Request for Further Information in order to:

- Clarify issues between parties.
- Protect clients' position.
- Show strength of clients' case.
- Highlight weaknesses of Claimant's case.

(2)   UNDERSTANDING THE PROBLEM

(a)   Cause of the problem
Claimant's business on ground floor at 83–87 Leeds Road, Wakefield, in financial difficulties. He blames financial difficulties on damage to premises caused when water escaped from burst pipe at first floor level on outside of building.

(b)   Clients' objectives
Resist claim by Claimant. Put Claimant to proof of loss and damage.

(3)   COLLECTING THE FACTS

(a)   Dramatis personae

Anthony Lowe the publicly funded Claimant and Tenant of Ground Floor and proprietor of snooker hall
Henry (Harry) Mainwaring 1st Defendant, Joint Tenant of First and Second Floors where he runs an upholstery business on premises
Elsa Mainwaring 2nd Defendant, Joint tenant with Husband Harry
Margaret Pike Landlord of the premises
Topspin Snooker Hall business carried on by Claimant on Ground Floor
Fraser & Co. Solicitors for the Claimant
Godfrey & Co. Instructing Solicitors for Defendants (Miss Pemberton)
Paula: helped to dry out Defendants' premises.

(b)   Chronology of events

18.10.95   Lease of First and Second Floors of 83–87 Leeds Road, Wakefield, granted to Defendants by Margaret Pike Landlord
Lease of Ground Floor of building to Claimant

30.12.00   Burst external water pipe discovered at First Floor level of premises and repaired

April 01   Distress Warrant for arrears of rent re Ground Floor premises issued

17.4.01   Letter before Claim sent to Defendants

19.10.01   Date of Particulars of Claim

27.10.01   Defendants Instructed Solicitors

(4)   AGREED/DISPUTED FACTS: GAPS AND AMBIGUITIES

Para. No.	Particulars of Claim	Defendants' Version	Notes/Queries
1.	C tenant of ground floor of 83–87 where ran snooker hall	admitted – see Instructions admitted – see letter of 27.10	
2.	Ds tenants of 1st and 2nd floors trading as upholsterers	admitted – see lease admitted – see letter of 27.10	
3.	23-30/12/00 Ground floor damaged by flood from external pipe at 1st floor level	Burst pipe on exterior 1st floor found 30.12. Probably burst on 30th see letter 27.10	Effect on ground floor? letter suggests that brunt of damage to 1st floor and that minimal
4.	Ds responsible for maintaining and repairing pipe	Landlord's responsibility? See lease preamble cl (4) Tenants' covenants cl 2(6) Schedule 'demised premises' and Landlord's right of entry to repair	Legal basis for allegation? Further legal research needed
5.	Ds knew/ought to have known that pipe carried mains water, not insulated/protected thereby in dangerous state of repair	all outside pipes insulated – see letter of 27.10	No particulars given why should have known?
6.	Flood caused by Ds' negligence in that failed to: protect against elements, inspect, maintain, repair, identify as danger to building, eliminate danger by relaying pipe inside building	Pipes adequately insulated	

Para. No.	Particulars of Claim	Defendants' Version	Notes/Queries
7.	As result C lost use/enjoyment of ground floor suffered loss and damage Flood damage £9,503.40 Loss of value of business £45,000 Loss of profits since 30/12/2000 £5,239.20	Other cause of losses – snooker hall in financial difficulties before flood Snooker hall in operation since flood – see letter of 27.10	Level of alleged damage very high. Compared with Ds' damage. What was damaged? How has this figure been calculated? When did business stop running? Net or gross? How were profits calculated?
8.	Interest		

(5) LEGAL FRAMEWORK

(a) Checklist for Action in Negligence:
Was duty owed by Defendants? Has there been a breach? Has any breach caused the incident? Has the loss and damage been suffered? Has any breach caused the loss and damage? Is the loss or damage suffered recoverable?

(b) Areas for Legal Research:
Tortious liability of landlords/tenants towards tenants of building in respect of burst pipes (Clerk and Lindsell *On Torts*, Charlesworth *On Negligence*). Repairing covenants in leases (Woodfall).

STAGE 2 ANALYSIS OF ISSUES AND EVIDENCE

(a) THE ISSUES

(1) THE FACTUAL ISSUES

See Stage 1(4) above and Particulars of Claim paras, 3, 4, 5, 6, and 7.

(2) THE LEGAL ISSUES

(i) Duty: Whether Defendants responsible for maintaining and repairing external water pipe?

(ii) Breach: Whether outside pipes insulated?

(iii) Knowledge: In particular whether Defendants knew or ought to have known of condition of the pipe?

(iv) Causation: Whether burst pipe caused by negligence of Defendants?

(v) Causation of loss and damage: Whether any loss or damage suffered by reason of the flood from the burst pipe?

(vi) Heads of damage: What heads of damage can be proved by the Claimant?

(vii) The amounts of each head of damage?

(3) THE POTENTIAL THEORY

Duty owed by Landlord, not Defendants under the lease; in any event no breach because pipe insulated, and pipe did not burst because of negligence of Defendants. Further, any loss suffered by Claimant, if it is proved, not caused by flood but by pre-existing financial difficulties.

(4) GAPS AND AMBIGUITIES

See Stage 1(4) above.

(b) THE EVIDENCE

At this stage the only evidence available is the lease and the letter of Mrs Mainwaring. Other sources of information are Instructions to Counsel, Particulars of Claim, letter from Claimant's Solicitors.

STAGE 3 PRESENTATION

(1) THE CHOSEN THEORY

See Stage 2(3) above.

(2) CARRYING OUT INSTRUCTIONS

A. Preparing to draft the Defence (see **Drafting Manual**).

(i) Parties — Paragraphs 1 and 2 — Admit

(ii) The Incident — Paragraph 3 — Admit bursting of pipe, do not admit effect. Clarify date.

(iii) Duty — Paragraph 4 — Deny. No duty under lease.

(iv) Knowledge — Paragraph 5 — Deny. Aver pipe insulated.

(v) Negligence/Causation — Paragraph 6 — Deny. If anyone's fault = Landlord's.

(vi) Causation/Loss and Damage — Paragraph 7 — Deny causation. Not admit loss and damage.

B. Planning the Request for Further Information (see **Drafting Manual**).

(a) Re Paragraph 3 — How was ground floor damaged?

(b) Re Paragraph 4 — Why does Claimant think Defendants responsible for repair etc?

(c) Re Paragraph 5 — Why should Defendants have known of condition of pipe?

(d) Re Paragraph 7 — Insufficient detail of how loss calculated.

(See **16.2** for completed Statements of Case.)

16.2 Advice on Merits

<u>IN THE WAKEFIELD COUNTY COURT</u>   Claim No. WF01 048972

BETWEEN:–

ANTHONY MALCOLM LOWE   <u>Claimant</u>

-AND-

(1) HENRY GEORGE MAINWARING

(2) ELSA ANN MAINWARING   <u>Defendants</u>

_____

INSTRUCTIONS TO COUNSEL TO ADVISE

_____

Counsel has herewith the papers previously before Counsel [only backsheet reproduced] together with:

4. Defence and Request for Further Information as settled by Counsel;

5. Response to the Request for Further Information;

6. Notice of Allocation;

7. Surveyor's Report prepared for the Claimant;

8. Legal Services Commission Certificates for the Defendants [extract only reproduced: both certificates are in substantially the same terms].

Counsel will recall this claim having drafted the Defence and a Request for Further Information. The Claimant's response to the Request appears at enclosure 5. The Defendants' business has not flourished in recent years, and their bank called in their loans some time ago. The effect has been to close down their business as they have been unable to pay their staff. It is hoped that the bank will be paid off more or less in full from sale of stock. The present litigation is a great worry to the Defendants, not least because if there is a substantial judgment against them the likelihood is that it will be enforced against their home, which has a substantial equity of redemption.

Counsel will see that public funding by the Legal Services Commission has been granted to the Defendants subject to a limitation. Counsel is asked to Advise on the Merits in this case for the purpose of removal of the limitation on the Certificate and to advise generally. Instructing Solicitors apologise that it has not been possible to arrange a conference with the Defendants as yet due to the ill-health of Mr Mainwaring.

There has been some slippage in the timetable, and the case management conference has been adjourned. A new date has not yet been fixed.

Counsel is instructed to Advise

Herewith:

(1) Defence

(2) Request for Further Information

      B. Barrister

      15.11.01

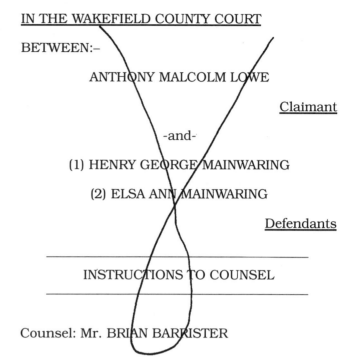

Claim No. WF01 048972

IN THE WAKEFIELD COUNTY COURT

BETWEEN:–

ANTHONY MALCOLM LOWE

Claimant

-and-

(1) HENRY GEORGE MAINWARING

(2) ELSA ANN MAINWARING

Defendants

_____

INSTRUCTIONS TO COUNSEL

_____

Counsel: Mr. BRIAN BARRISTER

Godfrey & Co.
27 Cressey St.
Wakefield
West Yorks
WF5 3SL

Ref: BB

Date: 29.10.01

<u>IN THE WAKEFIELD COUNTY COURT</u>   Claim No. WF01 048972

BETWEEN:–

ANTHONY MALCOLM LOWE   <u>Claimant</u>

-and-

(1) HENRY GEORGE MAINWARING

(2) ELSA ANN MAINWARING   <u>Defendants</u>

<hr>

DEFENCE

<hr>

1.   Paragraphs 1 and 2 of the Particulars of Claim are admitted.

2.   Save that it is admitted that the pipe burst, paragraph 3 of the Particulars of Claim is not admitted. The First Defendant arranged for the pipe to be repaired within a few hours of the occurrence of the burst.

3.   Paragraphs 4 and 5 of the Particulars of Claim are denied. The pipe was at all material times properly insulated. Further, under their Lease with Mrs Margaret Pike dated the 18th October 1995 the Defendants had no obligation to repair or maintain the pipe.

4.   For the reasons set out in paragraph 3 it is denied that the Defendants, their servants or agents were negligent as alleged in paragraph 6 of the Particulars of Claim or at all. It is further denied that the flood was caused by the alleged or any negligence on the part of the Defendants, their servants or agents.

5.   Further or alternatively, the flood was caused by the negligence of Margaret Pike.

PARTICULARS OF NEGLIGENCE

(a)   Failing to insulate or otherwise protect the pipe against the elements whether by lagging or otherwise adequately or at all.

(b)   Failing to inspect, maintain or repair the pipe whether adequately or at all.

(c)   Failing to identify that the pipe was a source of danger to the building.

(d)   Failing to eliminate the danger to the building presented by the pipe by relaying it inside the building.

(e)   The Defendants will further rely upon the doctrine of res ipsa loquitur.

6.   No admissions are made as to the loss and damage particularised in paragraph 7 of the Particulars of Claim, and no admissions are made as to the amounts claimed. Damage sustained by the Defendants as a result of the flood was to a value of about £800, and it is estimated that the Claimant's loss would have been at about the same level.

BRIAN BARRISTER

Statement of Truth

The Defendants believe that the facts stated in this Defence are true. I am duly authorised by the Defendants to sign this statement.

SIGNED   *F Godfrey*

Defendant's Solicitor

DATED the 19th day of November 2001.

Messrs. Godfrey & Co., of 27 Cressey Street, Wakefield, West Yorkshire, WF5 3SL, Solicitors for the Defendants.

To: The Claimant

and to the Court Manager

IN THE WAKEFIELD COUNTY COURT   Claim No. WF01 048972

BETWEEN:–

ANTHONY MALCOLM LOWE   Claimant

-and-

(1) HENRY GEORGE MAINWARING

(2) ELSA ANN MAINWARING   Defendants

DEFENDANTS' REQUEST FOR FURTHER INFORMATION AGAINST
THE CLAIMANT PURSUANT TO THE CPR, 1998, PART 18
DATED 19 NOVEMBER 2001

Paragraph references in this Request for Further Information are references to paragraphs in the Particulars of Claim.

Under paragraph 3.

Of: '. . . the Ground Floor sustained severe flood damage . . .'

REQUEST

1.   Please give full information on all the damage alleged to have been sustained to the Ground Floor by reason of the alleged flooding.

Under paragraph 4.

Of: '. . . the Defendants were responsible for maintaining and repairing the pipe'

REQUEST

2.   Please state whether it is alleged the Defendants were responsible for maintaining and repairing the pipe by reason of contract or otherwise.

3.   If by contract, state the contract relied upon, the parties to the contract, its date and the clauses relied upon.

4.   If otherwise than by contract, state the basis of the Claimant's contention that the Defendants were responsible for the repair and maintenance of the pipe.

Under paragraph 5.

Of: '. . . the Defendants knew or ought to have known that the pipe carried mains water at mains pressure, was not insulated . . .'

REQUEST

5.   State every fact and matter relied upon by the Claimant in support of the contention that the Defendants knew, alternatively ought to have known, that the pipe:

   (a)   carried mains water; and

   (b)   was not insulated

Under paragraph 7.

Of: '(a)   Flooding damage to the Ground Floor £9,503.40'

REQUEST

6.   Please specify how the alleged loss of £9,503.40 is made up.

Of: '. . . the Claimant's snooker hall business that he ran from the Ground Floor was worth £45,000 . . .'

REQUEST

7.   Specify each and every fact and matter relied upon in support of the contention that the business was worth £45,000.

Of: 'Before the flood the Claimant's snooker hall business generated profits of £6,500 per annum.'

REQUEST

8.   Specify how the figure of £6,500 is made up.

9.   State the period used in calculating the figure of £6,500.

10.   State whether the figure of £6,500 is:

(a)   before or after trade expenses;
(b)   net of tax.

BRIAN BARRISTER

NOTE: This request should be answered by 4 pm on 10th December 2001.

DATED the 19th day of November 2001.

Messrs Godfrey & Co., of 27 Cressey Street, Wakefield, West Yorkshire, WF5 3SL, Solicitors for the Defendants.

To: The Claimant

and to the Court Manager.

IN THE WAKEFIELD COUNTY COURT   Claim No. WF01 048972

BETWEEN:–

ANTHONY MALCOLM LOWE   <u>Claimant</u>

-and-

(1) HENRY GEORGE MAINWARING

(2) ELSA ANN MAINWARING   <u>Defendants</u>

CLAIMANT'S RESPONSE TO THE REQUEST FOR FURTHER
INFORMATION OF THE PARTICULARS OF CLAIM
DATED 19 NOVEMBER 2001

<u>Under paragraph 3.</u>

Of: '. . . the Ground Floor sustained severe flood damage . . .'

<u>REQUEST</u>

1.   Please give full information on all the damage alleged to have been sustained to the Ground Floor by reason of the alleged flooding.

<u>ANSWER</u>

1.   The matter requested has already been sufficiently set out. Full particulars will be given in a surveyor's report which will be mutually exchanged in accordance with directions.

<u>Under paragraph 4.</u>

Of: '. . . the Defendants were responsible for maintaining and repairing the pipe'

<u>REQUEST</u>

2.   Please state whether it is alleged the Defendants were responsible for maintaining and repairing the pipe by reason of contract or otherwise.

3.   If by contract, the contract relied upon, the parties to the contract, its date and the clauses relied upon.

4.   If otherwise than by contract, the basis of the Claimant's contention that the Defendants were responsible for the repair and maintenance of the pipe.

<u>ANSWER</u>

2.   Contract.

3.   Lease between the Defendants and Mrs Margaret Pike dated the 18th October 1995. The Claimant cannot identify the requested provision thereof until after disclosure of documents.

4.   Not applicable.

<u>Under paragraph 5.</u>

Of: '. . . the Defendants knew or ought to have known that the pipe carried mains water at mains pressure, was not insulated . . .'

REQUEST

5. State every fact and matter relied upon by the Claimant in support of the contention that the Defendants knew, alternatively ought to have known, that the pipe:

(a) carried mains water; and

(b) was not insulated.

ANSWER

5. The pipe is and was at all material times located on the outside of the building and is and was open to view. Access to and viewing of the pipe can and could be achieved by way of a nearby emergency escape staircase on the outside of the building and from a flat roof over the rear of the Ground Floor. The Defendants or their servants or agents viewed the pipe and thereby its condition and the fact that it was a mains pipe, or should have viewed the pipe and ought to have known of its condition and that it was a mains pipe.

Under paragraph 7.

Of: '(a) Flooding damage to the Ground Floor £9,503.40'

REQUEST

6. Please specify how the alleged loss of £9,503.40 is made up.

ANSWER

6. The loss of £9,503.40 comprises the following:

Repairs and refelting of snooker tables	£2,760.00	
VAT at 17.5%	£483.00	
Sub-total		£3,243.00
Replastering ceilings	£1,835.00	
Repairs to floors	£1,110.00	
Repairs to electrics	£1,437.00	
Redecoration	£946.00	
VAT at 17.5 %	£932.40	
Sub-total		£6,260.40
Total		£9,503.40

Of: '. . . the Claimant's snooker hall business that he ran from the Ground Floor was worth £45,000 . . .'

REQUEST

7. Specify each and every fact and matter relied upon in support of the contention that the business was worth £45,000.

ANSWER

7. The matter requested has already been sufficiently stated. Full particulars will be given in an accountant's report which will be mutually exchanged in accordance with directions.

Of: 'Before the flood the Claimant's snooker hall business generated profits of £6,500 per annum.

REQUEST

8. Specify how the figure of £6,500 is made up.

9.   State the period used in calculating the figure of £6,500.

10. State whether the figure of £6,500 is:

   (a) before or after trade expenses;
   (b) net of tax.

ANSWER

8.   Full particulars will be provided in the accounts disclosed on disclosure of documents.

9.   1st August 1999 to 31st July 2000.

10. (a) After trade expenses
     (b) yes

ALISON COUNSEL

Statement of Truth

The Claimant believes that the facts stated in this response to the request for further information dated the 19th November 2001 are true.

Full name: Graham Harding

Name of Claimant's solicitor's firm: Fraser & Co.

Signed: *G Harding*

Claimant's Solicitor

DATED the 6th day of March 2002.

Messrs. Fraser & Co., of Bank Chambers, Ripon Road, Wakefield, WF1 9GR, Solicitors for the Claimant.

To: The Defendants

and to the Court Manager.

Notice of Allocation	IN THE WAKEFIELD COUNTY COURT
to the Multi-track	Claim No. WF01 048972
	Claimant ANTHONY MALCOM LOWE
	(including ref) TBC/DH/00.0247
To [Claimant's] [Defendants'] Solicitor	Defendants HENRY GEORGE MAINWARING
Godfrey & Co.,	(including ref) ELSA ANN MAINWARING
27 Cressey Street	JTG/AP
Wakefield	
West Yorkshire	Date 10th January 2002
WF5 3SL	

Seal

District Judge Hodges has considered the statements of case and allocation questionnaires filed and allocated the claim to the multi-track.

The District Judge has ordered that:—

1. Any request for further information based on another party's statement of case shall be served no later than 4.00 pm on Thursday 7th February 2002.
Any such request shall be dealt with no later than 4.00 pm on Friday 8th March 2002.

2. Each party shall give to every other party standard disclosure of documents by list.
The latest date for delivery of the lists is 4.00 pm on Friday 22nd March 2002.
The latest date for service of any request to inspect or for a copy of a document is 4.00 pm on Tuesday 2nd April 2002.

3. Each party shall serve on every other party the witness statements of all witnesses of fact on whom he intends to rely.
There shall be simultaneous exchange of such statements no later than 4.00 pm on Friday 26th April 2002.

4. A case management conference shall be held at 2.00 pm on Tuesday 7th May 2002.

5. Costs in the claim.

The claim is being transferred to the [Civil Trial Centre at   County Court]
[Division of the Royal Courts of Justice] where all future applications, correspondence and so on will be dealt with.

[The reasons the judge has given for allocation to this track [is] [are] that the value of the claim exceeds £15,000 and the multi-track is the normal track for the claim.]

Notes:

You and the other party, or parties, may agree to extend the time periods given in the directions above provided this does not affect the date given for any case management conference, for returning the listing questionnaire, for any pre-trial review or the date of the trial or trial period.

If you do not comply with these directions, any other party to the claim will be entitled to apply to the court for an order that your statement of case (claim or defence) be struck out.

Leaflets explaining more about what happens when your case is allocated to the multi-track are available from the court office.

The court office at The Crown House, 127 Kirkgate, Wakefield, W. Yorkshire WF1 1JW is open between 10 am and 4 pm Monday to Friday. Address all communications to the Court Manager quoting the claim number.

CHRIS HODGES FRICS
CHARTERED SURVEYOR
43 High Street, Wakefield WF1 6YM

Facsimile: 01924 412020 **Telephone 01924 412019**

Solicitor's Ref: TBC/DH/00.0247

Our Ref: GH/AMT   12th March 2002

Court's Ref: WF01 048972

Wakefield County Court
The Crown House
127 Kirkgate
Wakefield
WF1 1JW

Dear Sirs,

Re: 83–87 Leeds Road, Wakefield: Mr T Lowe

I have been instructed on behalf of Fraser & Co., the solicitors for Mr Lowe, to inspect the above premises and to report on their condition and the damage which is alleged to have occurred as a result of a flood caused by a burst water pipe at the end of December 2000. I carried out all inspections personally.

SITUATION AND DESCRIPTION:

The premises form part of continuous shopping parades built 80 years ago or thereabouts. It comprises the whole of the ground floor of a three–storey terrace unit generally of substantial stock brick construction under a pitched slated main roof with iron guttering.

In respect of the shop front and return display, these are of old timber with large windows mainly sheeted over. Decorations are fair and condition of woodwork is generally reasonable for its age. There is a dwarf tiled stall riser. There is a lead flashing above the fascia box projection probably replaced and an illuminated fascia board to the front corner and side. Immediately to the rear is a door and entrance and iron staircase leading to workrooms on the upper floors.

INTERNALLY:

GROUND FLOOR:

Front lobby (carpeted). Main snooker hall 32' 6" wide by 39' 9" long rear bay, false ceiling, parquet floor.

Bar area to side (number 87) leading to store rooms (both with linoleum flooring) and office. Office 15' by 14' 2" and carpeted.

Small back addition Rear lobby 2 WCs & washbasins.

REAR:

The rear external staircase presumably part of Landlord's liability is somewhat poor with various rusted sections. The rear main wall is of solid stock brickwork with a metal casement window to the ground floor of the subject property and modern concrete lintel over. Directly above is part of the old iron fire escape landing which has a bearing into the wall. Rust expansion of the steelwork going into the brickwork has caused flaking to pointing and slight gaps underneath the steel landing.

Gerald Walker MA FRICS (Consultant)   VAT Reg No. 405 189622

I enclose copy sketch of the rear showing the staircase and landing and the external half–inch mains water pipe with a brass compression fitting which I understand was replaced as this was the source of the burst. The upper section of the pipe has been partly lagged but not to a good standard and the section below the iron staircase still remains unlagged to this day! Below the joint are streaks to the paintwork where water has washed down. A certain amount of water does drip from the staircase but not directly against the wall. It appears to me that the source of water damage was indeed this defective pipe as I could see no other water pipes to the ground floor and clearly there was a considerable amount of water in the ground floor causing sporadic lifting and damage to the parquet flooring.

There is a flush backdoor to the subject property which appears to be in fair order.

INTERNALLY:

GROUND FLOOR:

Lobby Section

Ceiling — false plaster ceiling with a few holes where fitments have been removed and otherwise satisfactory.

Floor — carpet — generally satisfactory.

Walls — wallpapered and generally in satisfactory condition. 9-light glazed double doors leading to:

Main Area

Ceiling — plasterboard painted black — from limited view appears generally satisfactory. More recent false ceiling under with extensive water streaking with many panels bowed and expanded by water.

Above the false ceiling towards the rear near the source of dampness there are a few cracks and small holes in the ceiling where water has percolated through. Behind the bar area are beer pumps and cooling apparatus with mains water supply for glass washing.

Walls — Papered and painted — condition generally good.

Floor — whole area parquet flooring about a quarter of an inch thick probably on sheet material. Clearly this was affected by a considerable volume of water as there are various sections dotted all over which are lifting and parquet material has become loose or is missing.

Decorations to the main area are generally reasonable but in reinstating the floor, checking electrics etc., a certain amount of disturbance would need to be made good.

Store rooms

Ceiling — generally satisfactory

Walls — plastered but patches of blown plaster from inherent dampness to the front and partly to side adjacent to number 89.

Floor — old linoleum probably on sheet material, lifting in places as a result of old dampness. This area is used mainly for storage. No apparent damage from the burst water pipe.

Office

Ceiling — plaster painted white — condition generally satisfactory.

Walls — wallpapered. Condition generally satisfactory and no apparent water damage.

Floor — carpet on concrete floor. Worn in places.

Decorations — fair only with some evidence of wear and tear.

Small Back Addition

Rear lobby

Ceiling — plasterboard — some of this is missing as a result of water damage also damaged plaster above the flush door and frame leading to the middle section and this area will need to be hacked off, rendered and set. Allow for renewing ceiling to this area and treating timbers above. Right-hand party wall covered with wall boarding. Bottom section rotted away clearly from recent water damage and the boards are noticeably warped from water damage and will need to be renewed.

Floor — blue tiles on sheet material — water damaged in places, therefore allow to take up and renew.

Ladies' lobby/wash basin and WC

Ceiling — plastered — surface lifting in places — allow for repair and redecoration.

Walls — stained by water and need redecorating

Floor — water damage in places to PVC tiles on concrete — strip and relay.

Gents' lobby/wash basin and WCs

Ceiling — plaster on concrete — make good where cracked and damaged by water ingress and redecorate.

Walls the WC areas are fully tiled and various sections are lifting as a result of water damage. Wall plastering at low level has blown as a result of dampness and the plaster between the WC doors has partly washed away as a result of dampness also extending between the lobby door and WC door — therefore allow 100% strip, render, set and fully tile WCs together with new splashback to wash basin and renew enclosure to wash basin which is water damaged.

Redecorate the whole of this area.

Floor — quarry tiles on concrete — appears satisfactory.

Electrics — there is some damage and disturbance to electrical wiring to the lobby and gents' WCs which will need to be renewed and to the ladies' lavatory where there was extensive water damage — it is likely that electrics may be affected and would need to be checked and properly reinstated where necessary.

I understand my duty to the court and have complied with that duty in compiling this report.

I believe that the facts I have stated in this report are true and that the opinions I have expressed are correct.

Should you require any further information or advice, please do not hesitate to let me know.

Signed:

CHRIS HODGES F.R.I.C.S.

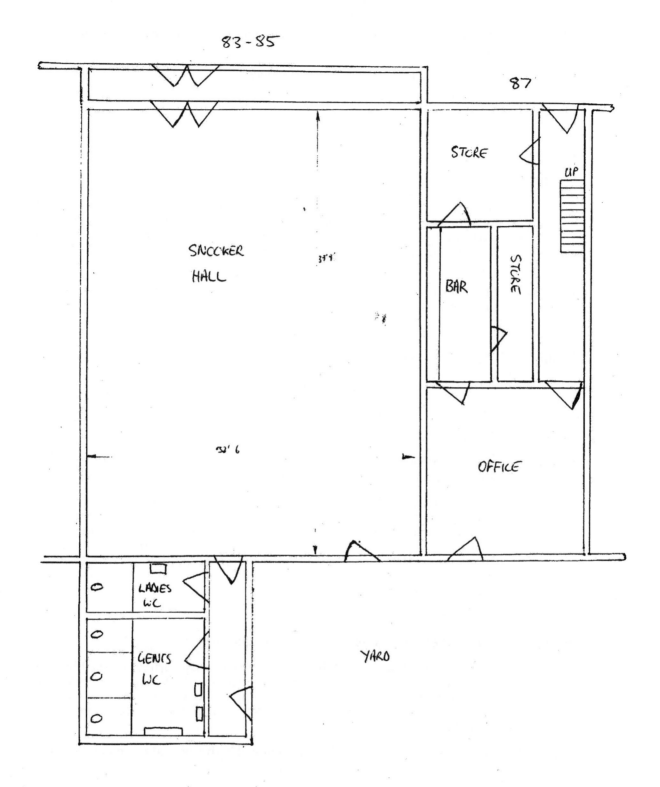

83-85

87

STORE

UP

SNOOKER
HALL

BAR

STORE

OFFICE

LADIES
WC

GENTS
WC

YARD

GROUND FLOOR

83-87 LEEDS ROAD, WAKEFIELD

SKETCH PLAN

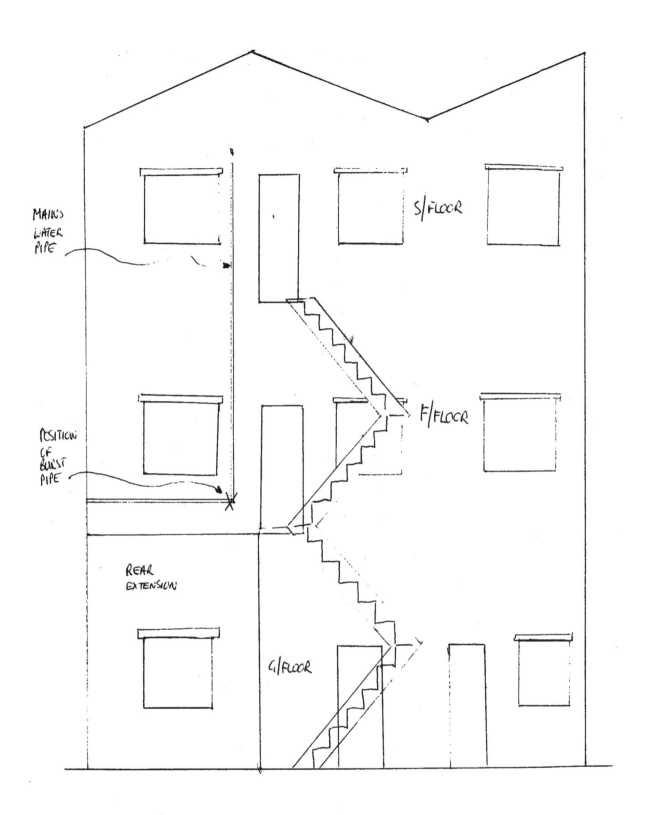

MAINS
WATER
PIPE

POSITION
OF
BURST
PIPE

REAR
EXTENSION

S/FLOOR

F/FLOOR

G/FLOOR

SKETCH OF REAR ELEVATION
83-87 LEEDS ROAD, WAKEFIELD
NOT TO SCALE

Extract

LEGAL SERVICES COMMISSION

COMMUITY LEGAL SERVICE CERTIFICATE

Assisted person: Mr Henry George Mainwaring

Level of service: Full representation

Description: To defend a claim in negligence brought by Anthony Malcolm Lowe seeking damages arising from an alleged flood at 83–87 Leeds Road, Wakefield, West Yorkshire, WF4 1AP between 23rd and 30th December 2000.

Conditions: It is a condition that the solicitor shall report to the area office if profit costs disbursements and counsel's fees exceed £2,500.

Limitations: Limited to all steps to track allocation, disclosure and asking Part 35 questions to experts, and to obtaining written advice from an independent advocate with higher rights of audience on merits.

12.12.01

16.2.1 **CAP IN ACTION**

Notes for advice on merits

STAGE 1   THE CONTEXT OF THE CASE

(1)   THE STAGE OF THE PROCEEDINGS

(a)   What steps have been taken?
Particulars of Claim, Defence, Request for Further Information served.
Copy Surveyor's Report prepared for Claimant.
Limited Community Legal Service Certificate granted to Defendants on 12.12.01.

(b)   Your Instructions
To advise on merits and quantum in order to:
- Advise on prospects of success.
- Identify further information necessary.
- Remove limitation from Community Legal Service certificate.
- Fulfil Bar Council's Guidelines. (See Code of Conduct: Miscellaneous Guidance.)

(2)   UNDERSTANDING THE PROBLEM

Defendants' business now closed down. Main remaining asset is their home. They are anxious that if they cannot defend action at trial, any award of damages may be enforced against their home. Certificate limited to steps to disclosure and exchange of witness statements.

(3)   COLLECTING THE FACTS

Only new sources of information are the Response to the Request for Further Information and the report of the Claimant's Surveyor. See below at 2(b)(1).

STAGE 2   ANALYSIS OF ISSUES AND EVIDENCE

(a)   THE ISSUES

(1)   THE LEGAL AND FACTUAL ISSUES

See Particulars of Claim, paragraphs 3, 4, 5, 6 and 7 and Response to the Request for Further Information, and Defence, paragraphs 2, 3, 4, 5 and 6. See also **16.1.1** above and (b)(1) below.

(b)   THE EVIDENCE

(1)   THE STRENGTH OF THE CASE ON EACH ISSUE

Note: Claimant bears burden of proof on each issue.

(a)   Issue (i) Responsibility for maintaining pipes: Depends on construction of lease: Claimant will rely on fact that no express covenant to repair on part of landlord. However, case law favours construction in support of Defendants (implied covenants to repair, contra proferentem). Terms of lease ambiguous (clause 2(6) of the tenants' covenants, paragraph 4 of preamble, Schedule Part I and Part III).

(b)   Issue (ii) Insulation of the pipes: Dispute between C. Hodges' report and statement of Mr Mainwaring reported by wife. Report of CH not contemporaneous and difficult to interpret. Need to get further statement from Mr Mainwaring and plumber called to repair pipe on 30.12. Need to refer CH's report to Mr Mainwaring to confirm location of burst pipe or identify it.

(c) Issue (iii) Knowledge of Defendants: Claimant's allegations in Response to the Request for Further Information need answering by Defendants, further information needed from Defendants as to knowledge of state of pipes, access to pipes, etc.

(d) Issue (iv) Causation of pipe bursting: Claimant will need to establish why pipe burst, i.e., because of failure to insulate?

(e) Issue (v) Effect of flood on Claimant's premises: Report of C. Hodges shows water damage on ground floor but inconclusive on causation of this. Several potential weaknesses, e.g., entry point of water, alternative reasons for damage. Defendant will need to instruct own surveyor to report.

(f) Issue (vi) Heads of damage: No evidence/detail of losses given. Possible alternative reason for closure of business — financial difficulty. In any event Claimant cannot claim both lost profits and lost value (double recovery).

(g) Issue (vii) The amounts of each head: Need to await disclosure for Claimant's accounts. Will also need inspection of Claimant's financial books and records, and to consider instructing an expert accountant to form an opinion on the value of the Claimant's business. Alternatively, could wait for the Claimant's accountant's report to see if it can be agreed without incurring the expense of a report on behalf of the Defendants. A further alternative would be to apply for an order that the Claimant answer Request No. 8. Details of the £9,503.40 damage to property claim need to be sought on disclosure, or should be given in exchange of witness's statements or expert reports. Need to consider seeking permission or an order for an expert (builder or surveyor) to inspect the ground floor for the purpose of giving evidence on the damage, cause and cost of repairs.

(2) GAPS AND AMBIGUITIES

Defendants should be asked to confirm position of burst pipe identified by C. Hodge. Further Information identified at 2(b)(1) above needed from Defendants, also witness statement from Plumber and report from Surveyor on behalf of Defendants. Unclear whether Paula, who helped dry out Defendants' premises, can assist on any of these issues, so a witness statement should be taken from her to find out what she knows.

Details of Claimant's losses etc. should be received on disclosure, if not may need to consider alternative options to secure information.

STAGE 3 PRESENTATION

(1) THE CHOSEN THEORY

Claimant overstating events, hoping to solve present financial crisis by blaming Defendants. Defendants not to blame and Claimant will not be able to establish either fault or loss. See **16.1.1**, Stage 2(3) above.

(2) SUPPORTING THE LEGAL FRAMEWORK

List of Authorities.

Construction of Lease: *Cockburn* v *Smith* [1924] 2 KB 119
Hope Brothers v *Cowan* [1913] 2 Ch 312
Quantum: *C. R. Taylor (Wholesale) Ltd* v *Hepworth Ltd* [1977] 1 WLR 659

(3) CARRYING OUT INSTRUCTIONS

Plan opinion. See *Opinion Writing Manual*.

(See **16.3** for completed Opinion.)

16.3   Brief for Application

<u>IN THE WAKEFIELD COUNTY COURT</u>   Claim No. WF01 048972

BETWEEN:–

ANTHONY MALCOLM LOWE   <u>Claimant</u>

-AND-

(1) HENRY GEORGE MAINWARING

(2) ELSA ANN MAINWARING   <u>Defendants</u>

BRIEF TO COUNSEL TO APPEAR ON CASE MANAGEMENT
CONFERENCE, 2.00 pm, Tuesday 7th May 2002

Counsel has herewith the papers previously before Counsel [not reproduced] together with:

9.   Counsel's Opinion dated 15th April 2002;

10.   Claimant's List of Documents;

11.   Defendants' List of Documents [not reproduced];

12.   Documents disclosed by Claimant on Disclosure;

13.   Application Notice;

14.   Witness Statement in support, and exhibits thereto;

Instructing Solicitors have settled the Application for Specific Disclosure and for an Order granting access to the Claimant's premises for the Defendants' surveyor. The Claimant has been very uncooperative on the questions of disclosure and obtaining access, and Counsel is asked to press not only for the Orders sought but also for suitable Costs Orders against the Claimant.

This application has been listed to be heard at the same time as a case management conference.

If counsel has any questions prior to the hearing, please do not hesitate to contact Miss Pemberton of Instructing Solicitors.

Lowe v Mainwaring

OPINION

1. I have been asked to advise Mr and Mrs Mainwaring, who are tenants of the first and second floors of 83–87 Leeds Road, Wakefield, on their prospects of successfully defending the claim brought against them by Mr Anthony Lowe (the Claimant), a tenant of the ground floor of the same building. Mr and Mrs Mainwaring have been granted public funding by the Legal Services Commission to continue to defend this action. However, at present, the grant of public funding is limited to proceedings up to asking Part 35 questions to experts, and to obtaining Counsel's advice on merits.

2. The action arose as a result of a burst water pipe situated on the outside of the building on the first-floor level and which it is alleged caused water to flood in and onto the ground-floor premises in December 2000, thereby allegedly causing considerable damage. The Claimant is alleging that Mr and Mrs Mainwaring are responsible for the upkeep of the pipe and that the pipe burst as a result of their negligence and that they are therefore responsible for the damage. I have not as yet seen Mr or Mrs Mainwaring in conference due to the ill-health of Mr Mainwaring but I have read a letter from Mrs Mainwaring explaining the relevant circumstances and the report of Mr Chris Hodges, the Claimant's surveyor.

3. In my opinion Mr and Mrs Mainwaring have good prospects of successfully defending this action. However, an initial question is to identify precisely where the burst pipe was located. Mr Mainwaring discovered the burst, so he should be asked to confirm that the location of the burst as identified by Mr Hodge in his report is correct. For the purpose of this opinion I have assumed this is so. The Claimant has provided very little evidence on quantum, so I am only able to give limited advice on the damages aspect of the case at this stage.

The Duty to Repair

4. Responsibility for the condition of the external water pipe in this case depends on the terms of the lease between the Mainwarings and their landlord, Margaret Pike dated 18 October 1995. I am however unable to give definite advice on whether the Mainwarings are responsible for the pipe, because the terms of the lease concerning who is responsible for the condition of the external water pipes are ambiguous.

5. By clause 2(6) of the lease the Mainwarings, as tenants of the first and second floors, covenanted 'to keep the whole of the demised premises and the conduits . . . in good and substantial repair and condition'. Conduits are themselves defined in paragraph (4) of the preamble as including supply pipes 'under or upon the demised premises'. The definition of the demised premises in Part 1 of the Schedule refers to 'all that first and second floors of the Building'.

6. On this wording it is unclear whether:

   (a) Paragraph (4) of the preamble includes pipes upon the outside of building as well as those within the premises.

   (b) The demised premises as defined in the Schedule includes pipes fixed to the exterior of those premises.

   (c) The landlord has retained the exterior of the Building and/or the pipes and other installations upon it.

7. In my opinion, a court is likely to construe clause 2(6) in favour of the Mainwarings and limit their obligation to repair and maintain to those conduits which are within the demised premises and for the benefit of the tenant. Being an external pipe, the Mainwarings will have no liability for its condition. There are two reasons.

First, terms in a lease are usually interpreted against the grantor and for the benefit of the tenant. Secondly the courts have long held that where the lease contains no express provision as to parts of a building, particularly where those parts are for the common benefit of a number of tenants, those parts will generally not be considered to be included in the demise. They will consequently remain in the control of the landlord who will therefore be under an obligation to take reasonable care of the parts of the premises retained (*Cockburn* v *Smith* [1924] 2 KB 119).

8. However, a demise of a floor in a building has in the past been held to include the exterior of a wall (*Hope Brothers* v *Cowan* [1913] 2 Ch 312). A favourable construction of the lease is therefore far from certain, although each lease must be construed on its own wording and case law is of limited value.

9. If the terms of the lease are construed in Mr and Mrs Mainwaring's favour the responsibility for the repair and maintenance of the pipe would be upon the landlord, and the Mainwarings as tenants would not be responsible for any damage that occurred when the pipe burst.

Breach of Duty

10. If it were established that the Mainwarings had any responsibility to insulate or repair the pipe, the Claimant would need to adduce convincing evidence to establish that they had in fact been negligent and that it was their negligence which caused the pipe to burst.

11. The allegation that the pipe was not insulated adequately or at all is disputed by the Mainwarings. However, the surveyor's report prepared for the Claimant states that on the date of his visit, the upper section of the water pipe at the rear of the property, was only partly lagged and not to a good standard, and that 'below the iron staircase' there was no lagging at all. As the report refers both to an iron staircase at the rear and an old iron fire escape, and the only staircase on the attached plan seems to extend over the whole height of the building, I have found it difficult to identify the area 'below the iron staircase' from the plan.

12. As requested above, could my Instructing Solicitors ask the Mainwarings to clarify the position of the pipe which burst and also the position of the staircase or staircases at the rear of the building? Obviously it is of the utmost importance to be absolutely clear where the burst pipe was located.

13. Mr Mainwaring's witness statement will need to describe in detail the insulation on the pipes at the rear of the building on 30 December 2000. He had apparently told his wife that all the pipes were insulated. This should also be covered in the witness statement from the plumber who repaired the pipe. Mr and Mrs Mainwaring should also be asked to comment on the ease of access to the pipe. A witness statement should also be taken from Paula (I have not been given her full name), who I see assisted in drying out the Mainwarings' premises.

14. If satisfactory answers are given to the points above I think it will be possible to refute the allegations of any negligence on the part of the Mainwarings in the event that they are held to have any responsibility for the condition of the pipe.

Causation

15. To date it has not been possible to obtain further details of the claim for loss and damage from the Claimant, but it seems very unlikely that he will be able to prove that these losses arose as a result of flood damage from the burst pipe.

16. The plumber who was called to fix the pipe on 30 December told the Mainwarings that he considered that the water may not have been escaping for more than a few hours. Further, Mrs Mainwaring was of the view that their premises took the brunt of the flood.

17.   The extensive claim made by the Claimant seems strangely in contrast with the Mainwarings' statement that the total loss they suffered from the flood was some £500 (taking into account the £300 salvaged). It is also difficult to reconcile the surveyor's plan with the presence of water inside the Mainwarings' premises.

18.   Mr Hodges' report, on the other hand, does describe considerable water damage to the ceiling and to the floor of the snooker hall. There appears from the report to be no water damage to the walls even at the point water from the burst pipe would be expected to have entered the hall, i.e., from the flat roof of the extension. The rear addition which includes a rear lobby and ladies' and gents' WC's appears to be badly affected by water damage. Mr Hodges has given his opinion that the water damage must have been caused by the defective pipe as he could see no other water pipes to the ground floor. There must, however, be a water supply for the WCs in the back addition. A survey of the ground floor on behalf of the Defendants will be necessary to try to discover accurately the condition of the Claimant's premises and whether the condition of the premises is consistent with any cause other than water penetration from the burst pipe.

19.   It will in due course be necessary for a detailed statement to be obtained from the Mainwarings and the plumber about these matters. As yet, not having seen Mr and Mrs Mainwaring in conference, I am unable to comment on the reliability of their evidence, but the only issues on which this may be relevant are on whether the pipe in question was lagged, whether Mr Hodges has identified the correct pipe and certain aspects on the Claimant's damages claim (see below). The report of Mr Hodges, however, leaves a number of matters uncertain. It is my opinion that the Claimant has a number of difficulties in establishing that the various alleged losses were caused by negligence on the part of the Defendants.

Loss and Damage

20.   The Claimant's claim for loss and damage is in the sum of about £60,000 together with some continuing loss. Of this sum only some £9,503.40 is for damage to the premises themselves. The remainder is alleged to arise from loss of profits and the lost value of the business. It is alleged that the Claimant has ceased trading as a result of the damage from the flood.

21.   The Mainwarings assert, contrary to the Claimant's pleaded case, that the snooker hall on the Claimant's premises has been in operation since the pipe burst. This would suggest that the 'flood' was not as extensive as the Claimant alleges and indeed that the reason the business ceased trading was not because of water damage from the flood. In support of this, Mrs Mainwaring has reported that a bailiff called to serve a distress warrant for arrears of rent which does suggest at the least that other factors may have been operating which affected the financial viability of the business.

22.   The lost value claim would include the profit-making potential of the business, and there is therefore a measure of double recovery in the Claimant's claim. The Claimant will not succeed in recovering all the heads of claim and will instead have to choose between the cost of cure together with the loss of profits while the property is being repaired, or the diminution in value of the business.

23.   The court will in general choose the measure of damages which provides fair compensation for the Claimant for any loss suffered but which results in the least damages being payable (*C.R. Taylor (Wholesale) Ltd* v *Hepworth Ltd* [1977] 1 WLR 659). At the present time it is uncertain whether, by the time of trial, the claim for lost profits would exceed that of lost value, but it is likely that the lost value claim of £45,000 would be taken as the maximum amount of the potential claim.

Public Funding

24.   I consider that the prospects of the Defendants in successfully defending them-selves from all liability to the Claimant are Good (Category B). Even if the issue of

liability were to be found against them I consider that on the limited information now before me there are serious issues as to quantum. The claim as formulated in the Particulars of Claim has a present value of £65,000 odd (including one year's alleged continuing loss of profits). That is considerably more than double the estimated costs of defending (see below). The cost-benefit criteria for public funding therefore appear to be satisfied, and I recommend the continuation of Legal Services Commission assistance for both Mr and Mrs Mainwaring.

25.   Once witness statements have been exchanged and disclosure has taken place, it will be necessary to reassess whether the Claimant will be able to adduce evidence in support of his sizeable claim for loss. In my view the limitation on the certificates should be altered to cover the exchange of witness statements and filing of listing questionnaires, and it would be sensible to increase the financial condition to (say) £7,500 or £10,000.

15th April 2002   BRIAN BARRISTER
Temple Court

IN THE WAKEFIELD COUNTY COURT   Claim No. WF01 048972

BETWEEN:-

ANTHONY MALCOLM LOWE   Claimant

-and-

(1) HENRY GEORGE MAINWARING

(2) ELSA ANN MAINWARING   Defendants

List of Documents

Standard Disclosure

Notes:
The rules relating to standard disclosure are contained in Part 31 of the Civil Procedure Rules.
Documents to be included under standard disclosure are contained in Rule 31.6.
A document has or will have been under your control if you have or have had possession, or a right of possession, of it or a right to inspect or take copies of it.

Disclosure Statement

I state that I have carried out a reasonable and proportionate search to locate all the documents which I am required to disclose under the order made by the court on 10th January 2002.

(I did not search for documents—
1.   Pre-dating 1995
2.   Located elsewhere than my office and that of my solicitors
3.   In categories other than the lease of the premises, repairs arising out of the flood, and papers relating to the conduct of this claim.)

I certify that I understand the duty of disclosure and to the best of my knowledge I have carried out that duty. I further certify that the list of documents set out in or attached to this form, is a complete list of all documents which are or have been in my control and which I am obliged under the court order to disclose.

I understand that I must inform the court and the other parties immediately if any further document required to be disclosed by Rule 31.6 comes into my control at any time before the conclusion of the case.

(I have not permitted inspection of documents within the category or class of documents (as set out below) required to be disclosed under Rule 31.6(b) or (c) on the grounds that to do so would be disproportionate to the issues in the case.)

Signed: Date: 4th March 2002
Claimant

I have control of the documents numbered and listed here. I do not object to you inspecting them/producing copies.

1.	Lease Claimant and Margaret Pike [not reproduced]	18.10.1995
2.	Estimate Snooker Restorers Ltd	3.1.2001
3.	Letter Claimant to WY Property Management Ltd	15.1.2001
4.	Copy letter WY Property Management to Belsize Loss Adjusters	19.2.2001
5.	Copy letter Belsize Loss Adjusters to WY Property Management	26.2.2001

6.	Copy letter Claimant's solicitors to WY Property Management	5.3.2001
7.	Letter WY Property Management to Claimant's Solicitors	19.3.2001
8.	Copy Letter Belsize Loss Adjusters to WY Property Management	23.3.2001
9.	Letter WY Property Management to Claimant's solicitors	2.4.2001
10.	Correspondence common to both parties [not reproduced]	Various
11.	Statements of case, orders [not reproduced]	Various

I have control of the documents numbered and listed here but I object to you inspecting them:

Communications between the Claimant and his solicitors for the purpose of obtaining or giving legal advice, communications between the Claimant's solicitors and third parties in relation to this action, instructions to, opinions of, and statements of case settled by Counsel.

I object to you inspecting these documents because they are protected by legal professional privilege.

I have had the documents numbered and listed below, but they are no longer in my control.

Originals of copy documents listed as items 1 to 11 above which were last in my control before being posted to their respective addressees.

SNOOKER RESTORERS LIMITED
48 Shaftsbury Road, Leeds, LS3 9IW
Tel: 0113 2879872

ESTIMATE

To:

Repairs and refelting Table 1	£1,350.00
Repairs and refelting Table 2	£850.00
Refelting Table 3	£560.00
Sub-total	£2,760.00
VAT at 17.5%	£483.00
Total	£3,243.00

Date: 3rd January 2001.

Mr Lowe
83–87 Leeds Road
Wakefield
West Yorkshire
WF4 1AP

Topspin Snooker Hall
83–87 Leeds Road
Wakefield
WF4 1AP

Mrs Bainbridge
WY Property Management Limited   15th January 2001

29 Commerce Street
Wakefield
WF1 8FJ

FOR THE ATTENTION OF MRS BAINBRIDGE

Dear Madam,

Re: TOPSPIN SNOOKER HALL, 83–87 LEEDS ROAD, WAKEFIELD

I enclose my insurance claim form together with the two builders' estimates you asked for. I also enclose an estimate from a specialist snooker table repairer with the estimated cost of repairing the felts on the three tables damaged in the flood.

Please pass the claims form and estimates on to the insurance company as quickly as possible. The snooker hall is in a shambles, and I cannot open for business with the place in this state. Could you please impress on the insurance company that this claim is urgent.

Yours sincerely,

Tony Lowe

W Y Property Management Ltd
29 Commerce Street, Wakefield, WF1 8FJ
Tele: 01924 433692

Our ref:	DB/4327
Your ref:	9328721
Date:	19th Feb. 2001

Mr D Beddoes
Belsize Loss Adjusters Ltd
8 Grovelands Road
London
EC4M 6YL

Dear Sirs,

Re: 83–87 Leeds Road, Wakefield

I refer to our telephone conversation this morning.

As I mentioned to you on the telephone, there are two matters arising out of that letter which I find quite extraordinary. The first is that there is a suggestion that if a pipe bursts outside then it is not covered by insurance, and the second is the suggestion that 'the escape of water has served only to bring to light the maintenance problem with the premises'. These suggestions are quite extraordinary and I wonder whether your surveyor has addressed his mind to this claim in any meaningful way.

A great deal of money has been spent in the last 3 years on maintenance of the exterior of the property, and whilst I would not suggest that problems might have arisen, I really cannot accept the proposition that the property had not been adequately maintained.

This is a valid claim, having resulted from an insured risk. Damage caused by a burst pipe is an insured risk.

Also covered under the policy is loss of rent and in that connection we are chasing the tenant for the quarter's rent due 25th December and the tenant is saying, probably quite rightly, that the rent should be paid by the Insurers until reinstatement of the property has taken place. He is also saying that in the event that the Insurers do not meet the claim, then he will be looking to the landlord to meet the claim as she should have had the property adequately maintained and insured.

It seems to me that my Client did have the property adequately maintained and insured, but if the Insurers wish to maintain their present stance and the tenant takes action against my client, then she will be making a claim to the Insurers under the Property Owner's Liability section of the policy. One way or the other therefore the Insurer will have to meet this claim and it seems to me that the claim can best be mitigated if dealt with quickly.

In the circumstances, therefore, can I ask you to take this matter up direct with the Insurer so that a satisfactory conclusion can be arrived at without further delay.

Yours faithfully,

Donna Bainbridge (Mrs) FRICS

Belsize Loss Adjusters Ltd
8 Grovelands Road
London
EC4M 6YL

Telephone: 0207 631 2971　　　**Facsimile: 0207 631 3111**

Date: 26th February 2001

Our ref:　　　9328721　　　Your Ref: DB/4327

Mrs Bainbridge
WY Property Management Ltd
29 Commerce Street
Wakefield
WF1 8FJ

Dear Madam

Re 83–87 Leeds Road, Wakefield

We acknowledge receipt of your letter of 19th February 2001 and comment on its contents as follows.

We have in fact given serious thought to this claim. We confirm that a burst pipe is an insured peril covered by the policy and it was never our suggestion that it was otherwise.

For a valid claim to arise, it must be shown that an insured peril had operated to bring about the damage for which the Insured is claiming. There are two points to make from this.

The first is that the Insured must take reasonable care to maintain his property and to prevent loss. From the information provided regarding this incident, it would appear that the pipe located externally to the premises had burst due to lack of insulation and protection against the elements and the Insured was by this very fact in possible breach of her policy in failing to take reasonable care in the maintenance of her property by failing to insulate the two external main pipes which led to the escape of the water.

Secondly, the policy does not cover damage caused by wear and tear, general weathering or gradual deterioration. Much of what we were shown by way of 'damage' did not appear consistent with having been damaged by water escaping from a burst pipe. In point of fact, there were several areas shown to our representative by Mr Lowe that were clearly by wear and tear.

We would only be too happy to make available a selection of photographs taken by our representative of the premises which in our view shows clear signs that the premises occupied by Mr Lowe are suffering from lack of maintenance. By this we are not suggesting in any way that the Landlord is not performing her repairing obligations or not adequately maintaining her premises but by way of illustrating the problem as we saw it at the time of our visit.

As regards the claim for loss of rent, it is our understanding from having spoken to Mr Lowe that the reason why he has been unable to trade from the premises is not solely due to the water ingress and in any event, the policy will only respond to indemnify the Insured for loss of rent if the Insured had taken all reasonable steps to mitigate her loss.

To date we have yet to receive the Insurer's instructions as to how to proceed with this claim and until then we are unable on behalf of Insurers to accept or deny liability and trust this letter has addressed fully your concerns.

Nevertheless should you wish to discuss any aspect of this matter, please do not hesitate to contact this office in the first instance.

Yours faithfully

Belsize Loss Adjusters

FRASER & COMPANY
SOLICITORS

Bank Chambers
Ripon Road
Wakefield
WF1 9GR
Tele: 01924 782364
Fax: 01924 807243
Ref: TBC/DH/99.0247

Date: 5th March 2001

Dear Sir,

Re: TOPSPIN SNOOKER HALL, 83–87 LEEDS ROAD, WAKEFIELD
Our Client: Mr A. LOWE

We have been instructed on behalf of Mr Lowe.

What progress has been made concerning our client's insurance claim in respect of the flooding on the 23rd–30th December 2000? Pending receipt of funds in respect of the claim our client is unable to reinstate the premises which are not fit for use at the present time.

Yours faithfully,

Fraser & Co.

Mrs Bainbridge
WY Property Management Limited
29 Commerce Street
Wakefield
WF1 8FJ

W Y Property Management Ltd
29 Commerce Street, Wakefield, WF1 8FJ
Tel: 01924 433692

Our ref:	DB/4327
Your ref:	TBC/DH/00.0247
Date:	19th March 2001

WITHOUT PREJUDICE

Messrs Fraser & Co.
Bank Chambers
Ripon Road
Wakefield
WF1 9GR

Dear Sirs,

Re: 83–87 Leeds Road, Wakefield

We thank you for your letter of the 5th March 2001.

We have heard further from the Loss Adjusters regarding the matter and, without going into too much detail at this stage, it does appear that what they are in fact saying is that the items of damage which your Client is claiming are the result of the lack of his maintenance rather than having been damaged by any water penetration.

However, we are arranging a meeting on site with the Loss Adjusters in an endeavour to get to the bottom of the situation and we hope therefore to be able to write to you more comprehensively following that meeting.

Yours faithfully

Donna Bainbridge (Mrs) FRICS

W Y Property Management
29 Commerce Street, Wakefield WF1 8FJ
Tel: 01924 433692

Our Ref: DB/4327
Your Ref: TBC/DH/00.0247

Date: 2nd April 2001

Messrs Fraser & Co.
Bank Chambers
Ripon Road
Wakefield
WF1 9GR

Dear Sirs,

Re: 83–87 Leeds Road, Wakefield

I refer to my letter dated 19th March and enclose a copy of correspondence received from Insurers' Loss Adjusters dated 23rd March 2001.

The contents are not very promising but whilst at the moment they are not prepared to agree to a compromise settlement, we are entering into further discussions in an effort to try and obtain some form of payment here.

As soon as there is any better news to report, I will contact you.

Yours faithfully

Donna Bainbridge (Mrs) FRICS

Belsize Loss Adjusters Ltd
8 Grovelands Road
London
EC4M 6YL

Telephone: 0207 631 2971   **Facsimile: 0207 631 3111**

Date: 23rd March 2001

Our Ref: 9328721   Your Ref: DB/4327

Mrs Bainbridge
WY Property Management Ltd
29 Commerce Street
Wakefield
WF1 8FJ

Dear Mrs Bainbridge,

Re 83–87 Leeds Road, Wakefield

I refer to the above matter and our meeting on Tuesday, the 13th March at 2.30 pm.

I have to advise regretfully, as per my conversation with you, that I was unable to see for myself from my external examination that there has been any real damage to this property.

I have seen both pipes which are alleged to have been the cause of the damage and from my examination cannot see that there is evidence of a burst nor can I see that there has been a recent repair.

I noticed that above the window where the suspended ceiling is alleged to have been damaged by water ingress there has been a recent fitting of a concrete lintel. There is also evidence of recent re-pointing above the lintel.

It does appear to me from the photographic evidence I have in my possession that a lot of the reinstatement works being claimed for by Mr Lowe are of a maintenance nature.

The Lease agreement is clear inasmuch as it places the responsibility upon the tenant to maintain the property and I fear that this has not been done properly.

Yours sincerely,

Belsize Loss Adjusters

Application Notice
You must complete Parts A
and B and C if applicable
Send any relevant fee and the
completed application to the
court with any draft order,
witness statement or other
evidence; and sufficient copies
of these for service on each
respondent

Claim No.	WF01 048972
Claimant	ANTHONY MALCOM LOWE
(including ref)	TBC/DH/00.0247
Defendants	HENRY GEORGE MAINWARING
(including ref)	ELSA ANN MAINWARING
	JTG/A
Date	3rd April 2002

You should provide this information for listing the application

1. Do you wish to have your application dealt with at a hearing?
Yes   No   If yes, please complete 2

2. Time estimate   0 hours   30 mins

Is this agreed by all parties?   Yes   No

Level of Judge   District Judge

3. Parties to be served   Claimant

Part A
We, Godfrey & Co., on behalf of the Defendants intend to apply for an order that:

(1) The Claimant do within 14 days of the date of service of such Order file and serve evidence stating whether the documents specified in the Schedule to this Application are or have at any time been in the Claimant's possession, custody or power, and if not now in his possession, custody or power, when he parted with the same and what has become of them.

(2) Unless the Claimant gives access to the Defendants' surveyor to the Claimant's property at the Ground Floor, 83–87 Leeds Road, Wakefield by 4 pm on the 14th day after the hearing of this application, the Claimant's claim be struck out and judgment entered for the Defendants with costs.

(3) The costs of this application may be provided for.

SCHEDULE

1. Accounts for the years ending 31.7.99; 31.7.00 and 31.7.01
2. Tax returns since 1.1.1999
3. VAT returns since 1.1.1999
4. All accounts books and financial documentation and invoices since 1.1.1999
5. All bank statements since 1.1.1999
6. Insurance claim form about January 2001
7. Builders' estimates (two) about January 2001

because the Claimant has not given full standard disclosure of documents, and has failed to allow the Defendants' surveyor access to the Claimant's premises for the purpose of reporting on the alleged damage to those premises.

Part B
We wish to rely on: tick one box
       the attached (witness statement)(affidavit)   my statement of case
       evidence in Part C overleaf in support of my application
Signed:
Applicant's Solicitor

Address to which documents about this claim should be sent (including reference if appropriate)
Godfrey & Co., 27 Cressey Street, Wakefield, West Yorkshire, WF5 3SL
Ref. JTG/AP

The court office at The Crown House, 127 Kirkgate, Wakefield, W. Yorkshire WF1 1JW is open between 10 am and 4 pm Monday to Friday. Address all communications to the Court Manager and quote the claim number.

Made on behalf of the Defendants
Witness: H.K.Jones
1st Statement of witness
Exhibits: HJK 1
Signed: 3.4.2002
Filed: 2002
Claim No. WF01 048972

IN THE WAKEFIELD COUNTY COURT

BETWEEN:–

ANTHONY MALCOLM LOWE <u>Claimant</u>

-and-

(1) HENRY GEORGE MAINWARING

(2) ELSA ANN MAINWARING <u>Defendants</u>

1. My name is Helen Katherine Jones. I am a Solicitor of the Supreme Court and employed as an Assistant Solicitor by the firm of Godfrey & Co. of 27 Cressey Street, Wakefield, West Yorkshire, WF5 3SL. I have conduct of this claim on behalf of the Defendants. I am duly authorised to make this statement in support of the Defendants' application for specific disclosure.

2. I have read a copy of the List of Documents served in this claim on behalf of the Claimant dated the 4th March 2002. It is my belief that this List does not disclose all the documents that are or have been in the Claimant's custody relating to the matters in question in this claim.

3. In my belief the Claimant has or at some time has had in his custody the various documents and classes of documents specified or described in the Schedule to the present Application Notice (referred to below as 'the Schedule').

4. My belief is based on the following matters. It is common ground that the Claimant was running a business at his premises, and the Claimant alleges this business has been damaged by the alleged flood. Anyone running a business will keep accounts (item 1 in the Schedule) and will keep books, invoices and other documentation (item 4 in the Schedule). He will be required to file tax returns and in all probability VAT returns (items 2 and 3 in the Schedule). Unless the business is very small (and the Claimant alleges that it generated profits, not turnover, of £6,500 per annum) it will need to operate a bank account, not least for paying in cheques. Therefore item 5 in the Schedule is likely to apply. The insurance claim form and estimates (items 6 and 7 in the Schedule) are expressly referred to in the letter dated 15th January 2001 referred to in the List of Documents at item 3. I refer to the bundle of correspondence marked '**HKJ 1**' and a true copy of that letter appears at page 1 of the exhibit.

5. The documents and classes of documents sought in this application all relate to matters in question in this claim. Items 1 to 5 of the Schedule relate to the Claimant's claim for lost profits and the loss of the value of his business, item 6 relates to the issue of liability and is also relevant to the claim on quantum, and item 7 relates to the claim for the cost of putting right the alleged damage.

6. At pages [2] to [4] of my exhibit are letters to the Claimant's solicitors requesting the disclosure sought in this application and access for the Defendant's surveyor, and the Claimant's solicitor's response.

7. I ask the Court to grant the orders sought in this application.

Statement of truth

I believe that the facts stated in this witness statement are true.

Signed: *Helen Katherine Jones*

Date: 3rd April 2002

Exhibit HKJ 1

Topspin Snooker Hall
83–87 Leeds Road
Wakefield
WF4 1AP

Mrs Bainbridge
WY Property Management Limited   15th January 2001

29 Commerce Street
Wakefield
WF1 8FJ

FOR THE ATTENTION OF MRS BAINBRIDGE

Dear Madam,

Re: TOPSPIN SNOOKER HALL, 83–87 LEEDS ROAD, WAKEFIELD

I enclose my insurance claim form together with the two builders' estimates you asked for. I also enclose an estimate from a specialist snooker table repairer with the estimated cost of repairing the felts on the three tables damaged in the flood.

Please pass the claims form and estimates on to the insurance company as quickly as possible. The snooker hall is in a shambles, and I cannot open for business with the place in this state. Could you please impress on the insurance company that this claim is urgent.

Yours sincerely,

Tony Lowe

[1]

GODFREY & Co.,

27 Cressey Street, Wakefield, West Yorkshire, WF5 3SL
Tel: 01924 985579   Fax: 01924 985877

Our Ref: JTG/AP
Your Ref: TBC/DH/00.0247
Date: 18th February 2002

Messrs Fraser & Co.
Bank Chambers
Ripon Road
Wakefield WF1 9GR

Dear Sir,

Re: TOPSPIN SNOOKER HALL, 83–87 LEEDS ROAD, WAKEFIELD

When compiling your List of Documents we would be grateful if you could provide full documentation in support of your client's claims for loss of profits and loss of the value of your client's business. These should include tax and VAT returns, bank statements and accounts.

Our expert surveyor needs to inspect the interior of your client's premises for the purposes of preparing his report, and we should be grateful if you could provide us with dates when this would be convenient to your client.

Yours faithfully,

[2]

FRASER & COMPANY
SOLICITORS

Bank Chambers
Ripon Road
Wakefield
WF1 9GR
Tel: 01924 782364
Fax: 01924 807243

Ref: TBC/DH/00.0247

Your ref: JTG/AP

Date: 20th February 2002

Dear Sir,

Re: TOPSPIN SNOOKER HALL, 83–87 LEEDS ROAD, WAKEFIELD

Further to your letter of the 18th February 2002, we are taking our client's instructions on the second paragraph of your letter. Our List of Documents is currently being prepared, and we hope to be able to serve this in the near future.

Yours faithfully,

Fraser & Co.

[3]

GODFREY & Co.,

27 Cressey Street, Wakefield, West Yorkshire, WF5 3SL
Tel: 01924 985579   Fax: 01924 985877

Our Ref: JTG/AP
Your Ref: TBC/DH/00.0247

Messrs Fraser & Co.   Date: 11th March 2002
Bank Chambers
Ripon Road
Wakefield WF1 9GR

Dear Sir,

Re: TOPSPIN SNOOKER HALL, 83–87 LEEDS ROAD, WAKEFIELD

We acknowledge receipt of the copy documents from your List. We consider your List to be defective in that it does not include the accounts, returns and bank statements that we referred to in our letter of the 18th February 2002. It also does not include the insurance claim form nor the two builders' invoices that your client submitted to the landlord's insurer in about January 2001. Kindly provide us with these documents within the next 7 days, failing which we will be making an application to the Court for an order for specific disclosure.

We still have not heard from you regarding access for our surveyor. Please may we hear from you on this also within 7 days, failing which we will be making an application to the Court.

Yours faithfully,

[4]

16.3.1   CAP IN ACTION

Notes on brief for application

STAGE 1   THE CONTEXT OF THE CASE

CHECKLIST

(1)   The stage of the proceedings

A.   What steps have been taken:

- Statement of case served/filed including request for further information. C's Expert Report served.
- Exchange of lists. Copies of documents exchanged.
- Directions re exchange of expert reports?

APPLICATION ON 9.1.2002

B.   Your Instructions:

- Appear at case management conference and obtain:
  Order for specific disclosure: of specific documents relating to C's loss.
  Order for inspection (for purposes of Ds' expert report).

(2)   Understanding the problem

A.   Cause of the problem:

- Why not get documents? C failed to disclose in list.
- Why not get access? C failed to allow.

B.   Client's objective

- Purpose of Disclosure: to enable proper preparation, encourage settlement and full argument on all issues, e.g., here on what losses actually suffered.
- Purpose of access: to enable Ds' expert to do survey and do report to ascertain damage done by flood and ensure C does not have an unfair advantage by depriving Ds of their own expert evidence.

(3)   Collecting the facts

A.   Application for disclosure

- Chronology:
  10.1.02   Direction requiring disclosure
  18.2.02   Letter D to C — requesting full disclosure of documents in support of financial claim
  20.2.02   Letter C to D — consider List served by D
  4.3.02   C's list of documents
  11.3.02   Letter D to C — asks for additional documents
  3.4.02   Application Notice
- Documents sought.
  Financial Info from 1.1.99: accounts, tax returns, VAT returns, accounts, books, documents, invoices, bank statements (to show loss of profit/value)
  Insurance Claim Jan 01: see letter 15.1.01 in List
  Two estimates: see letter 15.1.01 in List

B. Application for inspection

- Chronology:
18.2.02   First request on behalf of D for access for surveyor
          C's survey done
12.3.02   C's surveyor's report
3.4.02   Application Notice

(4) The legal framework

A. Disclosure: CPR, r. 31

- Procedure: application on notice supported by evidence
- Grounds: party not disclosed document(s) which leads applicant to conclude that documents exist, are disclosable, and within control of C.

B. Inspection: CPR, r. 25.

- Procedure: application on notice
'Unless order' (attached to application for inspection): empowers court to strike out unless order obeyed
- Grounds: party not allowed inspection of property:
— which is subject matter of the cause or to which any question may arise therein
AND
— is in possession of a party to the cause

STAGE 2 ANALYSIS OF LEGAL AND FACTUAL ISSUES AND EVIDENCE

A. Grounds fulfilled – Disclosure:

Application:
— sets out documents sought (schedule)
Evidence — Witness Statement:
— states belief list not complete (para. 2)
— states belief C has had in possession, custody or power (para. 3)
— states grounds for belief (para. 4)
— states relate to matters in question; relate to issues (para. 5)
— exhibits relevant evidence/requests (para. 4, 6)

B. Grounds fulfilled — Inspection:

Application:
— correct address
— seeks access by surveyor
— to inspect to do report
Evidence — Witness Statement:
— exhibits letters requesting access (para. 6)

STAGE 3 PRESENTATION OF THE CASE

A. ORDERS SOUGHT

1. Disclosure: Seek Order: C file/serve written evidence stating whether has docs in schedule in control, if not when parted & what became of them.

2. Inspection: Seek Order: C give access to D's surveyor by 4 pm, 14 days of hearing date to do inspection for survey report. If not strike out.

B. ARGUMENTS

(i) Disclosure: In C's possession etc.
— Docs 1, 4, 5: normal business requirement
— Doc 2: required by Inland Revenue
— Doc 3: required by Customs & Excise
— Docs 1–5: all recent, see para 4 writt st
— Doc 6, 7: C's own documents refer to these: see HKJ1 & C's list
Relate to Issues
— Doc 1–5: C claim loss of profit/value; these docs give information by which can be calculated
— Doc 6: insurance claim form; relevant to liability & quantum
— Doc 7: estimates of repair cost; relevant to quantum
Failed to disclose see list, correspondence — Exhibit

(ii) Inspection
Arguments: Have C expert report exchanged
D request access: see exhibits
C refuse
D no access/no report — denial by C serious issue so C suffer serious penalty if fail

SEVENTEEN

THE CRIMINAL BRIEF

Notes for the Bail Application

Stage 1   The context of the case

    (1)   The stage of the proceedings
    (2)   Understanding the problem
    (3)   Legal framework

Stage 2   Analysis of issues and evidence

    (a)   The Issues

        (1)   Legal and factual issues
        (2)   Potential theory
        (3)   Gaps and ambiguities

    (b)   The evidence

        (1)   The strengths and weaknesses of the case

Stage 3   Preparation of case

    (1)   Chosen theory
    (2)   Carrying out instructions

Stage 1 The context of the case

(1) The stage of the proceedings
(2) Collecting the facts
(3) Agreed and disputed facts
(4) Legal framework

Stage 2 Analysis of issues and evidence

(a) The Issues

(1) The legal and factual issues
(2) The potential theory
(3) Gaps and ambiguities

(b) The Evidence

(1) Strengths and weaknesses of case

Stage 3 Presentation

(1) Chosen theory
(2) Carrying out instructions

Stage 1 The context of the case

(1) Stage of proceedings
(2) Collecting the facts
(3) Agreed/disputed facts
(4) Legal framework

Stage 2 Analysis of issues and evidence

(a) The Issues

(1) Legal and factual issues
(2) Gaps and ambiguities

(b) The Evidence

(1) Strengths and weaknesses of case

Stage 3 Presentation

(1) Chosen theory
(2) Chosen themes
(3) Consider your audience
(4) Carrying out instructions

(i)   The plea and directions hearing
(ii) The trial

17.1   Bail Application

IN THE COLCHESTER MAGISTRATES' COURT

THE QUEEN

Vs

COSTAS GEORGIOU

INSTRUCTIONS TO COUNSEL
TO MAKE A BAIL APPLICATION

Public Funding

Counsel: Ms Nicola Grey

Brown Dingle & Slattery
27 New Buildings,
Chelmsford, Essex

100/NG/19/6/02

IN THE COLCHESTER MAGISTRATES' COURT

THE QUEEN

Vs

COSTAS GEORGIOU

INSTRUCTIONS TO COUNSEL
TO MAKE BAIL APPLICATION
ON 19TH JUNE 2002

Those Instructing apologise for the lateness of the Instructions to Counsel.

The above-named defendant was remanded into custody on 11th June 2002, charged with an offence of Section 18 wounding with intent, following a full bail application having been made by our Mr Johnson. The CPS's objection to bail was on the basis that the client may fail to surrender as he had only recently arrived in this country from Greece and he was charged with a serious offence. We have since then managed to take our client's instructions through the services of an interpreter on matters which might be pertinent to the making of a second bail application — please see proof of evidence enclosed. Furthermore, our client's uncle, Mr Demetri Ionides, who will be at court that morning, has also, since the application made last week, offered to stand surety up to the sum of £1000. Mr Georgiou's girlfriend will also be attending court.

Counsel is instructed to use his best endeavours to obtain bail for the client. Public funding was obtained at the hearing last week and a copy of the Representation Order is enclosed with these instructions.

Brown Dingle & Slattery

<u>COSTAS GEORGIOU</u>

PROOF OF EVIDENCE

I am Costas Georgiou and I live at 27 White Hart Lane Tottenham, N15 OHE. I arrived in this country from Greece at Easter of this year. I am currently studying English at a language school and I hope to go on and study engineering at the University of North London when my English is proficient enough. In order to make ends meet, I help out at my relatives' kebab vans in Colchester on most weekends.

I share the above address with my girlfriend, Anna Constantinou, who holds both a British and a Cypriot passport and who has been living in this country on and off for the past 5 years.

I strongly deny committing this offence. My cousin Alexis Ionides has already told the police that he did it. Given the way that Mr Canning and his friend behaved, it is, in my opinion, hardly surprising that Alexis behaved in the manner that he did.

I have no previous convictions either in this country or in Greece and I have found the past few days in prison to be an awful shock.

Signed: Costas Georgiou   14th June 2002

Colchester Magistrates' Court (Code 12343)

Representation Order No.2656-6088-02

In accordance with the provisions of Section 14 and schedule 3 Access to Justices Act 1999, a right to representation is granted as follows

DATE OF GRANT	12.6.02	DATE OF FIRST HEARING AFTER GRANT (M.C.)	12.6 at 10am
NAME	COSTAS GEORGIOU		
ADDRESS WHERE IN CUSTODY	COLCHESTER POLICE STATION		
NAME AND ADDRESS OF SOLICITOR IF APPOINTED	BROWN, DINGLE & SLATTERY 27, NEW BUILDINGS CHELMSFORD, ESSEX		

TERMS OF REPRESENTATION delete as necessary	MAGISTRATES' COURTS PROCEEDINGS	CROWN COURT PROCEEDINGS
	~~(1) SOLICITOR~~ (2) SOLICITOR AND JUNIOR COUNSEL	(1) SOLICITOR & JUNIOR COUNSEL

PURPOSE OF ORDER	~~(1) Proceedings before Magistrates' Court in connection with (state nature of proceedings)~~ ~~(2) Appealing to the Crown Court against a decision of the said Magistrates' Court~~ ~~(3) Resisting an Appeal to the Crown Court against a decision of the said Magistrates' Court on~~ (4) Proceedings before (both a Magistrates' Court and*) the Crown Court in connection with (state nature of proceedings) Including in the event of a person to whom this order relates being convicted or sentenced in those proceedings, advice and assistance in regard to the making of an appeal to the criminal division of the Court of Appeal. ~~(5) Other (state nature of proceedings)~~

Distribution **Legal Services Commission Copy** **Crown Court** **Solicitor's File** **Court File**	

CRIMINAL DEFENCE SERVICE **Representation order**	**Justices' Clerk** **Officer Designated to Act on Behalf of Justices' Clerk**

17.1.1 **CAP IN ACTION**

Notes for the bail application.

STAGE 1   THE CONTEXT OF THE CASE

    (1) THE STAGE OF THE PROCEEDINGS

        (a) What steps have been taken?

            Defendant arrested. Police bail refused.

            Defendant remanded in Custody on 11.6.02.

            Representation Order granted on 11.6.02.

            Application for bail made by IS refused by magistrates on 11.6.02.

            (Objection to Bail – likely to fail to surrender to custody, only recently arrived in this country from Greece, charged with serious offence.)

        (b) Instructions: to see Defendant and make Bail Application on his behalf at

            Colchester Magistrates' Court on 19.6.02 at 10.00 am.

NOTE: Interpreter will be at Court. Query client's understanding of/use of English.

        (c) Objective: to secure release of Defendant on Bail.

            Will need to show that either prosecution objection without foundation or can be overcome.

    (2) UNDERSTANDING THE PROBLEM

        Defendant in custody since 11.6.02. Last chance for defence to apply for bail as it is second fully argued application before magistrates.

    (3) LEGAL FRAMEWORK

        (i)   Offences against the Person Act 1861, s. 18. (See **Table 14.5**.)

        (ii) Bail Act 1976.

Refusal of bail – if court satisfied that there are substantial grounds for believing that the defendant, if released on bail (whether subject to conditions or not) would . . . fail to surrender to custody etc. (sch. 1, part I, para. 2).

Matters to be considered by court in deciding whether grounds applicable (sch. 1, part I, para. 9):

    (a) nature and seriousness of offence,

    (b) character, antecedents . . . community ties of defendant,

    (c) . . .

    (d) strength of evidence of his having committed offence.

Conditional bail – imposition of such requirements as necessary to secure that defendant surrenders to custody etc. (s. 3), e.g., residence at particular address, reporting to police, curfew, surrender of passport, provision of surety, security for surrender to custody.

Unless material change in circumstances, only two fully argued Bail Applications can be made before magistrates. Thereafter Application must be made to Crown Court (sch. 1, part IIA).

STAGE 2   ANALYSIS OF ISSUES AND EVIDENCE

(a)   The Issues

(1)   LEGAL AND FACTUAL ISSUES

Validity of prosecution objection on basis that Defendant has only just arrived in UK and therefore has limited community ties (and there is therefore a greater incentive to abscond to avoid custodial sentence which is the likely outcome if convicted of such a serious offence). See **Figure 14.3** — Mind-map.

(2)   POTENTIAL THEORY

Law abiding, strong community ties, unlikely to abscond, strong incentive to clear name, intention to strengthen links in UK.

(3)   GAPS AND AMBIGUITIES

(a)   Points to clarify with Client
When did he arrive in UK? Where is he presently studying? Has he enrolled at University? How many relations does he have in UK? How many close relations in Greece? Details of arrest.

How long has Anna Constantinou lived in Tottenham? Is she likely to return to Cyprus in near future? How long has relationship lasted?

(b)   Points to clarify with Mr Ionides
Can he show that he has necessary funds to pay amount promised if defendant absconds, e.g., building society passbook?

His suitability to act as surety, e.g., his influence over his nephew, whether he has any previous convictions.

(b)   The Evidence

(1)   THE STRENGTHS AND WEAKNESSES OF THE CASE

Defendant Greek national, short period of residence in UK, speaks little or no English: inference of risk of return to Greece. Custodial sentence almost certain if convicted.

Has number of close relatives in England, long-term plans to study in England, lives with girlfriend, Anna Constantinou (holder of British passport), in Tottenham: inference that Defendant has strong incentives to remain in UK, stand trial and clear his name — no previous convictions. Probably undesirable to reveal nature of defence to prosecution at this stage.

Likely outcome — Conditional bail. Possible conditions — surrender of passport, condition of residence, Mr D. Ionides to stand as surety.

STAGE 3   PREPARATION OF CASE

(1)   CHOSEN THEORY

See above at Stage 2(2).

(2)   CARRYING OUT INSTRUCTIONS

    (a)   Prepare for Conference

       See *Conference Skills Manual*, **Chapter 5**.

    (b)   Prepare to interview Mr Ionides if Solicitor not present.

    (c)   Prepare for Hearing

       See *Advocacy Manual*, **Chapter 10**.

       Mr Ionides will need to give evidence if acting as surety.

17.2 Advice on Evidence

<u>IN THE CHELMSFORD CROWN COURT</u>   No. T 02/0656

THE QUEEN

v

COSTAS GEORGIOU

INSTRUCTIONS TO COUNSEL
TO ADVISE

---

1.   Counsel will please find enclosed the following:

(a)   Papers previously before Counsel [only back sheet reproduced]

(b)   Indictment

(c)   Prosecution witness statements

(d)   Prosecution Exhibits

(e)   Unused material disclosed by Prosecution on 19 September 2002

(f)   Defendant's proof of evidence.

2.   Those Instructing act on behalf of the Defendant, Mr Costas Georgiou, who was committed to the Crown Court from the Colchester Magistrates' Court on 13th September 2002 under the provisions of Section 6(2) Magistrates' Courts Act 1980. The Defendant is currently on conditional bail, the one condition being to reside with his uncle Mr D. Ionides at 51 Piggott Close, Colchester.

3.   The Prosecution, in view of the statements of their witnesses, have taken the decision to proceed against Mr Georgiou despite the admission of Mr A. Ionides, which they consider unreliable.

4.   Mr Georgiou is the cousin of Mr Ionides. Mr Georgiou has only recently come to live in the United Kingdom and speaks little English. However, both his interview and the statement he has given to those Instructing have been properly translated.

5.   Counsel is instructed to draft Defence Statement and advise those Instructing on what further steps should be taken in preparation for the forthcoming hearing.

Brown, Dingle & Slattery
27 New Buildings
Chelmsford
Essex

<u>IN THE COLCHESTER MAGISTRATES' COURT</u>

THE QUEEN

Vs

COSTAS GEORGIOU

INSTRUCTIONS TO COUNSEL
TO MAKE A BAIL APPLICATION

Public Funding

Corain: Lay JJ
Ms Smith for CPS
Client attends in custody
Full bail app. made
c/bail granted
Conditions: Residence with
D. Ionides at 51 Piggott
Close, Colchester
R on c/bail to 1.8.01
target committal date

N. Grey 20/6/02

Brown, Dingle & Slattery
27 New Buildings
Chelmsford
Essex

100/NG/19/6/02

<u>INDICTMENT</u>　　　　　　　　No. T 02/0656

<u>IN THE CROWN COURT AT CHELMSFORD</u>

THE QUEEN v COSTAS GEORGIOU

COSTAS GEORGIOU IS CHARGED AS FOLLOWS:

<u>STATEMENT OF OFFENCE</u>

Wounding with intent contrary to section 18 of the Offences against the Person Act 1861.

<u>PARTICULARS OF OFFENCE</u>

Costas Georgiou on the 1st day of June 2002 unlawfully wounded Andrew David Canning with intent to do him grievous bodily harm.

Officer of the Court

Statement of Witness (C.J. Act, 1967, s. 9; M.C. Act, 1980, ss. 5A(3)(a) and 5B; M.C. Rules, 1981, r. 70)

STATEMENT OF   ANDREW DAVID CANNING

Age of Witness (date of birth)   Over 18

Occupation of Witness   Casual Labourer

This statement (consisting of 2 pages each signed by me), is true to the best of my knowledge and belief and I make it knowing that, if it is tendered in evidence, I shall be liable to prosecution if I have wilfully stated in it anything which I know to be false or do not believe to be true.

Dated the 5th day of June 2002   Signed: Andrew David Canning
                                                 Signature Witnessed by: Richard Jones

1.   I am Andrew Canning and I live at the address overleaf. I have never been in any very serious trouble with the police before.

2.   At about 7.45 p.m. on Friday 31st May 2002, I arrived at the Nine Bells Public House in the Oakridge Centre, Colchester, having walked from my home address. I was met there 20 minutes later by my girlfriend Jackie Perry. We stayed in the pub until 9 p.m. where I had drunk 1 1/2 bottles of Budweiser. I think that Jackie had a mineral water or an orange juice because she was driving.

3.   At 9 p.m. we got into Jackie's car, which is a white Nissan Micra, L36 YYT, and we drove to the Haven Public House at Thorpe to celebrate the landlord's (Mr Patrick du Pont) birthday. We had met a friend of mine at the Nine Bells and he travelled to Thorpe with us. His name is John Archer.

4.   We stayed at the Haven until about 10.30 p.m. and I had drunk about 3 or 4 bottles of Budweiser whilst there. John was drinking pints of lager. Jackie still drank non-alcoholic drinks. We then drove to the Rabbit Public House at Kirby, arriving at about 10.45 p.m. where I chatted to Lee, the landlord's son. John was chatting to the landlord. We stayed there until just gone midnight where I drank another 2 bottles of Budweiser and a large vodka. John had another pint of lager and a large whisky.

5.   We then drove back towards Colchester. I felt fine, John seemed fine and we decided to get something to eat. I was sat in the back of the Nissan and I fell asleep. I had already given my food order and I knew that we were going to the Shetland Road kebab van in Colchester for a chicken kebab.

6.   The next thing I remember is being woken up by Jackie. We were parked right next to the van. Jackie looked panicky and said, 'The geezer's threatening John with a knife'. I got out of the passenger side, got onto the grass and walked up to the kebab van.

Signed: Andrew David Canning   Signature witnessed by: Richard Jones

CONTINUATION OF STATEMENT OF ANDREW DAVID CANNING

7.   I saw John stood at the right-hand front of the van, backing away. Inside the van I saw 3 people. Directly in the front of the van was a male who I'd seen working there before. I would describe him as a Greek male, about 5'10" to 5'11", with a muscular build, about 16 years looking. He was wearing a shirt with his arms showing. He was waving an orange-handled knife with about a 12" blade. He appeared to be threatening John with the knife. Both he and John were shouting abuse at each other. It was a slanging match but I could not understand what it was all about. The Greek kept saying 'I'm going to cut you'.

Also in the van was a Greek female who was positioned just to the side of the young male. She appeared to be hysterical, and was grabbing the young male by the arms and by the neck. She appeared to be trying to pull him away from the front of the van. The young man kept trying to throw her off.

9.   There was a second Greek male in the van, and he was stood at the back, to the left of centre. He was about 25 years old, about 5'9", and with a wiry build. He had stubble on his face, and eyes that made him look older. His face was drawn. He wasn't involved at this point and I didn't take much notice of him.

10.   I went to the front of the van just left of centre, and started remonstrating with the younger Greek. I rested my left arm on the front of the counter, and waved my right arm towards the young Greek, and was saying, 'Look there's no fucking need for this, put the knife down', and I looked towards the older Greek saying, 'Look, fucking sort him out'. This carried on for less than 30 seconds, and I was concentrating mostly on the young bloke with the knife.

11.   I then saw the older Greek move. He was carrying a large knife in his right hand, the one they use for cutting the meat, with a blade about 16" long. He moved around to my left, and I felt a pressure on my left arm just above my elbow. I didn't see the blow, and I thought he had hit me with the handle or the back of the knife. I moved to try and grab him with my left hand, but he pulled back.

12.   I was then pulled back from the front of the van by one of my friends. At this point I was very angry, and I punched the perspex at the front of the van 4 or 5 times with the right fist, causing a graze to my knuckle. The three in the van were standing back by this point, and the girl was screaming.

13.   I realised I was bleeding from my left arm at this point, but I didn't realise how bad it was. I asked for the car keys off Jackie, and I stormed to the back of the Nissan to fetch the wheelbrace to hit the perspex with. Once at the back of the car I was approached by John and Jackie, and I could see how bad the cut was. I was then taken in the car up to the North Essex Hospital at Colchester. In Accident and Emergency I realised that my jeans and shirt were soaked in blood. I was treated in casualty and then moved up to the ward. I underwent emergency surgery to stitch up the arteries and was later informed that the cut was to the bone. I was discharged on Monday 4th June in the evening. I can't remember any of the doctors' names. My arm is now in a sling and I have no feeling in my lower arm. I am on painkillers and I am likely to be off work for about two months.

14.   On the Friday I was dressed in blue jeans, a cream and red T-shirt and red shoes. John was dressed in blue jeans, a shooting jumper with two dogs on it and a denim jacket. Jackie had boots, ski pants and a beige waistcoat.

Signed: Andrew David Canning   Signature witnessed by: Richard Jones

Statement of Witness (C.J. Act, 1967, s. 9; M.C. Act, 1980, ss. 5A(3)(a) and 5B; M.C. Rules, 1981, r. 70)

STATEMENT OF   JOHN FREDERICK ARCHER

Age of Witness (date of birth)   Over 18

Occupation of Witness   Self-employed Roofer

This statement (consisting of 2 pages each signed by me), is true to the best of my knowledge and belief and I make it knowing that, if it is tendered in evidence, I shall be liable to prosecution if I have wilfully stated in it anything which I know to be false or do not believe to be true.

Dated the 6th day of June 2002   Signed: John Archer
                                            Signature witnessed by: Richard Jones

1.   I am John Archer and I live at the address overleaf. I have been in trouble with the police before but that was some time ago.

2.   At 8.10 p.m. on Friday 31st May 2002 I went to the Nine Bells Public House in the Oakridge Centre, Colchester. Inside I met Andrew Canning, a friend from the pub. After 10 or 20 minutes, Andrew's girlfriend Jackie arrived. I had a pint of light and Kronenburg and Andrew had a bottle of Budweiser. I'm not sure what Jackie was having.

3.   The pub was quiet, and the three of us decided to travel to the Haven Public House at Thorpe. We travelled in Jackie's car and arrived there between 9 and a quarter past. Andy knows the landlord and it was his birthday. We stayed there until about 10 or 10.30 p.m. I drank 3 pints of Stella lager, Andy had 3 bottles of Budweiser. Jackie was on soft drinks and she also had a meal.

4.   We left and went to the Rabbit Public House at Kirby. I know the landlord, Roger Mates. He used to be a gamekeeper. We stayed there until about half past midnight, talking to the landlord and friends. I drank 2 pints of Lowenbrau and a large whisky and coke. Andy had another couple of bottles of Bud, and a couple of large whiskies. Jackie stayed on soft drinks.

5.   We left and got into Jackie's car and we decided to go and get a kebab. I sat in the front passenger seat and Andy was sat in the back. We drove to the kebab van in Shetland Road, Colchester, which is the one that we usually use. We parked up next to the kebab van and myself and Jackie got out. I think Andy was asleep in the back at this stage.

6.   I went to the front of the kebab van, and I could see that there were 3 people inside. There was a male, about 18 or 19 years old, smooth skin, standing just right of centre, from whom I was to order. I've seen him working there before. Behind him was a girl, sat on the bar at the back, young looking, wearing an orange T-shirt and jeans. I've seen her working there before as well. The third person was standing to the left, next to the kebab on the spit. He looked about 25ish, with stubble on his face, about the same height as the younger one, and the same build. He was carrying a large knife and was cutting meat.

Signed: John Archer   Signature witnessed by: Richard Jones

CONTINUATION OF STATEMENT OF JOHN ARCHER

7.   I stepped up and said, 'I'll have a small chicken kebab'. Jackie asked for a large mixed. I spoke to the younger Greek, who then spoke to his mate by the meat, who then started cutting up the chicken. The younger Greek was carrying what looked like a steak knife, with an orange handle and a twelve-inch blade. The older Greek had a wooden-handled knife with a two-foot blade.

8.   After I'd ordered, the younger Greek turned to the girl and spoke to her in a foreign language. I thought that they were talking about me and I said, 'If you've got anything to say about me, say it in English'. With that he said, 'I wasn't fucking talking to you, I was talking to the girl'. He turned to me and brandished his knife in his right hand. He waved it around in front of my face, and I stepped back. He was shouting and abusive and I was abusive back.

9.   During the slanging match I noticed Andrew had arrived. By this time the young girl was trying to hold the young Greek back, and she was hysterical. Andrew leant on the van with his left arm, and started pointing at the young Greek who was arguing with me. He said, 'Put the knife down, you're not going to use it, so you might as well put it down'.

10.   All of a sudden, I saw the older Greek move forward from the left-hand side, and chop down on to Andrew's left arm with the large knife. I saw it strike just before his elbow, and I saw the flesh open up. It started bleeding almost immediately. I saw Andy punch the van twice with his right fist as I went across to pull him away. We tied some clothing around his arm, and got him in the car, and took him straight up to hospital.

11.   That night I was wearing a pair of black jeans, Doc Marten shoes and a blue woollen jumper with two dogs and a man embroidered on the front. I am of stocky build and at the time was sporting a day's growth of stubble.

Signed: John Archer   Signature witnessed by: Richard Jones

Statement of Witness (C.J. Act, 1967, s. 9; M.C. Act, 1980, ss. 5A(3)(a) and 5B; M.C. Rules, 1981, r. 70)

STATEMENT OF   JACQUELINE ELIZABETH PERRY

Age of Witness (date of birth)   Over 18

Occupation of Witness   Trainee Hairdresser

This statement, (consisting of 2 pages each signed by me), is true to the best of my knowledge and belief and I make it knowing that, if it is tendered in evidence, I shall be liable to prosecution if I have wilfully stated anything which I know to be false or do not believe to be true.

Dated the 6th day of June 2002   Signed: Jacqueline Perry
                                            Signature witnessed by: Richard Jones

1.   I am Jackie Perry, and I live at the address overleaf. I am the girlfriend of Andrew Canning, and we have a two and half month old son. I have no previous convictions.

2.   At 1945 hrs on Friday 31st May 2002 I drove to the Nine Bells public house, Oakridge, Colchester, where I met Andrew and a friend called John Archer was also there. I was driving a white Nissan Micra, index number L36 YYT, and I was wearing black ski pants and a cream waistcoat. I had an orange juice. Andrew drank one or two bottles of Budweiser. John had one Kronenberg top whilst I was there.

3.   We left at about 8.45 p.m. and I drove to the Haven public house at Thorpe. We were going to have a meal there, and it was Patrick, the landlord's birthday. I had something to eat, but Andrew and John didn't. Andrew had one or two bottles of lager, I think, and John about the same.

4.   We left the Haven about 10 or half 10, and I drove us to the Rabbit public house at Kirby. John said that it was a good pub and he knew the landlord. I played on the fruit machine while Andrew and John spoke to the landlord. I think both had a pint of lager each, followed by a short each. We finally left the Rabbit shortly after midnight and got back into the car. Andrew got into the back. As we travelled back we decided to go for a kebab at the van in Shetland Road, Colchester. I drove into the road and pulled up next to the van.

5.   Andy didn't want anything to eat, and he offered me his shirt to put on because it was cold. It was a denim shirt which was mine anyway. He then tried to go to sleep, while myself and John got out. There were 3 people just getting their kebabs in front of us before they walked off. I think there were 2 girls and a boy.

6.   There were 3 people in the caravan. The first was about 5'11", clean shaven, about 18 to 20 years old, wearing a T-shirt and jeans. I've seen him working there before. The second male was shorter, about 5'8", about 24 years old. He had stubble, and was wearing a pastel vest. The third was a female, wearing a yellow T-shirt.

7.   John ordered a large kebab from the younger man, who then turned to me, and I asked for a large mixed kebab. I was standing on the grass waiting. The younger man then turned to the girl and started talking in a foreign language. They were laughing and looking at John.

John said, 'What was that mate?'

Signed: Jacqueline Perry   Signature witnessed by: Richard Jones

CONTINUATION OF STATEMENT OF JACQUELINE PERRY

The younger man replied, 'Private conversation'

John said, 'What are you talking about?'

He replied, 'It's none of your business'

The argument then escalated, and both began swearing at each other, and then I saw the man pick up an orange-handled knife with a 14″ blade, which he held high in his right hand, and said, 'Just fuck off mate, just leave'.

8.   John laughed when he picked the knife up, and I could see that the girl was now crying, seated in the corner. The older man was still stood over by the meat and looked upset. I got scared and went to get Andrew. I banged on the window and he got out. Andrew walked across to the left-hand side of the van, and I stood about six feet behind him, just to the left. John and the younger man were still arguing with each other to the right-hand side of the van. By this time the young girl had got up, and was trying to pull the young man back from behind, and I think he pushed her off. She became more hysterical.

9.   Andrew tends to use his arms to talk, and they were on the ledge as he talked to the older man. The older man was now holding a large knife in his hand. It was the long one that they use for cutting the kebab. Andy said, 'You're not going to use that, just put it down'. I don't know who he was talking to. The next thing I could see was blood coming from Andrew's left arm. The older man was just in front of him. I could see a deep gash across Andrew's arm. I grabbed hold of John and pulled him towards Andrew. John grabbed Andrew, and as he pulled away, he punched the van.

10.   I took off my shirt, and it was wrapped around Andy's arm. He then went to the back of the car, where I persuaded him to get into the car, and drove him to Colchester Hospital.

Signed: Jacqueline Perry   Signature witnessed by: Richard Jones

Statement of Witness (C.J. Act, 1967, s. 9; M.C. Act, 1980, ss. 5A(3)(a) and 5B; M.C. Rules, 1981, r. 70)

STATEMENT OF   P.C. 250 RICHARD JONES

Age of Witness (date of birth)   Over 18

Occupation of Witness   Police Constable

This statement, (consisting of 1 page signed by me), is true to the best of my knowledge and belief and I make it knowing that, if it is tendered in evidence, I shall be liable to prosecution if I have wilfully stated in it anything which I know to be false or do not believe to be true.

Dated the 5th day of June 2002   Signed: Richard Jones
                                        Signature witnessed by: Thomas Bright

1.   At 1.25 a.m. on Saturday 1st June 2002 I was on uniformed duty in a marked police car with PC 807 Smith, when we responded to an assault allegation, the location being given as the kebab van at Popley Way, Colchester. At 1.32 a.m. we arrived at the kebab van which was in fact in Shetland Road. The shutters on the kebab van were up, and the occupant of the van could be clearly seen in the street lighting and interior lighting of the van.

2.   I went to the front of the van and spoke to one of the occupants, a man I now know to be Alexis Ionides. Also in the kebab van were a female crying, Sophia Ionides, and a second male, Costas Georgiou. The female, who was standing on the right-hand side of the van as I looked at it, by the door, was very upset. Alexis Ionides stood next to her, but nearer to the front counter and he spoke to both myself and PC Smith. The male Costas Georgiou stood on the left side of the van next to the kebab meat. I did not speak to this male, as Alexis Ionides told me that he could not speak English.

3.   Alexis Ionides was very excitable and told me that he had an argument with a customer some 15 minutes earlier. He stated that 3 to 4 males approached the kebab van, and a fat male, quite tall, about 30 years old, with a beard, who was drunk, began telling him not to talk with Sophia Ionides in their own language. Mr Ionides refused to serve the fat male, and as a result says that the fat male punched him on the nose, but did not cause him any injury. He then said that the fat male tried to climb into the kebab van through the serving hatch area.

4.   He then showed a long kebab knife, with which he stated that he cut the fat male's arm. I seized the knife as an exhibit, which I now produce as Exhibit RJ/1. Alexis Ionides stated that he warned the fat male that he would cut him if he didn't withdraw, but he claims that the fat male carried on trying to climb into the van, and ended up cutting his arm with the knife. I saw that there was fresh blood on the top of the counter on the left hand side of the counter, directly in front of where the kebab spit was situated, and where Costas Georgiou stood.

5.   As a result of enquiries that I made, Alexis Ionides and 2 juvenile female witnesses agreed to accompany us back to the Police Station, at Colchester. At the Police Station PC Smith arrested Alexis Ionides on suspicion of s.18 grievous bodily harm at 2 a.m. Alexis Ionides was booked into the custody area, but continued to behave in an excitable manner, making comments to the effect that he meant to take the fat male's head off with the knife.

Signed: Richard Jones   Signature witnessed by: Thomas Bright

Statement of Witness (C.J. Act, 1967, s. 9; M.C. Act, 1980, ss. 5A(3)(a) and 5B; M.C. Rules, 1981, r. 70)

STATEMENT OF   JOHN GOLDSTEIN

Age of Witness (date of birth)   Over 18

Occupation of Witness   General Surgeon, Fellow of the Royal College of Surgeons

This statement, (consisting of 1 page signed by me), is true to the best of my knowledge and belief and I make it knowing that, if it is tendered in evidence, I shall be liable to prosecution if I have wilfully stated anything which I know to be false or do not believe to be true.

Dated the 8th day of June 2002   Signed: John Goldstein
                                            Signature witnessed by: Richard Jones

1.   At 2 a.m. on Saturday 1st June 2002, Mr Andrew David Canning was admitted to the Casualty Department of the Colchester Hospital. I had to be called out because of the seriousness of the injuries that he had suffered.

2.   On examination at 3 a.m. I noticed that he had a deep cut to his left arm just above the elbow. The wound required some 21 stitches to close. A small piece of bone had actually got knocked off the distal humerus and this was replaced back with some periosteal sutures and the wound closed. He was placed in a plaster at this stage to help splint the muscles whilst they healed. He was discharged on the following Monday, 4th June, to be seen in clinic some 4 weeks later.

Signed: John Goldstein   Signature witnessed by: Richard Jones

Statement of Witness (C.J. Act, 1967, s. 9; M.C. Act, 1980, ss. 5A(3)(a) and 5B; M.C. Rules, 1981, r. 70)

STATEMENT OF   SCOTT LESLIE

Age of Witness (date of birth)   Over 18

Occupation of Witness   Police Photographer

This statement, (consisting of 1 page signed by me), is true to the best of my knowledge and belief and I make it knowing that, if it is tendered in evidence, I shall be liable to prosecution if I have wilfully stated in it anything which I know to be false or do not believe to be true.

Dated the 3rd day of June 2002   Signed: Scott Leslie
                                            Signature witnessed by: Richard Jones

1. I am a civilian photographer employed by the Essex Constabulary, stationed at Colchester Police Station.

2. At 4 p.m. on Saturday 1st June 2002, I attended Ramsey Close, Colchester where I photographed a kebab trailer. In total I took 2 photographs which I produce as Exhibit SL/1.

Signed: Scott Leslie   Signature witnessed by: Richard Jones

Statement of Witness (C.J. Act, 1967, s. 9; M.C. Act, 1980, ss. 5A(3)(a) and 5B; M.C. Rules, 1981, r. 70)

STATEMENT OF	STEPHEN JOHN CAREY
Age of Witness (date of birth)	Over 18
Occupation of Witness	Detective Constable

This statement, (consisting of 1 page signed by me). is true to the best of my knowledge and belief and I make it knowing that, if it is tendered in evidence, I shall be liable to prosecution if I have wilfully stated in it anything which I know to be false or do not believe to be true.

Dated the 14th day of June 2002

Signed: Stephen J. Carey
Signature witnessed by: Thomas Bright

1.   At 12.16 p.m. on Saturday 1st June 2002, together with DC Dingwall, I interviewed Alexis Ionides at Colchester Police Station in the presence of his solicitor Mr Melville-Walker. The interview was tape recorded and a copy of the tape is produced as Exhibit SJC/1. A summary of the interview is produced as Exhibit SJC/1A. The interview concluded at 1 p.m.

2.   On Monday 10th June 2002, Mr Costas Georgiou attended Colchester Police Station by pre-arranged appointment at 12.30 p.m. At 12.33 p.m. I attended the front desk and arrested and cautioned Mr Georgiou on suspicion of unlawfully wounding Andrew David Canning on 1st June 2002. He made no reply to the caution.

3.   At 1.42 p.m. on 10th June 2002, together with DC Johnson, I interviewed Costas Georgiou, in the presence of an interpreter, Mrs Dorothy Hove. The interview was tape recorded and I produce a copy of the tape as Exhibit SJC/2 and a summary of that interview as Exhibit SJC/2A. The interview concluded at 2.26 p.m.

4.   I was present the same day (10th June 2002) when at 7.49 p.m. Georgiou was charged with wounding with intent contrary to section 18 Offences against the Person Act 1861.

Signed: Stephen J. Carey   Signature witnessed by: Thomas Bright

THE QUEEN

v

COSTAS GEORGIOU

EXHIBITS

(1) Exhibit SL/1 (photographs)

(2) Exhibit SJC/2A (summary of interview)

(3) Exhibit SJC/2 (interview tape) is available if required

(4) Exhibit RJ/1 (knife) can be viewed by arrangement.

RECORD OF TAPE-RECORDED INTERVIEW

Person Interviewed: Costas Georgiou

Place of Interview: Colchester Police Station

Date of Interview: 10/6/02 Time commenced: 1.42 pm   Time concluded: 2.26 pm

Interviewing Officers   DC Carey   DC Johnson

Other Persons Present   Mrs Dorothy Hove (Translator)

PERSON SPEAKING	TEXT
	Introduction and caution. Rights explained.
	Mr Georgiou explained that on the night in question he was working in the kebab van in Shetland Road, Colchester. They had opened up for business at approximately 8 p.m. He was cutting the kebabs and cooking chickens and was assisted by Alexis Ionides' sister-in-law, Mrs Sophia Ionides. As he speaks no English, he was not able to take orders from the customers and this was done by Alexis. He explained that there were 3 knives in the kebab van on the night in question, namely a salad knife, a knife with which to cut the chickens and the kebab knife.
DC Carey	Right, at about 1 o'clock in the morning, a large man who's been described as having a beard but in fact has got stubble came to the kebab van and ordered two kebabs. Does he remember that?
Translator	He remembers being asked by Alexis to prepare 2 kebabs and than an argument developing between Alexis and this man who was enormous over Alexis speaking to Sophia in Greek. He remembers this man punching Alexis on the nose and then Alexis picking up the salad knife and threatening the man with it.
DC Carey	And then what happened?
Translator	The girl that the fat man was with ran and got another man from the car. That man came up to the van and he was angry. During that time he was holding the knife that he uses to cut the chickens and the man thumped the back window of the van and he thumped the glass and he tried to take the knife away from him.
DC Carey	And what did Alexis do at this point?
Translator	Alexis picked up the kebab knife which was by the spit and then he didn't actually see the cutting taking place, but he knew that the man had been cut. The man continued to be violent and aggressive even after he was cut.
DC Carey	How did Ionides manage to get past you in the small confines of the kebab van to pick up the kebab knife?
Translator	He doesn't know how he managed it but he just did. The man

had been holding on to his arm in which he was holding the chicken knife and he had just broken free of the man's grip when Alexis picked up the kebab knife.

The interview concluded at 2.26 p.m.

CROWN PROSECUTION SERVICE

UNUSED MATERIAL DISCLOSED UNDER

S. 3 Criminal Procedure and Investigations Act 1996

THE QUEEN

v

COSTAS GEORGIOU

(1)   Statement Tracey Collins

(2)   Exhibit SJC/1A – Interview with Alexis Ionides

(3)   Exhibit SJC/1 (interview tape) is available if required

RECORD OF TAPE-RECORDED INTERVIEW

Person Interviewed: Alexis Ionides

Place of Interview: Colchester Police Station

Date of Interview: 1/6/02 Time commenced: 12.16 pm   Time concluded: 1 pm

Interviewing Officers   DC Carey

Other Persons Present: David Melville-Walker (Solicitor)

DC Dingwall

PERSON SPEAKING	TEXT
	Mr Ionides recounted how they had just served two regular customers (2 teenage girls) when an enormous man came up to the van together with a female and placed an order. He described how the argument started and how the female went and got another male with blond hair who came and remonstrated with him. He described how violent and aggressive they were and how scared they all were inside the van, in particular his sister-in-law, Sophia Ionides. He arrived at the point where the blond-haired male was holding on to Georgiou's arm with his left arm and Georgiou in turn was holding on to the knife that they use to cut the chickens.
DC Carey	Where were you at this point and what knife did you have in your hand?
Ionides	I was on the left-hand side of the van facing out and I had the salad knife in my hand.
DC Carey	Then what did you do?
Ionides	I rushed over to where the kebab spit is and picked up the big kebab knife. I told the blond man to let go but he would not. I then rested the knife on his left arm and he continued to pull at my friend's arm and therefore was cut. He only let go of Costas's arm when his friends told him that he was bleeding.
DC Carey	So you cut him with the big kebab knife?
Ionides	Yes, but it was in self-defence.
	General discussion then ensued with regard to reasonableness and self-defence and the interview concluded at 1 p.m.

Statement of Witness (C.J. Act, 1967, s. 9; M.C. Act, 1980, ss. 5A(3)(a) and 5B; M.C. Rules, 1981, r. 70)

STATEMENT OF	TRACEY COLLINS
Age of Witness (date of birth)	26th January 1985
Occupation of Witness	Schoolgirl

This statement, (consisting of 1 page signed by me). is true to the best of my knowledge and belief and I make it knowing that, if it is tendered in evidence, I shall be liable to prosecution if I have wilfully stated in it anything which I know to be false or do not believe to be true.

Dated the 4th day of June 2002   Signed: Tracey Collins
                                        Signature witnessed by: Richard Jones

1.   I am the above named person. At approximately 1 a.m. on Saturday 2nd June 2001 I was with my friends Kelly Longyear and Aaron Constantine at the kebab van in Shetland Road, Colchester.

2.   I noticed behind me in the queue for kebabs a white male, approximately mid to late thirties. He was of very big build and at least 6' tall. He had a beard and dark hair. My friend Kelly spoke to this man briefly and offered him a piece of her kebab, but the male refused.

3.   Inside the kebab van was a man I know as 'Smiles' who is of Greek appearance. Smiles was putting the meat into the kebabs and taking orders from the customers. There was also another Greek male inside the kebab van who is known as 'Rambo', and a Greek woman.

4.   We were served our kebabs and left the van and walked up Popley Way towards the local infants' school. Aaron and I were together but my friend Kelly had to run back to the van as she had left her purse on the serving counter.

5.   I heard shouting and looked around to see a man punching and kicking the screen of the kebab van and trying to get inside. I had not seen this man before. He was probably in his early 20s, blond hair, wearing a white top with jeans. He was shouting, 'C'mon then, I'll give you a fight, I'll have you'. Kelly was already within the vicinity of the van as myself and Aaron started walking back towards it. The large man who was originally behind me in the queue was trying to rock the van.

6.   I then saw 'Smiles' come out from the back of the kebab van carrying a long knife with about a 2' blade. The knife looked to be the same one that they use to slice the meat for the doner kebabs.

7.   I saw the white man with the blond hair, who had been banging on the van, holding his right arm to his body and he was bent over. He was being helped by the man who was originally behind us in the queue and a woman who was with them. At the time we were queuing for our kebabs, this woman was sat in a car near the van.

Signed: Tracey Collins   Signature witnessed by: Richard Jones

COSTAS GEORGIOU

PROOF OF EVIDENCE

1. I, Costas Georgiou (date of birth 12th August 1977) of 27 White Hart Lane, Tottenham, London N15, deny the charge of wounding with intent which has been laid against me.

2. The incident in question took place in the early hours of the morning of Saturday 1st June 2002. That evening, I had been assisting my cousin Alexis Ionides in his kebab van in Colchester.

3. At approximately 1 a.m., we had just finished serving 2 young girls and a boy when an enormous man with a beard came up to the van and placed an order. He was accompanied by a young woman.

4. He started an argument with Alexis because (so I was later told) he objected to Alexis speaking to Sophia (his sister-in-law) in Greek. The argument escalated with the man raising his voice and banging and thumping the kebab van. After he'd punched Alexis on the nose, Alexis picked up the salad knife and threatened the fat man with it saying, 'Go away or else I will cut you'.

5. At this stage, the woman who the fat man was with went to their car and fetched a blond-haired man who came out and leant on my side of the van (the right-hand side of the van looking out). He was being just as aggressive as the fat man, and fearing for my safety, I picked up the chicken knife in my right hand and gestured to the blond man to go away.

6. The blond man then grabbed hold of my arm with his left hand, and seeing this, Alexis came behind me and picked up the big kebab knife that was to my right. I'd managed to free myself from this man's grip by the time that Alexis had picked up the kebab knife. I did not actually see the man being cut but I did see him holding his arm afterwards.

7. I have no previous convictions either in this country or in Greece.

8. I am very concerned to avoid a conviction as I have recently become engaged to a Greek girl from a very respectable family who might not consider me a suitable fiancé if I were convicted.

Signed: Costas Georgiou

Date 19th September 2002

17.2.1   CAP IN ACTION

Notes for advice on evidence

STAGE 1   THE CONTEXT OF THE CASE

(1)   THE STAGE OF THE PROCEEDINGS

    (a)   What steps have been taken?

        Bail application 19.6.02

        Defendant on conditional bail — residence with D. Ionides

        Committal on 13.9.02 for Trial on Indictment – Chelmsford Crown Court

        Charge – Offences against the Person Act 1861, s. 18

        Primary Prosecution disclosure 18.9.02.

    (b)   Your Instructions: to draft defence statement and to advise on further steps before trial.

    (c)   Objectives: Meet defence disclosure obligations, evaluate strength of defence case and identify any further evidence necessary.

(2)   COLLECTING THE FACTS

    (a)   Dramatis personae

Costas Georgious (CG)	The Defendant, inside the kebab van on 1.6.02
Alexis Ionides (AI)	Cousin of Defendant, inside van on 1.6.02, arrested on 1.6.02
Sophia Ionides (SI)	Sister-in-law of AI, inside van on 1.6.02
Andrew Canning (AC)	Injured in incident
John Archer (JA)	Friend of AC and with him when AC injured
Jackie Perry (JP)	Girlfriend of AC and mother of his child. Drove AC and JA to van
Tracy Collins (TC)	Schoolgirl, gave witness statement to police
Kelly Longyear (KL)	Friend of TC, with her at kebab van on 1.6.02
Aaron Constantine (AaC)	Friend of TC, with her at kebab van
John Goldstein (JG)	Doctor who treated AC on 1.6.02
Richard Jones (RJ)	PC attended incident on 1.6.02 and arrested AI
Scott Leslie (SL)	Police photographer
Stephen Carey (SC)	DC who interviewed AI, and arrested and interviewed CG

(3)   AGREED AND DISPUTED FACTS

Prosecution Version	Witness	Defendant's Version	Witness	Notes/Queries
AC, JP, JA visited 3 pubs on evening of 31.5.02. Left Rabbit public house by car approx 12.00 a.m. and JP drove them to Shetland Rd to get kebabs	AC			Witnesses vary re times and amount drunk.
AC asleep in back of car.	AC			
JP parked car next to kebab van. JP and JA got out.	JA JP			TC says JP did not get out of car with JA.

Prosecution Version	Witness	Defendant's Version	Witness	Notes/ Queries
3 people getting kebabs in front of JP and JA. 2 girls 1 boy.	JP	TC, KL and AaC in front of big man in queue for kebab. Served two teenage girls.	TC AI	Why no statement from KL or AaC?
JA went to front of van 3 people in van. Male, 18, to right of centre, girl at back, male on left next to kebab spit about 25, stubble, cutting meat with large knife.	JA	CG was working in the kebab van on 2.6.01, cutting kebabs and cooking chickens, assisted by AI and SI. AI took orders as CG speaks no English. Smiles was taking the orders, there was another Greek male in the van known as Rambo and a Greek woman.	CG TC	JA only one to describe two men as of same height and build. It seems that Smiles is AI, CG is Rambo?
		3 knives in van – salad knife, chicken knife and kebab knife.	CG	Size of each knife?
JA ordered a chicken kebab from the younger male, older male started to cut up the chicken.	JA	Enormous man with girl came up to van and placed order. CG asked to prepare two kebabs.	AI CG	
The younger male was holding an orange-handled knife. The older Greek had a wooden-handled knife with a two-foot blade.	JA			Salad/ chicken/ kebab
Young Greek spoke to girl in Greek. An argument ensued between the younger male and JA.	JA JP	Argument between enormous man and AI about speaking Greek. Fat male told AI not to speak in Greek to girlfriend. AI refused to serve him.	CG RJ	
		The argument escalated with the man raising his voice and banging and thumping on the van. Enormous man punched AI on nose.	CG CG RJ	Any damage to van?
Younger man brandished knife in right hand at JA.	JA JP	AI picked up salad knife and threatened man with it, saying, 'Go away or else I will cut you'.	CG CG	
JP went to get AC	JP			

Prosecution Version	Witness	Defendant's Version	Witness	Notes/Queries
		Fat male tried to climb into van through serving hatch.	RJ	
		AI warned fat man that he would cut him if he didn't withdraw. Fat man continued to try to climb into van.	RJ	
AC woken by JP. She said, 'The geezer's threatening John with a knife'. AC walked up to van.	AC	Girl with fat man ran and got other man from the car. He came up to van, he was angry.	CG	
During slanging match AC arrived.	JA			
Male 5′ 10″, muscular build, 16, waving orange-handled 12″ bladed knife shouting at JA saying, 'I'm going to cut you'	AC			
Greek girl trying to pull young male from front of van by arms.	AC JA			Why no statement from SI?
Older Greek, 25, to left of centre about 5′ 9″ wiry, stubble.	AC	CG holding chicken knife.	CG	
AC went to front of van, left of centre.	AC	Blond-haired man came and leant on my side of the van (right side looking out). CG picked up chicken knife and gestured to man to go away.	CG	
AC leant his left arm on the van counter and spoke to the young man to get him to put down the knife. The older man was holding a large knife in his hand, it was the long one that they use for cutting the kebab.	AC JA JP	Man was very angry and thumped on back window and on glass.	CG	

Prosecution Version	Witness	Defendant's Version	Witness	Notes/ Queries
		Heard shouting, looked around and saw man punching and kicking the screen of the van and trying to get inside. He had blond hair. He shouted 'C'mon then, I'll give you a fight' etc.	TC	
		The large man who had originally been behind me in the queue was trying to rock the van.	TC	
The older man moved forward carrying knife with 16″ blade used for cutting the meat to AC's left	AC	Man tried to get chicken knife away from CG and held on to his arm. CG managed to break away from man's grip. AI picked up kebab knife from near spit. Told man to let go. Smiles came out from the back of the van carrying a knife with a 22″-blade like the ones they use to slice the kebabs. AI rested knife on man's left arm. Man continued to pull on CG's arm and was cut. Man did not let go until he was told he was bleeding	CG AI CG CG AI TC AI	Dispute between CG & AI as to when CG freed. How did AI get behind CG to pick up kebab knife?
AC felt pressure on arm above elbow.				
Older Greek chopped down on to AC's left arm with large knife. Flesh opened up. Started to bleed.	JA	AI cut fat man's arm with long kebab knife. Ex RJ/1.	RJ	
AC tried to grab him with left hand but he pulled back.	AC			
The older man was just in front of AC.	JP			
AC pulled away from the van.	AC JA			
AC punched the van with his right fist as he was pulled away by JA.	AC	Man continued to be aggressive even after cut.	SJC A	Dispute about how often van punched?

Prosecution Version	Witness	Defendant's Version	Witness	Notes/ Queries
AC taken to hospital.	AC			
AC treated in hospital. Piece of bone which had been knocked off distal humerus replaced, 21 stitches required to close deep cut to left arm just above elbow, arm put in plaster.				How hard a blow necessary to chip bone?
Police called to van, arrived about 1.32 a.m.	RJ			
Kebab knife seized as Ex RJ/1.	RJ			Any fingerprints?
Fresh blood on top of counter on left in front of kebab spit	RJ			
RJ spoke to AI.	RJ			
AI interviewed by police on 1.6.02.	SJC			
Photographs taken of kebab trailer.	SL			
CG interviewed by police on 10.6.02.	SJC			

(4)   LEGAL FRAMEWORK

(i)   The Offence (See **Table 14.5**.)

(ii)   Criminal Procedure and Investigations Act 1997
Section 3   Primary prosecution disclosure of previously undisclosed material which might undermine the case for the prosecution.
Section 5   Defence disclosure within 14 days of primary prosecution disclosure by service of written defence statement setting out nature of defence and indicating the matters on which Defendant takes issue with the prosecution and the reasons why.
Section 7   Secondary prosecution disclosure of additional prosecution material which might reasonably assist the disclosed defence.
Section 8   Defence can apply to court for disclosure of undisclosed material which might be reasonably expected to assist the defence disclosed.

STAGE 2   ANALYSIS OF ISSUES AND EVIDENCE

(a)   The Issues

(1)   THE LEGAL AND FACTUAL ISSUES

(i)   Identification — Whether it was the Defendant who cut AC?

(ii)   Self-defence — Whether, if it was the Defendant who cut AC, he acted in self-defence?

The witnesses describe a very confused situation — there are a number of discrepancies, e.g., JP's whereabouts before and during the incident. Which knife was held by whom? See above at Stage 1(3). The fact that there are discrepancies in the prosecution evidence is of positive benefit to the Defence.

(2) THE POTENTIAL THEORY

It was Alexis Ionides, acting in self-defence, not the Defendant who cut Andrew Canning who had been acting in a violent and threatening manner towards those in the kebab van in what was a very confusing situation.

(3) GAPS AND AMBIGUITIES

See table at Stage 1(3) above.

No statement from Sophia Ionides, Kelly Longyear, Aaron Constantine. Only prosecution statements from Alexis Ionides and Tracey Collins. No forensic statement on condition of van or examination of knife Exhibit RJ/1.

(b) The Evidence

(1) STRENGTHS AND WEAKNESSES OF CASE

(i) Strength of identification evidence depends on credibility of prosecution witnesses — obvious weaknesses in discrepancies, amount of alcohol consumed, previous convictions. (Check on previous convictions of defence witnesses.) Defence version might be strengthened by statements from other eye witnesses, from site visit to van to view width of van, from viewing knives. Do police have any further evidence pointing to identification, e.g., comments of Alexis Ionides/Defendant recorded on custody records?

(ii) Strong evidence of self-defence — weakness appears to be seriousness of injury and original behaviour of Alexis Ionides. Opinion of Doctor might be sought and proof of evidence from Alexis and Sophia Ionides.

STAGE 3 PRESENTATION

(1) CHOSEN THEORY

See above at Stage 2(a)(2).

(2) CARRYING OUT INSTRUCTIONS

(i) Draft the Defence Statement
(See General Council of the Bar: The Preparation of Defence Case Statements: Guidance on the duties of Counsel.)
Identify nature of defence, indicate matters on which defence take issue with reasons.

(ii) Plan and Write the Advice on Evidence
Identify and explain what further evidence required.

(See **17.3** for completed Advice on Evidence and Defence Statement.)

17.3   Brief for Hearing

THE QUEEN

Vs

COSTAS GEORGIOU

_____

FURTHER INSTRUCTIONS TO COUNSEL

_____

Further to Counsel's written advice, a copy of which is enclosed, together with the Defence Statement, Counsel will also please find enclosed the following documents namely:

(a)   Proof of evidence from Sophia Ionides.

(b)   Proof of evidence from Alexis Ionides.

(c)   Proof of evidence from Aaron Constantine

(d)   Previous convictions of Andrew Canning, John Archer, and Tracey Collins. [Reproduced on one page for convenience.]

Counsel will note that there has, as yet, been no secondary disclosure by the prosecution.

With regard to the other items requested by Counsel those Instructing can state the following:

(a)   Full statement from Tracey Collins. She was contacted by those Instructing but she has nothing further to add to her original statement. Counsel will no doubt take note of her hitherto undisclosed previous conviction.

(b)   Statement from Kelly Longyear. Despite exhaustive efforts by those Instructing it has not been possible to trace this witness. It would appear that she left her last address several months ago to travel around Australia and is not contactable in that country.

(c)   Viewing of knives. Counsel will no doubt recall the recent viewing of these items. The knives were much as the witnesses have described, the lengths of the salad, chicken and kebab knives being 12", 16" and 24" respectively. The salad knife has an orange handle and both the chicken and kebab knives have wooden handles.

(d)   Scientific report on knife. This confirmed that it was in fact the kebab knife which cut Mr Canning on the night in question. The prosecution have informed those Instructing that the report will be included in the prosecution secondary disclosure.

(e)   Forensic report on van. Unfortunately, no such report was carried out by Essex Police, although Counsel will no doubt take note of the fact that fresh blood was seen on the kebab van counter by PC Jones.

(f)   Expert medical evidence of force needed for injury. Those Instructing discussed this matter with Mr Goldstein and he felt unable to give a conclusive opinion on the subject.

(g) Interview tapes. Those Instructing have requested the tapes and these will be forwarded to Counsel as soon as they are received. We would be grateful if Counsel could inform those Instructing when she has listened to them as to whether the transcript is a fair and accurate summary of same.

(h) Following the recent site visit, the sketch plan is not yet completed. However, the inside of the van is 3′ in width and 10′ in length. The width of the work surfaces inside the van is 18′.

Counsel is now instructed to attend the Pleas and Directions Hearing on 25th October 2002, prepare this matter for trial and use her best endeavours to secure an Acquittal at the forthcoming Hearing due to start on 26th November next.

Brown Dingle & Slattery   18th October 2002
27 New Buildings
Chelmsford, Essex.

IN THE CHELMSFORD CROWN COURT   T02/0656

THE QUEEN

Vs

COSTAS GEORGIOU

ADVICE ON EVIDENCE

---

1.   Mr Georgiou currently stands indicted for an offence that he on the 1st June 2002 unlawfully wounded a Mr Andrew David Canning with intent to do him grievous bodily harm. I would advise that the following steps are taken in readiness for the forthcoming trial on the basis that Mr Georgiou is intending to plead Not Guilty.

2.   Mr Georgiou maintains that he was not the person who wounded Mr Canning on the night in question. Indeed, this version of events is supported by his cousin, Mr Alexis Ionides, who has already confessed to the Police that he was the person who carried out the wounding. Although we have the transcript of interview to hand, it would appear that no proof of evidence has been taken from this person and I would therefore advise that this be done as soon as possible.

3.   Also in the kebab van on the evening in question was Mr Ionides' sister-in-law, Sophia. It is hoped that she would support our client's version of events and therefore a proof of evidence should be obtained from her. I note that Tracey Collins's statement has been disclosed by the prosecution on primary disclosure as Unused Material. Although she does not see exactly what happened, her evidence, in my opinion, is useful in demonstrating the unacceptable manner in which Mr Canning and Mr Archer behaved, which might in turn assist any suggestion of self-defence that we make at the trial. She should therefore be contacted, asked if she wishes to add anything further to the statement that she made to the Police, and then requested to attend court and give evidence at the trial.

4.   Miss Collins was with two friends on the evening in question, namely Kelly Longyear and Aaron Constantine. I am particularly interested in any evidence that Kelly Longyear might be able to give as it would appear that she was much closer to the kebab van than her friends when the wounding actually took place. Having said that, I feel that both of them should be contacted and proofs of evidence obtained.

5.   I note that only one of the prosecution witnesses, namely John Archer, allegedly saw our client wounding Mr Canning. Even if the witnesses from whom I have requested proofs of evidence do not support either the defence or the prosecution version of events, they can be used to depict what I am sure was a fairly chaotic situation. The obvious question for Mr Archer would then be, 'How can you be sure that it was Mr Georgiou who wielded the knife on Mr Canning?'

6.   I am sure that it would be of assistance in re-constructing the events of 1st June last, if a site view of the kebab van could be arranged. At the same time we could also take exact measurements of the inside of the van and draw up a floor plan. I am particularly concerned with regard to the question as to how Mr Ionides managed to squeeze past Mr Georgiou in order to pick up the kebab knife. I would therefore be grateful if those Instructing could liaise with my Clerk to arrange a mutually conveni-ent date and time for the visit.

7.   The Police currently have in their possession Exhibit RJ/1, the kebab knife. If possible, I would like to have sight of this prior to the trial. There were also apparently two other knives in use on the evening in question, namely the chicken knife and the salad knife. As these were not seized as exhibits, I presume that they are still in the possession of the Ionides family. Perhaps these could be shown to me at the same time as the site view.

8.   I note that PC Jones observed fresh blood on the counter of the kebab van when he was called to the scene. Can enquiries be made of the Police as to whether a forensic

examination was carried out on the van? At the same time they can perhaps be asked whether a similar examination was carried out on the knife.

9.   There can be little doubt that the injury inflicted on Mr Canning was a serious one, it requiring some 21 stitches. Alexis Ionides states that the wound was inflicted by him resting the kebab knife on Mr Canning's left arm. Mr Archer states that the injury was inflicted by a chopping movement. The surgeon, Mr Goldstein, might be able to shed some light on whether or not the wound is consistent with either or both of the above versions.

10.   It would appear from their statements that both Andrew Canning and John Archer have previous convictions. Exact details of these should be requested from the Police. Furthermore, all the witnesses from whom I have requested statements should be asked whether or not they have previous convictions.

11.   Could those Instructing ask formally for the interview tapes of Mr Georgiou and Mr Ionides to be forwarded to the Defence. We shall also require the custody records of Mr Georgiou and the Computer Aided Dispatch message (CAD) and Crime Report (CRIS) dealing with the incident and I have included a request for these in the Defence Statement. If these are not included in the prosecution secondary disclosure I shall make a formal request for same at the forthcoming Pleas and Directions Hearing under s. 8 of the Criminal Procedure and Investigations Act 1996.

12.   Whilst I have not taken specific instructions from Mr Georgiou with regard to the contents of his Defence Statement, which as those Instructing are no doubt aware, needs to be served on the Prosecution no later than 1st October 2002, I feel that as I have had conduct of this case throughout, I am well acquainted with the nature of our client's defence. I have therefore prepared a draft Defence Statement pursuant to s. 5 of the Criminal Procedure and Investigations Act 1996, which should be shown to the client for his approval prior to its service on the Crown Prosecution Service.

13.   In summary, therefore, the following steps need to be taken in preparation for the forthcoming trial namely:

(a)   Proofs of evidence to be obtained from:

    (i)   Alexis Ionides,

    (ii)   Sophia Ionides,

    (iii)   Tracey Collins,

    (iv)   Kelly Longyear,

    (v)   Aaron Constantine.

(b)   Site view of kebab van to be arranged.

(c)   Floor plan of kebab van, showing exact measurements, to be drawn.

(d)   Viewing of exhibit RJ/1 and other 2 knives in use on evening in question to be arranged.

(e)   Enquiries to be made as to whether a forensic report was prepared on the kebab van and also Exhibit RJ/1.

(f)   If possible, expert medical evidence on the force required to inflict the injury, to be obtained.

(g)   Defence statement to be served on Prosecution.

14.   Please do not hesitate to contact me if you have any queries on this matter.

Nicola Grey   27th September 2002

<u>IN THE CHELMSFORD CROWN COURT</u>   T02/0656

THE QUEEN

v

COSTAS GEORGIOU

DEFENCE STATEMENT
PURSUANT TO s. 5 CPIA 1996

---

1. The Defendant admits that he was working at a kebab van in Shetland Road, Colchester during the early hours of the morning of 1st June 2002.

2. The Defendant denies inflicting any injury on the alleged victim, Andrew David Canning. He asserts that any injuries caused to the victim were as a result of actions taken in self-defence by his cousin, Alexis Ionides.

3. Paragraph 2 above is without prejudice to any submission that might be put at the trial with regard to the Judge leaving the issue of self-defence to the jury in the Defendant's case.

4. It is submitted that the above case disclosed by the Defendant might reasonably be assisted by the following documents and a formal request is made for same:

   (a) Incident Report Book of PC 250 Richard Jones.

   (b) Custody record relating to the Defendant.

   (c) CAD message.

   (d) CRIS report.

5. This statement has been prepared on the basis of evidence supplied by the Prosecution to date and the Defendant reserves the right to add to or amend his Defence at trial, in the light of any further evidence that might be served by the Crown.

Dated 1st October 2002

Brown Dingle & Slattery,
27 New Buildings,
Chelmsford, Essex.

SOPHIA IONIDES

PROOF OF EVIDENCE

I am Sophia Ionides (date of birth 10th February 1981) and I live at 51 Piggott Close, Colchester CM10 OAU. I have no previous convictions.

On Friday 31st May 2002 I was assisting my husband's brother Alexis Ionides serve customers at our kebab van which was that evening parked at Shetland Road, Colchester. Also present in the van that evening was my husband's cousin, Costas Georgiou.

We opened up for business at approximately 8 p.m. and everything went smoothly until about 1 a.m. when the van was approached by a big fat man in his late twenties, early thirties, who appeared to be growing a beard. He was accompanied by a girl who I would say was in her early twenties.

After they had placed their order, Alexis turned round to me and said in Greek words to the effect that the gentleman who had just ordered was a bit of a drunken slob. The fat gentleman appeared to take offence at this although I am almost certain that he did not understand what Alexis had said. An argument then developed between Alexis and the fat man. The girl who was with the fat man then went and got a third man who also joined in the argument in support of the big fat man.

I became quite hysterical whilst all this was occurring and for a lot of the time I had my face buried in my hands. I therefore cannot say who cut the arm of the man who joined the argument later on. I saw both Costas and Alexis holding knives whilst the fight was in progress. I can state that the fat man and his friend were both swearing, rocking the van and banging the perspex window whilst the argument was in progress.

Signed: Sophia Ionides

Date: 17th October 2002

<u>ALEXIS IONIDES</u>

PROOF OF EVIDENCE

I am Alexis Ionides (date of birth 26th March 1984) and I live at 51 Piggott Close, Colchester CM10 0AU. I have no previous convictions.

I confirm that all that I said in my interview of 1st June 2002 was true and accurate to the best of my knowledge and belief. In particular, I was the person who cut Mr Canning by means of the kebab knife. I did this by resting it on Mr Canning's left arm when he would not let go of my cousin Costas's right arm. I only did this in self-defence. At the time I felt that I had no other option given the behaviour of Mr Canning and his friend Mr Archer.

I would further add that Mr Archer punched me in the nose fairly soon after he started to argue with me.

Signed: Alexis Ionides

Date: 17th October 2002

AARON CONSTANTINE

PROOF OF EVIDENCE

I am Aaron Constantine (date of birth 16th October 1981) and I live at 63 Hillside Drive, Colchester CM6 2YP. I have no previous convictions.

On Friday 31st May 2002 I, together with my friends Tracey Collins and Kelly Longyear, had been to the Green Man public house and then on to a nightclub. We decided to buy a kebab on the way home. The time must have been approximately 1 a.m. when we ordered our food. I remember that there was a fat man and a woman behind us in the queue although I didn't take much notice of them at the time.

When we were about 50 yards away from the van, I remember hearing a lot of screaming, shouting and banging. I turned around to see the fat man who had been behind us in the queue rocking the van backwards and forwards. I also saw another man whom I'd not seen before banging the perspex windows on the kebab van with his fists. I don't remember seeing any of the Greek occupants of the van holding knives. This might have been due to the fact that my attention was primarily focused on the men outside the van.

On seeing what was happening, we started walking back towards the van. However, by the time that we got there, the people who had caused the disturbance had driven off.

Signed: Aaron Constantine

Date: 18th October 2002

CRO 02/633421

PREVIOUS CONVICTIONS OF
ANDREW DAVID CANNING

DATE	COURT	OFFENCE	SENTENCE
12th June 2001	Colchester Magistrates	Drunk and Disorderly	Bound Over to Keep the Peace — £100 for 12 months
6th March 2002	Colchester Magistrates	Section 5 POA 1986	Fine: £100 Costs: £50

CRO 96/492178

PREVIOUS CONVICTIONS OF
JOHN FREDERICK ARCHER

DATE	COURT	OFFENCE	SENTENCE
7th February 1996	Winchester Crown Court	S.2 POA 1986	CSO 240 hours

---

CRO 01/305125

PREVIOUS CONVICTIONS OF
TRACEY BERNADETTE COLLINS

DATE	COURT	OFFENCE	SENTENCE
20th November 2001	Colchester Magistrates	Theft (shoplifting)	Fine: £50 Costs: £25

17.3.1   **CAP IN ACTION**

Notes for plea and directions hearing and for trial

STAGE 1   THE CONTEXT OF THE CASE

(1)   STAGE OF PROCEEDINGS

(a)   What steps have been taken?

Defendant committed for trial 13.9.02.
Defence disclosure made. Secondary prosecution disclosure not yet made.
Defence Witness statements taken from SI and AaC and AI.

(b)   Your Instructions

(i)   To appear at the PDH on 25.10.02.

(ii)   To prepare for trial on 26.11.02.

(c)   Objectives

(i)   Of the Plea and Directions Hearing
Agree and settle plea, issues in case, prosecution witnesses required, number of Defence witnesses, length of trial, further information required, to be inserted on standard form. (*Practice Direction (Crown Court: Plea and Directions Hearings)* [1995] 1 WLR 1318.)

(ii)   Of trial
Represent Defendant on Not Guilty Plea, examine and cross-examine witnesses.

(2)   COLLECTING THE FACTS

Further information obtained by Instructing Solicitors does not alter significantly the previous position. However, note previous conviction of Tracey Collins, difference in size of chicken and kebab knives (although both have wooden handles) and narrowness of van.

(3)   AGREED/DISPUTED FACTS

Table in **17.2.1** shows witnesses who can give evidence on issues of identity and self-defence.

The new information in statements of SI, AI and AaC, obtained by Instructing Solicitors, needs to be included in that analysis but although useful it is not decisive in any way.

(4)   LEGAL FRAMEWORK

Elements of offence. Prosecution must prove that:

Andrew Canning was wounded.
It was Costas Georgiou who wounded him.
CG intended when he wounded him to inflict really serious harm.
The wounding was unlawful, e.g., not inflicted in self-defence.

Burden of proof. On Prosecution throughout but note Prosecution do not have to prove absence of self-defence unless the possibility of self-defence has been raised; but note Defence Statement.

Standard of proof. Beyond reasonable doubt.

(See **17.3** for completed Advice on Evidence and Defence Statement.)

STAGE 2   ANALYSIS OF ISSUES AND EVIDENCE

(a)   The Issues

(1)   LEGAL AND FACTUAL ISSUES

See Defence Statement.

(a)   Identity of the person who cut AC. Was it CG or AI?

(b)   There is evidence of violence in support of self-defence. Also the Defence might want to raise sufficient possibility of this to necessitate the Judge leaving the matter to the jury but note s. 11, CPIA 1996.

(c)   *Mens rea* not in issue as such. Defendant denies wounding. If issue of identity decided in Prosecution's favour, i.e., on JA's evidence, his statement of nature of blow, i.e., a chop, sufficient for jury to infer intent.

(d)   No dispute that AC wounded in incident.

(2)   GAPS AND AMBIGUITIES

Further information required — forensic report, interview tapes, custody record, computer aided dispatch (CAD) message/crime report.

(b)   **The Evidence**

(1)   STRENGTHS AND WEAKNESSES OF CASE

A.   Weaknesses of Prosecution case
The Prosecution case relies on the evidence of AC, JA and JP. Their evidence can be undermined by cross-examination of:

(a)   AC, JA, and JP on how much AC and JA drank between 8.00 and midnight, to show that JA and AC's evidence on detail is not reliable.

(b)   AC and JA on previous convictions to show lack of credibility.

(c)   JP on accuracy of statement — delay in joining JA in queue, left to get AC, 6 feet behind AC at time of wounding, and on credibility, relationship with AC (and mother of his child) has motive to withhold full story.

(d)   AC as to behaviour — trying to get into van, punching, kicking van before wounding to show clear vision of what happened unlikely.

(e)   JA about rocking van — how could he have seen what was happening clearly?

(f)   JA about possible confusion between two Greeks, both same build and height.

(g)   AC, JA and JC about knives to show possible confusion — AC sees CG holding 16″ knife — chicken not kebab?

(h)   Establish violence and confusion of incident from all witnesses.

B.   Strength of Defence case
Independent witnesses support Defence story of attack on van. TC supports D's version that it was AI who was holding the kebab knife.

C.   Weaknesses of Defence case

(a)   AI's initial story that it was fat man he cut (i.e., JA not AC).

(b) TC was not close to van (50 yards away according to AaC). Statement does not give description of 'Smiles' or 'Rambo' identifying AI clearly as person holding the kebab knife.

(c) TC has previous conviction for offence of dishonesty.

(d) Van very narrow. (But if CG pulled forward by AC, might not be difficult for AI to get behind, when CG breaks away and AI comes forward. AC who has not seen AI's movement thinks it is CG.)

(e) SI's statement that AI made derogatory remark might, in minds of jury, justify to some extent behaviour of AC and JA.

(f) Need for interpreter might affect jury's perception of CG as witness.

STAGE 3 PRESENTATION OF THE CASE

(1) CHOSEN THEORY

CG and young relatives in van in early hours of 1.6.02. Argument developed between large male customer (JA) and AI. CG not involved (English poor). AI tried to get JA to leave. JA became violent. Tried to climb into van, rocked van.

AC Joined JA in attack on van. He was angry and aggressive, he thumped on the back window and on the glass and tried to climb in while JA continued to rock the van.

It was very frightening and SI became hysterical.

Costas gestured to AC to go away. AC grabbed his hand in which he was holding the chicken knife. CG tried to pull away. AI moved behind CG, picked up the kebab knife, rested it on AC's arm. AC tried to recapture CG and arm cut in confusion.

(2) CHOSEN THEMES

Occupants of van in very vulnerable position.

Attack by two angry, violent, drunken lager louts.

Scene of confusion.

(3) CONSIDER YOUR AUDIENCE

Tactics: Consider how to deal with Tracey Collin's previous conviction.

Best approach to this case in terms of its theory? Self-defence is inconsistent with client's denial of blow and presenting alternative theories reduces persuasiveness and gives rise to inferences under s. 11, CPIA 1996.

(4) CARRYING OUT INSTRUCTIONS

(i) The Plea and Directions Hearing
       Plea: not guilty.
       Issues: identity, self-defence.
       Prosecution witnesses required: all except Dr and photographer.
       Defence witnesses: defendant plus 4 (AI, SI, TC, AaC).
       Length of trial: 3–4 days.
       Make s. 8 application if secondary prosecution disclosure not made.

Note: Check with Instructing Solicitor if interpreter needed at Trial.

(ii)   Trial
        Prepare for Trial (see ***Advocacy Manual***).
            Desirable to make opening speech in this case?
            Prepare to cross-examine Prosecution Witnesses.
            Prepare to examine Defendant and Defence Witnesses.

EIGHTEEN

DEALING WITH FIGURES

18.1 Introduction

Dealing with figures is part of dealing with the facts of a case. This chapter introduces the role of figures in the work of the barrister, and the contexts in which work with figures may be required.

18.2 Importance of Numeracy

Numeracy is vital to the barrister. Some people are quite confident in dealing with numbers, others are rather less confident, but in professional terms, no barrister can tell a client or solicitor, 'I never was much good at arithmetic' — the client wants to know what will be recovered in damages, and the solicitor can take briefs elsewhere. This chapter is designed to show you in what ways numeracy is important, and to help you develop your own skills.

Your immediate reaction to the proposition that you need to be numerate may well be 'Why?'. The law is about words, not figures — you see very few figures in legal textbooks — and also there will in any event be an accountant there if necessary. The student who has got a law degree or diploma without doing any addition or multiplication may well express the view that arithmetic was left behind happily at GCSE with no intention of ever returning to it.

Unfortunately for those who do not feel comfortable with figures, any suggestion that a barrister can get by without a facility with numbers is not true in practice. Although legal textbooks may have few figures in them, they do include substantial coverage of the legal principles for dealing with figures. A contract law textbook may not include figures, but most of the text ultimately relates to how much money you will get if you are successful in a claim for damages, so that when you have a contract case all the principles for the award of damages must be dealt with in terms of figures, not just words. Also, as outlined below, the barrister will most certainly not always have an accountant to help just because there are figures in the brief.

Thus although the immediate impression may be that a barrister can get by with limited numerical ability, a little thought should make it clear that this is not the case, and there are many contexts in which a lawyer will have to deal with figures every day. If you are not confident with numbers, now is the time to get to grips with the problem for the sake of your future clients and your career. If you are fairly confident with numbers, you can now start finding ways to develop your numeracy skills in a professional legal context.

In the simplest terms, as a barrister you must be able to tell the client what he or she might hope to get: you need to be able to deal with figures given to you: you need to be able to identify what further figures you need: and you need to be able to talk intelligently about figures to a solicitor or an accountant. Appreciating this is part of the vital move from the academic approach of university or college to the practical approach of the real barrister in practice.

18.3   Relevance of Figures in a Barrister's Practice

18.3.1   TYPES OF PRACTICE

Numeracy is going to be important to a barrister in any area of practice from the solely civil to the wholly criminal, albeit in slightly different ways. To provide some examples:

(a)   *Commercial practice.* The relevance of figures is obvious in dealing with companies or partnerships, especially as regards a detailed knowledge of accountancy and tax.

(b)   *Chancery practice.* The relevance is clear in actions for breach of trust, or for the administration of an estate, including claims for provision from the estate. Again this will specifically require a thorough knowledge of relevant tax provisions and how to read a set of accounts.

(c)   *General common law practice.* This has many elements, but to give some basic examples:

   (i)   *Contract.* You need to be able to deal with all figures relevant to a contract and to damages. Companies and partnerships will often be parties to the contract. Again a good knowledge of accounts and relevant taxation principles will often be required.

   (ii)   *Tort.* The importance of figures should be equally obvious here — damages assessment can be very complex in cases of severe injury or fatal accident. You should not be deflected from this by the possible complexity of the facts.

   (iii)   *Landlord and tenant.* Many financial issues arise in connection with leases and rent.

   (iv)   *Employment law.* Many questions relating to pay arise, and in some cases there will be a need to deal with statistics.

   (v)   *Family law practice.* Clearly the greatest relevance is to financial provision, both maintenance and capital payments. There is not simply the question of how much to pay, but also of how much is really available, how much a person needs to live on, the tax consequences and so on.

   (vi)   *Welfare law.* Clearly complex numerical issues can arise with regard to benefits, etc.

   (vii)   *Compensation.* There are various types of compensation, for example in discrimination cases, where numeracy is important.

(d)   *Criminal practice.* The importance of numeracy here ranges from the complex fraud trial to the small-scale fiddling of the books. Complete understanding is essential for clear presentation to the judge and the jury. There are also other possibilities, from being able to deal with tracing the monetary proceeds from the sale of illegal drugs to simply finding out what fine a defendant may be able to afford.

In addition, there is a pervasive need to deal with figures with regard to costs, interest etc.

18.3.2   WORKING WITH AN ACCOUNTANT

When dealing with a case that has a substantial financial factor it is possible that assistance will be available from an accountant. An accountant may actually be called in as an expert witness and you will see him or her in conference. If the client employs an accountant you may direct questions to the client's accountant through the client.

An accountant can be of great assistance, but having an accountant to help is not necessarily an answer, it is simply another element. You will still have to talk to the accountant, to know what to ask about, exactly what questions to ask, and you will have to be able to understand the answers.

However, in the vast majority of cases there will be no accountant to help, for the very simple reason that having an accountant costs money and the client either may not be able to afford this, or the financial issues may not be substantial or vital enough to justify the expense of an accountant. In a legally aided case the cost of an accountant may not be covered, although money issues may be especially important to the client in such a case even if the sums involved are small.

Whenever there is no accountant you will have to deal with all the figures and financial issues personally, finding the figures, analysing them and coming to conclusions that can be communicated to the client and be presented in court. You will personally have to deal with any relevant accounts and tax issues.

18.3.3 PROFESSIONAL ABILITY

A numerical ability is a matter of maintaining good professional standards. When you represent a client you have the duty to do the best you can, which includes not only winning the case if possible, but achieving the best result. You should get the highest figure that you properly can for a claimant. You must properly protect the position of a defendant.

This relates not just to the issue of damages, but to every arithmetical aspect of a case. If you think it is legally correct for a husband to pay £20,000 to his former wife you need to check with him whether he can afford to raise the sum without ruining his own financial position. If you advise your client that he or she can expect £40,000 in damages it is verging on the negligent not to advise that the money will be liable to 40% tax, if that is the case.

More personally, you need to impress each client, and each solicitor, with the range and quality of the advice that you give. A barrister can build up a reputation for good and thorough work with figures just as quickly as a reputation for a Marshall Hall style of advocacy, and probably on a sounder basis.

18.3.4 PERSONAL RELEVANCE

There is also a personal relevance for the barrister in practice having a reasonable arithmetical ability and a knowledge of the principles of accounting and taxation. The point is simply that as a self-employed person each barrister will be responsible for drawing up a set of accounts each year and will be personally liable for paying his or her own tax.

Again the reaction of those starting to train for the Bar tends to be that this point is in fact not very important — you employ an accountant to do your accounts and you get a good accountant so that you pay as little tax as possible, so why does a barrister need to be personally concerned? Such a reaction again shows a lack of practical appreciation of how things really work. Even if you are going to have an accountant to draw up your annual accounts, you need to keep all the records on which those accounts are to be based. Indeed with the introduction of self-assessment there is a legal duty to keep such records. You need to know what is taxable and should be entered and what is not. It is also in your interests to know what is tax-deductible so that you know what to keep receipts for. Tax rules mean that there is sometimes a choice of doing things in a tax-effective or a non-tax-effective way, and it is in your interests to know which is which. In addition to income tax, the barrister with sufficient income will be liable for value added tax, with the need to make quarterly returns.

18.4 Stages in an Claim when You May Need to Deal with Figures

These notes provide a brief and simple outline of those stages in a case at which a barrister may need to deal with figures. This is intended to give you an awareness of when to look out for numeracy issues on this course: a numeracy issue will not always come clearly labelled — it is for you to appreciate it is there. As general fact management skills inter-relate closely with other skills, so does the need to manage figures.

18.4.1 IN A CONFERENCE

When planning for or carrying out a conference, dealing with relevant facts must of course include all the relevant figures. This is so not only where figures are an important element of the case, for example, when you are interviewing a client for whom you are seeking maintenance, but in any case where figures arise.

Any figures that the client provides should of course be noted. In addition you should identify the figures that will be required to pursue the case and ask the client about them. Often the client will not be able to provide the figures personally, in which case you will have to consider with the solicitor how the figure might be obtained.

18.4.2 IN PREPARING A CASE

Fact management principles cover figures as well as facts. In dealing with the facts of a case the barrister will need to identify:

(a)   in what areas of the case figures will be needed,

(b)   precisely what figures will be needed,

(c)   what figures are already known,

(d)   what figures need to be ascertained,

(e)   how each figure will be ascertained,

(f)   how each figure will be used,

(g)   how each figure can be proved.

18.4.3 IN WRITING AN OPINION

A good solicitor will send you most of the figures that you need, but a less good solicitor might not, and even a good solicitor is unlikely to send all the figures you need in the initial brief. At that stage the main issue is whether there is a case and the strength of the case. But figures will still need to be dealt with — the client will want to know not only whether he might win but also at least in general terms how much.

Thus in analysing a brief you must consider in what areas figures are relevant. In writing the opinion you should deal with figures as far as possible. All figures that are provided in the brief should be dealt with, and other areas where figures are relevant should be dealt with in principle if not in detail. You also need to decide on a suitable way to present the figures in the opinion, whether as part of the text or in a tabulated form.

In writing an initial opinion, it is easy to underestimate the numerical and arithmetical side of a case simply because detailed figures are not always provided. This feeling must be resisted — the barrister is not there simply to accept what is provided, it is for the barrister to decide what is important and to indicate what information is needed and how the case should progress. Areas where more detailed figures are required should be indicated in an opinion.

18.4.4 IN DRAFTING

When planning a draft you must consider to what extent figures should be set out in the draft. Just to give a few general examples, in the particulars of claim, figures may need to be given for damages — figures for special damages should be listed in some detail, and the basis of the financial claims for general damages must at least be alleged in outline. While damages remain at large until trial, the increasing tendency is to include the figures for a claim for damages in more detail. However, you must of course hesitate to include a figure until you are reasonably sure of it.

An affidavit or witness statement in a case may require figures to be included in great detail, or, for example, a Form E supporting an application for financial relief on divorce. A draft order will of course need to have any relevant figures specifically included. If the figures are complex they should be presented in a schedule.

18.4.5 IN ADVOCACY

When presenting a case to a judge or jury it goes without saying that it is vital for the barrister to have total command of any figures in the case, be they sums of money, measurements or anything else. Only if the barrister has personally gathered all the relevant figures and mastered them will he or she have any chance of explaining them clearly, let alone convincing anyone of the strength of the case. Even someone who is confident in dealing with figures in writing may have more difficulty in dealing with them orally.

There are various ways in which a barrister may have to deal with figures in the course of presenting a case in court. First and most simply, figures may need to be dealt with in opening and closing speeches. Secondly, figures will need to be dealt with in offering evidence, whether it be documents or witnesses. Clearly the barrister must be capable of examining or cross-examining a witness on figures. At every stage you need to be able to present any numerical information in a way which really communicates your meaning to the jury and the judge. Even if you understand the figures, helping someone else to understand them can be very difficult.

If you have complex figures to get across you need to find the best way of doing it. Long and complex documents are difficult to understand, and the good barrister should always try to look for summaries or clear ways of presentation that will help comprehension. Computers and video display units are already finding their way into court, and it is quite clear that they will increasingly do so in the future, and this is another area where facility may help with the presentation of the case.

18.4.6 IN NEGOTIATING A SETTLEMENT

Before attempting to negotiate a settlement you must have all the relevant figures to evaluate the case and identify the most and the least that the client might expect to win or pay. It is important to stress this. Sometimes the settlement is seen as a quick and easy way of avoiding a legal claim, but of course no settlement should be contemplated until one has a clear idea of what the case might hope to achieve.

18.5 Collecting Evidence of Figures

Figures need to be ascertained just like other matters of fact, and admissible evidence will need to be found to prove them just as much as any other fact in the case. Having identified an area where figures are relevant, you need to sort out precisely what evidence you need and exactly where it may be obtained. Some the client will be able to provide. For others it is for the barrister to indicate to the solicitor what figures are required and for the solicitor to endeavour to find them.

The sources of figures, and of evidence of figures, are wide-ranging, from a full set of accounts to cash books, vouchers, receipts and even the backs of envelopes. In looking at figures it is important not to be blinded by big figures. The fact that a figure is large is not impressive — large figures can appear in the accounts of a company that is about to go into liquidation. You still need to be able to detect the truth behind the figures.

You also need to be aware of the procedural ways of getting figures that your client does not have. An obvious possibility is disclosure, but there are many others that you should watch out for during the civil litigation course.

Not only do you need to identify a source for evidence on figures, you need to be aware of the problems that can arise in presenting such evidence. If you need to take an accountant through his or her evidence you will have to be familiar with all the appropriate terminology. You need to be able to present evidence in a form in which it can be understood. Most important of all, you will sooner or later need to be able to cross-examine on the figures presented by the other side, which requires a most thorough understanding.

It is important to be realistic about what figures may be available and what may not, and to bear in mind what figures may be available to your side and what figures will be available to the other side.

Having stressed the importance of figures, it is equally important for the barrister to be able to deal with the lack of figures — you will often come across a case where you need certain figures to advise in detail and they are simply not obtainable. You can only do your best. Try to think of all the sources from which figures might be obtained. If there are no sources, or if the figures are in any event theoretical, you will have to do your best to argue what the figure should be, from common sense, analogy or some other source. This can, for example, be a problem in arguing for loss of future profit.

This is a point that students often find difficult. If in a contract claim there is a claim for future loss of profits, students tend to think that the claim is weak if it is difficult to assess what the potential profits might have been. This is of course a problem, but it is by no means fatal. The fact that a figure is difficult to assess simply means that you need to set about constructing a good argument for how it might be assessed. Look at profits over recent years, or profits of similar businesses.

18.6 Typical Numeracy Issues in Practice

Dealing with figures is not just a matter of addition and subtraction. It may require an agile mind. A few practical points to watch out for are summarised here.

(a) *What numerical issues are there in a case?* Never be happy with just dealing with the obvious possibility of damages, or with simply dealing with the issues for which figures are given to you. Look out for all the possibilities. For example, there may be tax issues, interest issues, costs, etc.

(b) *What financial resources are there?* If your client is seeking maintenance you need to know not only what your client wants but also how to find out what might be available to claim from. If you are suing for damages, you need to look not only at what your client hopes to recover but also at what a potential defendant can afford to pay. If you are representing a defendant the question may well be what resources your client has to meet the claims against him.

(c) *Where has money come from?* This may arise as a legal issue in a trust case, but can equally be an important factor in other circumstances.

(d) *Where has money gone to?* A question you may well wish to ask if your client's money has disappeared in the hands of the other side! It may also be something you want to know of your own client's resources, or in a criminal case possibly not.

(e) *What is the relevance of an individual figure?* This may sound a strange question, but it may be important in analysing a case or tax question. What exactly does a particular figure given to you consist of? For example, is it capital or income, or can the figure be broken down in any way?

(f) *Is a particular figure reliable?* Don't accept any figure without question. Any figure may or may not be accurate, and may or may not be the right answer to the question you asked about figures. How good is the source of the figure?

(g) *How accurate can a figure be?* The difficulty of assessing figures in some circumstances has already been mentioned. Never give up just because a figure is difficult to assess. Real professional skills are being called on when a figure is not obvious.

(h) *What does a figure really mean?* Is a business really strong or weak? Don't be mesmerised by big figures or long lists of figures. Learn to know what each figure means and what figures are most important.

(i) *What can you do with the figures available to you?* Get the most you can out of a set of figures for the client. Figures are not often going to win or lose a case, but they may well make a vital difference to the client and to the professionalism of the job you do.

(j) *Be specific about figures.* Even if the figures given to you are vague, this is no excuse for you to be vague.

(k) *Be comprehensive with figures.* You do an inadequate job if you give a figure for damages without saying that interest will be recoverable too. It is no good giving a figure for damages without warning that it is likely to be liable for tax.

(l) *Be realistic about figures.* It is no use settling for a figure for maintenance for a client if you are not sure it will really cover client's needs. It is no good offering a figure to settle a claim if you are not sure that your client can raise it.

(m) *Know what is suspicious in a set of figures.* There can be many factors in a set of accounts that could do with inquiry — a set of accounts is only a basic summary of the position of a business. Learn what may be suspicious and what to look for. Learn to find figures hidden in a set of accounts but which are not clearly labelled for what they are.

(n) *Always keep figures in context.* Although the emphasis here is on figures and money, always keep the relative importance of figures in context. A large possible figure for damages still needs to be seen in the perspective of how likely it is that the case will succeed. And remember that money is not always the most important thing for the client — sometimes they do have other objectives that need equal attention.

18.7 Statistics and Graphs

18.7.1 WHEN MAY THE USE OF STATISTICS BE HELPFUL TO YOU?

Statistical methods and statistical terms are used in reporting the mass data of social and economic trends, business conditions, opinion polls and the census. You should get used to reading statistics and utilise them whenever you seek to prove by inference that in your submission a state of affairs exists. Such information is particularly useful when seeking to establish racial or sexual discrimination, risk factors in such areas as sentencing, parole release from mental hospital, danger from chemicals and other environmental pollutants, risk factors in giving informed consent to medical treatment, future profit forecasts, blood test evidence, genetic fingerprinting evidence, etc.

18.8 The Language of Statistics

18.8.1 WHAT IS AN AVERAGE?

There are three different kinds of average: the mean, the median and the mode.

The mean is the arithmetic average arrived at by totalling the number of each of whatever it is you want to average and then dividing that by the total number in the sample. For example, you want to know the average (mean) number of cigarettes that Bar students who smoked, smoke on a particular Monday. If 400 of you smoke, and the total smoked by all 400 on the Monday in question was 8,120; the mean would be $8,120 \div 400 = 20.3$.

The median, using the same example, is the number of cigarettes which half the smokers smoke more than, and half smoke less than. In this example the figure could be less than the mean, and might be about 19.

The mode, again using the same example, is the number of cigarettes which the largest number of people in the sample smoke, so that if the greatest number of people in the group actually smoked 16 cigarettes on Monday then 16 is the modal number.

If presenting an average to the court always know what kind of average you are using, and if you are confronted with statistical information by your opponent, always ask what kind of average is being used.

18.9 What may Influence the Reliability of Statistical Information?

The major difficulty with all statistics is that they may be biased or based on too small a sample to give anything like a reasonable or believable result. Statistical data are generally developed from information collected in questionnaires. It is important to know: how many were sent out, how the respondents were selected, how many were returned, who did not return them and whether the respondents were likely to respond truthfully to the questions posed or whether there may have been a desire to give a pleasing answer. To be valid the sample must be representative and randomly selected.

18.10 Can the Significance of Statistical Conclusions be Tested?

Yes, it can: a test of significance lays down a set of rules for deciding when sample results are inconsistent with a hypothesis. You should check whether the statistics you want to use have been tested. These tests are tests of probability and in most cases nothing poorer than a 5 per cent level of significance is good enough, that is, 95 chances out of 100 that the result is real.

18.11 What Sources of Information Are There?

The government's statistics department provides monthly and annual figures which may be of use to you. Such publications as *Social Trends, Home Office Statistical Bulletin, Annual Abstract of Statistics, Regional Trends, Key Data, United Kingdom National Accounts, Economic Trends* and *Monthly Digest of Statistics* may all be of use to you. The *Guide to Official Statistics* will enable you to decide which of the published statistics may be particularly relevant to a case you are pursuing.

18.12 What is the Best Way to Display this Information?

Explaining this kind of information to a court is something you should plan carefully. One way of doing so is to prepare a graph which can be displayed on an overhead projector, or on a large flip chart. Do not be timid in seeking to use presentational methods that will really assist understanding.

18.13 Numeracy Areas Dealt with on the Course

18.13.1 DAMAGES

Methods of assessing damages will be dealt with in the remedies course (see the *Remedies Manual*). The remedies course will give most emphasis to practial points on approaching the assessment of damages, and particularly complex issues in the assessment of damages. You are expected to know the principles for assessing damages in the core subject areas, and this may be an area where you need to do extra work. You will be expected to deal with general principles for assessing damages and with more detailed questions of whether particular heads of damage are recoverable in a particular case.

18.13.2 INTEREST

The recovery of interest will be dealt with where relevant in the remedies course, the civil litigation course and the drafting course.

18.13.3 COSTS

The recovery of costs will be dealt with where appropriate in the civil litigation and criminal litigation courses.

18.13.4 REVENUE LAW

There will be lectures on revenue law for all students (see the *Remedies Manual*). This course will provide a basic grounding in the principles of tax law that are most relevant for the barrister. Students who have already studied revenue law are still advised to take this course because of the practical professional content.

18.13.5 ACCOUNTS

Although there will be no lectures on accounts, the *Remedies Manual* contains a section entitled The Principles of Accounts. This should familiarise you with the basic terminology of accounting, the elements of a set of accounts and the principles of and interpretation of a set of accounts. It is not intended that you will actually be able to draw up a set of accounts, simply that you will have enough knowledge to be able to deal with a set of accounts. A set of accounts can be a useful source of information once you know what it may contain. It can, for example, show how many of a man's possessions are actually owned by his company, and whether he is employing relatives in the business.

18.13.6 OPTIONS

All the above areas will be developed as appropriate in the option subjects. For example, the *Family Law in Practice Manual* will look at particular tax implications in family cases, and the *Property Disputes in Practice Manual* will look specifically at tax and accounts points relating to wills and trusts.

18.14 Helping Yourself to Deal with Figures

Always carry a calculator, be familiar with how to use it, and use it when figures arise. (A calculator may be taken into classes, assessments and examinations and will be expected to be used whenever appropriate.) Also, make sure you have a calendar available. When you are dealing with cases that happened some time ago a calendar covering more than the current year can be valuable.

Many other things can help with numeracy, the particular requirements depending on a barrister's practice. A ready reckoner can help with calculations. Tax tables are available, as are tables of current levels of social security benefits and so on.

In terms of doing personal accounts, the simple expedient of buying suitable business books for records pays dividends, and increasingly good software packages are available to help with the assessment of personal tax.

18.15 Dealing with Figures during the Course

You will be expected to deal with all numeracy issues whenever they arise on the course. Such issues will not always be obvious but must be spotted in dealing with an exercise, just as they would have to be in practice.

Once the teaching on revenue law has been completed, you will be expected to integrate such issues into any problem presented to you.

You will always be expected:

(a)   to spot a numeracy issue,

(b)   to deal with figures provided in a question,

(c)   to deal intelligently with a situation in which figures are not provided,

(d)   to do any necessary analysis of figures,

(e)   to do any appropriate calculations.

18.16 Numeracy Problems

General numeracy problems are included in the Self-assessment exercises in **Chapter 20**. These are provided to illustrate the type of issue you may be required to deal with during the course. Some may be used in class, the rest can be used for private study.

(See also the **Remedies Manual** for remedies problems.)

NINETEEN

IT USE IN CASE PREPARATION AND PRESENTATION

19.1 Introduction

The use of computers both in legal offices and in the courts themselves has increased at a very fast rate in recent years. Further developments will increase their use dramatically in the near future since the pressure for modernisation is coming from the judiciary and the Lord Chancellor's Department as well as from the legal profession itself. Computerisation is seen not just as an aid to individuals but also as a means of cost-cutting in the long term. Certainly any methods which will assist in reducing preparation and court time is likely to reduce the cost of legal proceedings.

The courtroom itself will in the next few years become far more computerised than it is at present. The 'Woolf' reforms contained in the Civil Procedure Rules are resulting in court administration increasingly being conducted through electronic methods.

The majority of Chambers have moved to the use of computers for a variety of tasks from simple office management to the replacement of secretarial support by barristers typing directly on to word processors or even dictating directly on to the screen using voice recognition systems. In urgent cases, modem links then enable paperwork to be sent directly into Instructing Solicitors' own computer.

Almost all chambers now expect their pupils and junior barristers to be computer literate and be familiar with the potential use of information technology within the legal system. It is therefore vital that those seeking to enter the legal profession have a working knowledge of how they can use computers to assist in the preparation and presentation of their own cases as well as having a general understanding of the situations in which they are likely to be encountered.

19.2 Word Processing

Many of the techniques of fact management set out in this Manual can easily be carried out using standard word processing packages such as Word for Windows. Lists of dates, events, witnesses, exhibits or issues can be prepared easily using the Tables feature. This not only assists in getting to grips with the facts of a case but reduces preparation time if the 'sort' feature is used which can arrange the information according to a number of different criteria such as date or alphabetical order so making it very easy to create chronologies or to draw up lists of witnesses which can then be handed up to the tribunal and used as an aid in court. If a skeleton argument is being prepared it is very easy to extract and create a list of the authorities to be cited using the tables of authorities featured in Windows which can then be handed in to the tribunal.

19.3 Databases

The use of computer databases for legal research has already been dealt with in **Chapter 8** but databases such as Idealist can usefully be used for storing and accessing key facts in a case. For instance, lists of documents with summaries of their contents can be created which can then be searched by means of keywords.

19.4 Spreadsheets

Spreadsheets can assist in carrying out elementary arithmetical calculations such as calculations of damages and interest in personal injury claims. Additionally they can be used as a simple database to assist with the analysis of documents.

19.5 Graphics

Graphic displays such as graphs, charts, family trees, company structures or diagrams can be created using the graphic or drawing function included in most standard word processing packages, which may aid one's own understanding of the case and assist in explaining difficult points to a tribunal by using them as visual aids thus making the understanding of evidence much simpler and indeed cutting the length of the trial and therefore its cost significantly.

19.6 Computerised Office Systems

A variety of standard programes are available which can be used both by individuals and chambers to deal with such matters as recording work done and payments received and maintaining an electronic diary.

19.7 Document Management

Document management systems enable both the storage and retrieval of documents in a case and their use as standard form precedents for future use. The systems allow for search of the document banks under different categories and for both protecting the original version whilst enabling modified versions to be created and added to the database.

19.8 Litigation Support Packages

Used primarily by solicitors these packages provide litigation support at a number of different levels.

Case management systems primarily concentrate on maintaining records of the current status of a case, recording the steps taken and to be taken and any known deadlines. Most systems are primarily diary-driven but they can be enhanced by including automated standard procedures into the system including the automatic production of county court summonses for routine transactions such as debt collection.

Documentary evidence management systems started simply as databases to list documentary evidence. The simplest systems merely index the documents in a searchable database together with short summaries describing the documents and their contents. A more advanced system provides additionally for the scanning of documents so that their image is recorded. However, while the image can be retrieved the system does not allow for the content of the document to be searched electronically. This still has to be done visually once the document has been recalled. However, such technology does enable several lever arch files to be reduced to disk form and so enable preparation to be carried out on laptop computers outside Chambers. The most advanced systems enable the full text of each document to be searched as a result of optical character recognition (OCR) technology.

The benefits of these systems are obvious but as yet the time and cost necessary to ensure completeness is usually only justified in cases such as fraud which involve a large number of documents. Moreover in most cases the decision as to what should be included in the system is not made by the ultimate user, i.e., the barrister, and some documents may not be included. The OCR technology is still developing and although it can recognise printed documents it cannot yet deal with handwriting nor is it yet 100% accurate which may, in a long document, mean a considerable degree of inaccuracy.

19.9 Multi-media Systems

In a suitably equipped courtroom CD-ROM technology can enable documents, charts, graphs, pictures, simulations and visual reconstructions to be shown simultaneously on monitors to the judge, jury, witnesses and to the lawyers and so enhance the accessibility of the information in a case. Some of these systems such as Showcase are very sophisticated indeed and have been used very effectively in a number of high profile fraud trials where all involved have been very impressed by the flexibility of the systems which, although expensive, made considerable savings in court time and therefore overall costs.

19.10 Transcript Analysis

In a long case, having a daily transcript of the trial is becoming increasingly common. If this is provided on disk as well as on paper, it is much easier to search for key words or passages than using a transcript. Software packages have been written specifically for litigation support, which allow for passages of the transcript to be highlighted and annotations made of important points. This can be very useful in preparing for the next day of the trial, whether this is further examination of witnesses or the making of a speech or submission.

Computer aided transcription (CAT), such as that provided by Livenote, enables the transcript of a trial to be transmitted to computers in court almost instantaneously so that the judge and lawyers no longer need to focus on notetaking but can instead concentrate on highlighting important pieces of evidence as the case progresses.

19.11 Computer and Video Conferencing

It is increasingly common for video links to be used to obtain expert evidence without the need for experts to travel to court or for lawyers to meet face to face.

19.12 Electronic Communications

The reliance on paper in the legal world is being replaced by electronic methods of communication. Court listings are now regularly transmitted to chambers electronically. Statements of case are now frequently being exchanged electronically as well as by paper. The organisation of the workplace itself is changing with many barristers increasingly preparing paperwork outside chambers and sending it into chambers via a modem link.

The legal profession, which has always been perceived as traditionalist, has quietly been learning to adjust to the new technology and to recognise its benefits. The next generation of lawyers, already comfortable with the new technology, will be able to develop its use in ways which hopefully will ensure more effective provision of legal services.

TWENTY

SELF-ASSESSMENT EXERCISES

20.1   Finding a Legal Framework

Your client is the mother of a nine-year-old child. She took the child on a picnic in the countryside. They ate their picnic at the side of a cultivated field near a stream. After eating their picnic your client fell asleep and was woken by her child crying out as he had fallen into the stream and cut his arm quite badly. It appears that the child had tripped on some rusty wire at the edge of the stream, but it is not clear how he cut himself. The client is worried that the water in the stream did not seem to be very clean. She took the child to hospital but had to wait some time to get attention for him. The child was not well for several weeks after the incident.

(a)   List the gaps and ambiguities that you would wish to pursue before trying to identify the possible legal framework.

(b)   Make a key list of as many potentially legally relevant factors as you can that might be involved in finding a legal framework.

20.2   Identifying Potential Theories

A man and a woman who are in the living room of the man's house, are heard arguing by a neighbour. Shortly afterwards two shots are heard. The man shouts for help, and the neighbour rushes in to find the man nursing the woman, who has a severe head wound. A doctor is called and the woman is taken to hospital but she later dies.

You have evidence that a handgun was found in the man's pocket shortly after the incident by a policeman investigating what happened. The man admits that he has owned the gun for several years. You also have evidence that the man and woman had been living together for several years, but their relationship had not been happy recently.

You are acting for the defence of the man on a charge of murder.

(a)   List the factual aspects of the case that will require investigation on behalf of the defence.

(b)   Construct as many potential theories of the case as possible which may show the man's innocence.

20.3   Lateral Thinking

1.   There are three witnesses who saw a woman running away from the scene of an armed robbery shortly after the robbery occurred. How many different factual reasons might there be for her conduct? How many different legal hypotheses can these factual possibilities lead to?

2. You are representing Cinderella's stepmother, who has been charged with ill-treating her stepdaughter. Tell the story from the point of view of the stepmother, offering possible lines of defence.

3. A man believes that he has developed a way of predicting how an individual's career may progress by looking at specific factors. He charges a fee for his service, which is popular with young people. He accepts that he is not infallible, and it is a term of paying for his service that if his prediction is wrong, he will return double the original fee. He makes a lot of money. He has just been arrested. What might he have been arrested for?

20.4   Analysing the Evidence

THE CASE OF *R* v *PETER PENNY*

Facts:
Report by PC Giles: dated 2 January 2002 In response to a call from a neighbour I visited 26 Acacia Court at 5 p.m. this afternoon. I spoke initially to John Thorp, the neighbour who called the police. I found the front door ajar. On entering the flat I discovered a body in the living room. I called for assistance and made a thorough search of the flat. There was no one else present. While in the flat I ascertained that there was no rear entry.
PC David Giles, 8.30 p.m., 2/1/02

Summary of police report on the body discovered by PC Giles on 2/1/02. The body has been identified as that of David Star, of 26 Acacia Court, London SE11. Medical evidence suggests that he was strangled between 4 and 5 p.m., on 2/1/02.

John Thorp will say: I was in my lounge on the afternoon of 2nd January 2002, watching out of the window. From here I have a good view of the flats opposite. At around 4.30 p.m. I saw a tall dark-haired man with a moustache run from the flat opposite: 26 Acacia Court. He appeared to be in a great hurry and this made me suspicious, so I telephoned the police. A constable arrived at around 5 o'clock. I told him what I had seen and he entered the flat and found poor David Star dead. I had been watching from my window for most of the time between 4 and 5 p.m., and I am sure that no one entered or left the flat apart from the man I have described.

Paula Lyle will say: I am a neighbour of Peter Penny, who lives at 32 Tamarisk Court, London SE11. I was returning to my own flat on 2nd January 2002, when, at 4.05 p.m., I saw Peter Penny enter the Flat at 26 Acacia Court. I know Peter and am confident that it was him I saw.

Alice Lion will say: I was at a party to see the New Year in, where I saw two friends of mine, Peter Penny and David Star. They were engaged in a heated argument, but I do not know what it was about as I did not want to get involved.

Police report on Peter Penny: Mr Penny is 6ft 2in tall, has dark hair and a moustache, and walks with a pronounced limp. He lives at 32 Tamarisk Court SE11, a block of flats on the same estate as Acacia Court. He is known to have been an acquaintance of the deceased.

The facts here are based on materials prepared by Professor Twining, which may be seen used in a different way in Anderson and Twining, *Analysis of Evidence*, and in Gold, Mackie and Twining, *Learning Lawyers' Skills*, at p. 253. These materials are used with the permission of Professor Twining.

Assignment
Draw a chart which analyses the evidence in respect of the identification element only of the potential murder charge. The chart should show the facts and inferences leading

to the conclusion that it was Peter Penny who killed David Star. It should also show the facts and inferences which weaken that conclusion.

An example of a completed chart in this case is shown in **Appendix 3**.

20.5 Preparing a Criminal Case

Your pupil-mistress has asked you to write notes on the case of *R* v *Juliet Stevens*, which:

(a)   set out the legal framework of the case;

(b)   identify the issues in the case;

(c)   identify what evidence there is on each issue;

(d)   identify any points to clarify with the client in conference.

You may find it useful to review **Chapters 13** and **14** before beginning any detailed preparation of this exercise. Further examples of analytical techniques can be found in **Chapters 16** and **17** in the preparation of the civil and criminal briefs.

<u>IN THE SOUTH LONDON MAGISTRATES' COURT</u>

THE QUEEN

v

JULIET STEVENS

BRIEF TO COUNSEL FOR THE DEFENCE

Public Funding

Starling & Co.
11 West Square
London WC1R 1AB

IN THE SOUTH LONDON MAGISTRATES' COURT

THE QUEEN

v

JULIET STEVENS

INSTRUCTIONS TO COUNSEL TO
ADVISE IN CONFERENCE

Counsel has herewith:

1. Copy of the charge.

2. Witness statements served under the Advance Disclosure rules.

3. Miss Stevens' proof of evidence.

Miss Stevens is charged with causing criminal damage to a motor car. The cost of repair is in excess of £5,000.

The facts appear from the statements of the prosecution witnesses and her proof of evidence.

Miss Stevens is a lady of good character, with no experience of the courts.

Miss Stevens will need advice as to her plea and she is very anxious to know whether it is better to elect trial in the Crown Court or to get the case over with quickly in the Magistrates' Court.

Counsel is instructed to advise Miss Stevens in conference.

CHARGE

Damaging property, contrary to section 1(1) of the Criminal Damage Act 1971

PARTICULARS

Juliet Stevens on the 11th day of August 2002, without lawful excuse damaged a car belonging to James Kirby, intending to damage such property or being reckless as to whether such property would be damaged.

STATEMENT OF WITNESS

(C.J. Act 1967 s. 9; M.C. Act 1980 ss. 5A(3)(a) and 5B; M.C. Rules 1981 r. 70)

Statement of: James Kirby

Age: Over 18

Occupation: Stockbroker

This statement consisting of 1 page, signed by me, is true to the best of my knowledge and belief and I make it knowing that, if it is tendered in evidence, I shall be liable to prosecution if I have wilfully stated in it anything which I know to be false or do not believe to be true.

Dated the 10th day of August 2002   Signed: James Kirby
                                                      Signature witnessed by: Jane Smart

I live at 23 Arcadia Mansions, Battersea SW11, with my girlfriend Paula Vernon. Until May of this year I had been living with Juliet Stevens. This relationship had lasted several years.

During the course of that relationship I had bought a BMW 323i motor car, index number P 564 RGT. We both used to drive it, but it was my car.

Juliet was very bitter when the relationship came to an end. She said I ought to compensate her for the fact that she had to move out and had nowhere to live.

She kept asking me if she could have the car, and I kept saying no. She seemed to be determined to have it.

Feelings between us remained very bad and there were many disputes over various items of property in the flat which we had acquired during the relationship.

In the early hours of Friday 9th August I was woken by a very loud banging in the street outside. My flat is on the ground floor. I looked outside and saw Juliet attacking the car with a sledgehammer.

I went outside to try to stop her, but she seemed to have gone berserk.

She had smashed all the windows and lights. All the body panels were dented.

She was really furious and kept saying, 'You said I could have the car, but all I ever see is the two of you in it. Well, it's mine and no one will drive it again.'

Shortly afterwards the police arrived. As far as I am concerned I had not given Juliet Stevens the car and it was not hers to damage.

I am willing to attend court and give evidence.

Signed: James Kirby   Signature witnessed by: Jane Smart

STATEMENT OF WITNESS

(C.J. Act 1967 s. 9; M.C. Act 1980 ss. 5A(3)(a) and 5B; M.C. Rules 1981 r. 70)

Statement of: James Kirby

Age: Over 18

Occupation: Stockbroker

This statement consisting of 1 page, signed by me, is true to the best of my knowledge and belief and I make it knowing that, if it is tendered in evidence, I shall be liable to prosecution if I have wilfully stated in it anything which I know to be false or do not believe to be true.

Dated the 24th day of August 2002   Signed: James Kirby
                                               Signature witnessed by: Jane Smart

Further to my previous statement, I have now obtained an estimate for repairs to the car. It will need new windows and lights, new body panels and a complete respray. The estimate is £5,500.

Signed: James Kirby   Signature witnessed by: Jane Smart

STATEMENT OF WITNESS

(C.J. Act 1967 s. 9; M.C. Act 1980 ss. 5A(3)(a) and 5B; M.C. Rules 1981 r. 70)

Statement of: Jane Smart

Age: Over 18

Occupation: Police Officer

This statement consisting of 1 page, signed by me, is true to the best of my knowledge and belief and I make it knowing that, if it is tendered in evidence, I shall be liable to prosecution if I have wilfully stated in it anything I know to be false or do not believe to be true.

Dated 10th day of August 2002   Signed: Jane Smart
                                                  Signature witnessed by: Paul Dunn

At 0200 on Friday 9th August 2002 I attended the scene of a disturbance at Arcadia Mansions SW11. On arrival I saw a person I now know to be Juliet Stevens repeatedly hitting a BMW motor car with a sledgehammer. The car appeared to be severely damaged. A man who I now know to be James Kirby was yelling at her and trying to stop her.

She appeared to calm down when she saw me, and I took her to one side to speak to her.

I asked her whose car it was and she replied, 'mine'. I asked her why she was smashing it up and she said, 'When I broke up with James, he said I could have the car since I'd been living with him for years and had lost out on the chance of getting my own place. I kept asking him for it, and he kept putting it off, saying I could have it soon. This evening I saw James and Paula driving around in it — my car — and I just saw red. It's my car'. Miss Stevens was very distressed.

I spoke to Mr Kirby who told me it was his car. He showed me the Vehicle Registration Document which was in his name. A check on the PNC also revealed him to be the registered keeper.

I went back to Miss Stevens and said, 'It appears that it is not your car. I am arresting you for causing criminal damage to that car.' I then cautioned her and she said, 'It's my car'.

She was taken to Battersea police station.

I was present at 7 a.m. when she was charged and further cautioned, to which she made no reply.

Signed: Jane Smart   Signature witnessed by: Paul Dunn

PROOF OF EVIDENCE

Juliet Stevens will say:

I am 25 years old. I am single and I live at 32 Malpas Road SW11. This is rented accommodation. I am a PR consultant.

I had been living with James Kirby in his flat for six years until May 2002 when we split up, because he met someone else.

During this time we both bought lots of things for the flat, and it was our home. We occasionally discussed what would happen if we broke up, since I had put a lot of money and time into making the flat our home, rather than buying somewhere of my own. He said we wouldn't break up, but if we ever did he would make sure I was all right financially by giving me the car. He bought the car, but we both drove it.

We always referred to it as my car, as a sort of private joke.

When we broke up I expected him to honour his promise to give me the car. I had taken the promise seriously. At first he said he would, but he kept putting it off. He never said I couldn't have it, but said I'd have to wait until he got another one.

I accept I was very bitter about the way he treated me.

In the evening of 9th August I was walking to a friend's house when I saw James and Paula drive past in the car. James hooted and waved. I was furious. By the time I got home I was even more furious. There is building work going on in the house where I am living, and when I saw a sledgehammer I decided I was going to wreck the car — my car.

By now I had decided he was not going to hand it over to me, so I decided if I couldn't have it, they certainly would not drive it.

I walked around to Arcadia Mansions, which is not far, and attacked the car.

I honestly believed it was my car and that I was entitled to do what I wanted with it.

I am worried about my employers finding out about this court case and want it dealt with as quickly as possible.

20.6   Preparing a Civil Case

Your pupil-master has asked you to write notes on the case of *Norman v Finings Engineering Ltd*, which:

(a)   set out the legal framework of the case;

(b)   identify the issues in the case;

(c)   identify what evidence there is on each issue.

You may find it useful to review **Chapters 12** and **14** before beginning any detailed preparation of this exercise. Worked examples of some analytical techniques can also be found in **Chapters 16** and **17**, in the preparation of the civil and criminal briefs.

IN THE CANTERBURY COUNTY COURT   Claim No. CT1/01306

BETWEEN:

MELVYN NORMAN   Claimant

v

FININGS ENGINEERING LIMITED   Defendants

_____

BRIEF TO COUNSEL ON BEHALF OF THE CLAIMANT

_____

Agreed Brief Fee £400

Blister & Co.
Ryder House
Park Lane
Sevenoaks
Kent

<u>IN THE CANTERBURY COUNTY COURT</u>   Claim No. CT1/01306

BETWEEN:

MELVYN NORMAN   <u>Claimant</u>

v

FININGS ENGINEERING LIMITED   <u>Defendants</u>

INSTRUCTIONS TO COUNSEL

Counsel has herewith:

1. Statements of case.

2. The agreed trial bundle (paginated [1] – [6]).

Instructing Solicitors act on behalf of the Claimant Melvyn Norman who was injured in an accident at his place of work on 3rd July 2001. The facts of the accident are straightforward. Mr Norman was walking across the press shop floor of the Defendants' premises when he slipped on a patch of oil and fell.

Counsel is asked to appear on behalf of the Claimant at the trial of this claim. Special damages have been agreed in the sum of £1,110. Unfortunately it has not been possible to agree general damages. However, the Claimant's medical report is agreed. The trial bundle contains the only two relevant extracts from the Accident Report Book, i.e., the Claimant's accident and one other similar accident in 2000.

It is also agreed that the oil can is to be an exhibit.

IN THE CANTERBURY COUNTY COURT   Claim No. CT1/01306

BETWEEN:

MELVYN NORMAN   Claimant

v

FININGS ENGINEERING LIMITED   Defendants

PARTICULARS OF CLAIM

---

1.   At the time of the accident described below the Claimant was employed by the Defendants as a service hand at their works at Eagle Road, Canterbury, Kent, which was at all material times a workplace to which the Workplace (Health, Safety and Welfare) Regulations 1992 ('the Regulations') applied.

2.   At about 3.45 p.m. on 3rd July 2001 the Claimant, in the course of his employment, was walking across the floor of the 'press shop' at these premises when he slipped on a patch of oil and fell.

3.   The accident was caused by a breach of statutory duty under the Regulations and/or negligence on the part of the Defendants, their servants or agents.

PARTICULARS OF BREACH OF STATUTORY DUTY

(a)   Failing to maintain the press shop floor in an efficient state, contrary to regulation 5(1) of the Regulations;

(b)   Failing to keep the floor free from a substance which may cause a person to slip, namely oil, contrary to regulation 12(3) of the Regulations.

PARTICULARS OF NEGLIGENCE

(c)   The Claimant repeats the allegations of breach of statutory duty above;

(d)   Causing or permitting the patch of oil to be and/or to remain upon the press shop floor;

(e)   Failing to carry out any or any adequate cleaning and/or failing to remove the oil from the press shop floor;

(f)   Failing to warn the Claimant of the dangers of the oil;

(g)   Failing to heed an oral complaint about the danger of oil on the floor made by the Claimant on 29th June 2001 to the Defendants' responsible servant one Andrew Jackson, the works foreman;

(h)   Failing to provide a safe system of work;

(i)   In the premises, failing to take any or any adequate care for the Claimant's safety and exposing him to the unnecessary risk of injury.

4.   By reason of the matters described above the Claimant suffered personal injuries and was put to loss and expense.

PARTICULARS OF INJURIES

The Claimant who was born on 18th March 1970 suffered bruising to and a ligamentous strain of his right knee. He was away from work for 3 weeks during which time he underwent a course of intensive physiotherapy. Pain, swelling and tenderness remained. The Claimant had a further 2-week course of physiotherapy in August 2001. During this 2-week period he was again absent from work. There is still some restriction of movement of the knee joint but this should fully resolve within 18 months from the date of the accident. There is no evidence of osteoarthritis. Full details of the Claimant's injuries are set out in the medical report of Mr Westside of St Hugh's Hospital in Sevenoaks, Kent, dated 3rd April 2002 a copy of which is served pursuant to Civil Procedure Rules, PD 16, para. 4.3.

PARTICULARS OF SPECIAL DAMAGE

Particulars of the Claimant's loss and damage appear in the statement of special damages served herewith.

5.   Further the Claimant claims interest pursuant to section 69 of the County Courts Act 1984 on such sum as may be found to be due to the Claimant at such rate and for such period as the Court shall think fit.

AND the Claimant claims:

1.   Damages.

2.   The aforesaid interest pursuant to statute to be assessed.

Statement of Truth

I believe that the facts stated in these particulars of claim are true.

Dated the 26th day of April 2002   *M. Norman*

SAINT HUGH'S HOSPITAL, SEVENOAKS, KENT

MEDICAL REPORT ON MELVYN NORMAN

Melvyn Norman aged 32

34 Copping Rise, Sevenoaks, Kent

Occupation: Service Hand at Finings Engineering Limited

Date of accident: 3/7/01

Date of Examination for this Report 27/3/02

Mr Norman tells me that whilst at work on 3/7/01 he slipped on a patch of oil and injured his right knee. He was taken to hospital where X-rays revealed no bony injury. There was severe bruising over the lateral aspect of the knee joint. A ligamentous strain was diagnosed, a supportive bandage provided and analgesics prescribed.

Mr Norman was off work initially for three weeks. During this period he had a course of intensive physiotherapy at Sevenoaks Hospital. At home he was restricted in his activities. He could not play with his two young children. He had difficulty negotiating stairs, his sleep was interrupted and he could not perform his normal household jobs. Mrs Norman therefore had to do more by way of jobs around the house and looking after the children in this period. Mr Norman says that when he returned to work he was still in pain. He worked for a week and then had a further two weeks off. In this period he had another course of physiotherapy. I have had the benefit of reading notes supplied by Mr Norman's GP, Mr Strange, and also from Mr Irwin the physiotherapist. There was an initial reduction in flexion of 40% in the joint, but this has steadily improved. Mr Norman still experiences pain when kneeling at work but this is a dull ache and not severe. He has needed pain-killing tablets intermittently since the accident but the instances of need have become less frequent.

Examination

General health: good

Height: 6ft 1″. Weight: 12 stone

Mr Norman presented as a pleasant if somewhat absent minded man. On examination his gait was normal. There was a 10% reduction in flexion of the right knee joint. Kneeling is still painful. There is no current bruising but there is a little residual tenderness over the lateral aspect of the joint.

Conclusion

There is a clear evidence of an initially severe ligamentous injury of the right knee joint. There is no evidence of osteoarthritis. I foresee no long-term effects and would anticipate full resolution of the injury within 18 months from the date of the accident.

TIM WESTSIDE
Consultant
3rd April 2002

IN THE CANTERBURY COUNTY COURT   Claim No. CT1/01306

BETWEEN:

MELVYN NORMAN   <u>Claimant</u>

v

FININGS ENGINEERING LIMITED   <u>Defendants</u>

SCHEDULE OF LOSS AND EXPENSE PURSUANT
TO CPR PD 16, PARA. 4.2

---

5 weeks' loss of earnings	£1,000
Taxi fares to and from hospital	£ 75
Damaged clothing	£ 35
	———
TOTAL	£1,110

Dated the 23rd day of April 2002

Blister & Co.
Ryder House
Park Lane
Sevenoaks, Kent

<u>Solicitors for the Claimant</u>

To the Defendants:
Finings Engineering Limited
Eagle Road
Canterbury, Kent

And to the Court Manager

IN THE CANTERBURY COUNTY COURT   Claim No. CT1/01306

BETWEEN:

MELVYN NORMAN   Claimant

v

FININGS ENGINEERING LIMITED   Defendants

DEFENCE

---

1. Paragraphs 1 and 2 of the Particulars of Claim are admitted.

2. It is denied that the Defendants were negligent or in breach of statutory duty as alleged in the Particulars of Claim or at all.

3. The Defendants aver that they maintained the press shop floor in an efficient state and did all that was reasonably practicable to keep the floor free from oil or any other substance which may cause a person to slip or fall. The Defendants' servant one James Stonehouse was charged with cleaning the floor twice each day and had cleaned the floor approximately 2 hours before the accident.

4. The accident referred to in the Particulars of Claim was caused solely or alternatively contributed to by the negligence of the Claimant.

PARTICULARS OF NEGLIGENCE

(a) Carrying an oil can with him across the floor in such a manner that oil was dripped on to the floor;

(b) Causing or permitting oil to fall onto the floor;

(c) Failing to look where he was going and slipping on the oil he had dropped;

(d) In the premises failing to take any or any adequate care for his own safety and exposing himself to the unnecessary risk of injury.

5. Further or alternatively, if, which is denied, the oil upon which the Claimant slipped was not dropped by him immediately prior to the accident, the Defendants will rely upon the failure of the Claimant to look where he was going and thereby avoid the patch of oil upon which he slipped.

6. The Defendants make no admissions as to the alleged or any injury, loss or damage, or as to the amount thereof.

7. Save in so far as has been expressly admitted the Defendants deny each and every allegation in the Particulars of Claim as if the same were set out in turn and specifically denied.

Statement of Truth

I believe that the facts stated in this defence are true.

Dated the 29th day of May 2002

D Temple, Director

for Finings Engineering Ltd

<u>TRIAL BUNDLE</u>

<u>INDEX</u>

[1]

Claimant
M. Norman
1st
4.9.2002

Claim No. CT1/01306

IN THE CANTERBURY COUNTY COURT

MELVYN NORMAN   <u>Claimant</u>

v

FININGS ENGINEERING LIMITED   <u>Defendant</u>

WITNESS STATEMENT OF MELVYN NORMAN

I, Melvyn Norman of, 34 Copping Rise, Sevenoaks, Kent, service hand, will say as follows:

1. I am the Claimant in this action. I make this statement concerning the accident that occurred at work on 3rd July 2001.

2. I am married with two daughters aged 5 and 7. I have worked for the Defendants for two years as a service hand at their Eagle Road works. My job involves me in looking after and adjusting the press machines on the press shop floor. At about 3.40 p.m. on the day of the accident I was adjusting a B/44 press machine in the press shop when I realised that I needed an adjustable spanner. I decided to go to the tool shop to get the spanner. I had just oiled a B/44 machine and had the oil can in my hand. As far as I can recall I was holding the oil can in an upright position. The can has a long, thin spout that points upwards. I believe that it was pointing upwards at the time of the accident. It is possible that a few drops of oil were dripping from the can as I made my way to the tool shop. If this was the case then they would most likely have dripped on to my overalls rather than the floor as I always carry the oil can very close to me.

3. I had reached the middle of the press shop floor when I slipped and fell. I had been chatting to workmates as I passed them. Simon Packer was working on a press near to where I fell and saw the whole thing.

4. James Stonehouse the press shop apprentice had been standing at the door of the press shop, some 20 feet away from the place where the accident occurred. After the accident I remember him coming over and helping me to the sickroom. I remember Simon Packer saying something about there having been a large patch of oil on the floor for some time.

5. Oil has always been a problem in the press shop. Lately the problem has got worse. On 29.6.01 I actually spoke to the works foreman, Mr Jackson, about it. It was a sort of general chat but I told him I thought the floor was dangerous.

6. I was in great pain when I fell. My knee was badly bruised. At hospital they said it was ligaments. I had the bandage on for three weeks. I was off work and couldn't play with the kids. Also I had difficulty getting up and down stairs and doing jobs around the house. The wife had to do it all. I went to physiotherapy for 3 weeks then I went back to work. The pain was still bad and after a week I had to have 2 more weeks off work and more physiotherapy.

7. I like a game of football now and again but I haven't played since the accident. I don't trust the leg. The same applies to the gardening which was one of my favourite hobbies. I was a very keen gardener and kept our front and rear gardens immaculately.

[2]

I was particularly keen on the bedded plants and shrubs and very proud of the way I'd arranged and groomed the flower beds. Since the accident I have had difficulty bending down to do the gardening. My wife has done most of the gardening but she isn't so much of a perfectionist as I am and the garden looks pretty untidy as a result.

STATEMENT OF TRUTH

I believe that the facts stated in this witness statement are true.

M. Norman
....

Dated the 4th day of September 2002

[3]

Claimant
S. Packer
1st
4.9.2002

Claim No. CT1/01306

IN THE CANTERBURY COUNTY COURT

MELVYN NORMAN   <u>Claimant</u>

v

FININGS ENGINEERING LIMITED   <u>Defendant</u>

WITNESS STATEMENT OF SIMON PACKER

I, Simon Packer, of 4 Blood Lane, Sevenoaks, Kent will say as follows:

1.   I am employed as a press operator at Finings Engineering's Eagle Road works. I know Melvyn Norman as a fellow employee but we are not friends. On the day of his accident I was in the press shop working on my press. When I returned from lunch at about 2.15 p.m. I noticed that there was a patch of oil by the side of my machine. The floor of the press shop is often oily. The apprentice is supposed to keep the floor clean but he often forgets. I do not remember him cleaning the floor on the day of the accident.

2.   It is difficult to keep the floor clear of oil. The machines shed some oil and the adjusting and maintenance work involves the use of oil. Really the floors should be inspected and, if necessary, cleaned every couple of hours just to be on the safe side. Even that might not solve the problem.

3.   I remember that Melvyn was carrying a can of oil as he approached my press. I can't say if it was leaking or not. He seemed to be walking in a line that would have taken him wide of the oil but he must have altered his course. When he fell the oil can went flying and Melvyn clutched his right knee in agony.

4.   James Stonehouse helped me to take him to the sickroom. I do remember that there were some oil stains down the front of Melvyn's overalls and on the top of his boots when we picked him up.

STATEMENT OF TRUTH

I believe that the facts stated in this witness statement are true.

S Packer
....

Dated the 4th day of September 2002

[4]

Defendant
J. Stonehouse
1st
4.9.2002

Claim No. CT1/01306

IN THE CANTERBURY COUNTY COURT

MELVYN NORMAN   Claimant

v

FININGS ENGINEERING LIMITED   Defendant

WITNESS STATEMENT OF JAMES STONEHOUSE

I, James Stonehouse of 39 Snargate Road, Sevenoaks, Kent, will say as follows:

1. I am 17 years old and work as an apprentice at Finings Engineering in the press shop. The foreman, Mr Jackson, asked me to keep the floor of the shop clean. I give it a clean twice a day. The problem is that oil gets all over the place and there isn't much you can do. Some of the lads are careless with their oil cans, and the presses spurt out a bit as well.

2. At about 3.40 p.m. on 3/7/01 I was standing by the door of the press shop. I saw Melvyn Norman walking across the shop towards the door. I particularly noticed him because he was carrying an oil can in one of his hands, I can't remember which. The spout was facing downwards and oil was leaking out. Melvyn didn't seem to realise. I was about to shout out when he slipped and fell. When we picked him up there was some oil on the front of his shoes. I was surprised that there wasn't more oil on his clothes and shoes. I usually clean the floor at about 1.30 p.m. at the end of the morning shift, and again at about 4 p.m. in the afternoon. A few days earlier Mr Jackson, the works foreman, had asked me to clean the floor carefully, that's why I'm pretty sure that I had cleaned the floor at 1.30 p.m. on 3/7/01.

STATEMENT OF TRUTH

I believe that the facts stated in this witness statement are true.

J. Stonehouse
....

Dated the 4th day of September 2002

[5]

Defendant
A. Jackson
1st
4.9.2002

Claim No. CT1/01306

IN THE CANTERBURY COUNTY COURT

MELVYN NORMAN   Claimant

v

FININGS ENGINEERING LIMITED   Defendant

WITNESS STATEMENT OF ANDREW JACKSON

I, Andrew Jackson, of 5 Rosebush Lane, Canterbury, Kent, will say as follows:

1.   I am the works foreman at the Defendants' premises at Eagle Road, Canterbury, Kent. I have worked at those premises for the Defendants since that particular factory opened in 1973. I started as an apprentice press operator and have been works foreman for the last five years.

2.   The press shop floor contains 10 presses in all. The maintenance of the presses involves them being regularly oiled to ensure that the moving parts move freely and do not grind causing wear. Any oil spillage from routine maintenance should be minimal.

3.   When the presses are operating there is some minimal release of oil. This is the oil used for maintenance which will sometimes escape from the moving parts when a press is working at full capacity. Most of the moving parts are boxed in, but occasionally oil escapes. The amount of oil is small, more in the nature of a few droplets than a pool or puddle.

4.   Melvyn Norman is a service hand at the Defendants' Eagle Road works. He is responsible for maintaining the presses on the press shop floor. This involves him regularly oiling the moving parts of the machine.

5.   On 29.6.01 he spoke to me about a number of maintenance matters. He mentioned in a general way that he thought that there might have been more oil on the press shop floor in the last few days. He did not say that he thought that this oil was causing a greater hazard than usual. The floor is cleaned twice a day by one of our apprentices, James Stonehouse. Even though Mr Norman had made no mention of a greater hazard being caused by the oil, following my discussion with him on 30.6.01 I told James Stonehouse to clean the floor particularly carefully.

STATEMENT OF TRUTH

I believe that the facts stated in this witness statement are true.

A Jackson
....

Dated the 4th day of September 2002

[6]

<u>ACCIDENT REPORT BOOK</u>

<u>Date/Time</u>	<u>Location</u>	<u>Details</u>
12/2/00	Press shop	F. Collins. Slipped on oil. Injured elbow and shoulder
. . .		
3/7/01	Press shop	M. Norman. Slipped on oil, injured knee.

[7]

20.7   Dealing with Figures

Problem 1

Examine the following facts in detail, and identify as many areas as you can where information about numbers must be sought and dealt with.

In each case, identify where information about relevant figures might be sought by yourself or by instructing solicitors.

Mr Duff, aged 59, was injured in April 2002 when he was driving his car and it was hit by another vehicle. His father was a passenger in his car at the time and was killed in the accident. The accident was caused by the driver of the other car, Mr Young, who has since been convicted of dangerous driving with regard to the incident. Mr Duff is suing Mr Young for negligence. As a result of the accident, which broke both his legs and caused serious internal injuries, Mr Duff could not work for six months. In order to be able to return to work as quickly as possible, Mr Duff used a substantial amount from his savings to pay for private medical treatment.

Mr Duff has had particular difficulties in that he is the manager of an interior design business. The business was incorporated in 1996 as Duff Decor Ltd, with Mr Duff as a 60% shareholder and his brother as a 40% shareholder. Business has suffered while Mr Duff has not been able to work. His brother is not good at business, so a manager had to be employed while Mr Duff was not there. In addition, a few months before the accident, £100,000 was borrowed to fund expansion of the business, and there have been problems keeping up with repayments on this loan.

Mr Duff's father left a will appointing Mr Duff and his brother as his executors. The main provisions of the father's will was to leave the residue of his estate in trust for his grandchildren.

Mr Duff left his wife and two children three years ago, and he has since lived in a flat. The wife and children are still in the former matrimonial home, and Mr Duff had been voluntarily paying maintenance to them. However, following his accident he has been unable to make such payments, and his wife is currently in receipt of social security benefits. Mr Duff has heard rumours that his wife has formed a relationship with another man who has done substantial work on the home.

Problem 2

A wife tells you that she needs maintenance from her husband. Both parties have made full disclosure of their financial situation and below you will find each party's schedule of income and expenditure. Is she right?

Wife	£
Gross income	15,708.00 p.a.
Net income, approximately	927.50 per month
National insurance	50.36 per month
Monthly expenditure:	
Gas	25.00
Electricity	15.00
Television licence	8.00
Contents insurance	13.00
Car tax and insurance	24.00
Car maintenance	34.00
Petrol	50.00
Dental treatment	10.00
House repairs, etc.	40.00
Investments: life assurance, etc.	154.25
Increase in national insurance contribution	68.00
Council tax, water rates, buildings insurance, etc.	136.50
Food	200.00
Clothes	100.00

Husband	£
Gross income	34,000.00 p.a.
Net income, approximately	1,845.00 per month

Monthly expenditure:

Expenses of former matrimonial home, council tax, etc.	136.30
Mortgage	719.00
Endowment policy	198.00
Gas	50.00
Electricity	20.00
Telephone	20.00
Contents insurance	10.00
Ground rent and maintenance charge	12.00
Television licence	8.00
Council tax and water rates	58.00
Hire purchase: car, furniture	135.82
Savings	152.00
Food	200.00
Clothes	20.00
Holidays	150.00

Problem 3

The XYZ Building Society is unwilling to advance money for the purchase of terraced houses without front gardens in an area where members of ethnic minority groups live. Your instructing solicitors have presented you with a copy of a report compiled by the Commission of Racial Equality whch states that 86% of ethnic minority families living in that area live in terraced houses without front gardens, and that 46% of white families living there live in terraced houses without front gardens.

Your instructing solicitors believe that their client (a member of an ethnic minority group) can successfully claim that she has been indirectly discriminated against on racial grounds by the Building Society, which has refused to advance her a mortgage to purchase a terraced house without a front garden in the area. Explain how you can use the figures supplied to help to prove discrimination.

Problem 4

The defendant is charged with fraud. The prosecution wishes to prove that in May of a particular year her level of income and expenditure rose significantly, and has obtained copies of her bank statements. Do they bear this out?

BARTLETT'S BANK PLC 27 Old Steet London EC8Y 2HR		Account : J Park 14278693			
Date	Details		Withdrawals	Deposits	Balance
					3,018.88
27 Mar		000621	50.00		2,968.88
28 Mar	CHEQUES			321.67	3,290.55
30 Mar		000620	98.27		
	PAYROLL			948.25	
		AC	30.00		4,110.53
3 Apr	HOLT FINANCE	SO	59.28		
	BROADWAY RENTALS	SO	22.90		4,028.35
5 Apr		000622	31.84		3,996.51

Date	Details	Withdrawals	Deposits	Balance
6 Apr	AC	75.00		3,921.51
7 Apr	W LONDON CTY CT SO	100.00		3,821.51
10 Apr	000623	1,260.55		2,560.96
11 Apr	CC 000624	80.00	13.60	2,494.56
14 Apr	AC 000627	50.00 142.88		2,301.68
17 Apr	WESTLAND B/SOC SO 000628	392.27 50.00		1,859.41
18 Apr	000625	27.00		1,832.41
19 Apr	AC L. B. LAMBETH SO CC	75.00 76.82	500.00	2,180.59
20 Apr	000626	60.48		2,120.11
21 Apr	000629	100.00		2,020.11
25 Apr	S.ELEC SO	43.00		1,977.11
26 Apr	000630	5,000.00		3,022.89 OD
27 Apr	CC		142.80	2880.09 OD
28 Apr	PAYROLL AC	75.00	948.25	2,006,84 OD
2 May	HOLT FINANCE SO 000632	59.28 50.00		2,116.12 OD
3 May	BROADWAY RENTALS SO CHEQUES	22.90	347.80	1,791.22 OD
5 May	000633	50.00		1,841.22 OD
8 May	AC W LONDON CTY CT SO	25.00 100.00		1,966.22 OD
9 May	CC		87.30	1,878.92 OD
10 May	000636	32.99		1,911.91 OD
11 May	000635	50.00		1,961.91 OD
12 May	BANK CHARGES AC CC	36.80 75.00	7.21	2,066.50 OD
16 May	WESTLAND B/SOC SO P. LANGTON	392.27	2,500.00	41.23
17 May	INTEREST 000634	36.67 186.21		181.65 OD

Date	Details		Withdrawals	Deposits	Balance
18 May	STAR CLUB	DD	32.00		
		AC	75.00		
		CC		500.00	211.35
19 May	L. B. LAMBETH	SO	76.82		134.53
22 May		000637	75.00		59.53
25 May		AC	75.00		
	S/ELEC	SO	43.00		58.47 OD
26 May		000638	21.95		
		CC		142.80	62.38
30 May	PAYROLL			948.25	
		000639	50.00		
		000640	17.90		
		000641	100.00		
	CHEQUES			338.92	1,181,65
1 Jun		AC	50.00		1,131.65
2 Jun	INTEREST		2.86		1,128.79
5 Jun	HOLT FINANCE	SO	59.28		
	BROADWAY RENTALS	SO	22.90		
		000642	50.00		996.61
7 Jun		000644	250.00		
	P. LANGTON			2,500.00	
	W LONDON CTY CT	SO	100.00		3,146.61
8 Jun		000643	44.99		3,101.62
9 Jun		AC	75.00		3,026.62
12 Jun		AC	50.00		2,976.62
13 Jun		CC		28.50	3,005.12
16 Jun	WESTLAND B/SOC	SO	392.27		
		000645	50.00		2,562.85
19 Jun	L. B. LAMBETH	SO	76.82		
		CC		500.00	2,986.03
20 Jun		000646	60.00		2,926.03
23 Jun		000647	23.90		2,902.13
23 Jun		AC	75.00		2,827.13

Key: SO STANDING ORDER   AC AUTOMATED CASH   OD OVERDRAWN
CC CASH AND/OR CHEQUES   DD DIRECT DEBIT

APPENDIX ONE

GLOSSARY OF MEDICAL TERMS

This glossary contains the meaning of certain technical terms commonly found in medical reports.

Abduction: movement away from the mid-line
Adduction: movement towards the mid-line
Amnesia: absence of memory
Analgesic: pain-relieving medication
Ankylosis: obliteration of a joint by fusion, either bony or fibrous
Aphasia: loss of power of speech
Arthrodesis: fusion of a joint by operation
Arthroplasty: production of movement in a joint by operation
Arthroscopy: direct vision inside a joint using a fibre-optic scope
Aspiration: sucking out fluid (e.g. from a joint or a cavity) through a hollow needle
Ataxia: unsteadiness of gait
Atrophy: wasting of a body part from lack of vascular or nerve supply
Avascular necrosis: death of tissue through deprivation of blood supply; refers particularly to bones — e.g. head of femur following fracture of neck of femur
Avulsion: wrenching away of a part, e.g. avulsion fracture, the wrenching away of a fragment of bone by force applied by an attached tendon
Axonotmesis: interruption of conductivity in a nerve by 'physiological' (i.e. not physical) division of the axons, resulting in paralysis and anaesthesia in the distribution of the nerve; spontaneous recovery can be expected but will take some months (cf. neurapraxia and neurotmesis)
Biopsy: microscopic examination of tissue taken from the living body
Bi-valve: removal of a plaster cast by cutting along each side of its length, permitting replacement if required
Brachial: pertaining to the arm
Brachioradialis: muscle of the forearm
B.S.R. (or E.S.R.): Blood (or erythrocyte) rate — a laboratory test upon the blood to detect the presence of an inflammatory process somewhere in the body
Bursa: a cyst-like sac between a bony prominence and the skin — e.g. prepatellar bursa, inflammation in which constitutes 'housemaid's knee'
Calcaneal: pertaining to the calcaneus
Calcaneus: the heel bone, or os calcis
Callus: the cement-like new bone formation which produces union of the fragments of a fracture
Cardiac: pertaining to the heart
Cephalic: pertaining to the head
Cervical: pertaining to the neck
Chondral: pertaining to cartilage
Chronic: long-lasting, the reverse of acute
Claudication: lameness; applied particularly to pain in the calf muscles resulting from defective blood supply owing to arterial disease
Comminuted: a type of fracture of a bone in which there are more than two fragments
Concussion of the brain: to establish the diagnosis the loss of consciousness must be immediate and complete though it may be of very short duration

Condyle: a rounded articular eminence

Cortex: the outer layer of a structure — e.g. the 'shell' of a bone; the surface of the brain

Costal: pertaining to the ribs

Crepitus: a creaking or grating, found in osteoarthritic joints; also in recent fractures and with inflammation of tendons and their sheaths (tenosynovitis)

C.S.F.: cerebro-spinal fluid, which lies on the surface of the brain and spinal cord and inside the ventricles of the brain

Cuboid: a small bone of the foot

Cyanosis: blueness from deficient oxygenation of the blood

Deltoid region: the outer region of the upper third of the arm

Diplopia: double vision

Disarticulation: amputation through a joint

Disc, intervertebral: fibro-cartilaginous 'cushion' between two vertebrae

Distal: farthest point from the centre (opposite to proximal)

Dorsal spine: that part of the spine from which the ribs spring; known also as the 'thoracic' spine

Dorsiflexion: movement of a joint in a backward direction (syn. extension)

Dorsum: back or top — e.g. back of hand, top of foot

Dupuytren's contracture: thickened fibrous tissue in the palm of the hand causing contracture of the fingers

Dys-: prefix meaning difficult, defective, painful — e.g. dyspnoea, meaning shortness of breath

-ectomy: suffix meaning surgical excision — e.g. patellectomy, removal of the patella

E.E.G.: electro-encephalogram (graph of electric impulses in the brain)

Effusion: extravasation of fluid in a joint (or any cavity) — e.g. 'water on the knee' (i.e. synovitis)

Embolism: blockage of blood vessel by a clot which has migrated

Emphysema, surgical: collection of air in the tissues through puncture of the lung by a fractured rib

E.N.T.: ear, nose and throat

Epiphyseal line: the cartilaginous plate near the end of a bone at which the bone grows in length

Epiphysis: the end of a bone during the period of growth

Erythema: superficial blush or redness of the skin — e.g. as from a very slight burn or scald

Erythrocyte: red blood corpuscle

Eschar: crust of dead skin

Extension: moving a joint into the straight position (opposite to flexion)

External: outer side, syn. lateral (opposite to medial)

Fascia: a fibrous membrane

Femoral: pertaining to the femur

Femur: the thigh bone

Flexion: moving a joint into the bent position (opposite to extension)

Flexor: a muscle that bends or flexes a part

Fossa: anatomical term for a depression or furrow

Gangrene: total death of a structure through deprivation of blood supply

Genu: the knee joint

Gluteal: pertaining to the buttock

Haemarthrosis: effusion of blood in a joint

Haematoma: localised collection of blood

Hallux: the great toe

Humerus: the bone of the upper arm

Hyper-: prefix meaning increase above the normal

Hypo-: prefix meaning decrease below the normal; anatomical term for below

Ileum: the lower half of the small intestine

Ilium: the main bone of the pelvis

Induration: hardening of a tissue

Infarct: a wedge-shaped haemorrhagic or necrotic area produced by obstruction of a terminal artery

Inguinal: pertaining to the groin

Intercostal: between the ribs

Interosseous: between bones

Intracranial: within the skull

Intubation: insertion of a breathing tube through the vocal cords

Ischaemia: reduction of local blood supply to a structure

-itis: suffix meaning inflammation — e.g. osteitis, inflammation of a bone

Keloid: a scar which is thickened and deep pink in colour

Kyphosis: posterior convexity of the spine

Laceration: physical tearing of a structure, e.g. lacerated skin

Lateral: outer side, or external (opposite to medial)

Leg: that part of the lower limb between the knee and ankle

Lesion: a structural change in a tissue caused by disease or injury

Leucocyte: white blood corpuscle

Ligamentous: pertaining to a ligament

Lipping: ridge of adventitious bone at joint edges in arthritis (syn. osteophytic formation)

Lordosis: anterior convexity of the spine

Lumbar: the 'small' of the back — i.e. situated between the dorsal (thoracic) and sacral levels

Lumen: the cavity of a tubular structure

Macro-: prefix meaning abnormally large size

Malar: pertaining to cheek

Mallet finger: inability actively to straighten the terminal joint of a finger

Mandible: the lower jaw

Maxilla: the upper jaw

Medial: inner side, or internal (opposite to lateral)

Medullary cavity: the soft interior of a bone

Meniscus: the semilunar cartilage of the knee

Metacarp-phalangeal: pertaining to the joint between the fingers and the bones of the palm of the hand

Micro-: prefix meaning abnormally small size

Motor: pertaining to movement (applied particularly to peripheral nerve function)

Myelo-: prefix meaning pertaining to the spinal cord

Myo-: prefix meaning pertaining to muscle

Necrosis: death of tissue

Neurapraxia: interruption of conductivity in a nerve owing to pressure thereon, resulting in temporary paralysis and anaesthesia in the distribution of the nerve; full recovery will take place spontaneously in a matter of days or very few weeks (cf. axonotmesis and neurotmesis)

Neurotmesis: interruption of conductivity in a nerve by anatomical division causing permanent paralysis and anaesthesia in the distribution of the nerve; recovery cannot take place unless the nerve is surgically repaired (cf. axonotmesis and neurapraxia)

Nystagmus: oscillatory movement of the eyes

Oedema: accumulation of fluid in the tissues

Oesophagus: the gullet, the muscular tube connecting the back of the mouth and the stomach

Olfactory: pertaining to the sense of smell

Oligo-: prefix meaning lack of

Optic fundi: optic disc, where the optic nerve enters the retina

Orthopaedic: pertaining to bony deformity

Os calcis: see calcaneus

Osteitis: inflammation of bone

Osteoarthritis: degeneration of a joint from wear and tear

Osteophyte: ridge of adventitious bone at joint edges in arthritis (syn. 'lipping')

Osteoporosis: loss of mineral salts from bones, the result of lack of use owing to injury or disease and causing softening of the bone

Palmarflexion: moving the wrist in the direction that the palm faces (syn. flexion)

Para-: prefix meaning by the side of, near, through, abnormality

Paramedian: pertaining to a vertical line parallel with the midline, i.e. a line drawn down through the xiphoid process and umbilicus

Paresis: incomplete paralysis

Patella: the knee bone

Periarthritis: inflammation round a joint, due to infection or injury, causing pain and restricted movement

Phalanx: a finger

Phlebo-: prefix meaning pertaining to a vein

Plantarflexion: flexing the foot — i.e. 'pointing the toes'

-plegia: suffix meaning paralysis

Plexus: a network of nerves or veins

Pneumothorax: air in the pleural cavity — e.g. from the puncture of the lung by a fractured rib — and causing collapse of the lung

Poly-: prefix meaning much or many

Prolapse: falling down, or extrusion or protrusion, of a structure

Pronation: twisting the forearm, the elbow being fixed, to bring the palm of the hand facing downwards (opposite to supination)

Proximal: nearest the centre (opposite to distal)

Pulmonary: pertaining to the lung

Quadriceps: the main muscle of the front of the thigh

Recurvatum deformity: bent backwards

Reduction: restoration to a normal position – e.g. of a fractured bone or a dislocated joint

Renal: pertaining to the kidney

Retro-: prefix meaning behind or backward

Rhomberg's Test: a test of balance — the patient stands erect with toes and heels touching and eyes closed; unsteadiness occurs if test positive

Sclerosis: increased density, e.g. of a bone, owing to disease or injury

Scoliosis: lateral (i.e. sideways) curvature of the spine

Sensory: pertaining to sensation (applied particularly to peripheral nerve function)

Sequestrum: a fragment of dead bone

Sinus: a track leading from an infected focus — e.g. in a bone — to an opening on the surface of the skin

Slough: tissue, usually skin, dead from infection

Spondylosis: degenerative changes in the spine

Sternum: the breastbone

Subscapular: beneath the shoulder blade

Subtalar: beneath the talar bone

Supination: twisting the forearm, the elbow being fixed, to bring the palm of hand facing upwards (opposite to pronation)

Supraclavicular: above the clavicle

Suture: stitch

Synovitis: inflammation of the lining membrane of a joint

Tachycardia: increased pulse rate

Talar: bone of the foot

Therapeutic: pertaining to treatment, the application of a remedy

Thorax, thoracic: the chest, pertaining to the chest

Thrombosis: clotting (thrombus) in a blood vessel or in the heart

Tissue: anatomically a complex of similar cells and fibres forming a structure

Tracheotomy: operative opening into the trachea (windpipe) to assist breathing in certain chest injuries

Traction: method by which fractures, particularly of the femur, are treated — the lower limb is suspended by weights and pulleys and a continously pulling force is applied by means of further weights and pulleys attached to a metal pin (Steinmann pin) passed through the upper end of the tibia

Trauma: an injury, e.g. physical, emotional

Ulcer: localised destruction, by injury or disease, of a surface tissue (i.e. skin, mucous membrane)

Umbilicus: the belly button

Valgus: outward deviation — e.g. genu valgum = knock knee (the tibia deviates outwards from the knee)

Varicosity: dilation and pouching of the veins

Varus: inward deviation — e.g. genu valugum = bow leg (the tibia deviates inwards from the knee)

Ventilation: the movement of oxygen in and carbon dioxide out of the lungs, mechanical ventilation is ventilation by means of a machine.

Vertebra: one of the backbones

Whiplash injury: strain of cervical structure from the head moving violently in one direction and then bounding back in the reverse direction

Xanth-: prefix meaning yellow

Xiphoid process: the lower most bony part of the sternum

APPENDIX TWO

WIGMORE ANALYSIS CHARTS

For an introduction to Wigmorean analysis, see **14.5.5** to **14.5.9**.

The aim of producing a Wigmore chart is to identify the chain of proof, including inferences which stengthen or weaken the main proposition to be proved. The chart is developed according to the purpose for which it is required and the standpoint of the person producing it. While there is often not time to produce this level of sophisticated analysis, for those who persevere it is well worth the effort. To produce a Wigmorean analysis chart:

(a)   Identify the ultimate probandum – the proposition ultimately required to be proved.

(b)   Identify the penultimate probanda – the matters leading directly to what must be proved.

(c)   List the facts in a key list which can include the whole case, or only certain elements in a case. Each proposition is then charted with a specific symbol. A square indicates evidence that can be directly perceived, e.g., the detective's statement in the example below. A circle indicates an inference from another source.

(d)   Draw the chart from top to bottom and from right to left. One item stands for one proposition and no more.

In the case example in **14.5.8**, the 'ultimate probandum' – the proposition that must be proved – is that Cassie Charnel stole a bottle of whisky from Super Stores plc. **Figure App 2.1** shows how this would look on a Wigmorean analysis. Note that items 1–4 represent the 'penultimate probanda', i.e., matters leading to the main proposition to be proved. Concentrating on the line of proof for the first item – (item 1 on the key list) that she appropriated a bottle of whisky – items 5, 7, 9 and 11 are only inferences from, respectively, 6, 8, 10 and 12. These last are facts to which you have direct access – the detective's statement – on the assumption that you either have the original statement, or a copy of it. The special nature of these facts is shown by the square, rather than the circle.

Figure App 2.1

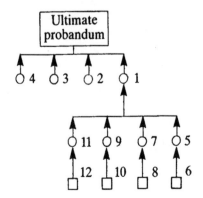

Key List:

1.   CC appropriated a bottle of whisky.
2.   The whisky belonged to Super Stores.
3.   CC appropriated the whisky dishonestly.
4.   At the time, she intended to deprive Super Stores of the whisky permanently.
5.   CC took the whisky from the display.
6.   Store detective's statement to this effect.
7.   CC put it in her coat instead of the basket.
8.   Store detective's statement to this effect.
9.   CC failed to produce or pay for the whisky at check-out.
10. Store detective's statement to this effect.
11. CC left store with whisky.
12. Store detective's statement to this effect.

Strictly speaking, there is another stage of thought which the chart might have shown. The move from the store detective's statement to the inference that what she stated was in fact the case involves a generalisation and could be charted as in **Figure App 2.2**.

Figure App 2.2

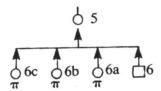

Key list:

5.   CC took the whisky from the display.
6.   Store detective's statement to this effect.
6a. In the absence of a motive to lie or opportunity for erroneous observation, a person's account of what he has seen is likely to be true.
6b. The store detective had no known motive to lie.
6c. He had no known opportunity for erroneous observation.

The symbol π is used to designate a fact noticed as a matter of general knowledge or inference without evidence being introduced specifically on the point. Here 6a takes the form of a generalisation about the trustworthiness of a particular type of evidence, whilst 6b and 6c may be inferred from the absence of evidence to the contrary.

The objective of the chart is to clarify, and since clarity is likely to be obscured by density of items it may be thought unnecessary to chart all the generalisations on which inferences depend. But care should be taken because some generalisations which are necessary to support an inference are a good deal more questionable than might at first appear. With or without explicit generalisations, the chart should always show the fact that a witness states something to be the case and the inference that that is indeed the case as two distinct items. One of the dangers of the Wigmorean exercise is that it can lead to the production of a rigid pattern of unnaturally solid 'facts', whereas reality is altogether more fragile and elusive. The point is well made in Peter Ackroyd's *Hawksmoor*. The detective in Ackroyd's novel had just been shown a number of witness statements, but:

> None of these apparent sightings interested Hawksmoor, since it was quite usual for members of the public to come forward with such accounts and to describe unreal figures who took on the adventitious shape already suggested by newspaper accounts. There were even occasions when a number of people would report sightings of the same person, as if a group of hallucinations might create their own object which then seemed to hover for a while in the streets of London. And

Hawksmoor knew that if he held a reconstruction of the crime by the church, yet more people would come forward with their own versions of time and event; the actual killing then became blurred and even inconsequential, a flat field against which others painted their own fantasies of murderer and victim.

Strengthening and Weakening Inferences

Suppose the evidence of the store detective's observation is not so clear-cut. There are difficulties because he admits in his statement that the store was crowded and so he did not have the defendant in view for the whole time at the spirits display. But an assistant manager who had been alerted was also observing the defendant and he confirms the detective's account that the bottle of whisky was taken. The appropriate section of the chart will look something like **Figure App 2.3**.

Figure App 2.3

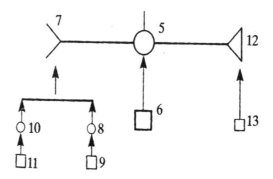

Key list:

5. CC took whisky from display.
6. Detective's statement to this effect.
7. His observation may have been mistaken.
8. Store was crowded.
9. Detective's statement to this effect.
10. Detective could not have defendant in view all the time at the spirits display.
11. Detective's statement to this effect.
12. Assistant manager confirms 5.
13. His statement to this effect.

(The numbers of the items shown in **Figures App 2.1** and **2.2** will have to be adjusted.) The symbol > shows something which weakens the effect of another piece of charted information. It appears on the left of the symbol which represents the weakened information. The symbol ◁ shows something which strengthens the effect of another piece of charted information. It appears on the right of the symbol which represents the strengthened information.

The most basic features of Wigmore's system have been shown. It should now be possible to construct a chart and key list either for a whole case or for part of one.

With the task completed you will have a better idea of how your information hangs together. The chart cannot, of course, tell you which propositions are likely to be accepted by the court but your own judgment will be greatly assisted in dealing with that problem by the construction of the chart. Wigmore observed that the use of this method came more readily to some than to others. Experience has shown, however, that initial difficulties disappear if the student persists in trying to make the method work. The best way to learn this technique is to use it.

Wigmore's ideas have since been elaborated by Terence Anderson and William Twining in *Analysis of Evidence*, Weidenfeld, 1991.

APPENDIX THREE

COMPLETED CHART FOR
R v PENNY

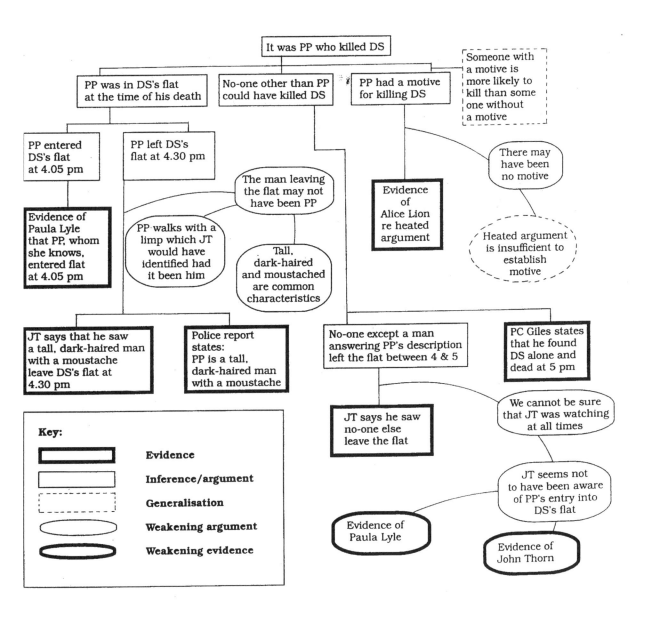

FURTHER READING

Anderson, T. and Twining, W., *Analysis of Evidence*, Butterworths, 1991.

Binder, D.A., and Bergman, P., *Fact Investigation: from Hypothesis to Proof*, West Publishing Co., 1984.

Bono, E. De, *Lateral Thinking*, Penguin, 1990.

Bono, E. De, *Po: Beyond Yes and No*, Penguin, 1990.

Bono, E. De, *Practical Thinking*, Penguin, 1991.

Bono, E. De, *Six Thinking Hats*, Penguin, 2000.

Bono, E. De, *Teaching Thinking*, Penguin, 1991.

Buzan, Tony, *Use Your Head*, BBC Books, 1995.

Constanzo, M., *Problem Solving*, Cavendish Publishing, 1995.

Gold, N., Mackie K., Twining W., *Learning Lawyers' Skills*, Butterworths, 1989.

Moore, A. J., Bergman, D., and Binder, D. A., *Trial Advocacy: Inferences, Arguments and Techniques*, American Case Book Series, West Publishing Co., 1996.

Nathanson, S., What Lawyers Do: A Problem-solving Approach to Legal Practice, Sweet & Maxwell, 1997.

Purver, J. M., *et al.*, *The Trial Lawyer's Book: Preparing and Winning Cases*, Lawyer's Cooperative Publishing, New York, 1990.

Sonsteng, J., Haydock and Boyd, *The Trial Book. A Total System for the Preparation & Presentation of a Case*, West Publishing Co., 1984.

Twining, W., *Theories of Evidence: Bentham and Wigmore*, Butterworths, 1985.

Twining, W., and Miers, D., *How to Do Things with Rules*, Butterworths, 4th ed., 1999.

Wigmore, J.H., 'The problem of proof', *University of Illinois Law Review*, 1913, vol. 8, p. 77.

Wigmore, J.H., *The Science of Judicial Proof*, 1937.

INDEX